MAJOR & MRS HOLT
Definitive Battlefield Guide to the
YPRES SALIENT &
PASSCHENDAELE
100th CENTENARY EDITION

YPRES

She was a city of patience; of proud name,
Dimmed by neglecting Time; of beauty and loss;
Of acquiescence in the creeping moss.
But on a sudden fierce destruction came
Tigerishly pouncing: thunderbolt and flame
Showered on her streets, to shatter them and toss
Her ancient towers to ashes. Riven across,
She rose, dead, into never-dying fame.
White against heavens of storm, a ghost, she is known
To the world's ends. The myriads of the brave
Sleep around her. Desolately glorified,
She, moon-like, draws her own far-moving tide
Of sorrow and memory; toward her, each alone,
Glide the dark Dreams that seek an English grave.

LAURENCE BINYON

Overleaf: St George's Memorial Church
Front cover: The Menin Gate at Night

MAJOR & MRS HOLT'S
Definitive Battlefield Guide to the
YPRES SALIENT &
PASSCHENDAELE
100th CENTENARY EDITION

Tonie & Valmai Holt
with foreword by the
Belgian Ambassador to the court of St James,
H.E., Guy Trouveroy

Pen & Sword
MILITARY

By the same authors:

Picture Postcards of the Golden Age: A Collector's Guide
Picture Postcard Artists: Landscapes, Animals and Characters
Stanley Gibbons Postcard Catalogue: 1980, 1981, 1982, 1984, 1985, 1987
Germany Awake! The Rise of National Socialism illustrated by Contemporary Postcards
I'll be Seeing You: the Picture Postcards of World War II
Holts' Battlefield Guidebooks: Normandy-Overlord/Market-Garden/Somme/Ypres
Visitor's Guide to the Normandy Landing Beaches
Battlefields of the First World War: A Traveller's Guide
Major & Mrs Holt's Concise Guide to the Ypres Salient
Major & Mrs Holt's Battlefield Guide to the Ypres Salient **+ Battle Map**
Major & Mrs Holt's Battlefield Guide to Gallipoli **+ Battle Map**
Major & Mrs Holt's Battlefield Guide to MARKET-GARDEN (Arnhem) **+ Battle Map**
Major & Mrs Holt's Definitive 100th Anniversary Battlefield Guide to the Somme **+ Battle Map**
Major & Mrs Holt's Definitive Battlefield Guide to the Normandy D-Day Landing Beaches
Major & Mrs Holt's Guide to the Western Front – North
Major & Mrs Holt's Guide to the Western Front – South
Major & Mrs Holt's Pocket Battlefield Guide to Ypres & Passchendaele
Major & Mrs Holt's Pocket Battlefield Guide to the Somme 1916/1918
Major & Mrs Holt's Pocket Battlefield Guide to D-Day. Normandy Landing Beaches
Violets From Oversea: Reprinted 1999 as Poets of the Great War
My Boy Jack?: The Search for Kipling's Only Son. Revised limpback 2014
Till the Boys Come Home: WW1 Through its Picture Postcards. 2014
The Best of Fragments from France by Capt Bruce Bairnsfather, 2014
The Biography of Capt Bruce Bairnsfather: In Search of the Better 'Ole. 2014
Major & Mrs Holt's Battle Maps: Normandy/Somme/Ypres/Gallipoli/MARKET-GARDEN

This book first published in 1996, Second Edition 1998, Reprinted 1999,
Third Edition 2000. Fourth Revised Edition 2003. Fifth Revised Edition 2007.
Sixth Revised, Expanded Edition 2008. Seventh Revised Edition 2011. This
8th Revised and Expanded 100th Anniversary Definitive Edition 2017

Pen & Sword Military

an imprint of Pen & Sword Books Limited 47 Church Street, Barnsley, South Yorkshire, S70 2AS

Text copyright © Tonie and Valmai Holt, 2017

ISBN 978 0 85052 551 9

Printed and bound in India by Replika Press Pvt. Ltd.

For a complete list of Pen & Sword titles please contact
Pen & Sword Books Ltd, 47 Church St, Barnsley, S Yorkshire, S70 2AS, England
email: enquiries@pen-and-sword.co.uk - website: www.pen-and-sword.co.uk

CONTENTS

LIST OF MAPS

FOREWORD

M. Guy Trouveroy, Belgian Ambassador to the Court of St James

On August 4th 1914, the armies of the Kaiser invade Belgium with their full might. The aim of the Germans was to turn the French defenses in Alsace-Lorraine and to head as fast as possible towards Paris. Belgium was a neutral country. Wilhelm could not care less. The German forces expected an easy passage through Belgium, a country that could only field a small, under-equipped army, probably consistent with its neutrality status. Nobody expected the Belgian army to put up a big fight. But in fact the Belgian forces did resist very well, defending and attacking, and by doing so distracting important German forces from their main goal. It has been written that this *"combat retardateur"* was a factor in allowing the French to regroup and stop the Imperial Army's advance at la Marne. Soon afterwards, an immensely long scar would deface Europe from the North Sea to Switzerland.

The violation of the neutrality of Belgium triggered the entry into war of our British neighbour. For the next four years, Belgium and the United Kingdom will join forces with many other allied countries: our two nations will suffer together tremendously, sharing the pain and but also the glory. We have started commemorating the centenary of these events as of August 2014. Mons and Ypres were the first names to appear. Many more books on WWI were published and quite a few new monuments were dedicated. I would like to mention two such dedications. On November 6th 2014, Their Majesties Queen Elisabeth II and King Philippe inaugurated the Flanders Field 1914-2014 Memorial Garden set immediately next to the Guards Museum, Wellington Barracks. The soil of the monument came from 70 WWI cemeteries where Guards are buried. The moment was extraordinary and very moving, highlighting as if necessary the strong bonds that unite our two countries. This commemoration period permits us as well to focus on individual stories related to the war. Edith Cavell remains a towering figure: Princess Anne and Princess Astrid were present last October at the unveiling of a new monument in Brussels on the hundredth anniversary of her execution by the German occupant. There were also books and seminars describing the unbelievable lives of British nurses such as Lady Dorothie Feilding, Elsie Knocker and Mairi Chisholm of Doctor Munro's Ambulance fame who worked for years immediately behind Belgian and French trenches.

The consequences of the conflict were so horrendous that everybody hoped for this nightmare to be the last, *"la der des der"* as we say in French. Unfortunately, a little more than twenty years later, the same were at it again. Today we live in peace in a united Europe where reconciliation and reconstruction took place. We should all strive to keep it that way.

….I would like to commend the work of Major Holt and Mrs Holt in describing with great precision the battle fields of Flanders. They have embarked on a major update and expansion of their famous Ypres & Passchendaele Guidebook as we prepare to commemorate next year (2017) the centenary of the terrible battle of Passchendaele (Third Battle of Ypres). The Guidebook will be your trusted companion to all these important places. Tears will come to your eyes in front of so much sacrifice by so many young men. But then a smile may come across your lips as you realize that all this has not been in vain.

Guy Trouveroy
H.E. Ambassador of HM the King of the Belgians
to the Court of St James.

NOTE: Ambassador Trouveroy was actively instrumental in the publication of the fascinating book, *Waterways of the Western Front: untold stories of World War 1*. Published by the London Canal Museum, where an exhibition of the same name was held in 2015, it was edited by Celia Halsey with a team of researchers led by Charlie Forman, Exhibition project Manager. It contains many superb photographs, including some of the Belgian Canals mentioned in this guidebook.

About the authors

Respected military authors Tonie and Valmai Holt are generally acknowledged as the founders of the modern battlefield tour in the 1970s.

Valmai Holt took a BA(Hons) in French and Spanish and taught History. Tonie Holt took a BSc(Eng) and is a graduate of the Royal Military Academy, Sandhurst and of the Army Staff College at Camberley. They are both Fellows of the Royal Society of Arts and Science and have made frequent appearances on the lecture circuit, radio and television. They are founder members of The Western Front Association and Honorary Members of the Guild of Battlefield Guides.

Their company, *Major & Mrs Holt's Battlefield Tours*, gradually grew, at first through their consultancy with Purnell & BCA Book Clubs, to cover battlefields as far afield as the American Civil War, Arnhem, the Crimea, El Alamein, Monte Cassino, the Normandy Landing Beaches, Vietnam, Waterloo, the WW1 Gallipoli, Italian and Western Fronts, the Falkland Islands, South Africa and other destinations.

In 1984 they acted as consultants to the cities of Portsmouth and Southampton, the *Département* of Calvados, Townsend Thoresen and British Airways to co-ordinate the first great commemoration of the D-Day Landings, the 40th Anniversary. In that same year they were appointed as ADCs to Congressman Robert Livingston of Louisiana for services in support of American veterans. Also in the 1980s they were asked to take over the organisation of the Royal British Legion Pilgrimages and greatly improved the standard for the benefit of the widows and families. They also acted as consultants to the Accor group as they began to receive more British groups in their hotels.

Their tours soon established a sound reputation for the depth of their research, which was then transferred to their writing. Their *Major & Mrs Holt's Battlefield Guides* series comprises, without doubt, the leading guide books describing the most visited battlefields of the First and Second World Wars and forms the only collected source of information about the memorials around Continental Europe that chronicle the achievements and actions of British and Allied forces in those wars. They have a unique combination of male and female viewpoints allowing military commentaries to be linked with the poetry, music and literature of the period under study and can draw upon 40 years military and travel knowledge and experience gained in researching and personally conducting thousands of people around the areas they have written about. In the early days they were privileged to be able to record the memories of veterans of the Great War and then World War Two, which have been incorporated into their books.

In December 2003 the Holts sponsored and unveiled a memorial to Capt Bruce Bairnsfather (the subject of their biography, *In Search of the Better 'Ole*) at St Yvon near 'Plugstreet Wood' and have supported many other military memorial and charity activities.

In 2007 an updated edition of their biography of John Kipling, *My Boy Jack?*, was published to

The Authors, holding two of the first bugles to be played under the Menin Gate, with Last Post Association Chairman, Benoit Mottrie

coincide with the ITV drama, *My Boy Jack*, starring Daniel Radcliffe and they acted as consultants for the IWM Exhibition of the same name. It has since been updated several times.

In 2008 they celebrated their Golden Wedding Anniversary.

In 2009, the 50th Anniversary year of the death of the cartoonist Bruce Bairnsfather, they updated their 1978 published collection of 140 of his most enduring cartoons, *The Best of Fragments from France,* and this, together with tribute cartoons donated by some of the world's leading cartoonists and sold at a Charity Auction, raised funds for 'Help for Heroes'. Bairnsfather would have been pleased. All authors' royalties from the sale of the book also go to the Charity.

In 2014 they were awarded the Department of the Somme's Centenary Medal for 'opening the door to the battlefields' and services to tourism.

In 2015 they mounted a petition to get official recognition for Bairnsfather's contribution to morale in WW1, with some success. It was a year of many articles, interviews in the media, lectures and exhibitions about him.

In 2016 they made a programme for BBC Welsh TV on the Welsh in the Salient, were proud to become Life Members of the Last Post Association and mounted an exhibition of their WW1 postcards in the Plugstreet Experience .

For more information and latest news VISIT THEIR WEBSITE:

www.guide-books.co.uk

ABBREVIATIONS

Abbreviations used for military units and acronyms are listed below. Many of these are printed in full at intervals throughout the text to aid clarity. Others are explained where they occur.

A/	Acting	kia	killed in action
ADS	Advanced Dressing Station	KRRC	King's Royal Rifle Corps
AIF	Australian Imperial Force	KOSB	King's Own Scottish Borderers
AM	Albert Medal	L/	Lance
Arty	Artillery	MC	Military Cross
Att/d	Attached	MGC	Machine Gun Corps
Aust	Australian	Mil	Military
BEF	British Expeditionary Force	NZ	New Zealand
Bde	Brigade	ORBAT	Order of Battle
Bn	Battalion	Pte	Private
Bty	Battery	QA	Queen Alexandra's
BWI	British West Indies	QMG	Quartermaster General
Can	Canadian	QRWS	Queen's Royal West Surrey
C-in-C	Commander in Chief		Regiment
CCS	Casualty Clearing Station	RA	Royal Artillery
CEF	Canadian Expeditionary Force	RB	Ross Bastiaan Plaque
CO	Commanding Officer	RBL	Royal British Legion
Coy	Company	RE	Royal Engineers
CWGC	Commonwealth War Graves	RFA	Royal Field Artillery
	Commission	RGA	Royal Garrison Artillery
DIV	Division	RHG	Royal Horse Guards
DLI	Durham Light Infantry	RIF	Royal Inniskilling Fusiliers
FOO	Forward Observation Officer	SLI	Somerset Light Infantry
HAC	Honourable Artillery Company	T/	Temporary
Imp	Imperial	RWF	Royal Welch Fusiliers
IWGC	Imperial War Graves		
	Commission		

INTRODUCTION

'The World has no other such battlefield'
The Times

The year 2017 sees the historic milestone of the 100th Anniversary of the bitter and costly battles, starting with the Messines Offensive in June and continuing in the long and desperate struggle from 31 July-10 November, which is collectively known as Passchendaele. The following year the Fourth Battle of Ypres in April 1918 will also be commemorated. The travails in Belgium, however, started, some three years earlier …

During the Great War of 1914-1918, most of Belgium was occupied. Apart from the small strip above Dixmuide to the west of the Yser, held by the Belgian army, only one other part of Belgium remained unconquered. This was a half-moon shape known as 'The Salient', and at its focus lay the old city of Ypres. For four years the British prevented the Germans from taking it and an eternal bond between the Belgian and British nations was formed. To this day that bond is movingly renewed every evening at 2000 hours when, under Sir Reginald Blomfield's impressive Menin Gate British Memorial, buglers from Ypres sound the Last Post in memory of their British allies.

In those four years of fighting for a few kilometres of land an average of 5,000 British soldiers died every month. By 1918 almost one million had been wounded. The ground was flat, the weather frequently wet and the trenches readily filled with water. Added to the dangers of cannon and machine guns were the Salient inventions of the *Flammenwerfer* and poison gas. To die there was easy.

Many who were to become famous in a future war served there, including Churchill, Montgomery, Wavell, Horrocks (who was taken prisoner during First Ypres) and Hitler. Others whose fame was cut short, like the poets Francis Ledwidge and 'Hedd Wyn' (Pte Ellis Humphrey Evans) still lie there. So do many holders of the Victoria Cross (including the double VC winner, Capt Noel Chavasse) and several men who were executed for supposed military offences. Many literary works were born out of the intensity of daily life in the Salient. R. C. Sherriff was badly wounded during Third Ypres and a decade later wrote *Journey's End* which was translated and performed in every European language. In a pill box on the Passchendaele ridge A. G. Macdonell, while talking to a fellow artillery subaltern, had the idea for the classic comic novel, *England, Their England*. Yet it was the common soldier who carried the heaviest burden as the terrifyingly vast lists of names on the Menin Gate and the Tyne Cot Memorial bear witness. There are almost 55,000 names on the first and nearly 35,000 on the latter. None have known graves.

The earliest tours of the area were for Americans in 1915. GHQ at St Omer ran some for the privileged few, including Conan Doyle (whose nephew was killed in the Salient) and Bernard Shaw. In 1922 King George V made his own pilgrimage in the company of the Imperial War Graves Commissioner, Rudyard Kipling. After the war several veterans based themselves in the Salient to run tours by motorcar or charabanc and the British Legion and other charitable and religious organisations (notably St Barnabas, whose Hostels Association did a two-night, return fare England and back, full-board stay with 3rd class rail and 2nd class boat for £3 11s 6d) offered organised pilgrimages for bereaved families. Several guidebooks to the Salient appeared.

One of the earliest was the *Michelin Guide* of 1920 (now reprinted). This was followed in the same year by *The Pilgrim's Guide to the Ypres Salient*, 'compiled and written entirely by ex-service men' and produced by Toc H. It contained an 'Advertisement Section' which listed details of 'The Battlefields Bureau Ltd – Association of Officers', which offered tours staying in the Château des Trois Tours, Brielen, whose '20 acres are left in their actual war state, gun positions, dug-outs mebuses [sic], light railways, duck board tracks and the innumerable souvenirs of modern warfare.' The Church Army also offered 'Escorted Parties of Relatives to Visit Graves on the Western Front'. The YMCA provided hostel accommodation for forty guests in its hut 'operational since August 1919'. Skindles Hotel in Poperinghe claimed to be 'the best hotel in the Salient', with bathrooms and central heating. 'Captain R. S. P. Poyntz (B.A. Oxon, B.E.F. 1914, and 1915-1918)' advertised 'Private Visits to Battle-fields and War-Graves ... From 10gns inclusive'. Thomas Cook also offered 'their services ... to those desirous of visiting the Ypres Salient'. Belgian Government Turbine Steamers and the Great Eastern Railway ran trips, as did the 'Franco-British Travel Bureau', which had 'Battlefield Tours de Luxe personally conducted by ex-Officers in High-Class Private Motor Cars'. The Introduction to the Guide was written by Capt the Rev Noel Mellish, VC (qv). It finished with the words that are still appropriate,

"Yours is a pilgrimage in memory of those who passed this way. You will tread reverently, for it is holy ground. It is the shrine of those who won the right for us all to have a country of our own."

There followed *The Immortal Salient* by Sir William Pulteney and Beatrix Brice, published for the Ypres League in 1925, *Good-bye to the Battlefields* by H. A. Taylor (Capt [Retd] Royal Fusiliers and General Staff), *Pill-Boxes of Flanders* by Col E. G. L Thurlow published for the British Legion in 1933, *Over There: A Little Guide for Pilgrims* published by Toc H in 1935 and so on, culminating in Rose Coombs's definitive work, *Before Endeavours Fade* first published in 1976.

The scars of that terrible war and its memorials remain, and interest in them continues to grow, although in recent years the culture of those visiting has begun to change. Immediately after the war it was mostly veterans and bereaved relatives who came, but by the time that World War II was threatening, visits had begun to tail off. After 1945 the effect of the Second War erased most thoughts of the First and travel to the Continent was difficult. It was not until the late 1960s, when World War I veterans were well into retirement, had the luxury of time to think back and had grandchildren to talk to (sons and daughters often told us that their soldier fathers never talked to them), that interest in returning to the battlefields revived. Organised tours, notably by the Royal British Legion Pilgrimages and *Major & Mrs Holt's Battlefield Tours*, began in the 1970s, but this time round the veterans were in the minority, honoured VIPs among travellers who were descendants of those who fought or who had some historical or particular personal interest in making the journey.

Inevitably, as the number of visitors to the battlefields grew, they became a significant factor in the economic calculation of the authorities in the areas they visited: museums opened or were improved in order to attract what were now seen as 'tourists' rather than 'pilgrims'. As the events of 1914-18 recede further into the past and the survivors have all gently faded away, so the war becomes a mere part of the stream of history (now on the school syllabi in the UK) to be viewed not as an event which is within living consciousness, but as a topic competing for attention with the Boer War, the Wars of the Roses, or the Franco-Prussian War. Indeed, the majority of visitors to the Salient are now students – as they are to the Imperial War Museum – currently encouraged by the Government's Centenary scheme to take a teacher and pupils from all primary schools in the country to visit the main Western Front battlefields.

This natural slipping of the war from the preserve of the veteran, or even the period enthusiast, towards the culture of tourism is reflected in the changing nature of the museums. They are moving away from the personal, object-orientated versions so beloved of the deeply interested 'buff' to the shallower, 'interpretative' designs that set out to attract new visitors (and the young) with high-tech presentations. The target market seems to be changing from the traditional British pilgrim, who came to remember the sacrifice of those who fought and often lost their lives to protect the freedom of the Salient, to the European visitor whose sympathies lie more easily with the celebration of peace - a fact recognised by the EEC which contributed a substantial grant to West Flanders to develop the In Flanders Fields museum in Ieper in 1998. Museums are now more usually known as 'Peace' Museums, not 'War' Museums. In Dixsmuide the Ijzer Tower is categorized as a 'Peace' Museum, in Péronne the World War One Museum is known as the '*Historial*' and in Caen the World War II Museum is a '*Mémorial*' (to Peace being implied).

To those whose hearts tell them that the war was fought by real people and not by images on TV screens or coloured panels, the changes were difficult to assimilate: but if newer and younger visitors, who might not otherwise even have heard of 'The Immortal Salient', are thereby introduced to the sacrifices made by those that went before them, then that is good, and provided the Commonwealth War Graves Commission is able to continue its caring and dedicated work, as its charter requires, 'In Perpetuity', then the respect that is due to those who fought and died for our freedom will never be lost and John McCrae's torch will have been taken up.

In the run up to the historic 90th Anniversary of Passchendaele in 2007 some major projects were realised – notably the new Interpretative Centre behind Tyne Cot Cemetery (updated again for the 100th), the Memorial Walk along the old Ypres-Roulers railway line from Zonnebeke to Tyne Cot, the complete refurbishment of the Passchendaele Museum at Zonnebeke, the Interpretative Centre at the German Cemetery at Langemarck, the trench system at Bayernwald, the Scottish Memorial on the Frezenberg to name but a few.

The succession of 100th Anniversaries commencing in August 2014 has prompted a spate of even more ambitious plans: another complete renovation of the In Flanders Fields Museum, the major extension of the Passchendaele Memorial Museum, the Interpretative Centre at Ploegsteert, the Visitors' Centre at Lijssenthoek Cemetery, an update of the Tyne Cot Interpretive Centre, the Welsh Memorial on the Pilckem Ridge, The Brothers-in-Arms Memorial Park near Polygon Wood and many more...

In the last few years the wind of change has been blowing over the Salient, especially in regard to the form that battlefield tourism is taking, becoming ever more technical. The museums along the Western Front seem to some to be too technical and often offer little more than what can be seen on the computer at home. Ypres has now moved against this trend under the title 'The ground is the last witness' and with an ambitious program of tree planting, unmanned Reception Centres placed in relation to trench lines and specific battle actions, is firmly anchoring its First World War history to the ground over which it played out. Cleverly, wifi links around the battlefield allow the now ever-present smart phone to be used to place the traveller at an exact location, and three pre-set clearly detailed tours can be self-conducted around the Salient.

Then of course there is the changing face of internationalism - the influx of migrants and the appalling terrorist attacks in Paris and in Brussels which have had a major effect on tourism in the Salient (and also on the Somme). These will have a lasting influence on the shape of tourism in the Salient after 2018.

But the interest and remembrance must not fade. We hope that this book, and the others in our Series, serve to form a base upon which a permanent public record of the Memorials to those who fought for our freedom may one day be created.

Tonie & Valmai Holt,
Woodnesborough, 2017

How To Use this Guide

This book is designed to guide the visitor around the main features, memorials, museums and cemeteries of the Ypres Salient, and to provide sufficient information about those places to allow an elemental understanding of what happened where.

It makes extensive use of extracts from contemporary accounts (letters, diaries etc), where available, to bring the sites, and past events, alive and to help the modern reader see them through the eyes of the 1914-18 protagonists. It also describes literary, artistic and other persons of interest (British and Allied, American, Belgian, French and German) who were engaged in the Salient during World War I.

Prior to Your Visit

Before setting out on a visit, read this section thoroughly and mark up the recommended maps (see below) with the routes that you intend to follow. Also look at the GPS locations given below and use any GPS information with care.

GPS Locations – Trench Maps

In view of the increasing use of 'satnavs' for navigation and for the convenience of readers who wish to go directly to specific locations, we have added GPS references to all the stops on the Battlefield Tour for this edition. The references refer to the closest parking place to the site. Though a satellite navigation system can be a great help, we do not recommend that you rely exclusively upon it as it may direct you away from a continuous route that is integral to an understanding of the 'shape' of a battle.

A very helpful tool is the searchable DVD set containing 750 British trench maps for France and Belgium produced by Great War Digital, called LinesMan. This innovative software permits navigation on screen between modern IGN French maps and trench maps, and when used with a GPS receiver the user's real-time position is shown over a moving map display. The software has to be registered by internet or phone to obtain full functionality and some patience and application are needed to become familiar with the system, but for the enthusiast this facility will become a must. Details can be found at www.greatwardigital.com

Another extremely useful reference source is the fully searchable (trenches and places) British Trench Map Atlas sourced from the National Archives and available from Naval & Military Press, www.britishtrenchmaps.com

Choosing Your Routes

In our experience, most people who visit the Salient have one or two days at their disposal. Three months might seem more appropriate for the enthusiast to tour it in detail.

This guide has been written to direct the traveller along the routes which we have found to be of greatest interest and give the most immediate atmosphere of the war to the majority. Three timed and measured itineraries are set out. Each offers five or more hours of touring and visiting, without including time for refreshments. They are presented in a deliberate order of interest and/or importance. Thus, if there is only time to cover one route, Itinerary One should be followed. If there is time for a second, then Itinerary Two and so on. Some items from Itineraries Two and Three can be seen *en route* to Ypres. Each itinerary begins and ends in Ypres.

If You Wish To Visit A Particular Place

Use the Index to locate what you wish to visit. If it is a particular grave, find the location from the CWGC or ABMC database before you set out (see War Graves section). Locate it on the Battle Map that accompanies this book. If you do not wish to make your visit by following an Itinerary, the GPS references can guide you directly to it.

Approach Routes

Modern dual carriageways have so altered the character of the ground that the traveller is highly recommended to approach the Salient through the old Flemish town of Cassel (used by both General Sir John French and Marshal Foch as an HQ). With its cobbled, narrow streets it gives a 1914-18 impression upon which to paint a mental picture of the Salient during World War I. This approach also visits Godewaersvelde, Mont des Cats and Mont Noir. Alternatively, a more direct approach for those with less time goes straight to Ieper via Poperinge. Both approaches are described from the Channel Ports/Tunnel.

Extra Visits/'N.B.s'

In addition **Extra Visits** are described to sites of particular interest which lie near to the route of the main itineraries. They are boxed with a grey background so that they stand out clearly from the main route. Estimates of the round trip mileage and duration are given. The three long Extra Visits at the end of Itinerary Three cover the sector from Ypres to Diksmuide, and the American National Cemetery, Flanders Field, at Waregem and areas around Comines-Warneton. Be aware of the total mileage and length of these visits before embarking upon them. Should you decide that you do not have the time to undertake them, we strongly recommend that you nevertheless read the sections that cover them as they contain much historical information that has a bearing on the Salient itself. Regular use of the Battle Map is strongly recommended when making the Extra Visits.

Other deviations from the main route to points of interest which do not have a circuit but are 'there and back' trips are prefaced by 'N.B.' These are slightly indented and boxed.

Miles Covered/Duration/OP/RWC/Travel Directions

A start point is given for each itinerary, from which a running total of miles is indicated. Extra visits are not counted in that running total. Each recommended stop is indicated by a clear heading with the running total, and the probable time you will wish to stay there. You may wish to stay longer at some and leave others out. For instance, each cemetery on the route is described. It is highly unlikely that you will have the time, or wish, to visit them all and a stop time is only given for cemeteries which contain some particular interest.

OP/RWC. The letters OP in the heading indicate a view point from which the salient points of the battlefield that may be seen are described. RWC indicates refreshment and toilet facilities.

Travel directions are written in italics and indented to make them stand out clearly. An end point is suggested, with a total distance and timing – without deviations or refreshment stops. Those wishing to devote the maximum amount of time to touring the Salient should consider taking a packed lunch. It is perfectly possible to follow the itineraries by bicycle – indeed, being so flat, it is ideal for biking (see the many cycle routes offered by the Tourist Offices) – but obviously fewer kilometres can be covered in the allotted time.

Motor Car Mileage Trip

It is absolutely essential to set this to zero before starting and to make constant reference to it. Distances in the headings are given in miles because the trip meters on British cars still operate in miles. Distances within the text are sometimes given in kilometres and metres, as local signposts use those measures. Conversion to kilometres from miles can be made by multiplying by 1.6. The printed distances may vary slightly depending on where you park etc.

Parking. Be careful not to park on one of the ubiquitous cycle paths when stopping outside cemeteries other than in the (sometimes very small) designated parking areas. You will be peremptorily moved on by any passing policeman.

Maps/Road signs/Place Names/ Hotels/Restaurants/Tourist Offices

This guide book has been designed to be used with the accompanying *Major & Mrs Holt's Battle Map of the Ypres Salient*, and the words 'Map —' in the heading indicate the map reference for that location. Frequent use of this map will also assist you in orientating, give a clear indication of the distances involved in possible walks and show points of interest which are not included in the itineraries or extra visits.

Map enthusiasts may wish to supplement the *Holts' Battle Map* with the detailed 1:25,000 IGN (*Institut Géographique National*) maps 28/1-2; 28/3-4; 28/5-6, 28/7-8 and 20/5-6. They are available from the Tourist Office in Ieper. Sites outside the area covered by the Battle Map (e.g. the Long Extra Visits and the Approaches) are covered by Michelin 51, 1:200,000.

Road signs and place names can be very confusing because of the dual use of Flemish and French languages. Some of the more important towns and their French equivalents are: Bergen-Mons; Brugge-Bruges; Doornik-Tournai; Gand-Ghent; Ieper-Ypres; Klijte-La Clytte; Kortrijk-Courtrai; Luik-Liège; Mesen-Messines; Rijsel-Lille; Passendale-Passchendaele. There is often a slight difference between the wartime spelling of place names, which tended to be French (eg Gheluvelt, St Julien) and the spelling used on modern maps, which tends to be Flemish (e.g. Geluveld, St Juliaan). This is reflected in the text where the spelling most appropriate to the context is used. The CWGC Cemeteries retain the wartime version of their names, and these are used in this guide. Otherwise, for the most part, current spelling is used.

Hotels/Restaurants/Tourist Offices *en route* are distinguished by a **distinctive typeface**.

History Of The Battles/Personal Stories

The historical notes given at each recommended stop and the personal anecdotes can in no way be continuous and sequential. It is therefore recommended that the visitor precedes his/her tour by reading the historical sections below. It is also strongly advised to make repeated use of the Index and the indication 'qv'. There are often multiple entries about, say, a regiment or an individual, each episode described on the spot where it occurred, which add up to a full picture.

A Warning

It is dangerous to pick up any 'souvenirs' in the form of bullets, shells, barbed wire etc. that may be found. To this day farmers in the Salient, when ploughing, turn up the sad remains of World War I soldiers, or bits of ammunition and equipment which they then pile up at the edge of the field, often under signposts or markers, to be collected by army explosives experts. Some years ago, gas shells started to smoke alarmingly in Hooge Crater CWGC Cemetery, for example, and had to be removed carefully. These remains of war are called 'The Iron Harvest' and are extremely dangerous to handle: explosions often occur with this volatile material, resulting in death or maiming. Cuts could cause tetanus or blood poisoning. Therefore active searching for 'souvenirs' should be discouraged. It also seems more fitting to let such items find their way to local museums where they can be seen by generations of future visitors and where safe souvenirs can be bought.

Telephoning to Belgium & France

NOTE: When phoning Belgium add the following prefix: 0032, indicated by '+' in the phone numbers listed. For France the prefix is 0033, for the UK 0044 and for the USA 001.

SOME EMERGENCY CONTACTS

Too often we all forget that we may need these contacts and, as we made that mistake,

HOSPITAL: Jan Yperman Hospital, Briekerstraat 12, Ypres. Tel: +(0) 57 35 35 35
[In 2016 one of the authors tested the facilities and standard of care in the Hospital. They are excellent!]
AMBULANCE: Use Emergency Tel No: 112
OUT OF HOURS PHARMACY: +(0) 903 99 000. Website: www.apotheek.be. E-mail: Info@ arroieper.be
OUT OF HOURS DOCTOR: Emergency Tel No: 112. Website: mediwacht.be
POLICE: Emergency Tel No: 112. Gen No. +(0) 57 23 05 30

The foyer of the Jan Yperman Hospital

HISTORICAL SUMMARY

A BRIEF HISTORY OF YPRES UP TO 1914

It is said that the first settlement in the area (near Langemarck) was by a British captain who moved there with 700 German slaves in about AD960 and that the Latin name Hypra, which gave Ypres its name, was in its turn derived from the captain's name of Hyperborus.

A cluster of villages then grew up around the stream known as the Yperlee and by the twelfth century the settlement had seven churches, a population of 20,000 (which was to swell to 40,000 during the town's apogée in the thirteenth century) and 8,000 looms. These worked to weave the town's main product – cloth, and the special pattern which gave its name to the word 'diaper' (from the French d'Ypres – 'from Ypres').

The Corporation of Drapers decided to build an imposing house for their successful trade. The resultant Cloth Hall, which has been compared to the Doge's Palace in Venice in importance, was built over many periods. The Belfry and the East Wing were begun in about 1200 in Gothic style; the Western and Northern parts were completed in 1304.

During the Hundred Years' War the martial Bishop of Norwich laid siege to Ypres. The inhabitants suffered from starvation and thirst, and the city was left in a sorry state. A great plague in the fifteenth century further reduced the population by one quarter. The despotic rule of the Duke of Alva continued the depopulation and by 1584 it had dwindled to 5,000. Thousands were homeless and jobless, and the citizens left in great numbers to make a new living elsewhere - many to East Anglia and Kent. The great cloth trade virtually died.

Ypres was occupied by the Spanish and in 1657 an Anglo-French military alliance was formed whereby Oliver Cromwell promised the French an expeditionary force and a fleet to attack the Spaniards. The English fought with success and distinction and as a result the French, under the terms of the alliance, had to hand over Dunkirk and Mardyke to the English Commonwealth. 'How many know that 6,000 of Cromwell's men – "The immortal 6,000" – captured Ypres by assault in 1658?', asked Captain J. C. Dunn (qv), DSO, MC & Bar, DCM, medical officer of the 2nd Battalion the Royal Welch Fusiliers, as the battalion returned to the Salient in October 1917.

A series of occupations of Ypres followed – by the French, who were granted the town by the Treaty of Nijmegen of 1678 and who benefited it by commissioning the famous military architect, Vauban, to build a series of ramparts and fortifications; by the Dutch, who were granted a Garrison in 1715 and who built more fortifications, and by the Austrians.

Ypres was then a completely walled city, surrounded by a moat. The roads into the town were through 'Gates' or 'Portes', named for the towns to which they led. Hence the Lille Gate, the Armentières Gate and the Antwerp Gate (for a while to be known as the Napoleon Gate after the Emperor's visit in 1804, then to change its name to what was to become the infamous Menin Gate).

Ypres' fortifications were reinforced by the British Royal Engineers under Colonel Carmichael Smyth on their way to Waterloo in 1815. But they were dismantled in 1852, 14 years after Belgium had gained her Independence, when Vauban's outer walls were destroyed and only the Lille Gate remained. Other entry roads were widened to take modern traffic and the railway came to the town.

The people had learned a variety of languages from the conquerors — French, Dutch and a smattering of English. These gradually gave way to the brand of Dutch known as Flemish, which is still the major language of the area.

In the nineteenth century a new industry started to grow up: agriculture. Ypres became a centre for hop, chicory, beetroot, corn and even tobacco growing. It also became one of the most important butter markets in Belgium, witnesses to which are the great Butter Hall in the Cloth Hall and the name Boterstraat (Butter Street). Lace-making was a cottage industry that thrived in Ypres, the lace-makers sitting outside their houses in fine weather, their nimble fingers creating intricate patterns. In 1914 the population had risen to 17,500. But the new prosperity was to be shattered by a war that was more terrible than anything Ypres had experienced in its nine centuries of existence.

THE BIRTH OF THE SALIENT

COUNTDOWN TO WAR

'The lights are going out all over Europe,
we shall not see them lit again in our lifetime'.
Edward, Viscount Grey of Fallodon

On 28 June 1914 Archduke Franz Ferdinand and his wife were assassinated at Sarajevo in Bosnia. The Archduke was the heir apparent to the throne of the Austro-Hungarian Empire, then ruled by the Emperor Franz Josef. He had gone to Austrian-occupied Bosnia on a tour designed to bolster up the Empire which was cracking under a rising tide of ethnic nationalism. The assassins were Serbs and the Austrians immediately accused the Kingdom of Serbia of harbouring the killers and others like them, and determined upon revenge. It also seemed an opportunity to crush the growing strength of the Serbs.

On 23 July the Austrians sent an ultimatum to Serbia demanding that anti-Austrian propaganda should be banned in Serbia and that the men behind the assassination be found and arrested. To these points the Serbs agreed, but they did not agree to having Austrian officials in their country to supervise the proceedings. On 28 July the Austrians, considering the response to be unsatisfactory, declared war on Serbia.

Sir Edward Grey, Foreign Secretary

Now the dominoes began to fall as old loyalties, tribal relationships and treaties toppled, country after country, into one armed camp or the other. Germany sided with Austria, Russia with Serbia. The French, still hurting from their defeat by Prussia in 1870 and determined to regain from Germany their lost provinces of Alsace-Lorraine, saw a victorious war as a method of achieving that objective.

On 31 July Russia ordered general mobilisation followed that same day by Austria. The British Foreign Secretary, Sir Edward Grey, asked both France and Germany if they would observe Belgian neutrality. France replied 'Yes'. The Germans remained silent and the Belgians ordered that mobilisation should begin the following day.

On 1 August the French ordered mobilisation, Belgium announced her intention of remaining neutral and Germany declared war on Russia. On 2 August German troops invaded Luxembourg and made small sorties into France. Belgium refused to allow German forces to cross her soil with the object of 'anticipating' (as the Germans put it or, as in the case of Iraq in 2003, making a 'pre-emptive strike') a French attack and the King of the Belgians appealed to King George V of Britain for help.

On 3 August, Bank Holiday Monday, Germany declared war on France, while in Britain bright sunshine warmed the holiday crowds and Sir Edward Grey told Parliament, that 'we cannot issue a declaration of unconditional neutrality'.

On 4 August, just after 0800 hours, German forces crossed into Belgium. The British issued mobilisation orders and the British Ambassador in Berlin told the Chancellor that unless Germany withdrew her troops by midnight their countries would be at war with one another.

The Germans did not withdraw. It was war.

THE SCHLIEFFEN PLAN

The German plan for the conquest of France began to evolve in the early 1890s under the direction of the chief of Staff, Field Marshal Count von Schlieffen. France and Russia, between whom Germany was effectively sandwiched, were allied against possible German aggression under the Dual Alliance of 1892 and so Schlieffen had to devise a plan that avoided fighting both enemies at the same time. According to German military intelligence estimates the Russians would be unable to mobilise fully for six weeks after the beginning of a war. Therefore, reasoned Schlieffen, if France were to be attacked first and defeated within six weeks, Germany could then turn around and take on Russia. That logic, however, only moved the goal posts to uncover another challenge: how to defeat France in six weeks?

Schlieffen had the answer to that too. The key element to a quick victory was surprise and simplistically the plan aimed to fool the French into maintaining their major forces in the area of Alsace-Lorraine to counter an invasion directly from Germany around Metz, while the actual assault descended on France from the north via neutral Belgium.

Ten German divisions were nominated to keep an eye on the Russians, while 62 were assembled to take on the French. Of these latter, five armies were assembled in a line facing west and stretching northwards from Metz to form a door hinged upon Switzerland. This door was to swing in a massive anti-clockwise movement through Belgium. At the top of the door was von Kluck's 1st Army and von Schlieffen had enjoined that the very last soldier at the end of the swing should 'brush the Channel with his sleeve'.

Von Schlieffen died in 1912, saying on his deathbed, 'Above all, keep the right wing strong'. His successor was Helmut von Moltke, nephew of the von Moltke of the 1870 War but made of different stuff to his eminent ancestor. A cautious man, lacking the ruthlessness upon which Schlieffen's plan depended and frightened by the possibility of a strong counter-attack by the French in the area of Alsace-Lorraine, he strengthened the hinge end of the door, thus weakening the force at the other end that was planned to sweep through Belgium.

General von Kluck, Commander Ger 1st Army, wounded 1915, retired October 1916, died 1934.

Nevertheless, when the invasion began, von Moltke had almost 1.5 million men forming his door and at the far end of his extreme right wing, there was the 1st Army, commanded by General von Kluck, who saw himself as Attila the Hun.

On 4 August 1914 the door began to swing and Attila invaded Belgium.

Britain, committed to defend Belgium by a treaty which Bethman-Hollweg, the German Chancellor, contemptuously called a 'Scrap of Paper', sent her Expeditionary Force to France and confronted the invader at Mons two weeks later, slowing the advance. Nevertheless it was not until the Germans were in sight of Paris that the invasion was stopped completely. Then, after the battles of the rivers Marne and the Aisne, the Allies began to push the Germans back to the north. Each side tried to outflank the other, extending the front line towards the Channel coast in what became known as the 'Race to the Sea'.

At the northern end of the line the British and Germans faced each other in the area of Ypres. At stake was control of the Channel ports and the British supply line. German cavalry scouts were pushed back from Poperinghe and at 1300 hours on 7 October 1914 the first of the invaders' shells burst in the Grote Markt in Ypres. 20,000 German troops marched into the square, exacting a toll of 75,000 francs and holding the Burgomaster hostage. They did not stay. Three days later they left and took up positions on the ridge facing Ypres from Passchendaele in the north-east to Messines in the south. There they met and fought the British advancing from Ypres to Bruges.

That contest, the First Battle of Ypres, came after less than twelve weeks of war. In that time the invader had travelled over 600km in a mobile contest ranging from the German border, across Belgium, and down to the gates of Paris and back. But now he stuck fast. Both sides dug in, shielding themselves from the deadly anger of the machine-gun and increasingly effective artillery fire. The British held on grimly to that part of Belgium which bulged out into the German line. That bulge, or salient, would never be conquered and Ypres (or 'Wipers' as Tommy would call it) would become to the British what Verdun was to the French. In 1935 a Toc H publication wrote of Ypres, 'To read its name was to see a flag flying, to hear it spoken was like the call of the bugle'. Nearly every division in the British Army would serve in the Ypres Salient before the final victory.

But preceding the struggles in Ypres there was a desperate bid by the Belgians between Ypres and the sea to stem the progress of the German steamroller through their newly united country, and under their King the Belgians stood on the River Yser.

THE INVASION OF BELGIUM & THE BATTLES OF THE YSER

'The fate of Europe, up to the time of Waterloo, has always been decided in Belgium. It is difficult to escape from this idea.' Marshal Foch. 19 November 1914

> *Ce n'est qu'un bout de sol dans l'infini du monde...*
> *Ce n'est qu'un bout de sol étroit,*
> *Mais qui renferme encore et sa reine et son roi,*
> *Et l'amour condensé d'un peuple qui les aime...*
> *Dixmude et ses remparts, Nieuport et ses canaux,*
> *Et Furnes, avec sa tour pareille à un flambeau*
> *Vivent encore ou sont défunts sous la mitraille.*

> Emile Verhaeren

> It's only a piece of earth in the infinity of the world...
> It's only a narrow piece of earth,
> But which still contains its king and its queen
> And the concentrated love of a people who love them...
> Dixmude and its ramparts, Nieuport and its canals,
> And Furnes, with its tower like a flame,
> Still live or are slain by the machine-gun.

Emile Verhaeren, born on 21 May 1855, was Belgium's best-known French language poet. Original, vital, lyrical, his three main themes were the improvement of humanity's lot, love of his wife, and of Flanders. Deeply moved by the outbreak of war, yet too old to fight, he lectured extensively throughout France on Belgian's cause. He was accidentally killed boarding a train after a rally in Rouen on 27 November 1916. After the Armistice his remains were transferred to his native town of Adinkerke.

Closely involved in their nation's bitter struggle were King Albert and Queen Elisabeth of the Belgians. Albert was a monarch of the old school, seeing himself as a conscientious and active Head of State and Head of the Armed Forces. Born in Brussels on 8 April 1875, the younger son of Philip, Count of Flanders, and brother of Leopold II, he succeeded to the throne on 23 December 1909, through a series of premature deaths. A graduate of the Brussels Ecole Militaire he served as an officer in the Grenadiers. In 1900 he married Elisabeth, second daughter of the Duke of Bavaria and they had three children: Leopold, Duke of Brabant (the future Leopold III), Charles, Count of Flanders, and Marie José.

On his accession, Albert was particularly concerned with social reforms, the patronage of arts and literature and, especially, the organisation of the Army. In May 1913 he consented to the raising of the Belgian Army to a strength of 350,000, but in July 1914, when World War I was moving inexorably to its outbreak, Belgium was still dangerously unprepared for war. She depended for her survival on the treaties signed by Great Britain, France, Prussia, Russia and Austria to preserve her neutrality - notably the 1839 Treaty of London, the famous 'Scrap of Paper'. It had been tested, and held firm, in 1870 during the Franco-Prussian War. But Leopold II mistrusted the strength of the protective treaty and reinforced the forts of Liège and Namur as a failsafe. Neither the treaties nor the forts were to save Belgium from German invasion in August 1914.

On 31 July Albert wrote to the Kaiser, in a letter carefully translated by his German-born wife, reminding him of the respect due to Belgian neutrality. Wilhelm replied with the ultimatum of 2 August and hostilities began when Germany's demand for free passage of her troops was refused. **At 0800 hours on 4 August the Germans invaded Belgium.** The fortified city of Liège was reached on 5 August, its last fort surrendering on the 16th; **Brussels surrendered on 20 August,** Namur capitulated on 25 August. Nearly 2,000 civilians were killed, 3,000 houses destroyed. The historic city of Louvain, with its famous library and cathedral, was destroyed, 79 inhabitants were shot. The Provinces of Brabant, Hainault and Antwerp were occupied and many more civilians executed.

Tales of German atrocities, many of them exaggerated, abounded, fuelling the propaganda campaign for the Allies to come to the help of 'Poor Little Belgium'. The concept of German Kultur equating to barbarism was perpetuated by the Dutch artist, Louis Raemakers, in a series of harrowing cartoons that chart the Germans' bloody progress through Belgium. Elsie Knocker, one of the 'Two at Pervyse' (qv) reported in her memoirs,

"Atrocities were at their height in those first months of the war, when the Germans were in a hurry to terrorise their way to a quick finish. Every unexpected resistance of the Belgian Army brought immediate reprisals against the civilian population... I did see Belgian children with their hands and feet cut off, and I saw one baby nailed to a door. The Germans forced Belgian civilians to walk ahead of them as they advanced to form a living screen... By the beginning of October nearly 1,500,000 people, or 20 per cent of the population, had left Belgian territory: a million went to Holland, 250,000 to Britain and over 100,000 to France."

Mrs Knocker seemed to be suffering from what one might call 'the Angels of Mons Syndrome' – when senior officers, men of the cloth and other supposedly trustworthy witnesses swore affidavits that they had seen mystical bowmen appear in the sky, preventing the Germans from annihilating the retreating British on 23 August, only to be embarrassed when the journalist Arthur Machen later confessed that he had fabricated the whole story when he had little else to write about. So strong was the power of propaganda in these early days of the war, so suggestible were the Allies, that spy mania was rife and everyone, yearning to support 'Poor Little Belgium', received with easy credulity any reason to do so. Elsie Knocker was an honest and intelligent woman. She obviously believed that she had seen a handless child - another story started by a newspaper, in this case *The Times*. The story was perpetuated by the French, and in Britain a Committee under Viscount Bryce, former British Ambassador at Washington, was set up to investigate the conduct of German troops in Belgium. The conclusions of the committee were that there had indeed been systematic massacres of civilians; that looting, wanton destruction and incendiarism had occurred; that the rules and usages of war had frequently been broken, particularly in the use of women and children as shields; that the Red Cross and White Flags had frequently been abused; that 'murder, lust and pillage prevailed over many parts of Belgium on a scale unparalleled in any war between civilised nations during the last three centuries.' The report even contained details of gross individual atrocities of the type reported by Elsie Knocker. Yet when the Belgian Cardinal Mercier held an enquiry in 1922, no substantiation of these atrocities was found and any real supporting evidence for them had mysteriously disappeared. No matter: mere belief in them served to fuel the Allied fervour for the war.

The Belgian Army fell back on Antwerp, from which it made sorties on 25 August and 9 September to divert the Germans from their main thrust, which was now into France. During the latter sortie the Belgians lost 6,000 men. On the 26th the Germans attacked Antwerp and again on 3 October. On the 9th the port surrendered. Winston Churchill's gallant attempt to relieve the Belgians in Antwerp with an expedition by the newly-formed Royal Naval Division (amongst them an excited Sub-Lieutenant Rupert Brooke) was too late, and a miserable failure. They left Dover on 4 October and were back in the port on the 9th.

Now the whole country, with the exception of the area around Ypres in South West Flanders, and a small part west of the Yser on the coast, was under German occupation. King Albert had withdrawn his army (now comprising four divisions in line and two in reserve) to positions along the Yser River, from Nieuwport on the coast to Ypres. General Foch, having visited the King at Furnes, wrote in his memoirs of the Belgian Army that 'the nervous force of its soldiers was all that remained to replace the deficiencies of their equipment'.

Many Belgian civilians fled in terror against the oncoming tide of German domination, bearing with them as many of their possessions as they could pack into carts, or carry by hand. France was the nearest refuge, but many found their way to the UK, often settling and integrating into the neighbourhood. A town grew up in Tyne & Wear called Elisabethville where four thousand Belgians lived in a sovereign area, who operated according to Belgian law, with their own police force, and worked in munitions factories at Birtley.

Belgian refugees departing by typical dog cart

On 6/7 October the British 7th Division landed at Zeebrugge, arriving at Ostend the following day. 3rd Cavalry Division landed that same day. After the battles of Mons, le Cateau and the Marne, and with the Aisne Line stabilised, the BEF was moving northwards to cover the Flanders crisis. After two months of mobile warfare and the 'Race to the Sea', the front line was soon to settle down into the stalemate of trench warfare.

On 14 October the King issued a last ditch command to his troops, comparable to Haig's

'Backs to the Wall' Order of the Day of 12 April 1918 (which in turn seemed to presage Churchill's stirring 'We shall fight them on the beaches' speech of 4 June 1940):

"You will now find yourselves alongside the gallant French and British Armies. Our national honour is at stake. Face to the front in the positions in which I shall place you, and let him be regarded as a traitor to his country who talks of retreat."

His divisional commanders were then personally visited and given the following instructions:

1. Any General whose Division gives way will be relieved of his command on the spot.
2. Any officer whose men abandon their trenches will be relieved of his command.
3. Under no pretext whatsoever, even if the line is broken, is there to be any retirement.
4. Officers of the General Staff will be distributed among the troops of the frontline. They will remain there during the fighting encouraging others instead of grumbling themselves.

King Albert and Queen Elisabeth installed themselves in a modest villa at La Panne (de Panne) on the coast to the east of Dunkirk, refusing to move with their Government to Calais and then to le Havre. From La Panne the King continued to play an active role as the leader of his Army and Elisabeth, who had been medically trained, took a practical interest in the care of the wounded in hospitals close to the front line. She was the active patron of the hospital that bore her name near Poperinghe and visited Ypres under severe shellfire. The dedication of this family was further proved when on 8 April 1915 the King made an 'Easter Present' of his 13-year-old son to the 3rd Division of the Belgian Army. The delicate-looking Prince Leopold was to act as a Private, getting

his hands blistered by digging (alternating with term-time spent in the rarefied atmosphere of Eton).

On 16 October the Battle of the Yser opened. Rear-Admiral Hood brought up a Royal Naval flotilla to Middelkerke and bombarded the German coastal batteries. Naval activity heightened and on 31 October a German submarine sank the British seaplane carrier *Hermes*.

Meanwhile repeated, inexorable, German attacks in the Nieuwport and Diksmuide areas continued through to the 23rd. Supported until this time only by 6,000 French Marines, the small Belgian force, deploying its entire army, was expected to hold a 22-mile front, from the sea to Zuydschoote (8km north of Ypres). And hold they did, until by 24 October the Belgian resistance started to fail. The troops were exhausted and running out of ammunition. Reinforcements in the shape of the renowned French 42nd (Grossetti) Division arrived to relieve them. Then, at the suggestion of General Foch (who declared, 'Inundation formerly saved Holland, and may well save Belgium. The men will hold out as best they can until the country is under water') Belgian engineers saved the day with a complicated plan to open the crisscrossed drainage system of canals and

The thirteen-year-old Leopold, future King of the Belgians

ditches (*watergands*) of the area to the sea, thereby flooding it against the advancing Germans. The land to be held was protected by damming twenty-two culverts under the Nieuwport-

Diksmuide railway, and then the Nieuwport sluicegates were opened to the sea. By 30/31 October the operation, assisted by the high tides caused by the full moon of 29 October, was successfully concluded. The Battles of the Yser were over, ending with a furious bayonet charge to the sound of bugles which repulsed the enemy at Ramscappelle. The Belgian Army, with 20,000 casualties in this battle alone, was reduced to 65,000 men. In one regiment only six officers remained.

According to the King's ADC, General van Overstraeten, the French feared their Belgian brothers lacked 'both ability and energy' and urged the distribution of the weak Belgian remnant amongst French units. As General Pershing was to dig in his heels later in the war, about the dispersion of his American forces, Albert 'would neither agree to being deprived of his constitutional prerogatives, nor let his army be split up.' They continued to hold the line between Diksmuide and the sea. The conditions they had fought in were horrendous (see the section on Diksmuide and Vladslo below). The land itself was forbidding:

"Water is everywhere: in the air: on the ground, under the ground. It is the land of dampness, the kingdom of water. It rains three days out of four. The north-west winds which, breaking off the tops of the stunted trees, making them bend as if with age, carry heavy clouds of cold rain formed in the open sea. As soon as the rain ceases to fall, thick white mists rise from the ground giving a ghost-like appearance to men and things alike."

wrote the Belgian author, le Goffic in *Dixmude*. Add to these natural miseries the man-made horrors of modern warfare and it is little short of a miracle that they held on so long.

But now the Germans diverted their attention southwards towards Ypres.

THE FOUR BATTLES OF YPRES

18 October 1914 – 29 April 1918

The area in which the British found themselves was known as 'Flanders', a centuries-old word meaning 'flooded land' and central to it is the city of Ypres. It sits on a wet plain astride a complex of small waterways whose main function is to drain the soil. Around Ypres, running in a broad sweep clockwise from Passchendaele at 2 o'clock, via Messines at 6 o'clock, to beyond Kemmel at 8 o'clock, is a low ridge forming the heights of a natural amphitheatre (see Holts' Battlefield Map). Observers on that ridge, known as the 'Passchendaele Ridge', can watch every movement around Ypres in the salient below.

During the next four years of bloody struggle, the British sought to climb up onto the ridge, while the Germans tried to come down from it and into Ypres. The fighting was continuous, and the town was reduced to rubble that reached no higher than a man's chest. Every building was damaged or destroyed. Only the gaunt skeleton of the clock tower of the Cloth Hall cast any real shadow by 1918, and a soldier on horseback in the Grote Markt could see from one side of the town to the other.

On four occasions the fighting in the Salient reached such depths of horror and destruction that it is possible to consider each in isolation and each is named as a 'Battle of Ypres' – the **First**, the **Second**, the **Third** and the **Fourth**. Below we take a brief look at them in turn, and a general understanding of what happened in each will be aided by frequent referral to the large **Holts' Battlefield Map** supplied with the book plus the in-text maps that accompany each account. More details are given in the battlefield tour pages.

First Ypres: 19 October–22 November 1914: 'A Close Run Thing'

Following the German invasion and its repulse at the Marne, the Allied Counter Offensive pushed the enemy back north and the BEF moved through Ypres in mid-October, pushing the Germans back onto the Passchendaele Ridge. Here the new German Chief of the General Staff, General Erich von Falkenhayn, initiated a series of savage counter assaults designed to break through to the Channel Ports. (The armchair analyst can divide them into neat and separate parts

– the battles of Armentières 12 Oct-2 Nov; Messines 12 Oct-2 Nov; Langemarck 21 Oct – 24 Oct; Gheluveld 29 Oct-31 Oct and Nonne Boschen 11 Nov).

They were, for the Germans, the opening moves in the 'Battle for Calais'. Confident of success, the Kaiser waited behind the lines in anticipation of a triumphal entry into Ypres. German newspapers reported that inspired by his presence, thousands of young Germans in student battalions marched uncaringly into battle with flowers adorning their spiked Pickelhaube helmets. Down towards Langemarck they came singing '*Deutschland, Deutschland über alles*' much as the British might sing 'Tipperary'. But the fanatical enthusiasm of the finest German youth exhausted itself against the professional military skills of the outnumbered British Expeditionary Force (BEF), with appalling casualties on both sides. The involvement of the student battalions in the fighting became a propaganda feature to bolster German morale and the '**Langemarck Myth**' of their battle prowess was an important plank of the National Socialist movement after the war with music, pilgrimages and poetry. So important a feature of German myth did Langemarck become that Adolf Hitler visited the area in 1940 to acknowledge the debt that the nation owed to those that had fought.

Von Falkenhayn opened his October attacks with the 4th and 6th Armies, on a wide front from Armentières north to Steenstraat, aiming their centre line down the Menin Road towards Ypres. On 29 October they broke the British Line along the road, but poised on the edge of success they were stopped two days later at Geluveld by a stubborn defence by the Welsh and a gallant bayonet charge by the Worcesters, Memorials to those Regiments stand in the village today and are visited on an itinerary below.

On 11 November the Germans tried once more along the same centre line, this time with a front of 9 miles with 12.5 Divisions. It was some 18,000 men versus 8,000, but it wasn't enough. The weather deteriorated with continuous rain and the ground turned to glutinous mud. The fighting died down as December approached and, when the dreadful scale of casualties became apparent, the Germans named the battle 'The Massacre of the Innocents' in memory of the thousands of slaughtered students. It had been a close run thing. In the final analysis, however, the situation was saved by the ability of the individual soldier and lower unit commanders to make decisions on the spot and to act upon them. Nevertheless, the historian General Edmonds wrote, 'The line that stood between the British Empire and ruin was composed of tired, haggard, and unshaven men, unwashed, plastered with mud, many in little more than rags.' Thus, weighted down with mud and casualties, the First Battle of Ypres ended. By then over half of those men who had arrived in France in August, the 'Old Contemptibles', were casualties. It should not be forgotten, in our inevitable concentration on the actions of the BEF, that both French and Belgian forces topped and bottomed the British lines, particularly de Mitry's cavalry between Ypres and Dixmuide with the Belgian Army beyond.

Both sides began to dig in and when the Belgians flooded the land from Diksmuide to the sea a front line which ran from the North Sea to Switzerland (the –◆—◆—◆– line on the Battlefield Map) was completed. The pattern had been set for a struggle that would change Europe's political and social faces. But Ypres had not fallen. It never would.

Second Ypres: 22 April-25 May 1915: Gas!

At the end of 1914, the German General Staff decided that, having failed to defeat France quickly and now being faced with enemies in both the east and the west, they would concentrate upon the Russian front. General Erich von Falkenhayn considered that Russia, struggling with internal political discontent, was the weaker of his two immediate protagonists and would succumb to concentrated German might. As far as the Western Front was concerned he instructed his commanders to do only enough 'lively activity' to keep the enemy occupied. One of the things that seemed likely to 'occupy' the French and British was to try out poison gas on them.

The use of chemicals in war was not new. During the Peloponnesian War of 431-404 BC, when they were setting siege to the cities of Platea and Pelium, the Spartans saturated wood with pitch and sulphur and set fire to it to produce sulphur dioxide. The first attempt was thwarted by rain but, when used again some five years later, it was a complete success. The first use of gas in World War I was in August 1914 by the French, who had a 26mm ethyl bromacetate grenade designed to be thrown through the loopholes of defence works, but it was ineffective and discontinued. At the battle of Bolimov in February 1915 the Germans fired several thousand shells filled with xylyl bromide, a lachrymatory gas, but the liquid failed to vaporise because of the low temperature. Perhaps, learning from this experience, the Germans looked for another delivery system

The simplest method of delivery of the gas was by cylinder, since that was the standard commercial container. Train loads of the heavy 3.5ft long objects were brought into the lines. It is estimated that some 30,000 cylinders were brought up into the forward areas and inevitably some were damaged – by accident or enemy action – so that the presence of the gas weapon was fairly common knowledge among German soldiers as time went on. Now and again German prisoners were taken who spoke about the presence of gas. However, neither the French nor the British authorities took the reports seriously enough to take any precautions, though early in April Canadian troops were warned about the possibility of a gas attack following the mention of gas in the French 10th Army's 30 March intelligence bulletin.

The cylinders were dug into their firing positions in groups of 20, each group covering 40 yards of front and, 24 hours ahead of the intended assault time, the German soldiers were given their final briefings and put on their gas masks. At 0500 hours on 22 April 1915 everything was ready – except the wind. It was blowing the wrong way.

As the German infantry waited, hoping for the wind to change direction, their field artillery pounded the front line defences and heavy 17-inch guns bombarded the rear areas. When the day matured it became warm and sunny, perhaps lulling the defenders into a degree of laxity and certainly making the Germans hot and uncomfortable in their heavy equipment. By late afternoon the attack was in the balance. Soon it would be dark. The offensive could not be made at night. Then, soon after 1600 hours, a breeze began to develop from the north-east and one hour later the Germans opened the nozzles of thousands of gas cylinders.

Thus, late in the afternoon of 22 April, the Germans' chlorine gas drifted towards the Allied lines north of Ypres in the area of Poelkapelle, Langemarck and Bikschote (see the –■—■—■– line on the Battlefield Map). The brunt of this deadly and unnerving assault was taken by French Colonial troops of the 87th Territorial Division and the 45th Algerian Division with the Canadian 3rd Brigade below the Pilckem Ridge. Apprehensive of the approaching grey-green coloured cloud, the French Colonials broke and ran. Luckily for the Allies, the Ypres assault had had only the limited aims set out by Falkenhayn, which did not include the capture of the town. By darkness the enemy's immediate objective of the Pilckem Ridge had been taken and the Germans began to dig in. It was

Cylinder released Gas Canisters

only in the morning light that the commanders of the two German Corps involved were able to assess the extraordinary impact of the gas attack and to see that, had they pressed their advance, Ypres would almost certainly have fallen and the road to the Channel Ports would have been open.

Overnight, Allied reinforcements were rushed in from the west to fill the gap and the 1st Canadian Division, holding the line south of the French, reformed. The Canadian 3rd Brigade under Brigadier General R.E.W. Turner put three battalions in line around Keerselaere (in the area where the Brooding Soldier Memorial stands) and began a series of holding actions and counter-attacks in conjunction with the Northumbrian Division. On 24 April the Germans again released gas, this time between St Julien and Passchendaele and, improvising masks from handkerchiefs soaked in water or urine, the Canadians fought tenaciously despite horrendous losses, giving up very little ground. The struggle continued in a series of engagements classified as the **Battle of s-Gravenstafel**, 22-23 April; **Battle of St Julien**, 24 April-5 May; **Battle of Frezenberg**, 8-13 May and **Battle of Bellewaerde**, 24-25 May. Overall the Germans made net gains, [See the –•–●–•–●–•–●–•– line and shaded area on the Battlefield Map.] On 4 May the British made tactical withdrawals in order to shorten their lines, reducing their frontage from 21,000 yards to 16,000 yards and reducing the greatest depth of the Salient from 9,000 to 5,000 yards.

The Canadian involvement in the gas attack was recorded in a painting by the official war artist William Patrick Roberts – *The First German Gas Attack at Ypres* – and by a Memorial at Kitchener's Wood (qv). The action of the Canadians is covered in detail by Sir Max Aitken, the Canadian Record Officer, (later as Lord Beaverbrook) in his book *Canada in Flanders*, the story of Canadian actions to 1916, including an entire chapter, with maps, covering the gas attacks

The most famous depiction of gassed soldiers is John Singer Sargent's 'Gassed' and the West Riding Woodcarvers' Association (an informal, altruistic fellowship of talented carvers) produced two superb panels of 95 carvings by a variety of artists depicting the First and Second World World Wars for permanent display at the Royal Armouries, Leeds. They were unveiled by HRH Prince Michael of Kent on 1 November 2010 and one of these panels, by Mike Chambers, shows an interpretation of what Sargent's picture represents.

In the World of 'If', the Germans might have taken Ypres and then the Channel Ports: 'If' they had not used the gas just as a tactical distraction, but part of a major attack: 'If' they had had reserves ready to follow up the initial success: 'If' the wind had been in the right direction early on 22 April they would have seen how successful the gas had been and could have called up forces to exploit the break in the French lines.

Casualties of Gas. Wood Carving by Mike Chambers

'If' they had used their secret weapon properly, say many, they could have won the war with it. The 'after-the-event' experts say the same thing about the British use of the tank on the Somme. Perhaps the most relevant 'If' belongs to the Canadians, courtesy of Rudyard Kipling, because they kept their heads when all about were losing theirs.

Third Ypres: 7 June-10 November 1917: Mud

In April 1917, General Nivelle, the hero of Verdun, began a battle on the Aisne which he had carelessly proclaimed to friend and foe alike would drive the German invader from French soil. It did not do so, and in the bitter disillusionment that followed the heavy casualties, mutinies broke out in the French army. 'Collective indiscipline' as the French put it, took place in over fifty divisions. Nivelle was replaced by General Pétain and official reports say that twenty-three men were shot as ringleaders — but historians agree that many more were actually executed. Richard M. Watt, in his book *Dare Call it Treason*, supposes that at least 100,000 men actively mutinied and even the official figures admit that between May and October 1917, 23,385 men were found guilty of offences. Yet, extraordinarily, the news of the mutinies did not become general knowledge.

French confidence at all levels was badly shaken. Maréchal Joffre went to America to seek reassurance that the US declaration of war on Germany would result in American armies coming to fight in Europe. It is possible that, without that assurance, France might have sued for a separate peace with Germany. In that uncertain environment, General Pétain needed a breathing space to rebuild the morale of the French army. It fell to the British to divert the Germans' attention away from the French front.

The British C-in-C, General Haig, believed strongly in keeping pressure upon the enemy, but that pressure had resulted in casualty lists that were making the War Cabinet, led by Lloyd George, uneasy, and they were not inclined to support the General's offensive plans. Haig was determined to launch a major attack in Flanders, perhaps to help Pétain, perhaps to seize the opportunity of accomplishing a single-handed victory before the Americans arrived that would vindicate his aggressive policies. Finally, persuaded by the Admiralty's assertion that the Navy 'could not keep going' unless the German naval bases on the Belgian coast were captured, by Haig's promise of a limited offensive that the French would support and his assertion that 'if the fighting was kept up at its present intensity for six months Germany would be at the end of her available manpower,' the War Cabinet agreed to his plans. These led to the Third Battle of Ypres which fell into two parts: firstly the fight for the **Messines** ridge by the 2nd Army under Plumer and secondly the struggle for **Passchendaele** by the 5th under Gough. Plumer planned a step by step offensive while Gough planned a flat-out general assault. Haig liked the latter best.

The Battle of Messines: 7-14 June 1917.
The small town of Messines lay at the southern end of the ridge and the enemy had occupied the high ground since the British withdrawal during Second Ypres. The Messines-Wijtschate area was of particular value to the Germans because from there they could enfilade much of the British trench system and harass the supply route from Poperinghe via Vlamertinghe to Ypres. It was therefore essential that this ridge should be taken before an attempt was made to bring up all the forces needed for the main attack. Plumer began his preparations in July 1916 by deep mining along the whole of the planned attack front from Hill 60 to Plugstreet. Though the Germans counter-mined the preparations they did not discover the totality of what was going on. See the map on page 298. In their book, *Tunnellers*, Grieve & Newman describe the minutes before firing. Here are selected extracts:

> "Hundreds of eyes constantly gaze at watches… No-one who has not undergone the experience can ever know how slowly the minutes before Zero can pass…At the firing posts stand officers; their pale faces show unmistakeable signs of the strain of suspense… at 0308 hours a hasty wipe of clammy hands… 0309 hours hands tremble slightly… 0310 hours ZERO… it seemed as if the Messines Ridge got up and shook itself… All along its flank belched rows of mushroom-shaped masses of debris flung high into the air … opening like a row of giant umbrellas spreading a dark pall over the yawning, cavernous craters below."

So at 0310 hours on 7 June 1917, nineteen giant mines were blown under the German positions and, capitalising upon their shock effect, the 2nd Army, supported by more than 2,000 guns, some 70 tons of gas and complete air superiority moved forward step by step and the whole of the objective was taken that day. The attack was a complete success. The 36th (Ulster) Division and the 16th (Irish) Division took Wijtschate and Messines fell to the New Zealanders [See the –●—●—●– line on the Battlefield Map.]

A major reason for the success of this operation, apart from the careful planning, was the explosion of the mines and we examine their use in the 'The War Underground Section' of the book from page 298.

Passchendaele 31 July-10 November 1917.
So far so good. So now on to the Passchendaele Ridge while the momentum of success was still warm? No. Now a long delay while preparations were made for the next attack. Why wasn't the Messines attack delayed until it could be followed immediately by the second phase? Were the French in such desperate straits that we had to grasp the Germans' attention in June? Perhaps. Perhaps too we needed to assemble and to reposition our artillery, something not done in a few hours, but the delay was fateful. It saw out the good weather and gave the Germans time to put the finishing touches to their new scheme of defence – defence in depth, now six lines in all. Gone were the old linear lines. Now trenches ran backwards and forwards in great depth and within the grid so formed were disconnected strongpoints and concrete pillboxes. The manning philosophy had changed too. The ground was covered by mutually supporting machine guns and forward

positions were lightly held with reserves well back and concentrated ready for counter-attack. On top of all that the Germans introduced mustard gas.

It was a further six weeks before the main assault began. Following an enormous ten-day preliminary bombardment by more than 3,000 guns, twelve divisions went over the top on an 11 miles front at 0350 on 31 July, heading initially for the Geluveld - Passchendaele Ridge with a view to breaking out to the North Sea beyond. It was raining heavily. North of Ypres advances of two miles were made, the Pilckem Ridge was recaptured, but further south and around the Menin Road the attack quickly stuck. The preliminary bombardment had totally destroyed the water table and the rain could not run away. Shell holes filled to overflowing with water and the earth turned into a thick glutinous mud, stinking and foul with the decay of dead horses and thousands of corpses. The mud reached out and sucked under any unwary soldier who left the duckboard paths. Gough advised Haig that the attack should be stopped, but the C-in-C, perhaps falsely buoyant from the success at Messines, or determined to demonstrate what Clausewitz called the 'Maintenance of the Aim', i.e. steadfastness of purpose, pressed on, through battle after battle and casualty after casualty.

When today's travellers stand at Tyne Cot Cemetery and look over the peaceful Flemish countryside towards the spires of Ypres, they should remember the purported words of Haig's Chief of Staff, Lt-Gen Sir Lancelot Kiggell. After the battle he visited the front, and seeing the endless pools of mud and slime, overlaid with the torn and twisted debris of war, he is said to have exclaimed, 'Good God, did we really send men to fight in that?' In his diary of 13 October 1917 Haig records that he was told by the Director General of Transport that the ground was so soft that light railway engines were sinking up to their boilers in mud and that many tracks had completely disappeared.

Haig defied the mud, and in doing so he may have played a major part in helping France to survive through 1917. The price, however, was 300,000 British casualties. Just a fragment of the evidence is there in Tyne Cot. No wonder Tommy called it 'PASSION DALE', a name redolent with the suffering of Christ on the Cross at Easter – Passiontide.

The Official History records the following episodes in the struggle:

Messines	*7-14 June*
Pilckem	*31 July-2 Aug*
Langemarck	*16-18 Aug*
Menin Road	*20-25 Sept*
Polygon Wood	*26 Sept-3 Oct*
Broodseinde	*4 Oct.*
Poelcapelle	*9 Oct*
First Passchendaele	*12 Oct*
Second Passchendaele	*26 Oct-10 Nov*

Fourth Ypres: 7 April 1918-29 April 1918: Backs to the Wall

On 21 March 1918, one million German soldiers attacked the British Third and Fifth Armies south of Vimy Ridge. It was the opening day of Operation Michael, the 'Kaiser's Offensive', an all-out effort to win the war. Despite extraordinary early success, Ludendorff did not make the gains that he wanted and when the next - Lys - phase of his plan, 'Operation George', opened on 7 April, he had to reduce the troops involved and the frontage of his attack to such an extent that one of his staff officers suggested that the offensive be renamed 'Georgette'. Nevertheless, following two days of concentrated gas attacks around Armentières, nine full-strength divisions drove directly at Neuve Chapelle, where a solitary Portuguese Division in the process of being relieved was no match for the Germans and Neuve Chapelle fell. (The Portuguese Memorial and Cemetery are at Neuve Chapelle.)

By the evening of 9 April the Germans had reached the Lys (see map below) and the next day they drove north of Armentières, taking the Wijtschate and Messines Ridges, and Ploegsteert village, despite determined resistance by the South African Brigade. The British 34th Division just escaped encirclement in Armentières and by the end of that day the Germans had driven a 10-mile salient into the British lines and were just 4 miles south of Ypres. See the map on page 30

Below Armentières the 51st Division was saved from near disaster by the 61st, another Terrritorial force, and frantic phone calls from London by the Prime Minister and others called for help from the French and the Americans. Both in London and at GHQ the view was forming that the Germans were on the edge of splitting the Allies and that Ypres could well fall. Haig wrote an 'Order of the Day' that was meant to stiffen the resolve of his troops, but it unintentionally revealed the level of his concern about the situation: 'Every position must be held to the last man: there must be no retirement. With our backs to the wall, and believing in the justice of our cause, each one of us must fight on to the end.' The message, which reached very few of the front line soldiers, is popularly connected with the near rout of Gough's Fifth Army on the Somme, but it was more likely prompted by the situation in Flanders.

On 12 April General Plumer assumed command of General Horne's First Army (responsible for Ypres) in addition to his own, the Third (responsible for the area south of the Lys), as the British attempted to co-ordinate their response to what was becoming a very confused struggle. Haig brought up the Australians from the Somme, his reserves dwindling. Formations and units fought for every inch of ground, often reduced to bullet and bayonet. Rear areas were prepared for defence and civilians and non-combatants were evacuated from Poperinghe. Ludendorff drove north-west, straight for Neuve Eglise *en route* for the Flanders Hills – Kemmel, Mont Noir, Mont Rouge and Mont des Cats (the area covered in Approach Two below) knowing that if he had them the British and Belgian positions between Ypres and the sea would become untenable and that the way to the Channel Ports would be open. The tired troops of 34th Division struggled backwards and the 2nd Worcesters held the Germans for a while in Neuve Eglise before the village fell.

But Ludendorff was confused too, and, short of the hills, changed the direction of his attack towards Langemarck, north of Ypres, in a pincer movement called 'The Tannenberg Plan' in which he hoped to repeat the envelopment that had worked so well in Russia in 1914. Meanwhile Plumer, in order to shorten his line, withdrew from the hard-won Passchendaele Ridge in the first phase of a movement that called for the evacuation of the Ypres Salient. As the Germans battered at Langemarck on 17 April, Sir Henry Wilson advocated a general withdrawal to a defensive perimeter around Dunkirk. Foch declined and Haig again asked for, and finally got, French support. The front held and Ludendorff again switched his effort south against Kemmel, which fell on 25 April, the French, who had taken over the hill just nine days earlier from the British, putting up little resistance. The way was open to roll up the British along the Flanders Hills, to encircle Ypres and to take Dunkirk. One final effort would do it.

The protagonists were like two tiring boxers, ducking and weaving, looking for gaps in the other's defences, but Ludendorff was now at a disadvantage. His lines of supply were longer and his deep salient into the Allied lines left his troops open to fire on three flanks. Back at home dissatisfaction with the conduct of the war had spawned endless strikes, food riots and the beginnings of armed revolution. Many troops were tired to the point of exhaustion, some formations diverted by looting and drunkenness. Ludendorff himself was worn out, and had never recovered from the death of his youngest son, Erich, in March. Finally, on 29 April, once again a finger's touch from success, the German commander ended the campaign. Ypres and the Channel Ports had been saved. The American historian, Brigadier General S. L. A. Marshall, said that in World War I there was '**no nobler or more decisive stand than that of the BEF in front of Ypres in April 1918**'. That stand is what we call 'Fourth Ypres'.

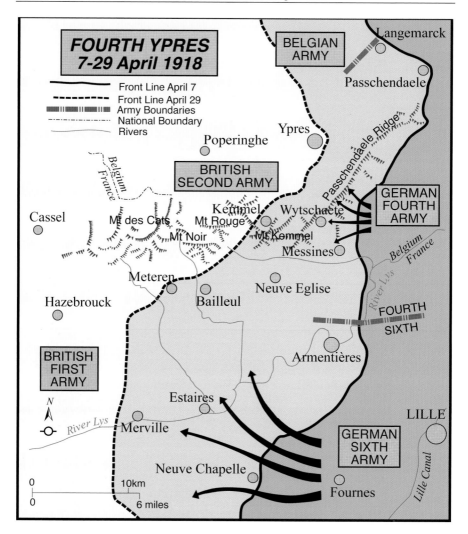

SOME STATISTICS ABOUT THE YPRES BATTLES

Military statistics are always suspect since they are frequently manipulated for propaganda purposes. The following figures for the first three battles are an amalgam of several sources.

Casualties	First Ypres Oct-Nov 1914	Second Ypres Apr-May 1915	Third Ypres July-Nov 1917
British	58,000	60,000	300,000
French	50,000	10,000	8,500
German	130,000	35,000	260,000
VCs	11	14	59

The Salient After World War I

You see why you should walk lightly if you ever go to Ypres, the very stones
of which are memorials to men who perished on the Field of Honour.

J. M. Halley, 62nd Field Coy RE

"Wipers! Does the mere name conjure up its pictures for you? Can you still see, in your mind's
eye, that long, long turnpike – slimy pavé between shell-torn poplars – leading out from 'Pop',
by the red ruins you knew as Vlamertinghe, to a skeleton of a city with its broken dog's teeth of
shattered spires?
Thousands living can still recall that picture."

Gilbert Frankau, who served with 107th Artillery Bde in Ypres, Jan-March 1916

The job of clearing up was daunting. But thanks to the dogged spirit of the local Flemish people
and the help given by the Allied armies with assistance from Chinese labourers and German
prisoners-of-war, the work soon began. Craters and shell holes were filled with the all-too
available rubble, roads were scraped out again. The Yprians came back to the sites of their
houses and tented villages sprang up, followed by more protective and durable wooden huts
which served as living quarters, shops, cafés, hostels. Pilgrims – mothers and fathers, sons and
daughters, brothers and sisters of the dead – began to arrive in their thousands.

By 1920 the first 200 cemeteries had been set up. By 1925 the Cathedral was in the course of
reconstruction. At this stage it was not planned to rebuild the Cloth Hall, a decision thankfully
later rescinded, and in 1934 it began to rise again in all its original glory, accurately reconstructed
to the medieval plans.

Everyone wanted a Memorial to the Missing in the Salient who had no known grave but the
site, conception and format of such an edifice caused more wrangling and dissent than any of the
other Imperial War Graves Commission's undertakings. Winston Churchill (qv) said, 'I should
like to acquire the whole of the ruins of Ypres ... a more sacred place for the British race does not
exist in the world.'

The Times of 30 January 1919 confidently reported that 'Ypres is to remain unrestored, as a
memorial of what Belgium has suffered in the war. The decision is so right that it seems to be
what we have always expected.... Another Ypres will arise near the old one, representing the
future, for the freedom and security of which the past has paid so great a price... these ruins will
mean more than the most splendid monument; they will mean a courage lasting through despair
into triumph.' But the Yprians were already returning and rebuilding their homes and businesses.

The Menin Gate

Finally Sir Reginald Blomfield, who had been appointed to design a memorial for the Commission,
chose the site of Vauban's old fortified gate, through which so many British soldiers had passed on
their way to the front, and whose ruins were known as 'the Gap' by Tommy. The Cabinet granted
£150,000 for its erection, but at the same time the Middleton Committee on National Battlefield
Memorials was also planning an important monument in Ypres. Theirs was to commemorate
'the national effort on the battlefields', the Commission's was to commemorate the missing.
Agreement was finally reached in June 1921 to build one memorial only in the form of an
architectural monument. Of all the Commission's Dominion members, only the New Zealanders
dissented. They erected their own memorials at s-Graventafel, Polygon Wood, Messines and
Tyne Cot.

Blomfield, perhaps the most classically influenced of all the Commission's architects, planned
a vast triumphal arch in the Roman style. When work began on the foundations in April 1923, he
was horrified to discover running sand and had to build a huge raft of concrete piles which were
sunk 36ft into the ground. The massive 'vaulted Hall' is made of French limestone and weighs
20,000 tons. It is 135ft long, 104ft wide and 80ft high.

On the Menin side it was surmounted by a proud British lion designed by Sir William Reid Dick (1878-1961) who was to look 'not fierce and truculent, but patient and enduring, looking outward' along the old Menin road, which has been termed the *Via Sacra* of the British at Ypres, comparable to *La Voie Sacrée* at Verdun or the Freedom Road to Lake Ladoga beside Leningrad. He was to be 'a symbol of the latent strength and heroism of our race', according to Blomfield's memoirs. Reid Dick went on to design the eagle which surmounts the RAF Memorial at Westminster and to sculpt many famous figures,

Menin Gate aerial view

including David Livingstone at Victoria Falls, President Roosevelt in Grosvenor Square, London and the effigies of King George V and Queen Mary for their tombs, designed by Lutyens, in St George's Chapel, Windsor.

On the Ypres side of the arch is a sarcophagus draped with a flag and surmounted by a wreath, a symbol to the citizens of Ypres of the sacrifice the Empire had made for them.

Problems with the Gate's construction continued. Blomfield failed to curtail building in the road leading up to it from the Grand' Place which he felt detracted from its impact on the Ypres side. The contractor was badly hit by the sudden fall in the value of the Belgian franc (in which currency he was being paid) in the summer of 1926. As the arch neared completion heavy rains held up the painting of the lettering, and electricity for the lighting was only installed at the last minute. But eventually it was completed in time for the official opening.

On 24 July 1927, Field Marshal Plumer, President of the Ypres League, unveiled the massive gate - probably the best-known of all the Commission's memorials world-wide, and a symbol of the British way of commemorating their dead – in the presence of the King of the Belgians, several thousand relatives of those whose names it bore, including a party of 700 mothers whose pilgrimage was organised by the St Barnabas Hostels Association (qv), a variety of bands and a BBC contingent. 'The broadcasting of the ceremony of the unveiling of the Menin Gate was quite successful, and, in view of the difficulties, the reception was good,' reported *The Times*. A procession, led by the King with the British Ambassador, Sir George Grahame, on his right and Lord Plumer on his left, marched from the Grand' Place to the Gate, the route lined with Belgian Cyclist Carabiniers (*Les Diables Noirs* – the Black Devils). En route the procession stopped so that the King could pop into the house of the Burgomaster, M. Colaert, to visit him as he was ill in bed. The Archbishop of Canterbury had composed a special prayer for the occasion and buglers of the SLI played the Last Post, followed by pipers of the 1st Bn the Scots Guards who played *The Flowers of the Forest*.

"Then came a terrible minute of silence - a silence so absolute that it seemed as if the whole Salient must be standing hushed in prayer ... As always, before the long minute was up it grew almost unendurable and the crash of bugles in the Reveille came as an immense relief. *The Brabanconne* was played, and then came a quite ineffaceable moment when once again the roll of British drums went out from the Menin Gate and the company sang *God Save the King*. They always make one shudder, those drums. But here, at such a place and in such surroundings, the splendour and the terror of them were beyond words,"

wrote the deeply moved *The Times* Special Correspondent. The frisson he felt so strongly can still often be experienced today when standing under the Menin Gate as the Last Post is played. Lord Plumer spoke with sincerity and emotion. 'His reference to each of the dead whose names are engraved on the gateway – "He is not missing. He is here," was most impressive,' it was reported. Wreaths of flowers (the artificial poppy had not yet become the symbol of remembrance) were laid until the whole 40yd-long interior of the gate was lined with a brilliant bank of flowers. The King was then conducted round the arch by its designers, Sir Reginald Blomfield and Mr (later to become Sir) William Reid Dick. He also met the two Englishwomen who represented the bereaved of the war – Mrs Emily Shrubhole of Clapham and Mrs Merriman of Croydon.

Despite its size, the gate was found to be too small to bear all of what Siegfried Sassoon called 'those intolerably nameless names' in his bitter 1927 poem entitled *On Passing the New Menin Gate*. Its panels only had room to inscribe the 54,900 names of those who were killed between the outbreak of war on 4 August 1914 and 15 August 1917. The remaining 34,888 names were inscribed on Sir Herbert Baker's memorial at the rear of Tyne Cot Cemetery.

On the same day Plumer laid the foundation stone of St George's Memorial Church (qv), next to which was built the school (qv), endowed by Eton College for the children of the growing colony (then numbering about 200) of British expatriates – mostly workers with the War Graves Commission.

Rebuilding

The rebuilding of the shattered towns and villages had been too large a task and financial liability for the communes to undertake themselves. On 8 April 1919, a law was passed enabling them to be 'adopted' by the State. An Office of the Devastated Regions was set up and architects were employed from all over the country. There was a heated debate about the style of the rebuilding. As Churchill had wanted to preserve the ruins of Ypres, so the Flemish community wished to preserve those of Diksmuide, and rebuild the town a couple of kilometres away, and what became known as the 'Modernist' faction subscribed to the idea of conserving at least some ruins (in Ypres especially the Cloth Hall and St Martin's Cathedral) but to rebuild in a progressive, modern 'socio-functional' style. Most inhabitants wished their towns, their homes and their business to be rebuilt exactly as they were. The traditionalists won the day, and when the devastated areas were turned into one enormous building site, local brick was used as it always had been - with the notable exception of the Château of Elzenwalle at Voormezele, which was rebuilt in concrete to what was then a futuristic design. New suburbs which sprang up round Ypres, Diksmuide and Nieuwport (which with Mesen were deemed to be totally destroyed and whose rebuilding had to start from zero) were not constrained by the traditionalists and traces of the influence of the *Art Deco* style then in vogue abounded. Farms were sometimes rebuilt nearer to roads and in the villages and towns roads were widened to cope with the increased motor traffic.

Happily the newly rebuilt Ypres suffered comparatively little damage during World War II. The Menin Gate had some panels chipped by bullets but the cemeteries, though neglected, remained mostly undisturbed. The townspeople hid the stained glass windows and other treasures from St George's Church, returning them all intact when the first members of the congregation came back on 5 October 1945. The Germans had removed the commemorative brass plaques from the chairs and kept them carefully. The town was liberated by the Polish Armoured Division on 6 September 1944, their arrival celebrated by sounding the Last Post (qv) again under the Menin Gate.

YPRES TODAY

After the 1944 liberation Ypres quickly returned to normality. For more information about present-day Ieper, see Tourist Information and In Flanders Fields Museum pages below. It is interesting to compare the post-World War I debate between the traditionalists and the modernists with that in the 1990s. In the 1920s the traditionalist view prevailed. In the years leading to the millennium it appeared to be the politically correct modernists who were subtly changing the attitude of the authorities of West Flanders in the Salient and its surrounds, from a spirit of perpetuating the remembrance of the sacrifices of war to the celebration of the concept of peace. This trend was evident in the design of the 'In Flanders Fields' Museum in Ieper, the promotion of Ieper as a 'Town of Peace' and the institution of a 'Peace Park' in the old war-devastated areas. Now that the last survivor of the fighting in the Salient has passed away (Harry Patch (qv) in 2009) and as preparations were made for the four 100th Anniversary years starting in 2014, there appears to be a reversion to a more traditional

The Cloth Hall and St Martin's Cathedral, Ieper

way of commemorating and remembering. The Land is truly, 'The Last Witness', to those four terrible years and it is being given ever more importance.

THE LAST POST CEREMONY

Summary provided by Ian Connerty, Secretary of the Last Post Association.

A high proportion of all of the visitors to Ypres are those interested in the 1914-18 theatre of war, and students. The highlight of their stay is undoubtedly the simple but highly moving ceremony of the sounding of the Last Post under the Menin Gate each night at 2000 hours. The local police stop the traffic and the bugle call is still played under the arch in 'the English style', as taught by Mr Dick Collick (qv), an early employee with the War Graves Commission. After the war, bereaved families streamed in their thousands to Ypres to find the graves or memorial names of their loved ones. When the Menin Gate was unveiled on 24 July 1927, the 'Last Post' - the British Army bugle call played to mark the end of the day's labours and the onset of the night's rest, and now traditionally used to commemorate the dead - was played under the great reverberating arches of the memorial for the first time. One of those moved by the haunting notes of the melody and the strong impression it made on those listening was the Chief of Police, Pierre Vandenbraambussche. He was so inspired by what he heard that he persuaded other influential local citizens to sponsor the regular playing of the Last Post under the Gate. According to the Foundation Rules of the Association, the purpose of the act was '... to commemorate and to express eternal gratitude towards the soldiers of the British Empire who fought and fell in the defence of the city and the Ypres Salient, thereby saving the independence and freedom of Belgium'. It was an act of sympathy, too, towards the relatives - a tangible gesture that the townspeople could make. The Last Post was played for two months after the unveiling of the Menin Gate, was sounded again on 8 August 1928, when the Prince of Wales took the salute under the Gate at the first major Royal British Legion pilgrimage, and then in 1929 became a daily ceremony. In 1930, the Last Post Committee was formed under the patronage of HM the King of the Belgians. It was a non-profit-making, totally independent association - and so it remains to this day. Funds were raised by gifts from influential local business people and from memberships, with contributions from the town of Ypres, the Belgian and other British Legion branches and many private gifts from relatives and old comrades. The original committee, whose Chairman was Pierre Vandenbraambussche, included Lieutenant General Pulteney, Major Paul Slessor (a leading light in the acquisition of Talbot House, qv) and Aimé Gruwez (the grandfather of the current honorary chairman, Guy Gruwez, and great-grandfather of the present chairman, Benoit Mottrie). The choice of who should supply the buglers fell, among others, between the Ypriana Band (of which Aimé Gruwez was chairman) and the Corps of Drums & Bugles of the Fire Brigade, commanded by Maurice Vergracht. It was decided to use the fire brigade buglers and so began the warm links with the fire service which have continued to this day.

In 1934, the Surrey Branch of the British Legion made what was then a considerable donation – £400 – which swelled the capital fund to produce a working income. In 1936, Richard Leclercq, head of the local telephone company, took over the chairmanship until the nightly ceremony was suspended on 20 May 1940, because of the German occupation at the start of the Second World War. Only two days before, 200 members of the British colony - men, women and children - fled to the Channel ports and thence to safety in England for the duration. The tradition of the Last Post was kept alive, weekly, at the Commonwealth war graves plot in Brookwood Cemetery and to this day members of the Brookwood Last Post Committee make an annual pilgrimage to Ypres. On 6 September 1944, a jubilant bugler repeatedly played the Last Post under the Gate as shots were still being exchanged on the other side of the town between the liberating troops of the Polish Armoured Brigade and the retreating Germans. Many British, Canadian and Polish soldiers attended this first post-World War II ceremony. In 1946, the Burgomaster, Jan Van der Ghote, became Chairman of the committee and was succeeded in 1953 by Florimond Vandervoorde. In 1966, the current honorary chairman, Guy Gruwez, who had served on the committee since 1953, took over the chairmanship just after the visit of HM Queen Elizabeth, which followed in a tradition of royal visits, including all the kings of Belgium since the First World War – King Albert I, King Leopold III, King Baudouin, King Albert II and King Filip. Many other members of the British royal family have visited, as did Pope John Paul II, Mother Theresa and Prime Ministers from around the world. Guy Gruwez was awarded the MBE in 1986 for his prodigious efforts and his dedication in making sure that the simple ceremony retains its purity and the atmosphere of sincere and dignified remembrance envisaged by the original founders. On 1 April 2006, after 40 years in post, Mr.Gruwez handed over the chairman's position to his nephew, Benoit Mottrie, who had served on the committee since 1990.

The organisation behind this unique act of tribute is now known as the Last Post Association. Anyone wishing to participate in the ceremony can send a request for an extended ceremony to the Association via its website, www.lastpost.be During extended ceremonies (when wreaths may be laid and the Reveille - the call traditionally played at the beginning of the day to rouse troops from their slumber – is also played) there may be up to six buglers, dressed in the smart navy blue uniform of the local Fire Brigade. The familiar and comforting words of what has come to be known as 'The Exhortation', a verse from Laurence Binyon's poem, *For the Fallen*, are also recited:

They shall grow not old, as we that are left grow old:
Age shall not weary them, nor the years condemn.
At the going down of the sun and in the morning
We will remember them.

The last line is traditionally repeated by those present
Now the Kohima Epitaph is often added to the ceremony:

When you go home,
Tell them of us and say:
For your tomorrow
We gave our today.

The Last Post Association asks for silence to be maintained throughout the ceremony and also feels that it is not appropriate to applaud at the end of the proceedings.

There have been many presentations of bugles to the Last Post Committee over the years. On 16 September 1928, buglers of the Guards handed over four silver bugles, presented by British Legion members who lived in Belgium. Thirty-nine years later, on 3 September 1967, one of those buglers, Drum Major Tom Simpson, returned with the Mid-Somerset branch of the Old Contemptibles to play his bugle under the Gate. More silver bugles were presented by the Blackpool and Fleetwood Old Contemptibles Association on 12 March 1950. The Last Post had always been played on bugles, but on 11 November 1959 Colonel John Whitaker, who had served during the war with the 31st (County Palatine) Division of the Royal Field Artillery, presented the Committee with two silver trumpets. He hoped occasionally to hear the call played on the trumpet, as is sometimes the case in the Royal Artillery and some cavalry regiments. Although the regular players practised assiduously with the new instruments, they returned to their familiar bugles. Two more trumpets were offered in 1961 by Lieutenant Colonel Keiller Mackay, Vice-Governor of Ontario. After years of use, it was noticed that the bugles were losing their tone and on 12 July 1992, the 65th anniversary of the inauguration of the Menin Gate, six new silver bugles were presented by 2 Group, Royal Corps of Transport. Eight further bugles – the current instruments – were donated by the Royal British Legion in June 2007.

The dedication of the Association's buglers is outstanding. The ceremony takes place every evening – come rain, shine, snow or heat wave – and irrespective of whether anyone is there to watch or not. Often they are called on to play at other ceremonies in and around Ypres and in recent decades have also been invited to perform in Australia and New Zealand. Several of the buglers have put in many years of service. Amongst the longest serving were Maurice Baratto, MBE (1944-1980), Daniel Demey, MBE (1945-1995), and Albert Verkouter, MBE (1966-2010), who was also a gardener with the Commonwealth War Graves Commission. But even these outstanding examples of devotion to duty were surpassed by Antoon Verschoot, who retired in 2015 after an outstanding 61 years of service, passing on his role as chief bugler to Rik Vandekerckhove. The Association's other buglers are currently Dirk Vandekerckhove, Tonny Desodt, Raf Decombel, Jan Callemein and Christophe Wils. It is always appreciated if visitors take the trouble to thank the buglers after the ceremony.

On 9 July 2015, the Last Post Ceremony was played for the 30,000th time – an unparalleled record of steadfast commitment in the cause of remembrance, and one that was rightly celebrated around the world. One hundred years after the First World War, the ceremony continues to attract widespread public interest. The number of people who participate each evening is still on the rise, in part inspired by the Great War centenary commemorations, and special ceremonies attended by high-ranking civil, military and political dignitaries are a regular occurrence. In this respect, perhaps one of the most symbolically important of these visits in recent years took place on 26 June 2014, when the heads of government of the 27 member states of the European Union – including David Cameron, François Hollande and Angela Merkel – came together under the Menin Gate to remember the outbreak in 1914 of a war that once threatened to tear the continent apart.

Yet despite this high-profile interest, in essence the ceremony remains what it has always been: a simple but inspiring daily tribute to those who died for our freedom, organised by a group of wholly independent private individuals, nearly all of whom are local Belgian people living in Ieper. It is remarkable to think that the ceremony, notwithstanding its well-deserved international reputation, receives no systematic public funding, but depends for its survival on the generosity of its members and other donors. It is a cause well worth supporting and new members are always welcome to join via the appropriate page on the Association's website: www.lastpost.be. The statutes of the Association declare its intention to maintain the ceremony 'in perpetuity'. With the help of us all, let us hope that it succeeds in this noble aim.

Please remember to thank the Buglers

APPROACH ONE

THIS ROUTE IS THE MOST DIRECT TO IEPER

From Calais via motorways E40-A16/E42-A25 to Steenvoorde and D948/N308/N38 to Poperinge and Ieper.

Approximate driving time, without stops: 1 hour 15 minutes. Approximate distance: 58 miles.

From Calais, as you leave either the tunnel terminal, or ferry port, follow blue motorway signs A16 Dunkerque. At Grande Synthe take Exit 28 to the A25 right signed Lille, Ypres. Take Exit 13 at Steenvoorde on the D948 signed Ypres (Ieper). Cross the old border station, beside which is a variety of shops and restaurants. Continue on the D948/N38.

At this point the very useful reference point of the tall wireless mast of Mont des Cats is seen to the right. Just less than a mile later is a sign to the left to Abeele and a green Commonwealth War Graves Commission (CWGC) sign to **Abeele Aerodrome Military Cemetery** on the N333 and the grass path which leads to the Cemetery. As the war began the main belligerents found immediate use for their aircraft as a means of seeing what their opponents were up to - but within one year the skies would turn into a major battlefield hosting a contest for air superiority. The rate of development of aircraft and tactics was extraordinary. In September 1914 the British first used air photography and airborne wireless was introduced to assist in artillery observation. During First Ypres the RFC was primarily concerned with reconnaissance and with liaison between commanders, RFC HQ being set up at St Omer. On 16 October, 6 Squadron moved to Poperinghe and 2, 3, 4, and 5 Squadrons settled at St Omer. Artillery commanders had come to realise the value of air observation for their guns and increasingly demanded it, but few aircraft were fitted with wireless. An alternative method of signalling existed using Very lights, but it was a complicated matter as this extract from an RFC instruction shows:

'The aeroplane flies at any convenient height immediately over the target. When the flyer is exactly above the target he fires a Very's light, and at this moment the battery rangefinders, who have been following the course of the aeroplane, take its range. At the same time an observer with the battery, who also has followed the course of the aeroplane with either a sextant and artificial horizon, or an inclinometer, takes the angle of elevation of the aeroplane. At the same time the guns are laid on the direction of the aeroplane. The two observations give sufficient data for ascertaining the horizontal distance between the battery and the target. By allowing for the difference in level between the battery and the target in the usual way, the exact range is given, and the batteries can open fire at once on the line obtained.'

Later experiments with electric lamp signalling proved to be much more successful.

At the end of November 1914 the RFC was reorganised into two 'Wings': No 1 under command of Lt Col H. M. Trenchard (in May 1915 to become Commander of the entire RFC in the field) and No 2 under command of Lt Col C. J. Burke. In December, 1st Wing was allocated to the new First Army and 2nd Wing to the Second Army. RFC HQ remained at St Omer together with base repair and maintenance support.

• *Abeele Aerodrome Military Cemetery (Map T6, GPS: 50.81489 2.65585)*

As the name of the Cemetery implies, Abeele was the site of an RFC airfield, from which Squadrons 4 and 6 worked. Prior to Second Ypres 6 Squadron had been based at Poperinghe but heavy

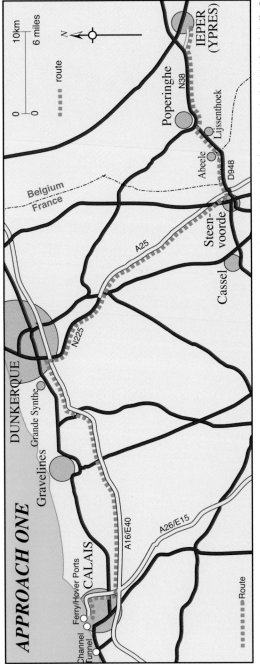

German shelling on 24 April forced the squadron to move further back from the line. Two days later, 5 Squadron based at Bailleul spotted the German armoured train near Langemarck that had been responsible for the shelling of Poperinghe and British heavy artillery was ranged on it (whether by Very, or wireless or lamp is not recorded) and it moved off. In that same month **2nd Lt Rhodes-Moorhouse** suffered fatal wounds during a raid over Courtrai and yet managed to bring his machine safely back to his field at Merville (France) and to report on his mission. He was posthumously awarded the **VC**, the first airman to receive the decoration 'for work in the air' and is buried in Dorset, where his son, Flying Officer W. Rhodes-Moorhouse, killed in the Battle of Britain, also lies.

The Cemetery contains 104 British burials, and was started by the French during the Battles of the Lys (Fourth Ypres) and taken over by the British in July and August 1918. The 91 French and 84 Americans originally buried here were removed after the Armistice. The burials are all from 1918 actions, either in April or in July/August, with many Notts & Derby, E Kents, Lancs Fusiliers and Cheshires. They include the interestingly named **Pte J. Foundling**, Notts & Derby, 17 July, age 20, **Maj R.W. Barnett, MC & Bar, KRRC**, age 26, 12 August 1918 and **2nd Lt P.V. Drake Brockman**, E Kents, age 19, 18 July 1918. The architect was Maj G. H. Goldsmith, who also designed the Memorial to the Missing at La Ferté-Sous-Jouarre on the banks of the River Marne and over sixty other CWGC cemeteries.

In 2011 the Cemetery underwent considerable renovation.

Continue on the D948/N38 and some 3 miles later, before Poperinge, turn right following signs to Lijssenthoek CWGC Cemetery and park in the Visitor Centre car park.

Abeele Aerodrome Military CWGC Cemetery

[Alternatively Lijssenthoek CWGC Cemetery may be visited on Itinerary Two from Poperinge.]

• *Lijssenthoek Military CWGC Cemetery & Visitor's Centre (Map T5/ GPS: 50.82840 2.701661)*

Visitors' Centre. On 21 September 2012 the unmanned Visitor's Centre, sited across the road from the small side entrance to the Cemetery, with parking area and WC, was opened. The architect Luc Vanderwynckel was influenced by the shape of wartime huts, barracks and hospitals. Its entrance is sunk 1 metre below grass level and it then rises to a glass structure with panoramic views. A path leads to the original entrance to the Cemetery, on one side of which is a row of 1,392 poles, representing the days on which at least one person was buried in the Cemetery.

The Centre tells the history of the Field Hospitals, of the CWGC and of how the Cemetery is a mirror of what was happening at the front, as for every day of the year there is at least one grave. Personal stories and photos etc were collected on a database system to tell a different 'Daily Story' 365 days of the year of men who are buried in this multinational cemetery. Visitors can print out a plan of the Cemetery showing the location of the subject of the day's story. A 9 metre 'Touch Table' gives access to the database and shows archaeological finds discovered during the construction, another shows contributions from relatives. One external wall is a 'Listening Wall' which recounts extracts from letters, diaries, hospital reports etc. Another is a 'Portrait Wall' with images of over 1,000 portraits of men buried here.

Open: 0900-1800, free entrance, disabled access. WC in car park. Drinks dispenser. For Group visits contact: toerisme@poperinge.be. Tel: + (0) 57 34 66 76.

The Visitor's Guide for Lijssenthoek, price 5.00, is available in the vending machine on site and in the Tourist Office Poperinge (qv). See www.lijssenthoek.be

Researcher Annemie Morisse wrote a superbly detailed article about the Cemetery and its history following the research project started at Talbot House (qv) in June 2009 which was published in the WFA *Bulletin* of Oct/Nov 2009.

Continue into the Cemetery.

At the back of the Cemetery was the old railway line. This spur from the Poperinghe line was built to carry supplies to the front and the wounded back to the CCS's. The Sidings were named from the adjacent farm owned by Remi (sometimes seen as Remy) Quaghebeur, whose buildings still remain today. During the war the farm's barns acted as a shelter. As at Godewaersvelde (see Approach Two), there were many air raids at Lijssenthoek. The French first used the farm as an

Visitor's Centre, Lijssenthoek CWGC Cemetery

Evacuation Hospital in May 1915 and theirs are the earliest burials in this cosmopolitan cemetery and some of the latest, as they used it again in August 1918. In July 1915 the British established CCSs here and in August 1916 the 2nd Canadian CCS took over from the French. By August 1918 the area had developed into four large Field Hospitals with some 4,000 beds. It was now a virtual village with huts, streets, electricity unit, vegetable gardens, concerts and football pitches. During the June 1917 Messines Battle alone 5,000 casualties had arrived at Remi Siding. It had become the second largest war cemetery in the area.

The post-war Cemetery, designed by Sir Reginald Blomfield, remains so today, with a total of 10784 burials - 7,369 known UK plus 23 Unknown, 1,131 Australian, 1,058 Canadian, 21 British West Indies, 3 Indian, 5 Newfoundland, 291 New Zealand, 28 South African plus 1 Unknown, 35 Chinese Labourers, 233 German – including many graves in which more than one soldier is buried, and 1 ex-soldier employed by the CWGC. There are 8 Special Memorials near the Stone of Remembrance to men Known to be Buried in the Cemetery.

There are also three American burials – **Lt James A. Pigue** and **Pte 1st Class Harry A. King** of the 3rd US Cavalry who died of pneumonia on 20 September 1918, and whose **brother, Private Reginald King** of the ASC, attd 25th Siege Battery RGA, killed on 17 October 1917, is also buried here. Our American friend Lil Pfluke (qv) referred us to research by Jerome Sheridan that revealed that Pigue, a VMI graduate, joined the US Marine Corps in 1904, took part in the construction of the Panama Canal and left the Corps in 1909. In 1916 he enlisted in the 1st Tennessee National Guard Regt and was promoted to 1st Lt. He then briefly left the service only to re-enlist, finally serving with the 117th IR, 59th Bde, 30th Division (a National Guard formation known as 'Old Hickory' after Andrew Jackson). Once arrived in Belgium, this experienced soldier served with British and Australian Arty Units of the depleted 2nd Br Army. On 15 July 1918 he was again serving with the 117th Regt who took over responsibility for the trenches east of Poperinghe. On 18 July he was shot through the heart by a sniper, the first casualty of the US 30th Div, and was initially buried in Gwalia Brit Cemetery (qv), being moved to Lijssenthoek's 'American Plot' in June 1919. When asked if she wished his body to be repatriated, his widow Jane stated that he should not be disturbed under any circumstances. As she did not reply to further communications, his father, Edward Pigue, came to Belgium to see his son's grave and had the words, 'Gave His Life for Humanity' added to his headstone. The third American is **Cpl William Leonard**, age 28, who served with the 27th (New York) Division. On 14 July 1918 Leonard persuaded a British patrol to let him accompany them to repair barbed wire entanglements. Attracting German attention, the party was hit by a shell, mortally wounding Leonard. Initially he was buried on the Scherpenberg Hill, but was later re-interred here, the first American to die on Flemish soil.

Other burials of interest (although each one, of course, was of immense interest to their friends and family) are: the only woman - **Staff Nurse N. Spindler of the QA Imp Mil Nursing Service**, killed on 21 August 1917, and **Maj Gen Malcolm Smith Mercer**, CB, killed on 3 June 1916, commanding the 3rd Canadian Division; **Brig Gen Hugh Gregory Fitton**, CB, DSO, killed on 20 January 1916, commanding 101st Inf Bde, 34th Div; Brig Gen A. F. Gordon, CMG, DSO, killed on 31 July 1917, commanding 153rd Inf Bde, the 51st Highland Div; **Brig Gen R. C. Gore** CB, CMG, killed on 13 April 1918, commanding 101st Inf Bde, 34th Div. Also buried here is the **Rev Charles Edmund Doudney** (qv) who died of his wounds on 16 October 1915. He was given a full military funeral, the Service being conducted by 6th Div's Senior Chaplain, which was attended by 'five or six of his fellow chaplains'. **Capt James Ernest Studholme Wilson**, MC, RAMC (attd Ox & Bucks), age 51, was the subject of a poem written by surviving comrades during a 1930 Pilgrimage. It describes how this much-loved MO was hit by a splinter during a raid from Piccadilly Hotel trench in the Ploegsteert area, taken back to Plum Farm dressing station at Wytschaete – overflowing with the dead and dying – where he died hit by a shell whilst undergoing surgery,.

There is a separate register for the 658 French burials.

The trees and shrubs are particularly beautiful in this forbiddingly vast Cemetery, especially the willows and wisteria, and many headstones are accompanied by splendid red roses. The CWGC nurseries which adjoined the Cemetery for many years have been closed as they were not competitive with local commercial nurseries.

During his May 1922 Pilgrimage, Lijssenthoek was the last Belgian Cemetery to be visited by King George V. In 1923 a huge pilgrimage was organised by the charitable society of St Barnabas with the help of Toc H. On Palm Sunday 850 (some accounts say it was 1,000) relatives from all parts of the UK, the majority of them women dressed in mourning black, arrived at the railway station at Abeele, were transferred into a cavalcade of motor-cars and then formed up 'a little distance away into a kind of ragged procession. Many of the women were very much affected, and the host of mourners slowly approaching the gate of the cemetery was most pathetic', reported *The Times*. During the Communion Service that was held, when the Stone of Remembrance acted as an altar, the altar vases were brass shell-cases and a shell-case supported the cross, 'many of the women began to break down for the first time. They wept silently, now that they were again so near their dead, and the scenes which they had passed can only have sharpened their grief.' The correspondent of the *Daily Express* crystallised the scene:

'No-one who was present at the memorial service at the Lijssenthoek Military Cemetery this morning will ever forget that slow-moving procession of a thousand lion-hearted bereaved parents, widows and orphans shuffling along the Poperinghe road under a hot sun, with shawls and rugs slung over their shoulders, artificial flowers and brown paper parcels in their arms, gathered from Ayr and Cornwall, Halifax and Lincoln, Balham and Barnstaple, to pay homage to their glorious dead. There were nearly a thousand of them – grey beards, infants in arms, school children, young (much too young) widows, and old, old women who looked too fragile to cross the village street. Not one of them had ever crossed the sea before, yet out of the love they bore their lost ones they were gladly ready to essay the great adventure. '

Reading these vivid descriptions of unbearable collective pain while overlooking the headstones of the men that were being mourned is to transport one back in time to share it. Carrying their dignity and their natural decency with them, immensely comforted by the beauty of the cemeteries and the flowers that abounded, the pilgrims moved on to other smaller cemeteries and to Ypres itself. 'Only such mothers could have given us such sons,' wrote one observer.

Turn round and return to the junction. Turn left.

As you turn left note the sign 'In De Leene Estaminet' on the hostelry ahead. The adjoining building is inscribed '1911'. From this one could safely deduce that this estaminet was active during World War I and it takes no great stretch of imagination to visualise tired and weary

*Undulating Line of
Headstones, Lijssenthoek
CWGC Cemetery*

"*We are coming, brothers, coming,
A hundred thousand strong!*"

"*Voici la République sœur,
Avec vous, frères d'armes, de cœur!*"

Our American allies join the fray

**German headstone
with two names**

*Headstone of an
American Doughboy
James A. Pigue*

Tommies here – perhaps overworked medical staff from the nearby CCS – eating 'oofs' and drinking the weak beer or sour 'vin blonk' that was the best on offer.

Continue to the main road. Turn right and continue to the junction with the R33 ring road.

N.B. At this point **Nine Elms Brit Cemetery** (Map T4, GPS: 50.85091 2.69762) may be reached by turning left on the ring road, going straight over the next roundabout and first left on Helleketelweg. Used by 3rd Australian and 44th CCS in September 1917 and then from March–October 1918, it contains 1,556 Commonwealth and 37 German WW1 graves plus 22 WW2 from the withdrawal to Dunkirk in May 1940. Buried here is **Serjeant David Gallaher**, 2nd Bn Auckland Regt, NZ EF, killed on 4 October 1917 age 41. He was a former Captain of the All Blacks Rugby Team. The Cemetery was designed by Sir Reginald Blomfield.

Headstone of Sergeant D. Gallaher, former Captain All Blacks, Nine Elms CWGC Cemetery

Turn right and follow signs to Ieper on the N38 to the roundabout with the following Memorial in the centre. Stop in the lay-by just beyond.

War Horse 'Agony' Statue. (Map G9a. GPS: 50.84986 2.8085)

This striking and very moving Memorial was in inaugurated on 11 May 2013. It was commissioned by the Ieper Town Council and is designed by local artist Luc Coomans (who died the following year). The two skeletal horses (reminiscent of the realistic puppet horses in the stage version of Michael Morpurgo's *War Horse*) rear in pain and agony from a ruined building. The forged steel horses are between 3.5-4.0 metres high on a 2.5 metre base. They symbolise the suffering of the thousands of war horses that were killed during the Great War. The site was chosen as it is on the border between the behind-the-line area around Poperinge and the hell of the front line around Ieper. The artist commented, 'Man dragged into war the whole of nature. My work is an indictment against war and any form of violence.'

Continue to the junction with the N308 and take it towards Ieper.

On house No 65, Poperingseweg is an

Advert for Earl Haig House (GPS: 50.84904 2.87083)

In early 2013, during the renovation on the house, the sign, covered (and therefore protected) since the late 1940s by tiles, was exposed and therefore became

Dramatic War Horses Statue, 'Agony', near Vlamertinge

Advert for Earl Haig House, Ypres

Earl Haig House, Ypres in 1935,
courtesy of Jacky Platteeuw

vulnerable to the elements. It advertises the British Legion (before it gained the word 'Royal') Earl Haig House round the corner from the Grand' Place, Ypres, at Korte Tourhoutstraat 9, which opened on 28 April 1932. The major ceremony was attended by VIPs, Legion Members with standards, pilgrims and large crowds. The House was a haven for pilgrims, where Poppy wreaths, luncheons and teas were available. The advert gives basic details, including the Telephone and Telegram numbers. The building still stands intact on the original site.

The Military Upkeep Preservation Society (Committee Members – Genevra Charnsley & Jacques Ryckebosch, Chris Lock & Milena Kolorikova and Iain McHenry) mounted a campaign to preserve it. Ieper Town Council, the Province and Flemish Heritage (Minister for Heritage Geert Bourgeois) helped funded the cost. Contact: Genevra on e-mail: info@ypres-fgt.com

Continue following signs into the Centre of Ieper.

APROACH TWO

This route has the option of either by-passing or going through St Omer. It then goes through Cassel, Godewaersvelde, Mont des Cats, Mont Noir, Reningelst, Lijssenthoek and via Poperinge to Ieper.

Approximate driving time, without stops: 2 hours. Approximate distance: 73 miles.

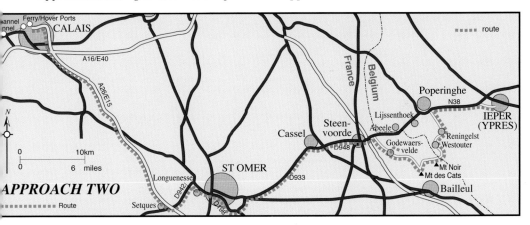

From Calais, as you leave the Tunnel or Ferry terminal, follow blue motorway signs to the A16 Paris (the key direction to follow at first) and St Omer. Continue to the fork to the right to the A26/ E15. Take it and follow it to Exit 3. Take it and continue direction St Omer to a roundabout. Take the 3rd exit signed St Omer on the D942, take it and follow it over a series to the Longuenesse exit. Take it and at the first traffic lights turn left signed Longuenesse on the D928 and continue to the parking area on the right for a group of cemeteries on the left.

Longuenesse Souvenir CWGC Cemetery 1914-1920 (GPS: 50.73119 2.25010).

On this site was an important hospital centre with the 4th, 10th, 7th Canadian, 9th Canadian and New Zealand Stationary Hospitals, the 7th, 58th (Scottish) and 59th (Northern) General Hospitals, and the 17th, 18th and 1st and 2nd Australian CCSs all stationed here at some time during the war. The Cemetery, which was set up to take casualties from the many hospitals, takes its name from the French Cemetery of the St. Omer garrison, called the Souvenir Cemetery (*Cimetière du Souvenir Français*). This is located next to the CWGC Cemetery (on the left of the entrance) which contains 2,874 Commonwealth burials of the First World War (6 unidentified), with Special Memorials commemorating 23 men of the Chinese Labour Corps (qv) whose graves could not be exactly located. Second World War burials number 403, (93 unidentified). There are also 34 non-war burials (e.g. CWGC) and 239 war graves of other nationalities.

We cannot recommend a visit here strongly enough. The Cemetery was designed by Sir Herbert Baker and must be one of the most beautiful Cemeteries in Flanders – especially when the shrubs and flowers are exuberant in June and July. The layout is interestingly irregular. It varies from long double lines of headstones, 'shoulder to shoulder', many with more than one name inscribed, to a Chinese plot close to the Stone of Remembrance and elegant shelters at the top (some of them, unusually, on French headstones), behind which is a plot of German graves.

The inscription on the Chinese headstones is very interesting. The central vertical column of Chinese characters represents the name of the casualty. To its right is inscribed the region of China from which he came. The epitaph at the top (repeated in English below) is one of six standard inscriptions: 'Faithful Unto Death', 'Endures Forever', 'Though Dead He Still Liveth', 'Bravely Done', 'True Till Death' and 'A Good Reputation Endures Forever'. See also Reningelst section following.

To the left as one enters there are semicircles of WW2 graves, many of them from a variety of Regiments from May 1940 and of RAF from 1941, among them Poles and Australians and IWGC/ CWGC Headstones from 1923 onwards.

Increasingly, as they have to be changed, the headstones are of the latest, crisply engraved style.

Buried here is 19 year old **Private Charles Nicholson** of the York and Lancs, **shot for desertion** on 27 October 1917. Seventeen days earlier, his twin brother John, of the 2nd Bn Essex Regiment, was killed in action and is buried at Poelcapelle (qv). Was the fact that his brother had been killed taken into account before Charles Nicholson was executed? The CWGC records show that some 20 pairs of twins in the UK Forces died in the war.

To the right of the entrance – which has magnificent wrought iron gates - is an **Information Board** describing the hospitals and the aerial activity in the area.

The French Plot is to the left as one enters, with a row of Muslim headstones at the front.

Turn round and return to the traffic lights at the cross roads.

Here you have two options which we consider in turn below.

1. *To visit the centre of* **St Omer** *go straight over at the traffic lights and follow signs to St Omer Centre.*
2. *To avoid the centre of St Omer.*

Chinese Headstones, Longuenesse Souvenir CWGC Cemetery (see text for details)

Longuenesse Souvenir CWGC Cemetery

1. St Omer/RWC. GPS: 50.75014 2.25062

Continue following signs to Centre and 'i' for information. Preferably park in the Place du Maréchal Foch in front of the Hotel de Ville.

In the area around the square is a brilliant choice of **restaurants, cafés and hotels** to suit all pockets and tastes.

Walk back to the rue du Lion d'Or.

At No 4 is the **Tourist Office** with helpful staff and tourist literature, notably a town plan.

Follow the plan on foot to rue Carnot, passing the Cathedral of Notre Dame.

In the **Cathedral** there is a **Tablet designed by H. P. Cart de Lafontaine** similar to the one in St Martin's, Ypres (see illus page page 71).

St Omer was GHQ for the BEF from October 1914 to March 1916. Sir John French was appointed its C-in-C, despite Sir Douglas Haig's doubts about his ability. Haig was to write in his diary on 11 August 1914, 'In my own heart I know that French is quite unfit for this great command at a time of crisis in our nation's history'. Nevertheless, French journeyed to Paris on 14 August, met Joffre at Vitry-le-Francois on the 16th, then established temporary GHQ in the Lion d'Or in Paris. The frequent moves of the succeeding few weeks reflect the mobile nature of the early days of the war. During the Retreat from Mons GHQ was established at Le Cateau, moving to St Quentin on 25 August, then to Noyon, to Compiègne on the 28th, to Melun in early September, to Fère-en-Tardenois, on 8 October to Abbeville and, finally, to St Omer after a brief stay in Cassel.

As the scene of action moved to the Ypres Salient, General Joffre, who was about to be appointed Commander *Groupe des Armées du Nord*, was based in Doullens and General Foch took over the Cassel HQ (see below) from French. The roads between the three HQs saw much to-ing and fro-ing, as hurried conferences between the Allied Commanders were called to solve each successive crisis.

The lonely grave of Field Marshal Viscount French of Ypres in Ripple churchyard, Kent

A later function of GHQ was to approve the work of the official war artists. Many chafed at the restrictions that were imposed upon them which cramped not only their artistic style, but the verity of what they were trying to report. Paul Nash (qv) complained, 'I was not allowed to put dead men into my pictures because apparently they do not exist. I am no longer an artist. I am a messenger who will bring back word from the men who are fighting to those who want the war to go on forever.' Frederic Villiers, the experienced artist who was studying in Paris during the Franco-Prussian War, had worked as a war artist in the Balkans, in South Africa, in the Sudan, and during the Russo-Japanese War and knowing the paranoid and restrictive attitude of the British towards war artists and correspondents, he worked for the French army. Occasionally he travelled with the correspondents Philip Gibbs of the *Daily Telegraph* and the *Daily Chronicle* or Gordon Smith of The Herald. Often he and Smith posed as Belgians to get into the British sector. To guarantee that his pictures got to the *Illustrated London News*, Villiers (now well into his sixties) delivered them in person, hidden in his boots! Otherwise they might have been blocked by the War Office Censors in London. Even when sketches were passed by them, they decreed that further pictures would have to be passed by HQ at St Omer as well. When told that one of his sketches showing a British soldier watering some daffodils with a jam tin would have to go for approval to St Omer, Villiers protested that ' ... if the jam pot was a give-away to the enemy, I could easily camouflage it as a beer mug'. Villiers died in 1922.

In August 1914 Lord Roberts, who despite his 82 years was still energetic and enthusiastic, had hinted to Lord Kitchener that he would dearly love to serve under him as C-in-C Home Forces, was given the consolation prize of being appointed Colonel-in-Chief of Overseas Forces. In view of his early service, he took a particular interest in the Indian Forces and raised a Comforts Fund for them.

As soon as the Indian Division landed in Marseilles on 26 September 1914, Roberts had wanted to visit them in France. Originally his visit was planned for 1 November, but the situation in Flanders was then so critical that French managed to postpone the visit until the 11th. The old Field Marshal travelled to France with his daughter Lady Aileen who reported that he 'was like a boy going on his holidays'. On landing at Boulogne he first visited an Indian hospital ship. The

drive to St Omer was bitterly cold: there was a smattering of snow on the hills. His first stop as they approached the town was 'to the flying field'. Major Maurice Baring, then Private Secretary to Sir David Henderson the first commander of the RFC, and later to become ADC to General Trenchard, had set up Flying Corps HQ on Monday 6 October 'in a small château on the hill between the town and the aerodrome'. Nos 2, 3, 4 and 5 Squadrons were established in the aerodrome on the top of the hill, billets were found in Longuenesse and the area became a hive of activity. 'A great quantity of guests used to stream through the house,' wrote Baring. 'Pilots, observers, staff-officers, administrative officers, experts, etc., used to arrive from London, and sometimes from Paris, and sometimes from the sky.' Baring reported having seen Lord Roberts 'as he walked round the Aerodrome one bitterly cold afternoon.'

On 12 November Lord Roberts started a gruelling day of long drives by inspecting the Indian Staff at Hinges, some 40km from St Omer. He then drove on to the various HQs of the Meerut Division, the Cavalry, where he met Hon Maj-Gen Sir Pertab (aka Pratap) Singh, Maharaja of Idar and Regent of Jodhpur, and the Lahore Division, before driving on to 'a place just two miles short of Armentières' for lunch with General Keir of 5th Division – roughly another 30 kilometres. They stopped

Field Marshal Earl Roberts

off at Fourth Army HQ to have tea with General Rawlinson and ended the day at Sir Henry Wilson's Mess back in St Omer. Lord Roberts commented that it had 'a much more cheerful and determined an atmosphere than had Sir John French's.' The next morning they set off with sandwiches to Cassel to see Foch, had lunch in 'a chemist's shop in Bailleul', visited the

No 52 Rue Carnot with detail of Lord Roberts plaque

Scherpenberg, where the party 'got out of the car and scrambled up a muddy track to a windmill at its summit' in an attempt to see the shelling at Ypres before driving back to St Omer in damp and freezing cold weather. It is small wonder that Roberts there developed a high temperature and, despite the administrations of French's own doctor and two Army nurses, died at 2010 the next evening. There is a **blue Plaque on the house at 52 Rue Carnot**, then the HQ of the Town Major where the great old soldier died. The impressive funeral was held on 17 November. Also on rue Carnot is the **Musée Sandelin**, on the exterior wall of which the sharp-eyed may make out graffiti from 1918.

A bizarre episode took place here in January 1916. A delegation comprising Lloyd George and Bonar Law went from GHQ to be shown round the workshops at Hazebrouck by Winston Churchill, then serving as a Lt Col in the 6th Royal Scots Fusiliers. Winston recounted how the previous day Sir F. E. Smith, Attorney General and a Cabinet member, had been arrested and brought back to GHQ for travelling from Boulogne through several sentry posts without a pass. Arriving at 2am he was installed in the Hotel du Commerce under arrest. Lloyd George and Bonar Law rushed back to GHQ in a panic, determined to hush up the story which had it got out would, they believed, have led to a spate of resignations. Smith was placated, the story contained and they left amicably for Boulogne the next day.

Leave Place du Maréchal Foch following Toutes Directions, past the Tourist Office on the left, downhill to the roundabout. Take the second exit, uphill. Continue over a series of roundabouts following Toutes Directions on the D928, over the A26 Motorway and rejoin the D942, direction Hazebrouck/Cassel.

2. To avoid the centre of St Omer.

Turn right at the traffic lights and take the D942 signed to the A25. Continue through several roundabouts following D942/A25 until you reach a roundabout with a white 'Cassel' sign to the

D933. Take it, continue and ascend the winding hill to the crest. Turn left following Panorama signs into the large square, Place de Général Vandamme, (Vandamme was a Napoleonic era French soldier of skill, but with unhappy social skills. He died in Cassel in 1830) either park and walk up the slope to the public park on the crest of the hill (on a path that is very slippery if wet) or drive up the narrow Rue Saint Nicholas following the one-way circuit to the park, signed Panorama/Jardin Publique/Statue Foch.

• *Mont Cassel Park/Panorama/Foch Statue/GPS: 50.80120 2.48489*

At 176m, Mont Cassel is the highest of the Flanders hills and its commanding strategic position has made possession of it the aim of many conquerors for more than 2,000 years. Its name derives from Castellum Morinorum, capital of the Celtic Morini tribe. The invading Romans turned the hill into a fortress, which was repeatedly attacked, captured and plundered and in 928 it was sacked by the Normans. Three notable battles were fought over it by three royal Philips of France: Philip I - defeated in 1071; Philip of Valois – who defeated the Flemish there and Philip, Duke of Orleans – who defeated the Prince of Orange in 1677, finally gaining Cassel for the French. During the English campaign with Austria against the French in the 1790s, the English under Frederick Augustus, Duke of York, were defeated, their prowess – or lack of it – derided in the familiar nursery rhyme, 'The Grand Old Duke of York, he had 10,000 men. He marched them up to the top of the hill and he marched them down again'. Cassel is purported to be the hill referred to, although the English army was nearer 30,000 than 10,000.

Today the imposing hill, with its attractively wooded slopes, still dominates the flat countryside around it in a dramatic fashion, looming imposingly as one approaches it over the plain. On 11 October 1914, **General Sir John French**, C-in-C of the BEF, set up his headquarters on that hill, moving to St Omer on 24 October. He was succeeded by General Foch. 'Apart from affording splendid observation over the Flemish plain, Cassel was a point of junction of some most important roads. Our transports would soon be filling these to their utmost capacity, thereby transforming the peaceful little town into a scene of feverish activity', he wrote. Here, during the afternoon of 30 October Foch was brought the news by Capt Bertier de Savigny, liaison officer attached to Sir John French, of a reported gap in the Allied line at Messines, ceded by the British 1st Cavalry. Foch dashed over to the British GHQ at St Omer to confer with Sir John French and agreed to plug the line with the newly arrived French XVI Corps. The crisis was temporarily solved. But it was only the first of many such crises. By the end of the following day French was wailing that there was nothing left for him but to 'go up and get killed with the British I Corps'. The bitter fighting of the next few days is described below in the sections on Hooge and Geluveld.

On 1 November Foch was summoned to Dunkirk to meet the French President, the French Minister of War, Millerand, General Joffre, and Lord Kitchener, who greeted Foch with the words, 'So we are beaten!' Foch answered, 'We are not'. But although Foch sent the President back to Paris (after a visit to Cassel where he was entertained with 'the restricted hospitality' that Foch was able to offer at the Hotel Sauvage) believing that victory was assured, Foch privately admitted, 'We were still far from that'.

On 13 November Foch was visited by Field Marshal Earl Roberts (qv). 'He was a fine figure of a soldier and patriot, a great Englishman in the best sense of the word. Notwithstanding his age, which was more than eighty,' wrote Foch, 'he was still wonderfully active and in keen possession of all his faculties'. It was after this visit to Cassel, following which he went to visit the Indian troops and took off his coat in the raw November air to pass them in review, that Roberts caught the chill which led to his death the following day in St Omer (qv).

Foch moved from Cassel in April 1915 to be succeeded in 1916 by General Plumer who commanded the Second Army. During the April and September/October 1918 Battles of the Lys, (Fourth Ypres), Cassel once more became a strategic observation point, with Foch making it his HQ again in April.

On 9 September 1918, Marshal (as he had then become) Foch held a conference at Cassel with Generals Haig and Plumer to plan the final offensive of the war in the north. Foch requested

King Albert of the Belgians to take command of the Belgian, British and French Forces engaged in the operation in Flanders. On 28 September Foch again visited Plumer at Cassel and, by the following day, Diksmuide, the whole of the Passchendaele Ridge, Messines and Wijtschate were in Allied hands, with 10,000 German prisoners and 200 guns taken.

In October 1918 **Sir William Orpen** (qv) painted Plumer in the 'little château' that was his HQ. 'A strange man with a small head, and a large, though not fat, body, and a great brain full of humour.' Today there is a numbered 'Orpen Walking Route' (qv), each stop illustrated with an Orpen picture painted in Cassel. Here is No. 8, a view of the Mont.

Maréchal Foch surveys the Ypres Salient from Mont Cassel

The **Tourist Office** (qv) originally had a leaflet describing the route but may be out of stock.

• *Statue of Marshal Foch*

The statue was sculpted by Edgar Boutry and the Marshal was present at its unveiling by President Poincaré on 7 July 1928. A replica of it stands in Grosvenor Gardens near Victoria Station in London in the area which was a tented camp for those soldiers leaving by train for France. The statue faces towards Ypres and Menin and on its base is inscribed a message from Foch, which translates, 'My concern in 1914 and my regard extended over the line between Ypres and Nieuwport. It was the fires of that line that I considered at night from the Cassel sector.' Below the statue, orientation signs to the Salient battlefield (restored in 1995) are set into the low wall. This spot affords magnificent views (foliage permitting) over the Salient and Ypres itself. Nearby, just visible are remains of a World War I bunker and beyond that a memorial to the many battles of Cassel which culminated in the French victory of 1677. The old hostelry, now demolished, was on the site of the Château, whose cellars were used by HQ staff. From the far side of the car park the flashing light of the radio mast on Mont des Cats may be seen.

• *The Windmill*

In summer the windmill is open daily. The original mill burned down in 1911 and was replaced in 1948 by one from Arneke. Once there were twenty-four windmills on Mont Cassel.
There is a Flanders Mill Route leaflet, probably available at the Tourist Office

> *Return to the main road, turn left and continue downhill into the centre to the Place Général de Gaulle. If you have driven to the top you will exit directly into the Place opposite the archway mentioned below.*

Cassel/RWC/GPS: 50.79946 2.48685

As the road leads into the square it becomes cobbled, much as it was when British soldiers marched along it on their way to the Salient. Around it is a great selection of eateries and hotels, from quick **bistros, crêperies to gourmet, 2-4 star**.

> *At the first junction to the right, look to the right.*

The Porte d'Aire today

'Household Brigade Passing to the Ypres Salient' by Sir William Orpen

• *Porte d'Aire*

The view you get through the archway is immortalised by Orpen in his painting, *Household Brigade Passing to the Ypres Salient, Cassel.*

> Continue on the road past the entrance to the Porte d'Aire.

• Tourist Office of Cassel Horizons,

20 Grand' Place. Tourist information on local events, a plan of the town, lists of restaurants (look carefully at the opening times, especially at lunchtime when times are irregular), and hotels in Cassel, are available here. Tel: + (0)3 28 40 52 55. E-mail: contact@cassel.fr Website: cassel-horizons.com. Closes for lunch.

• *Museum of Flanders, 26 Grand' Place*

Closed for several years for renovation, the Museum reopened in October 2010.

The Renaissance style building is the Hôtel de la Noble Cour which dates from the end of the sixteenth century. The museum covers local history (including the period of the '14-'18 War) art and folklore. Many interesting exhibitions and events.

It was here that during the early months of the War that Maréchal Foch had his office. Lt Col (later General) Maxime Weygand of the 5th Hussars, his Chief of Staff throughout the war, had his office in the next door room. Col Bentley Mott, who translated Foch's memoirs, described the two as 'the most efficient team for the conduct of a great war that history has reported ...

It was not so much that Foch conceived and Weygand executed, as was the case with Lee and Stonewall Jackson, but rather that the two minds seemed to constitute a single entity whose capacity was double that which any man working alone could furnish. General Weygand once said to me: 'The Marshal is the locomotive; I am the tender that furnishes him with coal and water'.

In 1940, as French Commander-in-Chief, Weygand was advised to surrender to Germany. Subsequently he became High Commissioner of North Africa, 1940-41, was imprisoned in Germany 1942-45 and was arrested after his return to France. Released in 1946, the sentence of 'national infamy' was quashed in 1949. Weygand died in 1965.

On the stairway are local memorials to the Crimean and Franco-Prussian Wars. It is interesting to note that on the former there are twenty-two names - out of a town population of only 2,000.

Open: Tues-Sat 1000-1230 & 1400-1800, Sun 1000-1800 (1 May-30 Sept 1000-1900). **Closed:** Mondays & Public Holidays). Tel: + (0) 3 59 73 45 60. E-mail: museedeflandre@cg59.fr

Walk across the road to the Mairie.

• Mairie

This is a new building. Its predecessor, dating from 1634, was destroyed in 1940 by the Luftwaffe during a three-day battle fought by the British rearguard before Dunkirk. Beside it at No 21 is the welcoming **Restaurant A l'Hotel de Mairie**. Tel: + (0) 3 28 42 41 38, www.restaurant-cassel.fr with varied menu and prices. Beyond it is the 2 star, 6 rooms, **Hotel/Restaurant Foch**. Tel: + (0) 3 28 42 47 73 with regional and Flemish specialities. Restaurant closed Fridays and Sun evenings.

(As an alternative to driving up the Place de Général de Vandamme (see above) you could walk from here to the crest of the hill up the Chemin du Château (or the steps nearby which lead to the same place.)

If you do, you will pass on the left the red brick, 5 storey-high, Castel Yvonne, where Plumer stayed. At the top, through the recently repaired Porte du Château, is the Public Garden described above.

Cross the road again and continue to walk along the Rue Maréchal Foch to the end of the Square.

• Hotel Sauvage

On the right at No 38 is **Le Sauvage**, no longer a hotel, but a popular **restaurant** Tel: + (0) 3 28 42 40 88. www.restaurantlesauvage.com

Sir William Orpen, RA, whose career as a war artist was to culminate with his often satirical portrayal of the Versailles Peace Treaty of 1920, described Cassel in June/July 1917 as 'being to the Ypres Salient what Amiens was to the Somme, and the little 'Hotel Sauvage' stood for the 'Godbert', the 'Cathedral' and 'Charlie's Bar' [favourite haunts in Amiens] all in one. The dining room, with its long row of windows showing the wonderful view, like the Rubens landscape in the National Gallery, was packed every night – for the most part with fighting boys from the Salient, who had come in for a couple of hours to eat, drink, play the piano and sing, forgetting their misery and discomfort for the moment.'

The hotel was managed by Madame Loorius and her two daughters, Suzanne (also remembered with affection for her smile by Lt Col Graham Seton-Hutchison) and Blanche, who were known as 'The Peaches'. The entertainment at the Sauvage was often boisterous and noisy, with Orpen's batman Green step-dancing and his chauffeur Howlett playing the mouth-organ.

Here other war correspondents like **Beach Thomas** of the *Daily Mail* and **Philip Gibbs**, 'his face drawn very fine, and intense sadness in his very kind eyes', gathered whenever there was something 'going on in the North'. In November 1917 Orpen returned after another spell based in Amiens to find at Cassel that 'hardly a night passed at this period that the Boche did not have a 'go' at St Omer' and Cassel afforded a grandstand view of the bombing and the searchlights. Sometimes, however, the show came dangerously close and 'one night they dropped three torpedoes in Cassel just as we were having dinner, but Suzanne, the 'Peach' at her desk, never fluttered an eyelid.'

Edmund Blunden (qv), the war poet, serving with the Royal Sussex Regiment in 1917, described in his memoirs *Undertones of War* how 'the cool streets of Cassel led between ancient shop-fronts and courtyards, maintaining their dignity that war was nothing to do with Cassel. There was one memorable inn in whose shadowy dining-room officers from highest to lowest congregated. Far below its balcony the plain stretched in all the semblance of untroubled harvest, golden, tranquil and lucent as every painter's eye rested upon.'

A new dining room (in use for groups and as the general restaurant on Sundays and holidays) has been built beyond the original one described by Orpen and Blunden, which still gives the same superb panoramic views over the plain. In it are photos showing Foch and other dignitaries entering the courtyard of the hotel, the *urinoir* clearly visible to their right! In this building Foch ate and entertained visiting dignitaries.

Continue out of the Square for about 150yd.

• *Hotel de Schoebeque*

On the right at No 32 is the old **Hotel Schoebeque** a private house during the war, now an operating hotel. Here **Maréchal Foch** slept. High up on the exterior wall is a **Plaque** commemorating the hotel's famous World War I visitors. Foch resided here from 24 October 1914 to 9 May 1915, then for frequent shorter stays, notably during the Battle of Mont Kemmel. Here he received **Albert, King of the Belgians, the Prince of Wales and Maréchal Joffre. King George V** stayed here 12-16 August 1916, and 3-7 July 1917, and **Gen Sir Douglas Haig** stayed 26-30 April, 9-12 May, 18-23 December 1916 and 27 February, 21-26 May, 15 August, 2-4 October, 8-15 October 1917, and also during 21-27 March 1919.

Châtellerie de Schoebeque. Beautifully restored 4 star Hotel de Prestige with individually and exuberantly designed luxury suites, spa and beauty treatments. See Tourist Information below for more details. Tel: +(0) 3 28 42 42 67. E-mail: contact@schoebeque.com Website: www. schoebeque.com

King George V in the courtyard of the Hotel Schoebeque

Return to your car and continue on the D933 down the cobbled hill following signs to Ypres and Steenvoorde.

Entrance to Châtellerie de Schoebeque

LE MARECHAL FOCH
ALORS GÉNÉRAL COMMANDANT EN CHEF
LES ARMÉES DU NORD
RÉSIDA DANS CETTE MAISON
DU 24 OCTOBRE 1914 AU 9 MAI 1915
IL Y REVINT ENSUITE
À DIVERSES REPRISES NOTAMMENT
PENDANT LA BATAILLE DU
MONT KEMMEL
IL Y REÇUT DE NOMBREUSES PERSONNALITÉS
S.M. ALBERT Ier ROI DES BELGES
S.A.R. LE PRINCE DE GALLES
LE MARÉCHAL JOFFRE
LE GÉNÉRAL DE MAUD'HUY
LE GÉNÉRAL MAISTRE

S.M. GEORGES V
ROI DE GRANDE BRETAGNE ET D'IRLANDE
EMPEREUR DES INDES
ACCOMPAGNÉ DE S.A.R. LE PRINCE DE GALLES
RÉSIDA DANS CETTE MAISON
DU 12 AU 16 AOÛT 1916 ET DU 3 AU 7 JUILLET 1917

LE MARÉCHAL DOUGLAS HAIG
COMMANDANT EN CHEF L'ARMÉE ANGLAISE
Y SÉJOURNA
EN 1916 DU 26 AU 30 AVRIL-DU 9 AU 12 MAI -
- DU 18 AU 23 DÉCEMBRE
EN 1917 27 FÉVRIER-DU 21 AU 26 MAI-15 AOÛT-
2 OCTOBRE-4 OCTOBRE-DU 8 AU 15 OCTOBRE
EN 1919 DU 21 AU 27 MARS.

Commemorative Plaque on Hotel Schoebeque

• Cassel Local Cemetery, Memorials & World War II CWGC Plot / GPS: 50.79904 2.49172

On the left is Cassel's local Cemetery with a parking area, in which is a Memorial, erected on 8 October 2014, to the Centenary of the repulsion of the Germans by the Gendarmerie and the Customs Officers. Around it is a colourful garden. This is Point No 11 on the 'Orpen Route' (qv).

In the Cemetery, on the left of the main pathway as you descend, is the tomb of **Lucien Devriendt**, soldier of the 310th *Régiment d'Infanterie*. This citizen of Cassel was taken prisoner in Verdun on 23 February 1916 and died in a POW camp in the namesake town of Cassel in Germany on 4 December 1918. To the right of the entrance is a plot containing CWGC headstones dating from the retreat to Dunkirk in 1940 and one French military cross of the same period. As you walk up again to the entrance you will see on the wall to the left a **Memorial to Brigadier the Hon N.F. Somerset, CBE, DSO, MC, and 228 officers and men of the 2nd & 5th Bns, the Gloucestershires** and their heroic struggle in the retreat to Dunkirk, 29 May 1940.

Gendarmerie & Customs Officers Memorial, Cassel

> *Continue down the D933 (noting that there is a 'rare' petrol station to the left). Turn left on the D948 direction Ypres and Steenvoorde. Go straight over the roundabout and continue through Steenvoorde on the D948. Turn right, signed A25/ D947 and continue to the roundabout. Take the D37 following white signs to Ypres, Godewaersvelde and Poperinge. Cross the motorway and continue on the D948 to the roundabout. Turn right on the D18 signed to Godewaersvelde. At the crossroads turn left on the D69 past the church on the right.*

In front of Godewaersvelde Church is the **WW1/WW2 War Memorial** with many plaques, including one from the 1st Polish Armd Div, 6 Sept 1944 (they reached Ypres the same day). The remains of a British Airman, a Canadian soldier and two unknown Indians originally buried in the churchyard were moved to the local CWGC Cemetery in May 1953.

Tomb of Lucien Devriendt, Cassel Local Cemetery

Plaque to Brig the Hon N.F. Somerset, CBE, DSO, MC and 2nd & 5th Glostershires, 29 May 1940

Continue, following CWGC signs along a winding road turning right and then bearing left. Ahead is Mont des Cats. Turn sharp right following the CWGC signs.

• *Godewaersvelde British CWGC Cemetery/GPS: 50.79611 2.6553*

This was started in July 1917 between the Battles of Messines and Passchendaele when three CCSs were moved to the village. The 37th and 41st CCS's used the cemetery for burials until November 1917 and the 11th until April 1918. From April to August 1918 during the German offensive, field ambulances and fighting units carried on the burials. There was a large plot of French graves on the raised terrace, but they were moved after the Armistice when the cemetery was enlarged by concentrations from the surrounding battlefields. It contains the graves of 894 UK, 65 Australian, 4 Canadian, 1 Indian, 2 New Zealand, 2 South African, and 19 German burials mostly in serried rows, shoulder to shoulder. Here is buried **Sister E.M. Kemp**, of the Territorial Force Nursing Service serving with 58th CCS killed in a bombing raid on 20 October 1917, as were eight members of the RAMC. The Cemetery was designed by Sir Herbert Baker.

Return to the village.

Headstone of Sister Kemp, Godewaersvelde Brit Cemetery

• *Godewaersvelde*

Known as 'God (or Gertie) Wears Velvet' to Tommy, this back area was the site of several Casualty Clearing Stations (CCS), and to its small station (the clearly recognisable station house still stands, but today is the village school) came the hospital trains bearing wounded and sick from the front. The cemetery you have just visited bears witness to the many who never travelled any further on the journey back towards the coast and Blighty. Although Orpen reports how friendly were the local French inhabitants of Cassel to Tommy, nearer the Belgian border, weary from three years of war, of requisitioning of billets and rations, the locals were often reported as hostile and resentful. Adding to the unpleasantness in this part of the world were the frequent bombing raids, aimed at the railway line and the nearby airfields at Abeele (qv) and Proven. From these airfields scouting forays were made. 'The Salient was never a gentleman's sector of the line; in the air it was as unpleasant in proportion to the numbers engaged as it was on the ground. The most important months there for the airmen were those of the summer and autumn of 1917,' wrote 'R. F. C.' in *The Pilgrim's Guide to the Ypres Salient* in 1920. 'From July 31st until November 6th, when the last ridge was taken by the Canadians, the sky was never empty of machines by day, and there were few nights when bombers on both sides did not drone over the lines and release their heavy loads on some dump or siding or billet.'

The CCS was a link between the field ambulance and lines of communication, normally sited 12,000 to 14,000yd from the front line, while those in the rear area were twice as far away. Here all sick and wounded were collected before being passed on to base hospital and thence, if necessary, to Blighty. It had three functions: to treat serious cases until fit for further transport; to evacuate at once to base all those fit to travel and to sort out and retain all those who were capable for early return to duty. It was designed as a mobile unit, capable of easy removal. In anticipation of, or to reinforce needs to support large battles, personnel were brought in from field ambulances and even from base hospitals. This was done in advance of the Messines and Passchendaele battles of 1917.

Here in CCS No 11, **Capt Francis Bernard Chavasse**, who won the **MC** for his actions at Hooge at the beginning of Third Ypres, younger brother of the double VC winner, Noel, and also a Medical Officer, served from 6 September 1917 until the end of the war. Before arriving on the Western Front in 1916, he had served in Egypt and Gallipoli.

Continue to the village crossroads and turn left on the D18 following sign to Meteren and Bailleul and watch out for the left turn signed Mont des Cats. Take the left turn, drive to the top of the hill and park opposite the Abbey wall.

• *Mont des Cats/Canadian Plaques/RWC /Map T7/GPS: 50.78587 2.66624*

On the summit of this 150m high hill is the Trappist Monastery founded in 1826 and adjoining it the Abbey which is open to the public. The origins of the name are obscure, but one theory is that it derived from the word 'Cattes' - a familiar greeting for the Frankish tribe, the Sueven, who settled here in 406.

In August 1914 a column of German cavalry passed through and some of the earliest skirmishes of the war took place here with the French. Ernest Leeuwerck, an inhabitant of Poperinghe, followed the early battles as a boy with great interest. On the night of 6 October the German Uhlans entered Ypres and then Poperinghe. On 7 October Ypres was occupied by the 8th German Cavalry Division under the command of Maj Gen von Unger, which then pressed on towards Calais via Steenvoorde and Mont des Cats. On the 12th, 3rd Cavalry Bde was ordered to dislodge the Germans from this strategic hill.

'The night was a real fireworks display', recorded M Leeuwerck. The 4th Hussars and the 5th Lancers attacked, dismounted, assisted by the 16th Lancers and succeeded in pushing the Germans off the hill (in 1922 the 16th and the 5th were amalgamated as the 16th/5th the Queens Royal Lancers and one of the authors served with them for a time). One of the casualties the retreating Germans left behind was **Prince Maximilian von Hesse**. 'Max', born on 20 October 1894, was the son of Princess Margaret, grandson of the Empress Frederick, nephew of the Kaiser, brother of the Empress of Russia and great grandson of Queen Victoria and cousin of Prince Maurice of Battenberg (qv). He is believed to have been carried into the Monastery when he was wounded, died there and was originally buried in the monastery cemetery. The story goes that his body was carried down to the village of Caestre in the valley below and secretly reburied by the English, and that the village priest later refused to tell the enquiring Germans (including members of the Hesse family) the location of the grave until 'there are no more German Soldiers in Belgium and when restitution is made for the crimes committed against our people'. To preserve the secrecy the body was once again moved. M. Leeuwerck interviewed several local inhabitants after the war who told him that in 1926 the grave was relocated and in November of that year Prince Max was exhumed in the presence of his brother Prince Wolfgang von Hesse, the Mayor of Caestre and the French Préfet. He was then transported to the family chapel in Kronberg, his final resting place. Copious correspondence by us with the German Embassy in London, the *Deutsche Kriegsgräberfürsorge* in Hamburg and the German Military Archives in Potsdam have failed to give official corroboration to this story.

In September 1917 **Captain J. C. Dunn, MO of the RWF** (qv), passed the monastery that was used in part as a hospital by the BEF and remembers seeing a young bearded friar, with his brown gown worn over khaki trousers, working in the adjacent field. The life of the monks continued unperturbed as far as possible by the fighting – until the war raged around the abbey again during the April 1918 German offensive, when it was completely destroyed. On the abbey walls a large **Plaque**, near the chapel entrance, unveiled on 20 March 1930, records the Catholic League of Remembrance's gratitude to **Canadian soldiers** and their French and Belgian allies. Beneath are bronze Plaques, including one recording the **visit of Gen Weygand** on his pilgrimage of 7 June 1936. A series of **Maple Leaf Plaques** record Canadian battle honours including Passchendaele.

The strong, dark beer made by the monks (a very strict order, whose name comes from the town in Normandy where they were founded, La Trappe) is on sale, as is the local cheese, in nearby hostelries, such as **L'Auberge du Mont des Cats** opposite. Traditional Flemish fare. Daily and

Franco–Belgian–Canadian Memorial Plaque, wall of Mont des Cats Abbey

Maple Leaf Plaque on Abbey Wall

varied menus. Pleasant terrace with magnificent views from the back of the restaurant. Closed Sun, Mon, Tues & Thurs evenings and all day Wed. Tel: +(0)3 28 42 51 44 www.montdescats.com

Turn sharp left downhill past the Auberge, following signs to Mont Noir through Berthen turn next right on the D10 then turn left on the D318 and continue along the winding road until you reach the crest of the hill, which is Mont Noir. Stop at the memorial on the left.

• *34th Division Memorial, Maginot Line Style Bunker, Mont Noir/ RWC/Map K1/GPS: 50.77915 2.73481*

Mont Noir was captured by the Cavalry Corps on 13 October 1914. In November 1914 3rd Division set up their HQ in Mont Noir Château and 'Billy' Congreve (qv), ADC to General Haldane, reported in his diary on 25 November 'We are going to keep the château as our night headquarters and use the Scherpenberg Hill as a day headquarters'. It was held throughout the 1918 Battles of the Lys (Fourth Ypres) but there were anxious moments when it looked as if the Germans were going to break through. The advanced HQ of 34th Div came to Mont Noir on the afternoon of 12 April and on 15 April General Nicholson, the divisional commander who was having trouble maintaining contact with his brigades in the confusion of the battle, brought the brigade HQs together in a large dugout on the hill and co-ordinated his artillery support from there. On 21 April the fighting in the immediate area died down and the division was relieved by the French 133rd Division. 34th Division went back to Abeele. In the period 8-21 April 1918, the division lost almost 200 officers and over 4,700 soldiers. A New Army division, the 34th had as its first commander Major General E. C. Ingouville Williams (Inky Bill) who was killed on 23 July 1916, and is buried in Warloy Baillon CWGC Cemetery on the Somme.

This handsome and well-kept **Memorial** of a victorious female figure, the Angel of Victory, is similar in style to the Division's Memorial at La Boisselle on the Somme, but there the figure no longer holds her laurel wreath. On the base is the Division's black and white checkerboard insignia and the Division's ORBAT. The memorial commemorates the

Memorial to 34th Division, Mont Noir

A glimpse of a 1938 Bunker, Mont Noir

officers and men 'who fought near this spot October-November 1918 and is on the site of the Divisional Headquarters during the Battles of the Lys' when the Germans captured Kemmel Hill, little more than 5km ahead, just over the Belgian border.

Behind the large building adjacent to the Memorial, on private ground, is a **Bunker** dating from 1938 with a Maginot Line style metal cupola, one of 7 that were built on Mont Noir.

Continue downhill, passing a well-preserved, ivy-covered, bunker on the right, to the CWGC sign. Turn first right and continue to the track leading to the cemetery. If it is not too wet and muddy the track is negotiable by car, but there is no turning area at the end.

• *Mont Noir Military CWGC Cemetery/Map K2 /GPS: 50.77663 2.73821*

The Cemetery was started in April 1918 during the First Battle of the Lys and used again in the Second Battle of September 1918. At the Armistice it contained 96 British and 33 French graves (all of the 26th Dragoons or the 88th Infantry Regiment). It was enlarged afterwards by the concentration of 57 more British graves (including some from November 1914) from the surrounding battlefields and more French graves (from March-May 1915 and April-May 1918), one Australian and two Newfoundlanders. There are 2 graves from WW2. The traditional CWGC

Mont Noir Military CWGC Cemetery

Cross of Sacrifice is mirrored by a French Cross to the *Morts Pour La Patrie* 1914 1915 1916 1917 1918. The Cemetery lies in a disused sandpit.

Turn round and return to the junction with the D318 and turn right signed Ypres.

NOTE: Some 3 miles to the southwest lies the village of Meteren. In this village on 13 October the 1st Bn the Royal Warwickshires made an attack on the enemy. One platoon was led by its lieutenant with drawn sword, who ran it through 'a large German' and then took him prisoner. The lieutenant was then shot through the chest and saved by one of his soldiers who ran to put a field dressing on the wound. The soldier was then shot in the head by a sniper, collapsing over his officer, and thereby saving him. The lieutenant was taken back to an ADS, where he looked in such bad shape that a grave was dug for him. He survived, however, to be transported back to base hospital and thence to the UK, returning to the front in early 1916 as a brigade-major. That 26-year old lieutenant, who had joined the regiment in 1908, was none other than **Bernard Law Montgomery**, who led the British to victory at El Alamein in 1942, and was promoted to Field Marshal on 1 September 1944. There is little doubt that Monty's horror at the loss of life in World War I led to the cautiousness that was sometimes criticised by his American colleagues in World War II.

Drive through the town of Mont Noir.

This is a typical old type border town, with many **cafés, restaurants, hotels**, *chocolatiers*, souvenir shops, amusement arcades etc.

Cross the border into Belgium and take the first (sharp) left signed Poperinge & Westouter on the D398 and enter the town.

• *Westouter*

This was another behind-the-lines area where tired troops were sent to get some rest before being sent into the front line once more. 3rd Division rested here for four days from 22 November 1914, exhausted from their participation in the First Battle of Ypres.

Continue past the Church and park by the extension on the right.

• *Westouter Churchyard & Churchyard Extension CWGC Cemeteries/ Map K4 /GPS: 50.79778 2.74634*

The local Churchyard, and then the Extension (at the back of the French graves and not in very good condition), were used by the British from November 1914 until April 1918. The Extension contains 64 UK, 1 Australian, 15 Canadian, 1 New Zealand and 3 German burials.

Continue, following the signs to Poperinge. On the right is

• *Westoutre British CWGC Cemetery/Map K3/GPS: 50.80048 2.74535*

Thus was begun in October 1917 during the Third Battle of Ypres. It contains 166 UK, 4 Canadian, 3 New Zealand and 3 Chinese burials. There is 1 French WW2 burial. **Maj Eric Stuart Dougall VC, MC**, 'A' Bty 88th Bde RFA, 14 April 1918, age 32, is '**Known to be buried here**'. Dougall won his VC on 10 April at Messines when he managed to maintain his line of gunners throughout the day, under intensive fire, thereby delaying the German advance. Dougall ran for Cambridge University in cross country events.

Continue following signs to Reningelst.

Headstone of Maj E.S. Dougall, VC, MC, Westoutre British CWGC Cemetery.

• *Reningelst*

This behind-the-lines area was used for the rare periods of rest enjoyed by Tommy and for quiet headquarter billets. It was far enough behind the lines to provide a suitable station for field ambulances. On 7 April 1915, 'Billy' Congreve (qv) reported in his diary that 'We [3rd Division HQ] moved to Reninghelst today. It is not such a bad place. The General and I share a little house and are quite comfortable. We are split up in billets all over the village.' They were taking over the village from General Snow ('about as much good as an old hen' – an ancestor of the broadcasters Jon and Dan Snow) and 27th Division. One anecdote recounted by Capt Dunn, MO of the 2nd RWF (qv), took place on Christmas Day 1917 when it was reported that a group of Chinese labourers from the 'Chink' camp near Poperinghe had walked over to Reningelst and there murdered their Sergeant Major. 'They said that he squeezed them too much, took 5 francs from each man on the voyage, and flogged them too readily: he was a bad man, the son of a half-caste woman and better dead'! The local people were apprehensive about these strange little yellow men whom they called 'Tsings'. Ernest Leeuwerck (qv) who also remembered seeing the Cape Coloured Labour Regiment that served with the South Africans who worked on road making, wrote:

'Their camp was called Pekin camp, No 101 CLC (Chinese Labour Corps). They were terribly afraid of the bombardments from which they fled crying, 'Boum-Boum. No Goedala'. They came into the town to buy provisions of onions, leeks, garlic and oranges, which they loved - their smell preceded them. They were special types, dressed in English jackets, old hats, trousers that were too short, like naughty boys. These coolies worked at the front, filling in trenches, levelling fields, taking away the materiel of war etc. All this was supervised by the English. The population was not at ease with them: they were thieves and when they had drunk too much, they fought. It was a great comfort when in September 1919 they returned to their own country.'

By autumn 1916 the demand for labour behind the lines had become critical and in October the Chinese (neutral) Government was approached, resulting in the formation of the Chinese Labour Corps. They were to carry out manual tasks such as building and repairing roads, railways and airfields, manning depots and unloading ships and trains. British missionaries helped in recruiting men, mainly poor peasants from Shantung and Chihli, to enlist for three years' service, who were enticed by promises of pay, clothing, housing and medical treatment beyond anything

Members of 29th Chinese Labour Corps in Poperinghe May 1919

they experienced at home. Formed into companies under British Officers and some Chinese NCOs for their training, the first contingent of 1,088 labourers sailed on 18 January 1917 via the Cape. Others took the three month journey to Vancouver and thence to Liverpool and France. By end 1917 54,000 Chinese labourers were working on the Western Front, some recruited from Chinese living in Canada. They were hard workers, but, as seen above, were open to various temptations resulting in bad behaviour. By the Armistice their ranks had swelled to some 140,000 (working for the British and the French), many of whom remained to work on clearing the land of explosives etc until well into 1919 (they also worked on the ferry ports of Calais and Boulogne and the sea defences at Orford Ness in Suffolk – known as 'the Chinese Wall') when they were prey to the deadly flu virus. Some 2,000 Chinese died during their service for the British in Europe. They were buried under the distinctive headstones bearing Chinese characters with various stock phrases. See Longuenesse Souvenir entry above. Several cemeteries in the Salient include a few Chinese Labourer graves: (Reninghelst New Mil (7); Meninghe Mil (8), Haringe (Bandaghem Mil (4); Gwalia (4); Poperinghe New I; (1); Poperinghe Old Mil (1) but there are cemeteries in France (e.g. Noyelles-sur-Mer, St Etienne-au-Mont, Les Baraques, Calais etc) that contain large Chinese plots.

Some remarkable research has been done on the Chinese Labour Corps (CLC) by historical researcher Dominiek Dendooven of the Ieper Documentation Centre with an expert on 20th Century Chinese history, Dr Philip Vanhaelemeersch of Howest University College, Bruges, firstly for the exceptional 'Toiling for War' exhibition at the In Flanders Museum. This inspired interest in their compatriots' part in the Great War by several historians in China and research is now underway to locate CLC descendants which is proving most successful. A delegation visited Ieper in May 2010. Attention is now focussed on a particular group of Chinese, known as The Busseboom Thirteen, who were killed by a bomb during an air raid on 15 November 1917. They were originally buried in the 'Chinese Cemetery' beside the Robaertbeek near Busseboom, then a major railway junction some 2.5 miles south-east of Poperinghe, and later reburied in Bailleul Comm CWGC Cemetery. On 29 May 2010, during the visit of a Chinese Delegation, a bronze Statue of a coolie with a bronze Plaque bearing the names of 'The Thirteen' was inaugurated in Poperinge. The statue was taken to China in August 2010 by Philip Vanhaelemeersch, then returned to Poperinge, to be installed in the presence Chinese dignitaries and relatives in a Special Memorial Garden (see Map F4a) on the site of the Chinese cemetery on the 100th Anniversary of their death on 15 November 2017.

More fascinating information about the CLC was obtained by research in Canada, notably from the letters, photographs and accounts of Capt Gordon R. Jones of 52nd Coy CLC provided by his grand-daughter, Ms Zamin of Toronto.

Continue, ignoring the first left turn to Poperinge, to the church. To the right of the church is

• *Reninghelst Churchyard Extension Cemetery/Map K6/GPS: 50.81426 2.76757*

The narrow plot, with a Cross of Sacrifice, consists of one long row of 58 headstones, including 2 graves from 1941. One of them, **Flt Lt Pilot Thomas Glyn Finlayson Ritchie** of 602 Sqn, RAFVR, 21 July 1941, was buried by the Germans with full military honours. The first grave is of the **Rev M. Bergin MC, Aust Army Chaplain** 3rd Class. (Only 7 Australians named 'Bergin' were killed during the war. Driver W. Bergin is buried at Lone Pine Cemetery in Gallipoli with the inscription 'A Mother's thoughts often wander to this sad and lonely grave.')

Michael Bergin was an extraordinary man, actually an Irish priest who never visited Australia, he was imprisoned in Damascus at the outbreak of WW1 by the Turks, released and reached the French Jesuit College in Cairo as the first Australians were arriving. He volunteered to join the military Chaplains and left for Gallipoli with the Australian 5th Light Horse. Officially appointed Chaplain on 13 May 1915, he was evacuated to the UK with enteric fever, returned to Lemnos but, being unfit, was confined to Hospital Ships. Evacuated to Alexandria in January 1916, he

Reninghelst Churchyard Extension Cemetery

joined the 51st Bn AIF and accompanied them to France. He served in Pozières and Mouquet Farm, the Hindenburg Line and Messines, being killed at Passchendaele on 11 October 1917. He was posthumously awarded the MC for his 'magnificent zeal and courage.

The last grave is of **2nd Lt Kenneth Theodore Dunbar Wilcox**, 8th Queen's (R W Surrey) Regt, 8 November 1915, age 20, who was buried by his father, the Rev Alfred G. Wilcox, MA, CF, Senior Chaplain of 15th (Scottish) Div. In the adjoining churchyard are 3 WW1 burials. These two sites were used for burials from March to November 1915.

At the junction turn left following signs to Poperinge on the N304. Continue to the grass path on the left leading to

• *Reninghelst New Military CWGC Cemetery/Map K5 /GPS: 50.81672 2.75953*

As the village was in British occupation from late autumn 1914 to the end of the war it was sufficiently far from the front line to provide a suitable station for field ambulances. The earliest burials took place in the village churchyard, but in November 1915 the New Military Cemetery, designed

Headstone of Rev M. Bergin, MC, Reninghelst Churchyard Extension

by Sir Reginald Blomfield, was opened. It remained in use until September 1918 and contains 452 UK, 104 Australian, 230 Canadian, 2 New Zealand, 1 South African, 1 British Civilian, 7 Chinese Labour Corps and 2 German burials. Two hundred and seventy five of the graves are of the Artillery and buried here is **Brigadier General C.W.E. Gordon** commanding the 123rd Inf Bde, 23 July 1917, age 39. Two brothers, **Lt Charles Richard** and **Lt John Lockhart Godwin**, killed three months apart in 1916, from Ottawa are buried here. The 31st Can Bn erected a wooden cross to forty-three of their men killed in 1916 in the Battle of Mount Sorrel (near Sanctuary Wood), but this has now disappeared.

Continue on the N304, direction Poperinge to the third (staggered) cross roads.

N.B. to Site of Pekin Camp, Chinese Cemetery and Planned Chinese Memorial Garden

Turn right along Singel Road and continue over the next main road, through a modern industrial complex and then take the small turning right just before the windmill to a Calvary. This is the area of the CLC Memorial Garden (qv) (**Map F4a. GPS: 50.84767 2.75601**) which is in the field beyond, along Sint Jansstraat. Here the bronze statue will find its resting place on 17 November 2017 (qv), the first Chinese Memorial on Belgian territory, with a Plaque bearing the names of the Busseboom Thirteen.

By turning right onto Visserijmolenstraat, crossing the tiny Roobaertbeek and following the left turn on the same road, the site of the Chinese Pekin Camp is reached on either side of the road at the next junction. Looking back down towards the Roobaertbeek, the site of the Chinese Cemetery may be seen on the near bank. Here were buried, among others, the '**Busseboom Thirteen**', according to fengshui logic, on a slope with their feet facing the water.

Busseboom.

It was in the vicinity of this hamlet (now difficult to find on a current map, but in this area) that 'The Busseboom Thirteen' (qv) were killed by a shell, and here Edmund Blunden was inspired to write his post-war poem *Concert Party: Busseboom*. The poem starts with a delightful reminiscence of a concert party but ends with a stark contrast with the 'show' put on by the war itself once the party was over. Here are the first, a central, and last verse of the six:

CONCERT PARTY: BUSSEBOOM
The stage was set, the house was packed,
The famous troop began;
Our laughter thundered, act by act;
Time light as sunbeams ran.
With generals and lame privates both
Such charms worked wonders, till
The show was over; lagging loth
We faced the sunset chill;
To this new concert, white we stood;
Cold certainty held our breath;
While men in the tunnels below Larch Wood
Were kicking men to death.

Statue representing the
'Busseboom Thirteen'

Continue to the R33 Ring Road. Turn right towards Ieper. Drive into Ieper town centre.

ITINERARY ONE

- **Itinerary One** starts in the Grote Markt Ieper, heads north-east towards the area of the October 1914 front line and the April 1915 gas attack, swings east and then south through the area of the 1917 Passchendaele offensive, the 1914 actions along the Menin Road and ends at the Menin Gate.
- **The Main Route:** Ypres – walking tour: Tourist Office, In Flanders Fields Museum, St Martin's Cathedral, Munster Memorial, Belgian Memorial, St George's Memorial Church, 'Two at Pervyse' Statue, French and Polish Plaques, Ramparts Walk; HQ of CWGC; Sint Jan - White House CWGC Cemetery, King Albert 'Barrack', Wieltje Farm CWGC Cemetery; Wieltje – Oxford Road CWGC Cemetery and 50th Northumbrian Div Memorial, Mousetrap Farm, Seaforth CWGC Cemetery, Cheddar Villa; St Juliaan – German Bunker, 15th Bn 48th Can Highlanders Plaque; Vancouver Corner – Lt Bellew VC Plaque, Brooding Soldier, Totemühle, Observation Point; 15th Bn 48th Can Highlanders Memorial; 's-Graventafel - New Zealand Memorial, Bunker, Beecham Farm; Tyne Cot CWGC Cemetery, Memorial Wall, NZ Memorial, Information Centre, KOYLI, Sherwood Foresters (Notts & Derby) & Bedford Memorials, Road to Passchendaele Marker; Passchendaele – Crest Farm Canadian Memorials, Town Hall Plaques, RB Memorial,

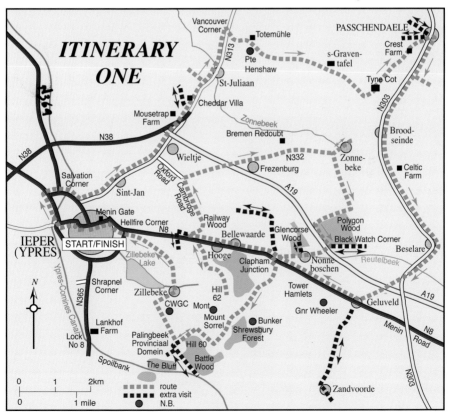

66th E Lancs SGW, 85th Can Inf Bn Memorial; French Memorial; 7th Div Memorial; Geluveld - Memorials to Lt Littleboy, S Wales Borderers, 2nd Worcesters; Tower Hamlets; Clapham Junction Gloucester Memorial, 18th (Eastern) Div Memorial; Hooge – KRRC Memorial, Château, Front Line Hooge Trenches/ Bunkers, Hooge Crater Museum, Hooge Crater CWGC Cemetery; Menin Road Museum; Sanctuary Wood - CWGC Cemetery, Museum and trenches; Can Memorial, Hill 62; Menin Road; Railway Wood - RE Grave, London Scottish Stone, Private Memorials to Capt Skrine and Capt Bowlby, site of Julian Grenfell's mortal wound; St Charles de Potyze - French National Cemetery; Aeroplane CWGC Cemetery; Frezenberg – Scottish Memorial; Zonnebeke – Passchendaele Memorial Museum, Can Arty Memorial Plaque, 'Archaeological Garden', Flemish Memorial Crypt; Polygon Wood CWGC Cemetery, Buttes New CWGC Cemetery, Australian 5th Div Memorial, New Zealand Memorial, 'Scott's Bunker'; Brothers in Arms/Peace Wood; Black Watch Corner & Statue; 4th Can Mounted Rifles/3rd (Toronto) Regt, Mount Sorrel; Hill 60 – Memorials to Q Victoria's Rifles, 14th (Light) Div, 1st Aust Tunnelling Coy, French Resistance 1944; Caterpillar Crater; Zillebeke Demarcation Stone; Hellfire Corner and Demarcation Stone; Site of White Château; Menin Road South CWGC Cemetery; Last Post at the Menin Gate, RB, & Indian Memorials, Model of Menin Gate.

• **Planned duration**, excluding stops for refreshments, Ypres Walking Tour, Extra Visits and N.B.s: 10 hours. **Driving time only: 1 hour 30 minutes**
• **Total distance: 38 miles**
• **Extra Visits** are suggested to: Kitchener's Wood Memorial; 3rd Bn (Toronto Regt) CEF Memorial; Passchendaele New British CWGC Cemetery, Albertina Marker & Cairns Plaque, 4th Can Mounted Rifles, 3rd (Toronto) Bn, Can VCs; Zantvoorde: British CWGC Cemetery, RWF 1st Bn Memorial, Local Churchyard and Turnor & Rose SGW, Household Cav Memorial, Bunker; Princess Patricia's Canadian Light Infantry Memorial; Birr Cross Roads CWGC Cemetery; Oude Kortrijkstraat: Sgt H.J. Nicholas VC Memorial, Plaque to Cox VC & Allen DCM; Capt Brodie Private Memorial, Glencorse Wood; Palingbeek Entry Point South, The Bluff.
• **N.B.** Visits are suggested to: Pte Henshaw Mem, Springfield Farm; Gnr Wheeler Mem, Zillebeke; Shrewsbury Forest Bunker; Memorial to 4th Can Mounted Rifles/3rd (Toronto) Rifles, Mount Sorrel; Larch Wood CWGC Cem.

• *Ieper/0 miles/90 minutes/RWC/Map H18*

A tour of the Salient is best begun by a Walking Tour around the centre of Ieper and a visit to the museum in the Cloth Hall. Park ('pay and display') in the Grote Markt or between St Martin's Cathedral and the Cloth Hall. Walk into the Grote Markt (known in French as the Grand' Place, the Market Square, which is the heart of the city).

Start at the Cloth Hall.

• *The Cloth Hall/The Grote Markt/Map H18/GPS: 50.85128 2.88683*

The massive structure, known as 'Les Halles', which served as market place, warehouse and offices during the boom days of the cloth industry and which contained many priceless works of art by some of Belgium's most accomplished artists, charting Ypres' history, now houses municipal offices, the tourist office and the magnificent museum. It encloses a space of more than 4,800sq m. The colonnaded structure on the side is the reconstructed 'Nieuwerck', the original of which was not finished until 1624. It is in Spanish Renaissance style. The completion of the rebuilding of this section to include the Council offices was commemorated by a plaque in the main entrance, unveiled by King Baudouin in 1967. The successive destruction of the original Cloth Hall is described in many contemporary accounts.

The imposing building facing the Nieuwerck across the square was originally the Notre Dame Hospital, built on ground given to the town by charter of 1187 by Philippe d'Alsace, Count of Flanders and is now the Court of Justice.

OP. Stand in the middle of the square, with your back to the Cloth Hall facing the fountain.

The Cloth Hall at Night

Adjoining, and at right angles to, the Nieuwerck is a series of restaurants - the **Klein Stadhuis** (originally the canteen for the officials working in the Cloth Hall), the **Anker** and the **Trompet**, all of which were taverns before the war and whose original buildings dated back to the seventeenth century. At 9 o' clock the imposing building facing the Nieuwerck across the square was originally the Notre Dame Hospital, built on ground given to the town by charter of 1187 by Philippe d'Alsace, Count of Flanders and is now the Court of Justice. At 10 o'clock is the road leading to the Menin Gate. Continuing clockwise around the Square, the **Tea Room/Patisserie** at No 9 (qv) was the first building to be rebuilt after the war. The family had located the site of the building in the rubble by finding a small white statue of the Virgin Mary. In the building lodged one of the workers with the Imperial War Graves Commission, William Dunn. He fell in love with one of the daughters of the house, Simone, married her and settled in Ypres, working with the Commission until he retired and, until his death in 1987, a staunch member of the congregation of St George's Church. They are both buried in Ypres Town CWGC Cemetery (qv).

Today the building still houses the excellent Family Vandaele Chocolaterie (which celebrated its 125th Anniversary in 2016) and is run by Simone's great-nephew Carl. The Virgin Mary statue still sits in the front bedroom upstairs. E-mail: vandaele.carl@skynet,be

At 4 o'clock is the old **Regina Hotel** and Rijselstraat, the road to the Lille (Rijsel) Gate. At 5 o'clock is the road leading to Poperinge and St George's Church. The shops are interspersed with **restaurants and cafés** - see Tourist Information page 324.

Walk along the façade of the Cloth Hall to the entrance to

• In Flanders Fields Museum/Regional Visitors' Centre & Shop, Cloth Hall

In the 40 years since we have been visiting the Salient the Museum has undergone a series of metamorphoses. Originally it was on the ground floor (where the Tourist Office currently is situated), was slightly fusty and dusty but full of fascinating exhibits. Its curator was the characterful Albert Beke who had started as a sweeper. Faithful regular visitors to Ieper had a strong affection for the old 'Salient Museum', with its simple, easily understandable presentation, its superb Anthony of Ypres photographs, its familiar displays of personal objects, of items returned by souvenir-hunting veterans (like the figures from the Cloth Hall belfry clock) and its homely, welcoming atmosphere. Many of these regulars were concerned when the Museum was moved upstairs, with a minimum of modernisation, but still with Albert, cigar in his mouth, glass of brandy in hand, waiting to welcome us warmly. The alarm deepened when in 1998 a massive joint investment of 150million Belgian Francs (equating to £3million in 1996) by the European Community, the Province of West Flanders, the Town of Ieper, the Flemish Community and private sponsors was made to create this large museum and Visitors' Centre in the Cloth Hall.

This completely revamped museum was named after John McCrae's 1915 poem (qv), emphasising the fact that the museum extends beyond the confines of the Cloth Hall to the battlefields which surround it.

IMPORTANT NOTE. A further major redesign of that Museum, **Tourist Office**, Boutique and designed for the series of 100th Anniversaries which started in 2014, was inaugurated in April 2012 in a project under the expert eye of Museum Director Piet Chielens. The new Museum occupies virtually the entire Cloth Hall (other than municipal offices), knocking through walls, thereby reverting it to its original vast, impressive open space.

The Flemish Chief Architect, heritage experts, local, regional and Government authorities were involved in the Euro 10 million project together with the competition-winning new architects. Cloakroom, elevator and cafeteria facilities were much improved.

Many changes in the occupancy of the great Cloth Hall are planned for the next few years, with a new City Museum in the old Town Hall in 2018, and Council Offices moving to a new dedicated building. Offices for municipal ceremonial and other functions will remain. Visitors enter through the ground floor of the Cloth Hall which contains the Visitor Centre with a plethora of useful information and leaflets describing the many attractions of this beautiful city and the surrounding countryside, walking and cycling routes, e.g. Ypres Salient Cycle Route, Ramparts Walking Tour…. Also lists of hotels, b&bs and restaurants, forthcoming events etc.

>

ENTRY POINTS – Walking, Cycling, Driving

It is thoroughly recommended to pick up the free detailed leaflets which describe the new **Interactive Entry Points to the Salient - North, East and South (qv)** to what are considered to be the most important wartime heritage sites in the old Salient. At each of them is an unmanned Information Centre with Introductory Film, describing the history and significance of that particular location and the following **Walking Routes** (parts of which can also be driven or cycled). The routes are marked by a series of interactive **Remembrance Trees**. These are hardy elm trees, partly to restock the region with this species which was decimated by Dutch elm disease, so traditional to it (the Flemish for elm was 'Iep'). The trees are enclosed by metal frames with colour-coded 'baskets' indicating the nationality of the front line - Red for German, Blue for Allied. The baskets on many of the trees contain **Information Boards**, with a wartime photo, which emit a signal, enabling one to locate the position on a map and aerial photos on a cell phone.

Entry Point North (see page 183) goes from Klein Zwaanhof via some small original cemeteries, along The Writers' Paths, to Yorkshire Trench. **Entry Point East** (see page 114) goes from the Hooge Crater Museum, around the old Château and Bellewaerde Ridge; **Entry Point South** (see page 125) goes from The Bluff, along the craters, Hill 60 to Caterpillar Crater.

The Ypres Salient 1914-1918 App indicates the position of all the trees.

Beside the Visitor Centre is the well-stocked **Boutique** with books, maps and souvenirs.

The **Museum** itself has changed from the old linear to a circular format. There is greater emphasis on landscape-related items, such as archaeological evidence, (using models of Hill 60, Bellewaerde Ridge etc), personal histories and encounters with events at specific places at a specific time. Although the latest cutting edge technology is used where appropriate, there is also a return to acknowledging the power of personal possessions, artefacts, ephemera etc. and impressions by poets, authors, artists, photographers and sculptors, both early 20th Century and contemporary. It is considered that as the last human witness of the war (Harry Patch (qv)) has now disappeared, the land itself will indeed remain – '**The Last Witness**' and there will be more need for material objects as evidence as time goes by. The scope of the Museum widened to cover the Belgian WW1 Front from Ostende and Nieupoort, through the Salient, Roeselare and Menin to the French border at Armentières and the Lys. The importance of aerial photography plays a large part in this understanding as can be further studied in the **Knowledge Centre** – see below.

Visitors may 'log in' giving their country and district of origin so that the stories they will see and hear in the various showcases and computer screens relate ingeniously to their personal and cultural experience. They receive a personal 'poppy bracelet' with a microchip to set the language of choice and enable 4 personal stories throughout the Museum. The stories are told chronologically, from the home front, from the opponent's point of view with chronological histories of the war covering:

1. The area pre-WW1: growing wealth; nationalism and the sensitive Flemish-Walloon situation
2. Visitors then cross over a huge steel plate, following the path of the German invasion through Liège to the Marne.
3. The story of the War on Belgian soil then unfolds

At the centre is an amazing Belfry Experience. Visitors (maximum 20 at a time, and with a small additional fee) are able to mount the 205 stairs with stops to catch breath at several platforms including the one from which cats have traditionally been thrown. At the top (provided they are svelte enough to get through the final narrow entrance) they are rewarded by stunning views over the Salient from beyond the Yser Tower to Cassel. Over 15,000 aerial photos are projected on multi-touch LCD

Ypres Tourist Director, Peter Slosse, in the Cloth Hall

Above: *National Gas masks, IFF Museum*

Left: *Memory and Sacrifice, IFF Museum*

Below: *Interior scene, IFF Museum*

screens which have the capacity of zooming in on monuments, cemeteries and important sites on the map of the entire front - even interesting architectural features of individual buildings.

Behind the medieval reproduction façade, the Belfry was constructed with then-modern techniques and construction material in the '20s, such as concrete beams, and the carillon are an interesting part of the story told in it.

An interesting series of temporary exhibitions, with emphasis on the Centennial, are regularly mounted in the Museum. From late 2016-2018 subjects include: **The Written War** (until 8 January 2017), **Archaeology from WW1** (4 February-30 April 2017); **Total War in Flanders** (7 June-31 December 2017); **3rd Battle of Ypres/Battle of Passchendaele** (12 July 2017, 100th Anniversary – Ieper & Zonnebeke); **From Mine Explosions to Floating Mud Sea** (7 June-31 December 2017 in In Flanders Fields, Memorial Museum, Passchendaele, and throughout the region); **The German 1918 Spring & Final Offensives** (April-November 2018).

Current Opening times: 1 April-15 November 1000-1800, every day. 16 November-31 March 1000-1700, closed on Mondays, Christmas and New Year's Day and the first three weeks after the Christmas holidays. Ticket sales stop one hour before closing time. Entrance fee payable with special rates for students and groups.

Contact: Cloth Hall, Grote Markt 34, 8900 Ieper. Tel: +(0) 57 23 92 20. E-mail: flandersfields@ ieper.be Website: www.inflandersfields.be

DOCUMENTATION/KNOWLDEGE CENTRE & ARCHIVES/ TECHNOLOGICAL BATTLEFIELD TOURISM

The Cloth Hall also incorporates these facilities which moved into spacious accommodation here from their cramped HQ in the Stedelijke Museum (qv) facilitating easy access to its enormous and important collections and archives. The dedicated and enthusiastic team of Museum Co-ordinator Piet Chielens, Curator Jan Dewilde, Scientific Research Assistant Dominiek Dendooven (who took a Sabbatical in 2016 to gain his Doctorate), joined by Historical Aerial Photography expert Dr. Birger Stichelbut of Ghent University (for the duration of the Centenary years) have taken the Centre to the very cutting edge of technology with the latest equipment.

The extensive library comprises some 15,000 books, including the extraordinary collection of Dr Canapeel. The 3,300 outstanding images of the photographer, Anthony of Ypres, many of them reproduced as prints, are now available at the Centre, the royalties for reproduction going to his family.

Perhaps the most impressive research continues to be undertaken on the aerial photography of the Great War and the Centre has built the most comprehensive collection of aerial photographs

from museums and other sources around the world. Piet Chielens and Dr Stichelbut have produced a fascinating book *De Oorlog vanuit de Lucht 1914-1918: het Front in Belgie* on the subject.

A significant project was to make cemetery registers for the Belgian, French, German and Missing of the Belgian Front available to the public for research (currently without appointment). There is also ongoing work on British casualties, which can be searched for by town or village.

Contact: Tel: +(0)57 23 94 50. E-mail: kenniscentru@ ieper.be. **Open:** 1 April-15 Nov – Mon-Fri from 1300-1800; Sat/Sun 1000-1800. 15 Nov-31 March - Mon-Fri 0900-1700; Sat/Sun – 1000-1700. **Closed:** 26 Dec-8 Jan.

The state of art technology now used in the Centre epitomises the use of interactive Information Boards, freely available apps etc which at a given spot can show the visitor images and give spoken information about

Museum Director Piet Chielens
in the Knowledge Centre

what happened there and how it affected those taking part in the action (e.g. on the Remembrance Trees (qv) etc).

• St Martin's Cathedral/Map H17

*Go through the archway at the corner of the Nieuwerke with the **Kleine Stadhuis** restaurant and continue left around the building to the Cathedral.*

The original Cathedral was started in 1221 on the foundations of a church built in 1083. It was completely destroyed during the war and is now rebuilt to the original plans in its harmonious ogive (pointed arches) style, in the shape of a Latin cross with three naves. The 100m Gothic spire was added, although the town had been unable to afford it in 1433! It contains the tomb of C. Jansenius, founder of Jansenism, the statue of Notre Dame of Thuyne, Patroness of Ypres and a rose window over the South door, which is the **British Memorial to King Albert**. There are also Memorials to the RAF, to the **French forces** and one of the **cathedral tablets designed by H. P. Cart de Lafontaine** and made by Reginald Hallward, 'To the glory of God and to the Memory of One Million dead of the British Empire who fell in the Great War 1914-1918 many of whom rest in Belgium'. Others were erected in Brussels, Malines, Mons and Antwerp. Hanging beside the tablet is a framed poem about Ypres which was found among the papers of Brig Gen Hordern, OBE, MC after the war and presumed to be written by him. The last verse reads,

French memorial and CWGC tablet in St Martin's Cathedral

> But still there lingers in this town of dreams
> Where every stone is sanctified by dead
> A breath of English lanes and hopes of youth.
> I sigh and then in silence bow my head.

There are public toilets in the wall of the Cloth Hall opposite the cathedral.

On the small lawn outside the south-east wall of the cathedral is a **Memorial** in the form of a Celtic cross to the casualties of the **Munster**

Regiments. The architect was T. A. O'Connell of Cork and the cross is a tribute from the Province of Cork.

Continue past the Cathedral and turn right. Continue approx 100m to the corner of Elverdingsestraat, passing the attractive restored Town Theatre on the right.

Beside it is one of the **International Peace Posts** designed by the Japanese artist **Mié Tabé** (qv) and erected at her initiative, not only throughout the Salient, but around the world. On 24 June 1982 at the United Nations in New York, Mayor Takeshi Araki of Hiroshima proposed that mayors around the world should join a campaign for the abolition of nuclear weapons. On 7 July 2006 a Mayors for Peace Office was inaugurated by the Burgomaster of Ieper in the City and a green Peace Pole

The Memorial to the Irish Munster Regiments outside St Martin's Cathedral, Ypres

was placed outside the Cathedral. **Contact:** Aaron Tovish, e-mail: 2020visioncampaign@ieper.be As early in 2007 there were 1,578 member cities in 120 countries and regions.

N.B. 'The Two at Pervyse' at the **Ariane Hotel** (GPS: 50.854392 2.883021). By continuing straight ahead here the Hotel (see also Tourist Information) may be reached at Slachthuisstraat 58. In its garden is a superb bronze statue of these extraordinary British ladies, Elsie Knocker (later the Baroness of T'Serclaes) and Mairi Chisholm, and in the foyer an important display of artefacts, photos, books etc which illustrate their story. These are here because academic and author Diane Atkinson, having written a detailed book about the pair and their brave work for the Belgian Army in their dugout in Pervyse (qv) (see www.dianeatkinson.co.uk) was then inspired to erect a statue of them in the village - but permission was refused. Diane had already raised sufficient funds with the help of Stefaan Vandenbussche and other locals and engaged the sculptress Josiane Vanhoutte. Hearing of this disappointment, Ariane proprietor, Natasja, offered it a home. The statue was unveiled on Saturday 22 November 2014, the Centenary of the pair's arrival in Pervyse and it was soon followed by the display cases which have been expanded in 2016. Well worth a visit.

The 'Two at Pervyse' with 'Shot'
their dog, Ariane Hotel

On the left around the corner is the entrance to a church.

• St George's Memorial Church/Map H15/GPS: 50. 85237 2.88288

In 1924 Field Marshal Sir John French made an appeal for a British church to be built in Ypres to act as a memorial, and to serve the thriving British community. On 24 July 1927, the day of the Menin Gate's unveiling, Field Marshal Lord Plumer laid the foundation stone. Sir Reginald Blomfield, designer of the Menin Gate, also designed the church (giving it the feeling of an English Parish Church), the adjoining school, Vicarage and 'Pilgrims' Hall. The latter two buildings were sold in the 1960s and it is now intended to buy them back from the present owner for conversion into an Ecumenical Study Centre for the growing number of young students of military history and for Parish/Ecumenical Groups from the UK who now visit the church.

The church was dedicated on 24 March 1929 and the 75th anniversary of the Church was celebrated in 2002. On 20/21 April ceremonies were held to mark this auspicious occasion including reunions of former pupils of the School, a special Sung Eucharist in the Church conducted by the Bishop in Europe and the erection of a commemorative Plaque by a current pupil of Eton College with the Provost of Eton and the President of the Old Etonians.

Almost every item in the Church is a **Memorial to an individual:** for example **Sir John French, Sir Winston Churchill, Field Marshal Montgomery, the poets John McCrae and 'Hedd Wyn'** and many lesser known men of all ranks; to a regiment or division which fought in the Salient. Most were gifts from relatives or regiments. King George V gave a bible and the Church Tower was endowed by Sir James Knott in memory of his two sons killed in the war and buried in Ypres Reservoir Cemetery (qv). In 1953 Plaques were unveiled to the **Australian and New Zealand Forces and in 1955 to the Canadians**.

In that year Canadian veterans paid for a new central heating system. In the choir stall there is a Plaque on the seat regularly occupied by Dick Collick (qv) a veteran of the war who came out to Ypres to work with the Imperial War Graves Commission as a carpenter in 1924. Dick became Church Secretary in 1946 - a post taken over by his daughter, Joan Mauret in 1975 and who served until 1994. He and his family, together with the other veteran stalwart of the Church and the War Graves Commission, WW1 Veteran Willy Dunn (qv), taught the authors everything they first knew about the Church - and much about the Salient. Later the function of conducting visitors round the Church was taken over by the 'Young 'Un', WW2 Veteran Sid Arnold, who died in 1995. His son, John Arnold is now the Treasurer of the Church.

Modern Plaques include those to the **Royal Marines**, the **Australians** mysteriously killed in Celtic Wood (qv) and, in November 1996, to **Ivor Watkins of the 38th (Welsh) Division** as well as a plaque to the **Chinese Labour Corps**. In May 2007 a **Plaque to Capt Bruce Bairnsfather** (qv) was inaugurated by Mark Warby and readers of the *Old Bill Newsletter*. A growing number of schools are now remembering the sacrifices made by their former pupils in the Great War and are donating plaques in memory of their Old Boys (many giving the number of their war dead) such as **Brighton College, Bury Grammar School** (24 in the Ypres Salient, out of total of 97 during the war, there being 165 boys in the school in 1914 and it is believed that the venerated, long-serving headmaster, Henry Howlett died of a broken heart in 1919), **Charterhouse** (687 WW1 and 339 WW2), **Cheltenham College** (675), **Gresham's Norfolk** (92), **Haileybury, King's Gloucester, King's Peterborough** (6), **Merchant Taylor's** (316 OMTS, 146 Staff), **Q Elizabeth Grammar Horncastle, St Dunstan's College, St John's Leatherhead** (154), **University College, London** (251), **Uppingham** (447 WW1, including **4 VCs – A/Capt A.M. Lascelles, T/Lt G.A. Maling, 2nd Lt T.H.B. Maufe and A/Lt Col J.S. Collings Wells** - and 250 WW1), *Wellington* (725) and **West Park Grammar** (6).

In the small chapel to the left of the altar, now used as a 'choir vestry', is a **Memorial Window to the Old Etonians the Grenfell twins**, Francis (buried in Vlamertinghe Mil Cemetery, one of the earliest VCs of the war - 16 November 1914- killed on 24 May 1915) and Riversdale (killed on 14 September 1914 and buried at Vendresse Churchyard on the Chemin des Dames), cousins of the poet Julian Grenfell. It also commemorates the 9th Queen's Royal Lancers.

Behind the altar is the beautiful Guards Window. The Organ (believed to be over 100 years old and originally built for a private chapel) is a **Memorial to Lt Durant of the Irish Guards**. By the organ is a Window dedicated to **Capt Loftus Jones**. Historic standards hang around the walls and a Bust of Field Marshal **Sir John French**, First Earl of Ypres, faces one on entering the main church. It was sculpted by J. Davidson and Blomfield designed the plaque beneath it. The twin pulpits also commemorate Sir John. Two of the Chair Plaques are dedicated to **Capt Bowlby and Capt Skrine** who have private memorials on Railway Hill (qv). Several chairs are dedicated by **Rutherglen and Cambuslang Girl Guides and Brownies**. There is also a Plaque to the English Cricket Board and a Prayer Desk dedicated to the **cricketer Colin Blythe** (qv). A list of memorials was compiled in 1963 as more than 100 more memorials had been added since the original list made in 1928. It was updated in 2001 to include the 200 beautifully embroidered kneelers, many of them with regimental badges and which were made in the space of three years, which provide a colourful microcosm of British History. In 1998, dedicated member of the congregation, Maurice McBride, made an extraordinarily comprehensive list of all the Memorials, Plaques, Kneelers, Chairs, Windows and other commemorative items in the Church. It is regularly updated. See: http://www.stgeorgesmemorialchurchypres.com/church-plaques/4587298334

One of the Church's most precious 'treasures' is an exquisitely **illuminated Service of Communion Missal in memory of 2nd Lt Charles Dean Prangley**, 3rd Bn the Lincolnshire Regt, always known by his nickname 'Doox'. It was commissioned by his father, also Charles, a parson, from a talented Downham Market corn merchant, George Smith. The colourful and extraordinarily detailed illustrations to each page record milestones of the young officer's life,

1. *Exterior St George's Memorial Church*

2. *SGW 1st Bn Monmouthshire Regt*

3. *SGW Grenfell Twins and 9th Royal Lancers*

4. *Earl French Memorial Font*

such as his school (Marlborough) and college (Jesus College). The highly polished wooden cover is made from a tree in his father's rectory garden with a golden cross made from his mother's wedding ring. In the book are the signatures of Randall Davidson, Archbishop of Canterbury, and of Geoffrey Fisher, a future Archbishop. The book was bequeathed to St George's Church by Charles Prangley Senior's will. 'Doox' was killed on Monday 25 September 1916, when the Linconshires attacked on the opening of the battle for Morval and is buried in the Guards' Cemetery, Les Boeufs on the Somme. Doox's story has been told by John Pollock, *Doox. A Soldier of the Great War and his Legacy*. Doox was his mother's cousin. Obviously the 'Doox Book' is too valuable to be on general display but a reprint may be seen in the glass display cabinet in the church.

During the German occupation of Ypres in World War II the residents of Ypres concealed many of the precious banners and other treasures. The Germans sometimes used the church as a place of worship. After the war the hidden items were restored and the British Legion paid to restore the church. It is also supported by the Friends of St George's (qv).

Postcards are on sale, there is a visitors' book to sign and a box for donations. The church is owned by the British Settlement & Ypres Memorial Trust. The town of Ieper now supports the Church. However there are many day to day expenses which are not covered by them and donations are welcomed. Services take place in the church every Sunday and on 11 November each year a moving Service of Remembrance is

Plaque to Civilian Victims, Belgian Memorial

Belgian Memorial, Ypres

French Memorial on the wall of the Cloth Hall, Ypres

held, when the church fills with pilgrims and the service is relayed to the Cloth Hall (or occasionally the theatre opposite).

A new Padre was appointed in late 2016.

Adjoining the church is the '**British School**' (originally named 'The Eton Memorial School' and wrongly renamed when the first Headmaster, himself a former master at Eton, retired) built as a tribute to the Old Etonians who fell in the Salient.

In the 1920s Eton College published its 'War List', giving details of all those who served in the Great War and it provides an extraordinary mirror to the social structure of the period where almost all those listed are officers and so many of them, in being killed, contributed to the 'Lost Generation' of the privileged class. Prefaced by Julian Grenfell's 1915 poem 'Into Battle', it records that 1,157 were killed (about one in five of those who served), 13 won the VC and that, amongst other notables, Lord Roberts, General Rawlinson, General Gough VC, Brigadier Fitzclarence VC and General Plumer were all Etonians. Many histories of the war tell the story of those for whom it was '*dulce et decorum est pro patria mori*'. They fought early, they died early in greater proportion to any other class it was said. In recent years some historians have sought to disprove this idea. In an attempt to offer the reader some guidance on the subject we have looked more closely at those who went to Eton College and where we have been able to identify a burial as that of an Etonian we have said so in the text. You may be surprised to find how often that occurs and we can only have touched the surface.

In October 1926 Mr M. R. James, the Provost of Eton, exhorted Etonians to subscribe the estimated £1,500 for the school which would be 'a very appropriate, effective and kindly service ...

Polish Memorial with name Plaques, wall of Cloth Hall

associated as it is with the name of the unforgotten friends of youth.' Inside the hall is a Memorial to all the Old Etonians (all officers except one) who gave their lives in the Salient. In 1928 there were over 100 pupils, aged 5 to 15, in the school whose then headmaster was Mr H. Morris, who had served (and been wounded) in the war. The children, the majority of whose parents worked with the Imperial War Graves Commission, were brought in by bus from the surrounding villages. Many of their mothers were local girls and their children often had to be taught enough English to read their text books. French was also taught but 'Flemish, so far, is not in our curriculum, although some of the children speak it', affirmed Mr Morris. In 1940 the school closed when the gardeners were evacuated to the UK as the Germans advanced on Ypres, not to re-open until 1946. It now acts as the Church Hall, shared by the CWGC Social & Welfare Club.

A major renovation of the Hall took place in 2007, with a new kitchen, bar, toilet block with disabled facilities, central heating system and a pleasantly landscaped garden.

Return towards the cathedral but continue along Coomansstraat to the T junction.

On the right is the impressive **Belgian War Memorial** which commemorates the dead of both wars. To the left of the main Memorial is a Plaque to the **13th Belgian Field Artillery**, incorporated in the British Army from 17 May 1915-17 May 1917. To the right is a bronze Plaque inaugurated in 2010 to the **Civilians of Ypres who died in both World Wars** which uses a new technique to incorporate a photograph of the ruined Cloth Hall.

On the left is the Cloth Hall.

Turn left along the side of the hall. Walk along the long facade with its tiers of pointed arches and acutely pitched roof.

Half way along, and immediately under the huge belfry tower, is the **Donkere Port** (Dark Gate. To the right of the opening is the **Memorial to the French Forces** killed in the Salient during World War I and a **Memorial to the Polish Forces** who liberated Ypres in September 1944. In September 2016 researcher Chris Lock (qv) discovered three Polish soldiers not mentioned on the Memorial. The Town has agreed to add new name plates for **Lt. S. Strachowski, Sgt S. Struzik and Pte B. Otreba**.

Return to the Grote Markt. From here walk up Meensestraat towards the great Menin Gate (visited later).

Walking up the road you will pass a variety of interesting shops and **cafés**, e.g. The British Grenadier (qv) bookshop, No 5; **Karamel**, No 9; the T'Iepertje souvenir shop, No 12; **Pizzeria Babilonia** No 29; **Coffee Break**, No 35; Over The Top Tours (qv) bookshop No 41; **Brasserie Kazematten**, No 1 Bollingstraat (on the corner).

Turn right just before the Menin Gate.

Ramparts from the Menin Gate.

Use the Ramparts Route Leaflet from the Tourist Office to visit some of the fascinating Casemates.

It details many of the uses these Vauban structures in the city walls were put to, including the De Kazematten working brewery, visitable on Saturdays 1500-1700. Entrance fee. www.kazematten. be During WW1 this was used as barracks and storerooms.

One of the best-known uses for the casemates was as a secure home for the printing works for the famous *Wipers Times* in one of the 3 **Kazematte Houten Paard** (Wooden Horse) Casemates.

Steve Douglas in the Grenadier Bookshop

Known as '**Hotel des Remparts**' it was used as an officers' mess, Command HQ and hospital. This humorous publication was started when Captain F. J. Roberts of the 12th Bn the Sherwood Foresters (who went on to win an MC on the Somme) found an old printing press in Ypres in January 1916. One of his sergeants who was a printer got the machine to work, despite the scarcity of the letters 'y' and 'e', which meant that only one page could be printed at a time. The first issue, of 12 February 1916, was a sell-out and a second was printed. Shortly afterwards the cellar, housing the press, was destroyed and with it the press itself. Another press was located at Hell Fire Corner and the new works moved into a casemate. Editions 3 and 4 were produced in March 1916, then the paper was re-christened the *New Church Times* when the battalion moved to Neuve Eglise. There was one edition of the *Kemmel Times* and then the battalion and the paper moved to the Somme. Reading its idiosyncratically laid out pages transports one immediately back to the 1914-18 period. It is full of soldiers' predictable jokes and wartime slang and the spirit of those men of World War I burns brightly through its pages. [The twenty-three editions were reprinted in a paperback in 1988 by Papermac]. There were some well-known contributors, notably Gilbert Frankau (qv). His piece for the first *New Church Times* began, 'I read in last month's *Wipers Times*, the Editor was sick of rhymes; the best of reasons, I suppose, that I should henceforth stick to prose', and continues throughout the article to rhyme. Capt Roberts wrote the Editorials, the Correspondence Column, the 'Advertisements' and many other features. Spoof articles were written by 'Belary Helloc', there was a serial about 'Herlock Shomes and Dr Flotsam' and many references were made to the provocative, scantily-clad ladies drawn by Raphael Kirchner which were pinned up in dug-outs, thereby coining the word 'pin-up'.

In his foreword to the 1973 bound edition, Henry Williamson (qv) wrote,

'Now more than fifty years later, I can feel myself to be surrounded by the spirit of the Western Front in the pages of Wipers Times, accepted as part of myself, for every item is gentle and kindly in attitude to what was hellish - and this attitude, its virtue, was extended towards the enemy. It is a charity which links those who have passed through the estranging remoteness of battle ... men who were not broken, but reborn.'

The Centenary of the first edition was on 12 February 2016 when the first of 10 films about this unique publication was launched on YouTube (see also www.visitflanders.com/en/themes/

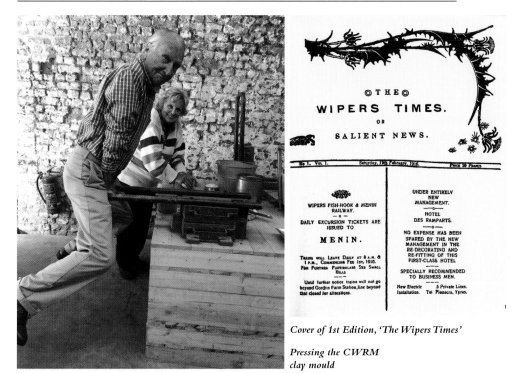

Cover of 1st Edition, 'The Wipers Times'

Pressing the CWRM clay mould

flanders_fields/wipers-times/ The films are introduced by Ian Hislop with contributions from Capt Roberts' grandson, Nick, from veterans and Peter Doyle.

Also in the Ramparts is the opportunity to take part in a unique **'Coming World Remember Me' (CWRM)** project to commemorate the 600,000 victims of WW1 in Belgium by creating a simple symbolic sculpture of a human figure which will form part of an art installation in the Palingbeek (qv). **Open:** Tues-Sat.1300-1800. Fee of 5.00. For details see: http://www.toerisme-ieper.be/en/page/334-360-569/cwrm.html

> *Return to your car. Set mileometer to zero. Drive, following the one-way circuit past St George's Church towards Poperinge along Elverdingsestraat.*

The town prison on the right was almost totally destroyed during the war, although the cellars were used as a main dressing station with individual wards constructed from elephant shelters, concrete and sandbags. A large tented area grew up there after the war providing support facilities for organisations such as the Church Army. Immediately afterwards at No 82 Elverdingsestraat is the

• HQ of the Commonwealth War Graves Commission. GPS: 50.85149 2.87738

Now that the CWGC Debt of Honour Register website (www.cwgc.org) lists all those who died in the Salient, it is strongly recommended that visitors look up any names they are interested in before coming to Ieper. In the meantime, if this is not possible and if (as is regrettably becoming quite frequent) the Cemetery Reports are missing from the bronze boxes in the cemeteries, then details may be requested here. Available at the office are various CWGC publications, Reports,

Information Sheets and videos and the Michelin maps overprinted with the cemeteries of Northern France and Flanders.

The Belgian MOD tends the **Private Memorials for Captains Bowlby and Skrine** and the local CWGC those of **Capt Brodie, Lt Rae and Maj Redmond** and the non-standard tombs of **2nd Lt de Gunzburg and Lt Lee Steere** in Zillebeke churchyard (qv). They also do the maintenance of the Island of Ireland Peace Park and the national, divisional and regimental memorials in the Salient. They employ about 140 personnel in their offices, their works department and as gardeners to maintain to their habitual high standard the cemeteries and memorials in and around the Salient. The original IWGC workers were almost exclusively ex-servicemen, many of whom married local girls and settled in Ypres, forming the congregation of St George's Church, providing pupils for the adjoining school and members of the local branch of the RBL. One family has provided four generations of gardeners in the Salient: Mr Leslie Brown's father and grandfather worked for the Commission; in 2002 he was Senior Head Gardener of the Lijssenthoek Group and his son, Thimothy, worked in the Bedford House Group of cemeteries. Traditionally CWGC workers (including several members of the Brown family) have been buried in Ypres Town Cemetery Extension (qv). This plot is now required by the Belgian cemetery authorities for more local burials and the CWGC graves will probably have to be removed into the adjoining main military cemetery. The military graves which are also in this plot, including that of Prince Maurice of Battenberg (qv) will not be affected.

The cemeteries in the Salient, especially the grass at the entrances, suffer (as do other historical sites) from the passage of the large numbers who visit them. Various remedies have been tried – such as the green plastic geo blocks under the grassy avenue that leads to the Australian 5th Div Memorial at Polygon Wood but the grass still wears beneath it and it can become slippery. Rubber crumbs are another solution now being experimented with.

Open: 0830-1230 and 1330-1700 Mon-Fri (closed 1630 Fri). Tel: 57 20 01 18. E-mail: neaoffice@ cwgc.org

Continue and at the first roundabout turn right on the N8 following signs to Diksmuide. At the next roundabout turn right on the N379 and at the following roundabout (once known as 'Salvation Corner') go straight on following signs to Centrum on the N379. Continue, passing the end of the Canal (known in the war as 'Dead End' or 'The Devil's Elbow') towards Roeselare on the N313 to the traffic lights. Go straight over. As the road crosses the small Bellewaardebeek stream and begins to rise to Sint Jan village, White House Cemetery is seen on the left.

• *White House CWGC Cemetery, St Jan/2.4 miles/10 minutes/Map H33/GPS: 50.86171 2.89955*

This was begun in March 1915 and is one of the many that were increased by concentration after the Armistice and designed by Sir Reginald Blomfield. In it there are 974 UK, 40 Australian, 1 Bermudan, 1 BWI, 73 Canadian, 5 South African, 322 unknown, 28 Special Memorials along the left hand side with a Memorial to them in the centre recording that they had previously been buried in other Salient cemeteries, and some World War II graves. Among them is **Pte Robert Morrow, VC,** of the 1st Bn the RIF who, on 12 April 1915 and under heavy fire, rescued several wounded men who had been buried alive in trenches. He was killed two weeks later. His VC is in the RIF Museum, Armagh. Also buried here is Brig Gen J. Hasler of the Buffs (qv), killed on 27 April while commanding 11th Inf Bde and **Lt Sir Richard W. Levine Bt**, KRI Hussars & 1st Life Guards, 24 October 1914, age 36. The body of Pte

Headstone of Pte R Morrow, VC,
White House CWGC Cemetery

Herbert Chase was one of those concentrated here after the Armistice from its original burial place near St Sixtus's Monastery (qv) where he was executed, for cowardice during a gas attack.

Continue on the N313 to Sint Jan (St Jean).

• Sint Jan

The village lies due south of the direction in which the German gas cloud of 22 April 1915, (Second Ypres) was travelling (see Battle Map). That day the 2nd Buffs and 3rd Middlesex were camped nearby and just after 1700 noticed firing in the distance and shortly after that a green cloud on the horizon. They took little notice, as they were in reserve waiting to go into the line at Boesinghe that night, but when hordes of French Turcos and Zouaves streamed south heading at full speed for Ypres, Lt Col E. W. R. Stephenson moved the two battalions astride the centre crossroads to form a stop formation. By noon the following day the 5th King's Own and the 1st York and Lancs had joined and the whole force was put at the disposal of the Canadian Division and under command of Col A. D. Geddes of the Buffs to form 'Geddes Detachment'. This force linked up with 11 other battalions strung out in haphazard formation left and right to fill the gap left by the French Colonials between the canal and where the Canadian Brooding Soldier (qv) now stands. Later that day, its own strength increased to some seven battalions, the Geddes Detachment counter-attacked to the north as part of a larger effort to stabilise the line. German attacks continued over the next few days and General Smith-Dorrien, the Second Army Commander, brought in the Indian Division and the 149th Northumberland Brigade, whose Divisional memorial is just ahead at Wieltje, Map I2.

On 27 April, at around 1700, a message in clear arrived from Sir John French ordering Smith-Dorrien to hand over the command of his Army immediately to General Plumer. Smith-Dorrien, who had only learned of his elevation to Army Commander at lunch with Sir John French on Christmas Day last, was not totally surprised, because relations between the two had been strained for some time, stemming primarily from Smith-Dorrien's decision to stand at Le Cateau against Sir John's orders. The counter-attacks in April had been costly and Smith-Dorrien was advocating a limited withdrawal. It was too much for Sir John.

Plumer immediately began a reorganisation (ironically including a planned withdrawal, much as Smith-Dorrien had advocated) including the disbandment of the Geddes Detachment. Colonel Augustus David Geddes was about to leave Sint Jan early on that morning of 28 April when he was killed by a German shell and is buried in Ypres Reservoir CWGC Cemetery. He was 48. At about the same time Brigadier-General J. Hasler was also killed here and is buried in White House CWGC Cemetery above.

As the front stabilised some 1.5 miles ahead, although the village had been destroyed by shell fire, the cellars were used as dressing stations and prisoner-of-war cages were established nearby.

Opposite the cemetery is house No 162 Brugseweg.

• Post-WW1 'King Albert' Wooden Barrack, St Jan/2.5 miles/5 minutes/Map H42a/GPS: 50.86197 2.89994

This beautifully preserved temporary home is the last known survivor of its kind in the actual Salient today (others have been found in De Lovie, De Panne and there is one at the Ijser Tower, Dixmuide). As the refugees came home in 1918 there was nowhere to house them in the devastated regions and King Albert set up a fund to fabricate temporary moveable wooden

Last known 'King Albert' wooden Barrack in the Salient, Sint Jan

homes to this pattern (an interesting forerunner to the 'prefabs' built in the UK after WW2). It was inhabited by Achilles Sedeyn and Emma Catry in 1918. They, with their two wooden barrack neighbours, bought their homes in 1927 for a joint price of 8,000 Belgian Francs. Achilles died in 1945 but Emma continued to live there until her death in 1980. It has been preserved, with simple furniture, by their descendants.

Continue on the N313. The basic direction is NE, directly towards the German lines.

• Wieltje Farm CWGC Cemetery/3.2 miles/Map H42/GPS: 50.86731 2.91189

This is signed to the left on leaving Sint Jan and is approached by a long, beautifully maintained, grass path. Designed by A.J.S. Hutton it was used from July to October 1917, particularly by 2nd/4th Gloucesters. One hundred and fifteen graves are recorded, including one German and 20 Special Memorials to unidentified casualties whose graves were destroyed. The Visitor's Book is in the wall at the back.

The road forward from here was known as 'Paradise Alley'.

Continue along the N313.

Ahead is the motorway bridge and clustered to the right the small village of Wieltje.

Take the small road to the right signed to Oxford Road Cemetery.

• Oxford Road CWGC Cemetery/50th Northumbrian Division Memorial/3.3 miles/10 minutes/Map I 1, 2/GPS: 50.86731 2.91189/50.87035 2.91776

The Cemetery, designed by Sir Reginald Blomfield, was established in August 1917. Burials continued until April of the following year. There is a total of 853 graves, including Australian, Canadian, German and 254 unidentified plus 3 Special Memorials. Here is buried **A/Capt Clement Robertson, VC**, of the QRWS, Special Res, Tanks Corps, killed at Polygon Wood on 18 Dec 1917 (qv). Also buried here is **Sgt Colin Blythe**, KOYLI, killed by a shell on 8 November 1917. Blythe was a left arm spin bowler who played in several Tests, including the Ashes series. In June 2009 the England Cricket Team visited his grave (upon which a stone cricket ball, a couple of other balls and a miniature bat had been laid) during their pre-Ashes Test Series battlefield tour. Captain Andrew Strauss described it as a 'Deeply moving and humbling experiencing'. Later the bat

Path leading to (inset) Wieltje Farm CWGC Cemetery

disappeared, and Kent County Cricket Club (for whom Blythe played) replaced it in a small but moving ceremony in December 2010. They presented Fr Llewellyn (qv) with a Kent bat and cap for display in St George's Church. The headstone bears the moving inscription, 'In loving memory of my beloved husband, Kent and England Cricketer.'

This is an interestingly laid out Cemetery with beautiful copper beach hedges and many sharply inscribed new-style headstones.

A further 200 yards ahead is the **Northumberland Divisional Memorial** which was unveiled by Plumer in 1929. It also commemorates the losses of WW2 and there is a Divisional plaque opposite Bayeux cathedral in Normandy. The Division, a territorial formation from Newcastle, Alnwick and Hexham, arrived in 'France' (units were often described as being in France when they were actually in Belgium) in April 1915 and within seven days its 149th Brigade was fighting in the Second Battle of Ypres. It served three-and-a-half years in France and played a major role in the breaking of the Hindenburg Line in October 1918.

New miniature cricket bat being laid by KCCC CEO Jamie Clifford on Colin Blythe's grave, Oxford Road CWGC Cemetery

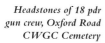

Headstones of 18 pdr gun crew, Oxford Road CWGC Cemetery

50th Northumbrian Division memorial, Oxford Road

Continue and take the first left to the crossroads with the N313. Ahead of you is Admiral's Road. Turn right.

• Wieltje

Here the British had sited a major ammunition dump before Second Ypres and on 13 May 1915, **L Sgt Douglas Belcher** of the 1/5th City of London Bn the London Regt won the **VC** for breaking up enemy attacks while under continuous fire. He is thought to have been the first Territorial other rank to win the VC. He survived the war as a Captain. His medals are in the Green Jackets' Museum, Winchester.

In 1917 the German defensive line ran across the N313 at this point and beside Wieltje were more than a dozen German pill boxes. The defences in this area were known as Cambrai Lane, Cambrai Trench, Call Trench and Call Support and formed part of the objective of the 55th (W Lancs) Division during Third Ypres. The dugouts had a reported thirteen entrances and were remembered by the 36th Ulster Division for 'the coughing and groaning of men in uneasy slumber, mingled with the click of typewriters'. Wieltje changed hands twice more before the Armistice.

Continue under the bridge to the junction with the by-pass road.

The buildings on the left, 200yd across the road under the pylons, are near the site of Mousetrap Farm.

• Mousetrap Farm.

The present buildings dating from the 1920s stand some 200m farther south than the originals. The area was known to the Germans as Wieltje Château, to the French and Belgians as Château du Nord and to the British as Shell Trap Farm. Its name was changed by Corps orders to Mousetrap Farm, which was considered less intimidating. During April 1915 the buildings were used as an HQ by the 3rd Canadian Brigade. Following the retreat of the French Colonial troops from the chlorine gas on 22 April 1915, the area became part of the front line and the German advance was stopped here by the 13th Battalion of the Brigade, the Royal Highlanders of Montreal, led by Major McCuaig. During a move to join up with reinforcements, McCuaig was taken prisoner.

Turn right in the direction of Poelkapelle on the N313.

Extra Visit to 3rd Bn (Toronto Regt) CEF Memorial (GPS: 50.88357 2.92281), Kitchener's Wood, 22 April 1917, Memorial (Map I33, GPS: 50.88738 2.91915).

Round trip: 0.7 miles. Approximate time: 15 minutes.

Turn first left along Wijngaardstraat (signed to Kitchener's Wood monument) and continue to the small Memorial in the bank on the right.

Unveiled on 12 June 2012 this black polished stone Memorial to the 3rd (Toronto) Bn, CEF. It is now in a somewhat neglected

Somewhat neglected Memorial to 3rd Bn Toronto Regt, 2016

state. It commemorates the Bn's action of 22 April 1915 in holding the line between Kitchener's Wood and the village of St Julien. Casualties were 19 officers and 460 ORs.

The Memorial after the unveiling, June 2012

Continue to the house on the right by a large commercial structure.

Memorial to Kitchener's Wood

Just within the garden (on land donated by the occupants) is a white stone **Monument, unveiled on 22 March 1997 to the 10th and 16th Bns of the CEF.** The imaginative Memorial represents a tree, with the rounded bushy top (and/or a gas cloud) standing on tree trunks. The idea for it came jointly from the Headmaster of St Juliaan School, Robert Missinne, and an officer of the 16th Canadian Scottish. The children of the 5th and 6th classes were actively involved in the production and erection of the Memorial. Today the Canadian flag flies proudly over it and there is an Information Sign. No trace of Kitchener's Wood now remains. However it was a commanding feature in 1915 and taken by the Germans on 22 April, the first day of the gas attack. A counter-attack at midnight by the Canadians, in which the 10th and the 16th (Can Scottish) played major roles in establishing a defensive line south of the Wood. The Wood was some 300 metres from the site of the Memorial at two o' clock. In recognition of their achievement both battalions wear a shoulder badge of an Oak Leaf with Acorns.

Return to the main road and turn left.

Immediately on the left is a cemetery.

• *Seaforth CWGC Cemetery & Memorials, Wieltje/4.2 miles/10 minutes/Map I21/GPS: 50.87961 2.92698*

Originally called 'Cheddar Villa Cemetery', this was named after the majority of burials from the 25/26 April 1915 Battle of St Julien (101 of the Regiment's 2nd Battalion out of 147 UK, 1 Canadian and 42 Special Memorials). On the rear wall is a Memorial to 23 additional 2nd Seaforths who have no headstones and there are Special Memorials to them and to the Northumbrian Fusiliers. It was designed by W.H. Cowlishaw.

The farm buildings beside it are on the site of

Memorial to 23 men of the 2nd Seaforths, Seaforth CWGC Cemetery

Cheddar Villa. As you pass the buildings, look back to see a large bunker incorporated into the farm structure.

• Cheddar Villa/Map I20/GPS: 50.88068 2.92764

Before Second Ypres this area was held by the Canadians. It was captured by the Germans following the gas attacks and a large concrete defence work was constructed. On the opening day of Third Ypres it was captured by the British and then used as a Regimental Aid Post. Being a German fortification, the entrance had faced to their rear. It now faced to the British front and just one week later a German shell burst near the entrance. Sheltering inside was a platoon of the Ox & Bucks and many were killed or wounded.

Cheddar Villa

Continue on the N313.

It was in this area that **Bruce Bairnsfather** (qv), the creator of the famous 'Old Bill', was wounded. His regiment, the 1st Warwicks, had been among those brought up to repair the line following the retreat of the French Colonials and had marched forward from Locre (Loker, Map K) on the afternoon of 23 April, the day after the first gas attack. Against a stream of retreating troops they reached Ypres that evening, stopping in a field just north of the town to issue rum and brew some tea. At midnight they moved off in driving rain, following the road that you have taken past the church at Sint Jan and on through Wieltje to the light rise before Mousetrap Farm. Then at 0400 they dashed forward in attack, the bullets 'flying like rice at a wedding', according to Bruce Bairnsfather in an evocative simile that compares to the description of German machine-gun fire hitting the water at the Waal River crossing in September 1944 as 'like trout rising'. Bairnsfather reached a farm (probaby Mousetrap) where he met a Canadian Colonel and, leaving his Corporal with two machine-guns (he was the machine gun officer), ran back to help a wounded officer. In his book, *Bullets and Billets* – much underrated as an accurate account of the early months of the war - in typically honest fashion he described what happened next:

> 'I heard a colossal rushing swish in the air, and then didn't hear the resultant crash ... I lay in a filthy stagnant ditch covered with mud and slime from head to foot. I suddenly started to tremble all over ... I had been blown up by a shell ... I lay there some little time ... All fear of shell and explosions had left me. I still heard them dropping about ... but I listened to them ... as calmly as one would watch an apple fall off a tree. I couldn't make myself out. Was I all right or all wrong? I tried to get up and then I knew ... I shook all over and had to lie still with tears pouring down my face.'

Bairnsfather was helped back down the Wieltje Road and eventually reached hospital in London where he began the series of drawings that led to the inimitable booklets of cartoons of life on the Western Front, *Fragments from France,* to fame and to an international career.

The incident haunted him for the rest of his life.

Continue.

Some 600yd further on from Cheddar Villa the road crosses at a right-angle the line where a formidable row of German pill boxes once stood. Running from the Steenbeek stream (to your right) westwards for about a mile to Kitchener's Wood, this virtually continuous wall of concrete and its trench system was named by the Tommy as 'Canteen' to the East of the road and 'Canopus' and 'Canoe' to the West.

Continue to St Juliaan and turn left up a small road, Peperstraat, beside a red bricktransformer tower. Stop after 150 yds beyond the houses on the right.

• St Juliaan German (Alberta) Bunker/5.2 miles/15 minutes/Map I18/ GPS: 50.89007 2.93353

To the right about 200m is a large German HQ bunker which formed part of the formidable Alberta defences during Third Ypres. Taking the direction of the road as 12 o'clock and the bunker as 3 o'clock, Canoe trench was 1km away at 9 o'clock, Kitchener's Wood 5km away at 10 o'clock and the main Alberta position 400m at 11 o'clock. In his diary, published by Leo Cooper as *Some Desperate Glory,* Edwin Campion Vaughan (qv) describes using, on 25 August 1917, what was probably this blockhouse: 'It was a very long pill box in which a corridor opened into about eight baby-elephant cubicles ... one was filled with

'My Dream for Years to Come', Bruce Bairnsfather

German flares and Very Lights ... the next I took for ... myself ... Into the remainder I crammed three platoons.' He was preparing for an attack to be made that evening but, before that could

take place, the position was shelled, the German flares were set on fire and he had to vacate the pill box. The officer with whom he was sharing a room was overcome with shock. 'He could not walk or even talk but lay shuddering on a wire bed. I gave him whacking doses of rum until he went to sleep.' If you do walk over to see the structure carry in your mind Vaughan's description: 'The ground about the blockhouse was a most ghastly sight. Dozens of English and German bodies were strewn about the entrances.'

These strong points were eventually taken during Third Ypres by the 29th Division, other blockhouses being overcome by the 17th Sherwood Foresters using 'a passing tank' and a trench mortar bombardment. Allow a further 15 mins for a walking inspection (making sure not to damage any crops) and be warned that the ground is usually damp.

Return to the N313, turn left and continue through the village.

'Alberta' German HQ bunker, St Juliaan

• St Juliaan

The village was taken by the Germans on 24 April 1915, the first day of the second gas attack and held by them for two years. It was then that the concrete defences were constructed. However, during the opening days of Third Ypres, following fierce fighting, it was recaptured by the 29th Division, who attacked in this direction. The road from St Juliaan to just short of Poelkapelle is effectively the eastern edge of the area directly affected by the first gas attack. Thus, late on the afternoon of 22 April 1915, the fields to the left would have been covered with a greenish-yellow blanket of deadly chlorine (see Battle Map).

Accidentally caught up in the gas attack were two FANYs. The First Aid Nursing Yeomanry Corps was founded in 1907 and its members were specifically trained to be highly mobile and to give first aid to the wounded. The girls whom Dr Harvey Cushing (qv) called 'horsy women – sporting females accustomed to ride and shoot and drive high-powered motors', bought their own smart uniforms and paid a subscription. They were anxious for official recognition on the outbreak of war, but like 'The Two at Pervyse' (qv) had to content themselves with working with the Belgians. The Corps set up a hospital in Calais from which they ventured forth towards the front line near Diksmuide to collect the wounded by ambulance. The following year they were still supporting the Belgians, several of whose batteries were set up around Ypres. The two FANYs, Lewis and Hutchinson, had delivered a soup kitchen to 7th Regt Belgian Mounted Artillery, attached to the British 5th Division, and were awakened at 0300 by their interpreter who rushed in with two respirators. Outside, as Lewis recorded, 'Out of the queer green haze that hung over everything came an unending stream of Tommies, stumbling, staggering, gasping, all a livid green colour. We dashed to the kitchen and prepared large quantities of salt and water to help them vomit the poison'. Some of the men were Warwicks, others from a Scottish regiment, and more and more poured in. The girls improvised respirators with cotton-wool and weak carbolic solution for those going forward and worked on until they too were affected by the gas.

They were then sent back to their hospital at Calais. There they were asked by the Assistant Provost Marshal of Cassel for a report on the efficacy of Belgian respirators and the type of chemicals they contained, as the British wished to 'remedy the absence of protection against gas in the future'. This recognition at last by the British made the girls feel 'exceedingly proud and important and our reply went back by despatch-rider'. Beryl Hutchinson's memories were recorded by the IWM in 1974. The FANYs celebrated their centenary in 2007, visiting the Salient in May during their annual camp.

Continue to the church. Turn right immediately before it and park in the car park on the right. On the wall of the modern red brick building is

• Plaque to 15th Bn, 48th Highlanders of Canada, Gas Attack, St Juliaan/5.3 miles/5 minutes/MapI19a/GPS: 50.88947 2.93712

This fine bronze Plaque commemorates the Gas Attack of the Second Battle of Ypres-St Julien and the 15th Bn (48th Highlanders of Canada), with a comprehensive description and sketch map. It was inaugurated on 24 April 2010.

Continue.

Plaque to 15th Bn, 48th Can Highlanders, Gas Attack, St Juliaan

On leaving the village the spire of Langemarck Church is seen left at 10 o'clock and a windmill at 2 o'clock.

Continue to the black St Juliaan/St Julien Memorial sign and crossroads. Turn right signed to Zonnebeke and park immediately on the left.

• Plaque to Lt Edward Donald Bellew VC, Brooding Soldier, Vancouver Corner/6.2 miles/10 minutes/Map D3a/3 /GPS: 50. 89916 2.94044

Walk over the road to the long red brick building.

On the wall is a **Plaque to Lt Edward Donald Bellew VC**, 7th Bn CEF, who won his VC near this site. It was unveiled on 8 September 2008. Bellew was born in Bombay in 1882, educated at Blundells School and Sandhurst, emigrated to Canada in 1903 and enlisted in the British Columbia Regiment when war broke out. He was renowned for sticking a loaf of bread onto his bayonet for the Germans to shoot at.

Plaque to Lt Bellew VC, Vancouver Corner

As machine-gun officer, Bellew held two guns with his sergeant (who was killed in the attack) when attacked from the front and rear. Bellew continued firing until he ran out of ammunition. He then smashed his machine gun and was taken prisoner and remained in captivity until 1919. He died on 1 February 1961 and sadly his VC medal was stolen from the Royal Canadian Military Institute in the 1970s. Bellew was the second cousin of Maj-Gen Sir Robert Adams KCB, who won the VC on 11 August 1897 in India.

At one time it was intended that this Plaque should be moved over the road near the Brooding Soldier and placed on a plinth.

Return to the Brooding soldier.

Brooding Soldier. This 35ft-high statue of a Canadian soldier with bowed head and hands resting on arms reversed was carved on a single shaft of granite. In its simplicity it is extremely moving and dramatic. 'Surely the memorial for all the soldiers of all wars?' wrote Henry Williamson when he revisited it in 1964 for an article in *The Evening Standard*. 'For the bowed head and shoulders with reversed arms emerging from the top of the tall stone column has the gravity and strength of grief coming from the full knowledge of old wrongs done to men by men. It mourns; but it

Detail of the 'Art Deco' head and shoulders of the Brooding Soldier

Detail of Plaque

Canadian Brooding Soldier, Vancouver Corner

mourns for all mankind…. The genius of Man rises out of the stone, and once again our tears fell upon the battlefield.'

The designer, Chapman Clemesha, was wounded during the war. The monument commemorates the 18,000 Canadian soldiers who withstood the first gas attack on 22-24 April 1915. Two thousand of them were killed and are buried in various CWGC Salient Cemeteries. The Monument was unveiled on 8 July 1923 by the Duke of Connaught. The cedars are trimmed to represent shells.

After the war Vancouver Corner was 'a featureless waste of dead men, mules, tanks and shell-holes linked together with five feet of water in each. Triangle Farm stood [more or less on the site of the small café across the road] solid with concrete and steel like a tooth decayed on its root, with other German pill-boxes in line [now disappeared]', commented Williamson.

Triangle Farm and the nearby Maison du Hibou blockhouses seemed impervious to shell-fire during the concentrated Allied attack of 16-19 August 1917. On the 19th eight tanks were brought up. One, training its guns on the entrance to the Maison du Hibou, fired forty rounds, driving the garrison out. Triangle Farm was finally captured by B Company of the 1/8th Worcesters in hand-to-hand bayonet fighting, supported by a tank. The success of this operation, the first time that tanks were used in the 1917 offensives, satisfied the Doubting Thomases that tanks would work and led to their successful use at Cambrai in November.

Continue for 200m towards Zonnebeke to the junction with a small road, O.L. Vrouwstraat, to the left.

N.B. Some 250m further, on the right of the road, is a stone Memorial to **Pte Stephen Henshaw** (Map I18a, **GPS: 50.89068 2.94406**) of the 1st Bucks Bn, the Oxs & Bucks which describes how he was wounded in the Battle of Langemarck on 16 August 1917, lay wounded on these fields for 6 days, was found on 22 August and moved to CCS 61 Dozinghem near Proven, died of his wounds on 23 August and is buried in Dozinghem Mil Cemetery. 'Lovingly remembered by all his family'. There is a moving story behind this.

During her researches on Pte Henshaw his grand-daughter, Jenny Hailstone, who told us the story, visited the area in 2000 and made contact with local historians who eventually led her to the owners (Marc and Hilde Vanderstichele-Neirynck) of the farm, 'Springfield Farm' (now Zonnebekerstraat 91) opposite the Memorial. In 2003 Jenny left *Memorial to Pte Henshaw, Springfield Farm* pinned to a fence post a laminated sheet with a photograph and some details of Pte Henshaw's participation in the attack on Springfield Farm.

When Jenny returned to Springfield Farm in 2004 she was overwhelmed to find that Marc and Hilde, with the aid of an engraver friend and using the information on her laminated sheet, had at their own expense erected this fine Memorial – between 1900 and 2000 hours on 15 June 2004. Pte Henshaw's 96-year-old son and 90-year-old daughter were very moved by this gesture of friendship and commemoration of their father.

Turn left onto O.L. Vrouwstraat past the glasshouses.

This leads to the mill.

• *Totemühle (Death Mill)/6.6 miles/GPS: 50.89740 2.94828*

The original mill on this site earned its title during its use by the Germans as an observation post. In such flat countryside even a few metres of additional height greatly increased visibility and Forward Observation Officers directing artillery fire often carried their own step ladders to climb upon.

Near the Totemühle served **Erich Maria Remarque**, author of the German classic *All Quiet on the Western Front*. He was born in Osnabrück in 1898 by the name of Kramer - which he reversed and 'gallicised' to become 'Remarque'. The book was attacked by the rising National Socialist regime in the 1930's and he fled from Germany. Remarque had an affair with Marlene Dietrich in Paris during World War II and married the film star Paulette Goddard in 1957. He died in Switzerland in 1970.

The mill may be visited and opening times are posted outside.

Continue to the right of the mill. Pass a small junction to the left and stop just before the next junction to the right opposite a calvary.

The Totemuhle

• Observation Point/6.9 miles/5 minutes/OP (crops permitting)/GPS: 50.89460 2.95418

You are in the middle of the battlefields of Second and Third Ypres. Take 12 o'clock to be your direction of travel. At 10 o'clock is the rectangular shape of Passchendaele water tower and at 11 o'clock the spire of Passchendaele Church. The Passchendaele-Messines Ridge runs from 11 o'clock to 2 o'clock. The bulk of Kemmel Hill may be seen on the horizon just to the left of Ypres which is at 3 o'clock, with the other Flanders hills behind it and Langemarck Church can be seen past the mill at 6 o'clock. On a clear day the tops of a group of four poplars may be seen between 11 and 12 o'clock through the buildings beyond the near horizon. That is Tyne Cot Cemetery. Before the beginning of Second Ypres the Germans held the ridge, the British the area you can see between Ypres and some 3km to your left. Following the success of the chlorine gas on 22 April 1915, the Germans released their next cloud at 0400 hours on 24 April in the area to your left. It swept across the road on which you are now standing, while German artillery kept up a continuous assault on British positions in the Salient. The German forces involved here were part of the 51st Reserve Division and, in particular, the 4th Marine Brigade which advanced through here on the following day. By the time that the repercussions of the assault had ended on 25 May 1915, the Germans had reached Cheddar Villa. At the beginning of Third Ypres in June 1917 this spot was just to the rear of the German

Sergeant Hans Marx of the German Marine Corps

third main trench line. It took the British two and-a-half months to get here from around Wieltje Farm. It probably took you 5 minutes to drive it.

In the 1970s when visiting the Ypres Salient, the authors were approached for information by a German couple, Hanns and Dorrit Marx, who were looking for the areas where Hanns' father, also called Hans (but with a single 'n'), had served. The postwar battlefields have seen the reconciliation of many former enemies - indeed the German War Graves Organisation emphasises 'Reconciliation through the Graves'. Over the years Hanns and Dorrit became friends of ours and we corresponded erratically, met and talked in Berlin and exchanged views about wars – First and Second. Hans Marx senior joined the Marine Infantry as a boy in 1900 (in one of those extraordinary coincidences that are almost common among battlefield visitors, the father of one of the authors joined the Royal Marines as a boy in 1900) and by 1915 was a sergeant in the 3rd Coy, 3rd Regt, 2nd Division of the German Marine Corps. On 8 April Marx's unit arrived in Flanders around Langemarck and on 25 April followed up the gas attack in this area and then moved to the Diksmuide sector. Hanns junior joined the German navy in 1941 and by 1944 was serving on a submarine hunter unit in Norway seeing much sea-air action, was later captured and repatriated after the war to Berlin where he subsequently served with NATO forces and became involved with the war archives.

Sadly Hanns died on 5 December 2007 and Dorritt on 12 January 2008.

Continue along the road to the memorial on the left.

• Memorial to 15th Bn, 48th Highlanders of Canada, Gas Attack, 's-Graventafel/7.4 miles/5 minutes/Map I24a/GPS: 50.89303 2.96507

On a clear bronze Plaque with badge, the Memorial tells the story of the 22 April 1915 Gas Attack (the first major engagement of 1 Can Div) in considerable detail. It was inaugurated on 24 April 2010.

Memorial to 15th Bn, 48th Can Highlanders, Gas Attack, 's-Graventafel

New Zealand Memorial, 's-Graventafel

Bunker, 's-Graventafel

Continue to

• 's-Graventafel Crossroads, New Zealand Memorial/Bunker/8.1 miles/10 minutes/Map I24,25/GPS: 50.89067 2.97855

The column on the left commemorates the men of the New Zealand Division in the battle of Broodseinde of 4 October 1917. On a front extending from around Geluveld to just short of Houthulst, an attack began at 0600 on 4 October in which Australian, New Zealand and English divisions took part. By chance the attack went in 10 minutes before the Germans planned to launch their own assault and the Germans thus suffered severely from artillery fire, much of the fighting then being finished off with the bayonet. The task of taking the Zonnebeke/s-Graventafel spur was given to the 2nd Anzac Corps and the stiffest opposition was faced in this area which was taken by the New Zealanders under Maj Gen Sir A. H. Russell. By the end of the day the division had taken over 1,100 prisoners and 59 machine guns. Among the dead was **Sgt David Gallaher** (also known as 'Gallagher') 2nd Bn, Auckland Regt, age 41, former Captain of the New Zealand All Blacks rugby team. He is buried in Nine Elms Brit Cemetery near Poperinge (qv).

To the right at the crossroads and some 100m down is a **Bunker** in the right-hand bank, now cleared and visitable.

Continue straight over the crossroads onto Schipstraat.

After the road takes a sharp bend to the right there is a large farm on the right with imposing iron gates. This was wartime **Beecham Farm (Map J1a, GPS: 50.88663 2.99128)** and in February 1999 the current farmer went out one morning and when he returned could find no trace of his wife. Eventually he found her, mercifully unhurt, in a large wartime dugout whose roof had collapsed under her kitchen. The ABAF (qv) excavated the extensive site, removing much of the well-preserved infrastructure which has been incorporated into the superb 'Dugout Experience' in the Ijzer Tower (qv). Naturally there is nothing to see of the dugout today as the area had to be filled in and the farm safely shored up!

Tyne Cot Cemetery is visible immediately to the left.

The main gallery, Beecham dugout, 1999 - now filled in.

Continue and turn left along Vijfwegenstraat then follow signs to the parking area behind the cemetery in which there are toilet facilities (for which you will require 50 cents) and from which one follows signs to the entrance of the Visitor Centre.

[The road leading to the front and original entrance to the cemetery, which had been widened to bear the traffic engendered by tour buses, has now been returned to the original narrow width with a grassy ditch.]

• Tyne Cot CWGC Cemetery, Memorial and Interpretative Centre/ NZ, KOYLI, Sherwood Foresters & Bedford Memorials/9.4 miles/45 minutes/Map J1/2, 3, 4, 5, 6, 7, 8, 8a, 8b/GPS: 50.88771 3.00113

On the 90th Anniversary of the Battle, on 12 July 2007, the unmanned **Interpretative Centre** was inaugurated by HM Queen Elizabeth II, as was the **KOYLI Memorial**, the initiative of the Leeds City Council and the Community of Zonnebeke. The Regiment was awarded Battle Honours for the Battles of Langemarck, Menin Road, Polygon Wood, Broodseinde, Poelcapelle and the Passchendaele Ridge. **Pte Wilfred Edwards** of the 7th Bn won the

Victoria Cross at Langemarck on 16 August 1917 and **Lt-Col Harry Moorhouse**, DSO, MiD, Légion d'Honneur, and his son, **Capt R.W. Moorhouse**, also of the Regiment were both killed on 9 October 1917 during the attack on Belle Vue Spur, the ground behind the Memorial. They are both commemorated on the Tyne Cot Memorial, Panels 108-111. Rupert Forrester, age 17, great-great grandson of Harry Moorhouse, was present at the unveiling. The Memorial pays tribute to all members of the Regiment who served in the Great War, 9,447 of whom were killed in action. In 1927 Queen Elizabeth, the Queen Mother, was appointed Colonel-in-Chief of the Regiment, her first such appointment. Sited to the right of the path to the Information Centre, the Memorial is now joined by a **Sherwood Foresters**

Memorial to the Sherwood Foresters (Notts & Derby), Tyne Cot

Memorial to the KOYLI, Tyne Cot

(Notts & Derby Regt) Memorial, the first WW1 Memorial to the Regiment in France or Belgium. Made of Derbyshire stone it was inaugurated on 24 October 2009. Sadly the first Memorial stones have not weathered well and inscriptions are hard to read. These were all constructed behind the Cemetery so as not to obstruct the fine vista of the approach. The latest **Memorial is to the Bedfords**, the stone coming from the Keep, donated by the Provincial Grand Lodge of Bedfordshire. This area is now designated as the site for new memorials, which should all conform to the same size.

The Euros 1,500,000 project of a Visitor Centre was jointly funded by the EEC, West Flanders Tourism, the Zonnebeke Community, the Australian Government and private finance. The low building does not obtrude above the Cemetery wall. The panoramic windows offer superb views over the Passchendaele Battlefield and *Tables d'Orientation* point out all the salient features in four languages. On the

Memorial to the Bedfordshire Regiment, Tyne Cot

remaining black-painted walls are panels featuring 'Remembrance' – the Cemetery is one of the most important sites in Flanders with thousands of visitors annually – the history of the Graves Registration Commission, the Imperial War Graves Commission and its founder Fabian Ware, the cemetery, its architecture and construction, the CWGC, the British (1 July-September 1917), Australian (September-October, notably 4-6 October) and Canadian (October-November) Phases of the Battle of Passchendaele and the result – 8 kms won, 245,000 Allied and 215,000 German casualties. There is a database with access to the CWGC and Passchendaele Archives (more information about which may be obtained from the Passchendaele Memorial Museum – see below) and an Australian CD rom for 3rd Ypres. The Centre is not manned but closes at night. One poignant display features a quotation from the fiancée of 2nd Lt John Low, KRRC, age 23, died 10 January 1918, commemorated on the Tyne Cot Memorial: 'The thought that Jock died for his country is no comfort to me. His

The New Zealand Memorial in the Tyne Cot Memorial Wall

Panoramic view of Tyne Cot CWGC Cemetery

Tyne Cot CWGC Cemetery: Entrance porch and the Cross of Sacrifice

memory is all I have left to love.' Beneath is a display case containing some of his personal belongings and letters, found in a car boot sale. Low was killed near a pillbox between Zandvoorde and Hollebeke.

During the winter 2016/2017 the Centre was renovated, with new information panels and an informative video.

Follow exit signs and walk along the elevated path around the cemetery wall to the original cemetery entrance.

This is the largest British War Cemetery in the world. It was designed by Sir Herbert Baker (1862-1946, knighted in 1926) who designed the tomb of Cecil Rhodes and had worked in New Delhi with Lutyens. In his work here he was assisted by Maj John Reginald Truelove. In its harmonious surrounding walls and shelters, in the elegant colonnaded peristyle of the memorial wall, it shows strong references to the Greek Revival style that was in vogue during the 1920s and was so favoured by this architect. Baker designed the war memorial at Winchester College and was greatly influenced by the design of local Winchester cemeteries, with their enclosing flint walls and covered entrance gates. This influence is strongly seen at Tyne Cot. Some of the flint used in the 168m-long enclosure wall came from England, the remainder from Italy. Trainload after trainload of this heavy stone was stacked along the road leading to the new cemetery and specialist Italian stone masons worked for months splitting the hard boulders which were attached to foundations of local Tournai grey stone (also used for the enclosure wall of Polygon Wood and Buttes New Cemeteries).

Aerial views of the Cemetery show (see photo on page 97) a remarkable resemblance to a great church or cathedral: the serried ranks of the lines of headstones in the first section resemble lines of pews, the choir stalls are to each side of the cross, the Stone of Remembrance represents the altar. The sketch on this page of the Cemetery plan in colour shows the developing stages of the Cemetery. The orange section shows the original battlefield graves from October 1917 - March 1918. The dark green section shows burials by 728 Labour Coy from June 1919-September 1920. The blue section shows burials by 126 Labour Coy from March -December 1920 and the lime green section shows burials by No 1 Exhumation Platoon from January-April 1921.

Plan of the Cemetery showing the various stages of burial - see text

In recognition of the harrowing nature of the fighting here, it was not thought appropriate to include a triumphant symbol such as the lion that surmounts the Menin Gate. Instead two mourning angels kneel on top of the dome-covered pavilions at either end of the Memorial Wall which, in its sickle shape, echoes the form of the Salient itself. The angels, designed by Baker, were sculpted by Joseph Armitage and F. V. Blundstone. The pavilions (which have echoes of the South African Memorial at Delville Wood, also designed by Baker) were built over two German blockhouses, now used as gardeners' sheds. Two other German block-houses can be seen, one to the right of the much-photographed entrance gate (through which the Cross of Sacrifice can be artistically framed), one to the left, each surrounded by poplars.

Aerial view of Tyne Cot Cemetery

Pill boxes played a major part in the Passchendaele affair. The Germans had started to use concrete in large quantities as early as 1915 in order to build bunkers and machine gun positions. The water table was so close to the surface that it was better to build above the ground rather than to dig into it. Many *MEBU (Mannschafts Eisenbeton Unterstände)* were made throughout the Salient and in 1933, under the auspices of the British Legion, Colonel E. G. L. Thurlow wrote a guide, *Pill-Boxes of Flanders*, in which he not only described those that remained, but also marked them on a detailed map. British military policy laid down that an offensive attitude must be maintained at all times. Thus the idea of using concrete defensive structures was not a popular one with the High Command and their construction was not officially sanctioned. While the British often found themselves paying local French and Belgian landowners for the materials needed to defend their own country, the Germans set up workshops to produce pre-cast concrete blocks that could fit together to form structures of a particular design and many blocks were made in a factory at Wervik. It has been estimated (*Pill Boxes of the Western Front* by Peter Oldham) that prior to the battle of Passchendaele there were some 2,000 concrete structures between Pilckem ridge and Hill 60.

The received story is that in 1917 the Northumberland Fusiliers saw a resemblance to Tyneside cottages in the new German pill boxes silhouetted on the horizon, which led to them calling them 'Tyne cottages' and hence the name Tyne Cot. Recent local research prefers the theory that contemporary trench maps show the use of river names in this area – such as 'Thames' and 'Marne' and including 'Tyne' - in use well before 1917 and that 'Tyne Cot' was originally attached to a barn that stood in the area. Trench maps show the square shapes of 5 or 6 German pillboxes in the cemetery area and the one in the middle was used as an Advanced Dressing Station after its capture by the 2nd Australian Division whose success is commemorated by a bronze plaque. At the suggestion of King George V, the Cross of Sacrifice was built over that pill box and a small part of the original fortification can be seen below the cross, framed by a bronze laurel wreath. It is said that with binoculars the cross can be seen from a ship in the Channel. Never managed it ourselves. Pillboxes 4 and 5 were under Plot LXV and the northern pavilion.

Headstone of Capt Jeffries, VC

At the end of October 1917 the ridge in this area (Broodseinde Ridge) was taken by the Australians and then the empty village of Passchendaele by the Canadians. On 12 October the 34th AIF attacked two German pillboxes at Hamburg Farm, some 700m north-west of the cemetery (50.88856 2.99583). **Captain Clarence Jeffries** led one attack, taking 35 prisoners and capturing 4 machine guns, he then took another machine-gun emplacement in the area behind where the Canadian 85th Infantry Memorial stands today, actions for which he was awarded the VC. In that action he was killed. He and five other **VCs** are buried or commemorated here including **Sgt Lewis McGee** of the 40th Bn AIF, who was killed taking a pillbox at Hamburg Farm. There is a Memorial Park to Captain Jeffries in Abermain NSW which was established in 1947 and in a clear-out at his old school a letter to his father, signed by King George saying how he regretted that he could not give the award personally and accompanied by a miniature VC, was found.

Another **VC, Pte James Peter Robertson** of the Manitoba Regt, is buried in the Cemetery. On 6 November 1917, he rushed a machine-gun position at Passchendaele, killed four of the crew and turned the gun on the rest. Later that day, having rescued one man, he was killed while attempting to rescue a second.

Standing on the steps of the cross and overlooking the graves is a sobering experience. The headstones facing you stand like men on parade and their numbers are numbing. The first 350 graves were made during the war and stand behind the cross. Among them are four German burials in two graves who were moved here from outside the original wall as a symbol of unity and fraternisation in death. There are also two brothers: **Pte Creighton Wellington Hatt, killed on 8 November 1917, and Pte F. Hatt**, killed on 6 November 1917. They both served with the 25th Bn Can Inf (Nova Scotia Regiment).

In all, 11,953 graves are registered on the CWGC website (including 8,901 UK, 1,353 Australian, 2 BWI, 966 Canadian, 6 Guernsey, 14 Newfoundland, 519 New Zealand, 4 German) of which 8,366 are unidentified (ongoing researches by the Passchendaele Memorial Museum show slightly different figures) – witness, in many cases, to the horrifying strength of the vile Passchendaele mud, which sucked into its morass a man and all means of his identity. Edwin Campion Vaughan had a close shave:

'I paused a moment in a shell hole. In a few seconds I felt myself sinking, and struggle as I might I was sucked down until I was firmly gripped around the waist and still being dragged in. The leg of a corpse was sticking out of the side and frantically I grabbed it; it wrenched off, and casting it down I pulled in a couple of rifles and yelled to troops in the gunpit to throw me more. Laying them flat I wriggled over them and dropped, half dead, into the wrecked gun position. '

Among the thousands of graves 'Known Unto God' are many personal inscriptions which are intensely moving. Although the majority are accepting, with biblical quotations or deeply felt expressions of family grief, some are more cynical. One such was noted by Sarah Shepherd via Instagram in July 2016. It is to **2nd Lt Conway Young** of the RIF, 16 Aug 1917, age 26, buried in IVG.21 and reads, "Born at Kobe, Japan 9th October 1890. Sacrificed to the fallacy that war can end war." This a version of the phrase used by H.G. Wells in his book, 'The War that Will End War', and was also used by Pres Woodrow Wilson as 'The War to end All Wars', by Lloyd George, by Field Marshal Earl Wavell at the Paris Peace Conference…even by Pres Nixon talking of the Vietnam War…

The eldest soldier to be buried in the Cemetery is **Pte J.N. Crowley**, 34th Bn AIF, 12 October 1917, age 52.

On the Memorial Wall at the back of the Cemetery are the names of almost 35,000 soldiers who have no known grave and who died from August 1917 to the end of the war — a continuation of the names inscribed on the Menin Gate. There are 33,750 from the UK and one from Newfoundland. In line with their decision to have their own national memorials, the New Zealand Memorial to the Missing, listing 1,176 names, is completely separated in the central apse. Note that there are no Australian, Canadian, Indian or South African names: they are all on the Menin Gate. On the wall are commemorated the war poets, **2nd Lt William Hamilton** of the Coldstream Guards, attd MGC, killed on 12 October 1917, **Lt Col J. E. Stewart, MC**, of the South Staffs Regt, killed on 26 April 1918 near Kemmel and **Capt Eric Fitzwater Wilkinson, MC**, of the West Yorks Regt, killed on 9 October 1917. There are the **VCs 2nd Lt (Temp Col) Philip Eric Bent, DSO**, killed on 1 October 1917 while in command of the Leicestershire Regt; **Cpl William Clamp** of the Green Howards, killed on 9 October 1917, and **LCpl Ernest Seaman**, MM of the Inniskillings, killed on 29 September 1918 at Terhand.

When looking at the Cemetery Reports here, and in particular at the Memorials where large numbers of soldiers are remembered, look for your own name. Over the years we have been in the company of many friends who have found, to their complete surprise, details of members of their family.

When the Cemetery was completed, thousands of bereaved pilgrims streamed out from Ypres to find the graves of their loved ones. A whitewashed wooden hut had been built opposite the entrance gate as a canteen for the cemetery workers and later it was converted into a tea room, serving not only tea but beer and postcards. For many years the landlady, Mme Irma Blanckaert, lived on in Zonnebeke.

OP: Stand with your back to the entrance gate (at the bottom of the cemetery). The two Zonnebeke chimneys should be visible at 11 o'clock and on the horizon to their immediate left is Kemmel Hill, briefly captured by the Germans during Fourth Ypres. To their right are the spires of Ypres and immediately behind the central spire (which is the Cloth Hall) on the horizon are the flashing lights of the wireless mast of Mont des Cats the last of the Flanders hills before the flat lands to the sea.

The front line at the start of Third Ypres ran roughly parallel to the road in front of you and some 8,000yd away - through the area of Cheddar Villa and, allowing for foreshortening, about halfway to Ypres as the eye sees it. Following the success of the Messines Phase of the operation the British readied themselves for the Passchendaele offensive watched by the Germans up here on the ridge. They took from 14 June to 31 July - over six weeks, giving the enemy ample opportunity to prepare his defences. The bombardment which preceded the attack completely destroyed the water table and the ground became a slick, foul morass, pocked with craters, littered with broken equipment, strung with barbed wire and made nauseous by countless dead bodies.

The Germans in their pill boxes had their machine guns ready - they could fire effectively about a quarter of the way to Ypres as the eye sees it — and yet another secret weapon, mustard gas, was waiting for the luckless Tommies.

The assault began on 31 July 1917, and within days it floundered in the mud. Rain fell incessantly and some commanders asked that the offensive be stopped, but Haig persisted and for fourteen weeks the Tommies laboured up the slope towards you, 300,000 of them becoming casualties. This area was taken by the Australians on 4 October 1917. Finally the Canadians took Passchendaele village on 6 November 1917, and the offensive that the C-in-C launched in order 'to be in a better position to start the New Year' was over. And then what did we do with the ridge? We withdrew from it in the spring in order to shorten our line.

The Germans occupied the area from April to September 1918 and then it was retaken by the Belgians.

Take the designated exit from the Memorial Wall and walk back into the car park. From the car park return to Tynecotstraat, turn left and then first left along Rozestraat. Immediately on the right as you turn is

• *Marker Stone to 'The Road to Passchendaele'/9.6 miles/5 minutes/Map J8b/GPS: 50.88521 3.00176*

This is one of the markers on the Australian trail following the 4 October 1917 battle.

N.B. By walking up the tarmacadam path beyond the Marker Stone for some 200yd an Information Board concerning the railway and some remnants of the track may be seen. Fighting took place here pretty well throughout the war but it was in German hands for a considerable time after 2nd Ypres and they ran a number of narrow gauge railways lines in this cutting. In 1917 the Australians retook the area. In 2005 a young Lancashire Fusilier was found buried between the tracks. His body had been covered with canvas and a Bible placed beside him. He is now buried in Tyne Cot Cemetery.

Marker Stone to 'The Road to Passchendaele'

Passchendaele Narrow Railway Line Info Board & Rail Remnants, Tyne Cot

The Cemetery is linked by a walking/cycling path to Zonnebeke along the old Ypres-Roulers railway line. Logically it should be followed from Zonnebeke – not from Tyne Cot – a visit to the Passchendaele Museum is first advised, as one then follows the path of the Australian attack of 4 October 1917. Excavations along the route have revealed German defensive dugouts, notably the Flandern 1 position, tunnels and other interesting features that are marked by well-researched Information Plaques on 'The Road to Passchendaele'. They describe, with photographs and sketch maps, 'The Battle of Broodseinde'; 'Thames Farm' (50.87976 2.99471 where a typical three-roomed bunker and trench system was found which was used as a German aid post – later as an Australian Field Ambulance aid post); 'Daring Crossing' – where Schipstraat crossed the Ypres to Roulers railway; 'Keerselaarhoek' – where there was a German cemetery. In the summer of 2005 some original railway line was uncovered just beyond this point and in a shell hole the remains of a Private of the Lancashire Fusiliers who, despite extensive research, could not be identified. He was re-interred in Tyne Cot Cemetery. A final Information Plaque summarises 'A Generation Lost, with photos of some of the 10th Aust Bde losses of 25 officers and 889 men, including the brothers L/Cpl J.B. and Pte G.B. Gavin of the 26th AIF, killed on 4 October 1917 and buried side by side in Ypres Reservoir Cemetery.

A fascinating programme, **The Platoon Experience**, officially inaugurated on 6 October 2007, is available at the Passchendaele Museum Zonnebeke, for students who can assume the persona and clothing of a particular soldier, walk the railway line using a 1917 map, and eventually find his grave in Tyne Cot Cemetery. The old Tourist Office at the entrance to the Passchendaele Museum serves as a changing room, housing uniforms specially made by the Belgian Army with shoulder flashes of a genuine Australian battalion, de-activated WW2 Lee Enfield rifles, small packs, army boots and 'rations'. The guides who lead the walk are superb and it is a moving and involving experience for students who enter into the spirit of the exercise.

Continue along the narrow road to a crossroads. Turn left signed as a cycle path and continue to the Canadian Memorial.

• *Canadian Memorial, Crest Farm, Passchendaele/10.8 miles/5 minutes/Map E3/GPS: 50. 89800 3.01410*

This is the standard Canadian octagonal granite stone erected on all sites where the Canadians performed with exceptional valour on the Western Front when it was deemed that the winning design for a Canadian monument (the Vimy Ridge Memorial) and the runner-up (the Brooding Soldier) were too expensive to duplicate. It commemorates the taking of Passchendaele village at the end of Third Ypres. It is surrounded by a landscaped park which for the 90th Anniversary in 2007 underwent major renovations and at the front of the existing Monument,

Crest Farm Canadian Memorial with, behind, Bronze Information Plaques & The Road to Passchendaele

facing Passchendaele Church, a new Memorial similar in design to that at Essex Farm (qv) was inaugurated by the Canadian Government on 10 November 2007. There are two bronze Plaques on the plinth telling the story of the battle. The work was undertaken by the CWGC who also maintain the site on behalf of the Canadians.

The farm had been originally named by the British in 1914 for it strategic position.

The 6 November 1917 attack here was launched at 0600 with 1st Can Division on the left and 2nd Division on the right. By forming up in no-man's-land the Canadians avoided the worst effects of the German artillery and little over an hour later had taken the village and the high ground. Crest Farm itself was first taken by the 9th Australian Brigade on 12 October but lost the same day. It was then retaken on 30 October by the 72nd Bn (Seaforth Highlanders) of Canada and it was from here that the final assault on the village was made.

The village itself, then merely rubble, was taken by hand to hand fighting. When the village was rebuilt after the war the road from the Memorial to the village was made, 'The Road to Passchendaele', symbolising the last few yards left for the Canadians to retake.

Round the other (looking towards Passendale) side there are Information Boards with interesting facts and map and a seat.

Continue towards Passendale Church. Park in the Square.

• *Passendale Town Hall & Plaques/RB & 66th E Lancs SGW in Church/11.2 miles/10 minutes/Map E4, 5, 6, 7/GPS: 50.90008 3.02057*

On the wall of the town hall are **Plaques to the 4th Belgian Carabiniers**, the **Belgian Grenadiers**, a **1944 Polish liberation** and **the Western Front Association**. In the car park of the square is a bronze Ross Bastiaan Australian Plaque unveiled on 1 September 1993. In St Audomar's Church opposite is a **Memorial Window** to the **66th East Lancs Division** donated by the people of Lancashire in 1928. The church, completely destroyed in the war, was rebuilt in its pre-war roman style form.

Ross Bastiaan Australian Plaque,
Passendale Square

Passendale Town Hall and WFA
Plaque. SGW to East Lancs,
Passendale Church

Extra Visit to Passchendaele New British CWGC Cemetery (Map E1/GPS: 50.90440 3.01100); Albertina Marker (Map E2); Cairns Plaque (1a, GPS: 50.91157 3.01129) & Can 3rd (Toronto) Bn/4th Can Mounted Rifles (GPS: 50.91420 3.00364).

Round trip: 3.5 miles. Approximate time: 30 minutes

Turn left past the town hall on 4th Regt Karabinierstraat and left again at the T junction. The cemetery is immediately over the road.

The entrance bears the distinctive minimalist style of architect Charles Holden (cf NZ Memorial, Polygon Wood). The Cemetery, built on three levels, contains 1,018 UK burials, 647 Canadian, 292 Australian, 126 New Zealand, 6 Guernsey, 3 South African, 1 Newfoundland and 7 Special Memorials.

The **Albertina Memorial** records the end of the Passchendaele Offensive on 28 September 1918. It is the last of the twenty-five diamond-shaped markers erected by the Belgians between 1984 and 1988 to commemorate the death of King Albert I. Each bears his monogram and marks a significant site or event of World War I.

Turn round, go past the T junction and take the first left along Haringstraat and continue to the second junction to the left and stop.

At the corner of the junction with Goadbergstraat and beside the road sign is a small hazel tree at the base of which is a metal Plaque. It is to commemorate **Pte Hugh Cairns, 16th HLI**, age 20. It was erected by the Commune of Zonnebeke and the Passchendaele Museum (who provided the tree and the land to plant it on) at the instigation of David Bartlett of Bartlett's Battlefield Journeys (who commissioned the Plaque) on behalf of Cairns's great-niece, Joanne Coyle, who planted the tree

Hazel tree and Plaque to Pte Hugh Cairns

on 11 August 2004. She sang The Bonnie Banks of Loch Lomond at the moving service here conducted by the Rev Ray Jones (qv). Later there was a commemoration for Cairns and **Pte Albert J. Atkins**, 3rd Queens, died 4 October 1917 age 31, at Tyne Cot Cemetery,

The striking entrance building of Passchendaele New Brit Cemetery

complete with Army Cadet Band and Bugler. Cairns was killed on 2 December 1917 and is commemorated on the Tyne Cot Memorial. Sadly in 2016 the Plaque was in a sorry condition and difficult to find in the long grass.

N.B. By continuing from the Cairns Plaque on Goedebergstraat to the T junction and turning right, and a further 100 yds on the left by a large farmhouse (known as Veal Cottages) with well-maintained garden are three flat **Canadian black marble Plaques**. They are to the participation in the **2nd Battle of Passchendaele** of the **4th Can Mounted Rifles, 3rd Can Div** and the **3rd (Toronto) Bn and VCs Pte T. Holmes and Cpl Colin Fraser Barron**. They were inaugurated in June 2014 by the current 'Perpetuating Regiments' for actions around Vine Cottage and Wolfe Copse.

Plaques to 4TH Can Mounted Rifles, 3rd (Toronto) Bn and VCs in the 2nd Battle of Passchendaele

Return to Passendale village and rejoin the main itinerary.

Take the N303 to the right, direction Zonnebeke.

After 0.75 miles in the field to the left is a Memorial. It is approached by a long grassy path (which is clearly signed) to the left just after the glass bus shelter.

• 85th (Nova Scotia Highlanders) Can. Inf. Battalion Memorial, Passendale/11.9 miles/10 minutes/Map J16/ GPS: 50.89081 3.01227

The Memorial commemorates the October 1917 Passchendaele battles, De Kleine Copse and Vienna Cottage, 28-31 October '17. The 85th, the Nova Scotia Highlanders, part of the 4th Canadian Division, reached this position on 30 October at the same time as the 72nd Bn took Crest Farm. The actions

7th Division Memorial, Broodseinde

Memorial to 85th (Nova Scotia Highlanders), Can Inf Bn, Passchendaele Ridge, with (inserted) CWGC sign

French Memorial, Broodseinde

on that day gained ground from which the final assault on Passchendaele was made. On one side there is a bronze Plaque with the names of the killed.

Continue to the roundabout. Drive straight over and stop immediately on the right. Walk back to the memorial.

• French Memorial/13.2 miles/5 minutes/Map J18/GPS: 50.86352 2.92592

The Memorial was constructed on 11 October 1977, to honour the 16,000 French soldiers who were killed between 23 October and 13 November 1914, in particular the 77th, 114th and 135th Regiments of the 9th CA (Army Corps). On 6 October 1978 the *'Questors [Magistrates] du Sénat de la République Francaise'* erected a small black plaque on the memorial. Written diagonally above the three white crosses, which are identical to those in St Charles de Potyze French Cemetery, are the words, *'Ici on ne passe pas'*, a reference to the famous rallying cry at Verdun. The architect was W. Barthier.

Continue in the direction of Beselare on the N303. After some 400yd stop on the right.

• 7th Division Memorial/13.4 miles/5 minutes/Map J17/GPS: 50.87141 3.00295

This obelisk, surmounted by a distinctive figure 7 on all four faces, commemorates the division's actions here in 1914 as well as in 1917 when it won the Zonnebeke Ridge in five days, suffering 2,672 casualties. Erected in 1924 on the site of a pre-war chapel, it is identical to that near Papadopoli Island which commemorates the Division's crossing of the Piave in Italy in 1918. The 7th Division landed at Zeebrugge on 7 October 1914, and Antwerp, their original objective, having fallen, they marched and counter-marched from their port of entry to Bruges, to Ostend, to Ghent through roads clogged with fleeing Belgian refugees, eventually arriving in the Salient on 14 October, having marched 40 miles in 40 hours. With the 3rd Cavalry Division they plugged the line between Houthem, Geluveld and St Juliaan, fighting without rest or reinforcement during the First Battle of Ypres.

Continue on the N303.

Some 500 yards to the left is the area of Celtic Farm and Celtic Wood where on 9 October 1917 a 'raid in force' was made by eighty-five young Australians, of whom forty-two disappeared. The mystery was examined in 1991 by Tony Spagnoly in his book Celtic Wood.

Follow the N303 as it bends right through Beselare. Continue and at the bottom of the hill turn right along the small Kasteelstraat towards Geluveld, over the motorway.

After the motorway, **Geluveld Château (a private dwelling**, for long the seat of the Keignaert de Gheluvelt family, and rebuilt after the war) may be glimpsed in the woods to the right. On 31 October 1914, a determined German attack from the east along the Menin Road had captured this area and the British line was in danger of breaking. German resolve to break through was strengthened by the news that the Kaiser was due to visit Geluveld at 1500 hours on 1 November. From 29 October the Kaiser had been staying at Thielt and, according to the 1920 *Michelin Guide to Ypres*, 'For 17 days the German regiments, elated by the presence of their Emperor, fought with unheard of frenzy and an utter disregard of losses in their frantic attacks against the Ypres salient.' The

J.P. Beadle's painting of the action of the Worcesters, Geluveld Château

Geluveld Château today

Duke of Wurttemberg commanded the Fourth Army, Prince Rupprecht of Bavaria commanded the Sixth (Rupprecht was a career soldier. He had joined the German army in 1886 and worked his way up to be a General by 1904. He was a descendant of Charles 1st of England and was said by some to be the rightful heir to the throne) and General von Deimling commanding XV Corps, all exhorted their men that 'the breakthrough at Ypres will have an importance which cannot be over-estimated'. The 2nd Battalion the Worcesters, however, made a remarkable bayonet charge into the Château and, joining up with the remnants of the 1st Battalion the South Wales Borderers who were still holding out, saved the day.

On 23 October 1914 **Drummer William 'Wee Wullie' Kenny** (later to become Drum-Major) of the 2nd Battalion, the Gordon Highlanders, won the Regiment's first **Victoria Cross** of the war in this village by rescuing wounded men on five occasions under heavy fire. This diminutive (5ft 3in tall) regular soldier, who had served in India and Egypt before the war, had twice previously saved machine guns by carrying them out of action and successfully delivered important messages under severe fire. Drummer Kenny survived the war. Later that month (on the 29th), his officer, **Lt James Anson Otho Brooke**, was also awarded the **VC** but was killed going back for support from the trench which he had taken from the enemy. Lt Brooke is buried in Zantvoorde Brit Cemetery (qv).

Continue uphill and turn right (before reaching the main road) to the Church. Park.

• *Geluveld Church Memorial Plaque to Lt Littleboy/17.1 miles/5 minutes/Map O4*

Inside on the right is a bronze Plaque to **Lt Wilfrid Evelyn Littleboy** of the 16th Bn the Royal Warwickshire Regt, killed in action near Polderhoek Château on 9 October 1917. He is buried in Hooge Crater CWGC Cemetery.

Outside the church is a fine local war memorial with **a bust of King Albert** and an Information Board describing the action at the Château.

Walk over the road to the memorials ahead. Stop.

Memorial Plaque to Lt Littleboy, Geluveld Church

• Geluveld Mill/Memorials to S Wales Borderers & 2nd Worcesters/5 minutes/Map O2, 3/GPS: 50.83455 2.99447

The mill, now un-recognisable as such, was brought here from Watou in 1923 to replace the original mill that was destroyed during the war. At its base are Memorials to the 1st South Wales Borderers and the 2nd Bn Worcestershire Regiment which commemorate the famous action of 31 October 1914. The Worcestershire Memorial was originally on a private house in nearby Herentage, as illustrated in early editions of Rose Coombs's *Before Endeavours Fade.*

Just after midnight on 30 October 1914, Marshal Foch woke Sir John French at his HQ at St Omer and warned him that a formidable German attack was under way. By morning a crisis had developed around the British 1st Division (part of Haig's I Corps). defences here at Geluveld astride the Menin Road. General Lomax, the 1st Division commander (who on learning about the situation at Geluveld said 'My line is broken'), and General Monro, commanding the 2nd Division, held an urgent conference at Hooge Château, their joint HQ, to discuss what to do.

Just after mid-day the Château was hit by a shell causing serious casualties (see below). Not only were the troops at the front in trouble but the command structure was crumbling too.

There was one stroke of fortune however. Less than half an hour before he was wounded, General Lomax had detached the 2nd Worcesters to Brigadier-General FitzClarence (qv) commanding the 1st Guards Brigade and this act, combined with the Brigadier's quick thinking, was to save the day.

Sir John went to see Haig, at White Château (qv). 'They have broken us in,' said Haig. Things looked desperate. In sombre mood (he was later to call the moment, **'the worst half hour of my life'**) French was

Memorial to SWB, Geluveld Mill

just walking away when the news came in that a counter-attack by the 2nd Worcesters had retaken Geluveld. 'England and the Empire', said Sir John later, had been 'saved from a great disaster.' Sir John had been under extraordinary pressure: not only was he attempting to fight a war that was quite different from anything that had gone before but he was also short of resources. Just a week earlier when he had asked for more guns and ammunition he was told by the Secretary of State to 'practise economy'. What a way to fight a war. No wonder French felt he had to confide in his mistress, Mrs Winifred Bennett. His regular letters to her (sold at auction in the 1980s) reveal his anxieties and his often stormy relations with some of his fellow officers.

The Worcesters' attack was a remarkable feat of arms whose sequence can be followed by using the Holts' Map. On the morning of 31 October the 2nd Worcesters were at the western edge of Polygon Wood (Map J) and formed just about the last reserve available for the defence of Ypres. Even so they had been in battle for about ten days and numbered less than 500 men, but while they were dirty from the mud at Langemarck and ragged from the brambles in the wood, their weapons were clean and they had

Memorial to 2nd Worcesters, Geluveld Mill

plenty of ammunition. Perhaps what was the most important factor of all was that their morale was high.

Around noon they learned that Geluveld had been lost and that the right flank of the South Wales Borderers in the Geluveld Château area had fallen back. Thirteen German battalions had attacked five depleted British battalions, overwhelming the Queens, the Royal Scots Fusiliers, the Welsh and the KRRC. Only the South Wales Borderers still held any ground, though the Worcesters did not know it. There was a large gap in the line and if the Germans were to pour through it in force the entire position of the BEF could be in jeopardy.

Brigadier-General FitzClarence (qv), ordered the Worcesters forward to mount a counter-attack, one company being given the task of sitting beside the Menin Road on the northern side of Geluveld to block any German advance down the road to Ypres. At 1400 the remainder of the battalion fixed bayonets and moved off in file to Black Watch Corner (Map I/J) at the south west edge of Polygon Wood, from where they could see the smoke of the burning village and the tower of the church. The ground ahead was open, falling gently to the Reutelbeek (Map J) and then rising in a bare slope towards Geluveld.

Down the slope to the beek went the Worcesters against a tide of stragglers and casualties going the other way. Beyond the beek the ground was littered with dead and wounded and German artillery was bursting on the slope ahead. Major Hankey, then in command of the battalion, deployed C and D companies in line, with B Company in reserve behind, and believing that the safest way to get over the ground was to do so in a rush, he launched his men at the double, with the officers leading, heading for the church. About 370 men set off in straggled lines through a rain of shrapnel and high explosives and men fell on all sides - more than 100 were killed or wounded as they climbed the slope but they kept going. Once they crested the rise before Geluveld the château became visible and the Worcesters charged into direct combat with the enemy. The Germans, young troops of new units, were forced back in disorder, and as the Worcesters chased after them they met remnants of the South Wales Borderers who had earlier recaptured the Château. Major Hankey met the CO of the Welsh and found him to be an old friend, Colonel Burleigh Leach. 'God, fancy meeting you here,' said Hankey. 'Thank God you have come,' replied the colonel. The Borderers, who had been in the area of the Château all day, had delayed and confused the German advance and the success of the Worcesters' bayonet charge owed much to them.

No attempt was made by the Germans to counter-attack and the British positions about the Menin Road were safe. It may be an exaggeration to say that the Worcesters' advance over almost a mile of open ground with fixed bayonets saved the BEF, but those who were there at the time thought so – and so did Sir John French. It is extraordinary in such circumstances that, although Major Hankey was promoted to Brevet Lt Col and other officers were awarded the DSO and MC, a VC was not given. It was probably too early in the war. If the year had been 1917 it is likely that there would have been a handful of them.

The historic meeting of the Worcesters and Borderers is commemorated in a painting by J. P. Beadle in the Worcester museum and a 'Gheluvelt Memorial Park' was opened in Worcester on 17 June 1922 by Field Marshal Sir John French. In it is a Plaque to Capt Gerald Ernest Lea who died on 15 September 1914 while commanding D Coy, 2nd Worcesters on the Aisne. He is buried in Vendresse CWGC Cemetery. On 14 August 2010 the renovated Park was re-opened in the presence of a delegation from Geluveld and Zonnebeke when a striking new Memorial was inaugurated. Made of weathered steel (which gives a rust-like finish) it comprises 27 panels, each representing two months of the war. The height has been calculated so that each centimetre represents 500 British and Commonwealth casualties. The involvement of the 2nd Worcesters is represented with, on the final panel, the names of the dead of 31 October 1914. The Steelwork artist is Lawrence Walker.

Continue to the main, Menin, Road.

Note: From here **Long Extra Visits 2 and 3** may be taken. See pages 290 and 293.

Extra Visit to Zantvoorde British CWGC Cemetery (Map N14, GPS: 50.81345 2.98351), RWF 1st Bn Memorial, Zandvoorde Churchyard and SGW in Church (Map N15a, GPS: 50.81327 2.98075), the Household Cavalry Memorial (Map N15, GPS: 50.81096 2.98364) & Zandvoorde Bunker (Map O1, GPS: 50.80847 2.98546).

Round trip: 4.4 miles. Approximate time: 30 minutes

Go straight over signed to Zandvoorde. Turn sharp left at the T junction, following signs to

Zantvoorde British CWGC Cemetery. Made after the Armistice by concentration of graves around the battlefield, it contains 1,525 UK burials, 2 Australian, 22 Canadian, and 1 Indian. 70 per cent of the burials here are unknown (1,135), probably because most of them were buried by the Germans. There are thirty-three Special Memorials and one WW2 burial. Here is buried **Capt J. H. Joseph** (described as 'from a well-connected Warrington family'), the commanding officer of D Coy, 17th Bn King's Liverpool Regt. He was mortally wounded at Clapham Junction on 31 July 1917, and died the next day. There are two **VCs** in the cemetery: **Lt James Otho Brooke** (qv) of the 2nd Gordon Highlanders, killed at Geluveld on 29 October 1914, who won the Anson Sword of Honour at Sandhurst and was the son of Sir Harry Vesey Brooke, KBE, and **Acting Sgt Louis McGuffie** (qv) of the 1/5th KOSB killed on 4 October 1918, a week after he won his award in the advance on Piccadilly Farm, near Wijtschate. The Hindu soldier, Sher Sing was a Cook in the 34th Div Followers' Central Depot, killed on 2 October 1918. Also killed on 11 October 1918, with just one month to go to the end of the war, is a row of **11 men of 72nd Bty, RFA, 38th Bde**, buried side by side with their **Sgt Maj, James Allen**.

Entrance to Zandvoorde British Cemetery

The Cemetery was designed by Charles Holden and contains a rectangle with a large Special Memorial in the centre to 32 men previously buried in Werviq Road German Cemetery.

Turn round and drive past the T junction to the next T junction signed Wervik.

By the Church and local War Memorial ahead to the right is

Royal Welsh Fusiliers Ist Bn Memorial. In the shape of a classic obelisk, the Memorial was inaugurated on 26 October 2014. It commemorates the Battalion's costly battles of 19-30 October 1914, (fought some 500m on the slope to the east of the village) when on 31 October only the Quarter Master and 89 men out of 1,350 reported for duty. It also remembers the 10,000 men of the Regiment killed in WW1. The Battalion, comprising mainly regulars and excellent reservists, was commanded by Lt-Col Henry Osbert Samuel Cadogan, who was among the dead of 30 October. He was 46, twice MiD and is buried in Hooge Crater CWGC Cemetery (qv).

Memorial to 1st Bn RWF, Zandvoorde

SGW to Lt Turnor, Capt Sir F. S. D. Rose, & 4 Troopers of the R Hussars, Zandvoorde Church

Beside it is **Zandvoorde Churchyard**. Here are buried side by side 4 men of the 10th Hussars, killed on 26 October 1914. They are **Lt C. Turnor, Capt Sir Frank Stanley Day Rose, L/Cpl J. Waugh and Pte R.S. McKenzie**. In the church is a **Stained Glass Window** in memory of **Capt Sir Frank Stanley Day Rose & Etonian Lt C. Turnor**. It was a gift of the Turnor family and is behind the statue of St Crispin, to the left of which is a Plaque describing the window. Capt Rose and his 3 brothers served in the Boer War.

In the car park beside the church is an **Information Board**.

Turn left and continue to the entrance on the right to

The Household Cavalry Memorial. In a box by the Memorial entrance the beautifully illuminated Roll of Honour of the Household Brigade which safely rested there for many years has been replaced by a plain listing but also contains a handsome leather-bound Visitors' Book. This elegant obelisk surmounted by a cross is on the site of the original grave of Etonian **Lt Lord Charles Sackville Pelham Worsley**, Lady Haig's recently married brother-in-law. On 30 October 1914, the Life Guards, attempting to hold the slopes of Zandvoorde Hill, were attacked by the enemy. Worsley, a member of the Royal Horse Guards, commanded a squadron of the 1st Life Guards. One of their machine guns had jammed and Worsley, after 'seven days of ceaseless strain in the trenches', was asked by the Brigade Major to remain for a further short spell of duty. '"All in a day's work", was the smiling reply of a young officer from whose lips a smile scarcely ever seemed to fade', reported the Regimental History. Worsley did not receive the order given to withdraw and instructed his men to fight on at their post. Many of them, including the brothers-in-law Capt Lord Hugh Grosvenor and Lt the Hon Gerald Howard (both commemorated on the Menin Gate), simply disappeared. 'The squadrons suffered almost total extinction, only a few prisoners being accounted for', recorded the Regimental History. Many of the dead were buried by the Germans who even sent a map to the family showing the site of Worsley's grave. After the war his body was recovered and reburied in Ypres Town Cemetery Extension (qv). The Memorial was unveiled by Field Marshal Earl Haig, Colonel of 'the Blues', 4 May 1924. Interestingly, the area opposite was known as 'Harrods Stores'.

Continue to the sign to the right along Gaverstraat to the entrance to

The Zandvoorde Bunker. This is an impressive 1916 German Command Post bunker, built by Pioneers who specialised in building reinforced concrete positions. Their plaque is above the entrance. It has six rooms, which are accessible, clean and dry (maintained by the Zonnebeke

Leather Visitors' Book, entrance to Household Cavalry Memorial, Zandvoorde

tourist authority who have erected an **Information Board** describing its construction) and the site has been cleared to make easy access, though it did look rather 'hairy' in 2016.

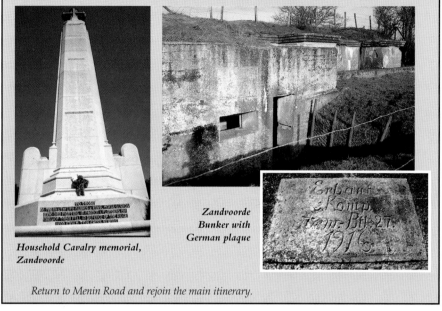

Household Cavalry memorial, Zandvoorde

Zandvoorde Bunker with German plaque

Return to Menin Road and rejoin the main itinerary.

Turn right. Continue. To the left some 500yds away was the area called Tower Hamlets.

• *Tower Hamlets*

In this area on 4 October 1917, Private Thomas Henry Sage of the 8th Bn SLI was in a shell hole with eight others, one of whom was shot as he threw a grenade, which fell back into the shell hole. Sage was awarded the VC for throwing himself on the grenade. Although badly wounded, Sage survived, unlike 'Billy' McFadzean who won a posthumous VC for a similar act on 1 July 1916, on the Somme and Joe Mann who won the American Congressional Medal of Honor on 18 September 1944, near Best in Holland. Pte Sage was tended by the Rev Bayley Hardy (qv), the Regiment's Chaplain, at a nearby Advanced Dressing Station. So dangerous was this section of road that the Germans created a virtual subway, a 1500m long tunnel that ran from here under the Menen Road almost to the entrance to the Bellewaarde Theme Park to enable their troops to get to the front line in safety. It was known as the 'Hooge Tunnel'.

Continue to the crossroads with Waterstraat on the left.

N.B. Private Memorial to **Gunner A.E. Wheeler (Map N13a. GPS: 50.83484 2.97244)**.

This may be visited by turning left here and first right along narrow, winding roads. The non-standard white Headstone of Gunner Wheeler, 345 Bty, RFA, died 7 May 1982, is in a small garden on the right. Wheeler was badly wounded on 1 July 1916 at Zillebeke and his experience affected him so deeply that he asked that his ashes should be scattered among his comrades. This was done at Bedford House CWGC on 1 August 1982 and the headstone was placed here in 1983, on land donated by the owners of the adjacent house.

Private Headstone of Gnr A.E. Wheeler, Zillebeke

Continue along the road as it dips and rises.

On the right is the **Protea B&B** with 5 simple rooms with en-suite facilities – very popular with battlefield tourists. Tel: + (0) 57 46 63 39. E-mail: the protea@belgacom.net Website: www. theprotea-ypres.be/

Continue to a crest with a garage complex on the right and the turning to Pappotstraat on the left.

• *Clapham Junction/Gloucestershire Memorial/18th Division Memorial/18.8 miles/5 minutes/Map I29, 30/GPS: 50.84347 2.96192*

This was a meeting point for roads and tracks, hence its name. The 1st Battalion of the Gloucestershires saw heavy fighting here during First Ypres and the 2nd Battalion during Second Ypres. Their Memorial obelisk is on the right. Opposite on the left is a similar one for the 18th (Eastern) Division which has others in Trones Wood and Thiepval on the Somme.

Memorial to the 18th Division with 1st Gloucesters Memorial behind, Clapham Junction, with detail of plaque.

Extra Visit to Princess Patricia's Canadian Light Infantry Memorial, Westhoek (Map I32, GPS: 50.85458 2.95027).

Round trip: 3.2 miles. Approximate time: 10 minutes

Continue and turn first right following the green CWGC sign to the memorial and continue following memorial signs to the village and turn left on the wiggly Princess Patricia Straat to the circular memorial.

The Plaque on the base of the Memorial, built beside a Canadian Maple tree, records that 'Here on 6 May 1915, the "Originals" of Princess Patricia's Canadian Light Infantry commanded by their founder Major A Hamilton Gault DSO held firm and counted not the cost.' On 4 May the Germans began an intense bombardment of the Frezenberg Ridge area that initiated 10 days of fighting that the Official History says 'was some of the most desperate fighting that ever took place in the Salient'. The Pats suffered badly, but by bringing up their orderlies, batmen, pioneers and others held on, though on 8 May Major

Hamilton Gault was wounded twice and had to give up command of the regiment. That same day they lost 9 more officers and 382 other ranks and were reduced to 4 officers and 150 other ranks. Their stand, says the Official History, 'is worthy to rank ... among the historic episodes of the war.'

The Memorial was unveiled by Mrs Hamilton Gault, on land offered by M. Jules Van Ackere of Wevelghem, in 1958. Another Plaque was unveiled on 13 August 1964, the fiftieth anniversary of the founding of the Regiment.

In 2015 the area was cleaned and landscaped and on 8 May a new **Plaque** was unveiled to commemorate the **100th Anniversary of the Battle of Frezenberg** by Col-in-Chief Adrienne Clarkson, together with an **Information Board and Map**.

Memorial to Princess Patricia's Light Infantry, Frezenberg

Turn round and return to pick up the main itinerary at Clapham Junction.

Continue downhill along the Menin Road, to the memorial by the entrance to the car park for Bellewaerde Leisure Park on the right.

• KRRC Memorial/19.4 miles/5 minutes/Map I31/GPS: 50.84575 2.94966

The Memorial, which is similar to one on the Somme at Pozières and another in Winchester, is placed here in acknowledgement of the Regiment's part in the battle of 30/31 July 1915, at Hooge Château (qv) and the later battle of Sanctuary Wood (qv) on 2 June 1916. During the war the Regiment grew to twenty-two Battalions, fifteen of which fought in Flanders.

• Site of Hooge Château/Crater

The leisure park is on the grounds of the original Château (family home of the Baron Gaston de Vinck,) whose destruction began on 31 October 1914, when a shell fell on Maj Gen Monro's Divisional Headquarters and several staff officers were killed. Others were wounded, including Gen Monro and Lt-Gen Samuel Holt Lomax, CB, of 1st Division, age 59, who was mortally wounded and eventually died on 10 April 1915. He is buried in the Aldershot Military Cemetery. Several of the casualties are buried in Ypres Town CWGC Cemetery (qv). The crater itself was filled in during the 1920s. It was formed by a mine sprung by 3rd Division on 19 July 1915. The gallery leading to the charge of 3,500lb of ammonal was 190ft long and was prepared by 175th Tunnelling Company RE.

Memorial to KRRC, Hooge

When new the crater measured 120ft across and 20ft deep. (For those who know the Lochnagar crater on the Somme, that took 60,000 lbs of ammonal.)

Continue to the Hotel Kasteel to the right.

• Front Line Hooghe Crater/Preserved Trenches/Bunkers/19.6 miles/15 minutes/RWC/Map I14a/14b/GPS: 50.84639 2.94624

From May 1915 the Château area was held by the Germans. It was the scene of continuous bitter fighting and some 50 mines were exploded in the grounds. The British recaptured the ruins in August 1917 were pushed back again in spring 1918 - almost to Ypres itself, finally stopping the Germans at Hell Fire Corner.

In 1918 the Baron returned to the ruins and rebuilt the château in the shape of the present Hotel. (**The Hotel Kasteelhof 't Hooghe and Restaurant**, Tel: + (0) 57 46 87 87, e-mail: kasteelhof.thooghe@belgacom.net Website: www.hotelkasteelhofthooghe.be. Owned and run by the Loontjens family it offers not the usual 'sea views' but 'crater views'!)

To the left of the hotel, three adjoining water-filled craters (blown by the Germans in June 1916 during the attack on Mount Sorrel) and blockhouses, both in and out of the water, have been excavated and may be visited. There is no formal entrance fee but there is a box by the entrance of the site for donations to its maintenance. The area where the path runs between the craters and the fenced border of the theme park is where in a surprise attack at 0315 on 30 July 1915, the Germans first used the flame thrower against British troops. At that time the crater and its immediate surroundings were held by the 8th Rifle Brigade and the 7th Bn KRRC, and jets of flame were sent against both sides of the crater from the direction of the theme park. The *Flammenwerfer* equipment that the Germans used was carried by one man and looked rather like a portable fire extinguisher. The liquid was ignited at the nozzle and produced a jet of flame some 25yd long accompanied by thick black smoke.

Both battalions were forced back beyond what is now the rear wall of Hooge Crater Cemetery. Despite further flame attacks that night the line was stabilised some 200yd beyond the other side of the Menin Road and in the two days of fighting the 7th KRRC lost 12 officers and 289 other ranks and 8th Rifle Brigade 19 officers and 462 other ranks.

Bitter fighting had taken place earlier in this sector in 'The Battle of Hooge' (or Bellewaerde) of 16/17 June 1915, and the Royal Fusiliers, the Royal Scots Fusiliers and the Northumberland Fusiliers, followed by the Lincolns and the Liverpool Scottish, assaulted enemy trenches between the Menin Road and the Ypers-Roulers railway line. An account of this action, which practically wiped out the Liverpool Scottish, appears below and also in Ann Clayton's biography of **Noel Chavasse** (qv), for it was here that their Medical Officer, who was to go on to win the **VC and Bar, won the MC** for 'untiring efforts in personally searching the ground between our line and the enemy's [for which] many of the wounded owe their lives'.

In February 1916 the poet **2nd Lt Robert Ernest Vernède** of the 12th Bn the Rifle Bde was serving in trenches here. He wrote vivid letters to his school and college friend, Frederick Salter, and to his wife Carol about his experiences after several days of particularly fierce bombardment during the second week in February. To Salter he described with horror how the 'men suffering from shock, flopping about the trenches like grassed fish, is enough to sicken one, and some of the face wounds are terrible'. To his wife he detailed more domestic

Bunker, Hooge Crater,
Kasteelhof grounds

situations, 'I'd been wet to the waist for about twenty-four hours ... and I had no feeling in my legs for about two hours... I sat up from 6 a.m. to 12 drying my drawers over a brazier ... without any trousers on.' Although Vernède commented that, in a physical sense, 'It's extraordinary how one doesn't feel the worse for this sort of thing,' this sensitive, over-age officer (39 when he enlisted in 1914), who need never have gone to war, wrote to his friend, 'Anyone hereafter who shows a tendency towards exalting war ought to be drowned straight away by his country.'

This area is noted for another innovation. It is said that here the first experimental use of portable wireless was attempted between division and brigade HQ. It is to be hoped that the army radios worked better then than they seemed to do at Arnhem in 1944 or even in early 2002.

Continue to the Hooge Crater Museum on the right.

• *Hooge Crater Museum /19.7 miles/20 minutes/RWC/Map I13/GPS: 50.84634 2.94338*

This is truly an atmospheric, traditional, enjoyable, classic style museum and justifiably proclaims that it is 'the best private museum in Belgium'. It is housed in the old Chapel at Hooge, built in 1927 by Baron Gaston de Vinck, as a memorial to those who fell in the Salient, and was acquired by Roger de Smul, who after extensive renovation, opened it as a museum at Easter 1994. In it he set up two superb private collections. One consists of World War I armour and equipment, handed down through members of the de Smul family (who during WW2 managed the Regina Hotel in Ypres in which they had a secret room where they hid downed RAF pilots and crews until they could be guided out through the German lines). The other, of uniforms and artefacts of the men who fought in the Salient, belongs to the collector Philippe Oosterlinck. There are some well-interpreted dioramas, clear commentaries and a dramatic stained glass window of the Cloth Hall on fire and outstanding displays of German helmets and decorated shell cases. There is a 1917 German Fokker DR1 and an authentic British 1916 Ford 'T' ambulance, audio-visual presentations, a section dedicated to the finds of 'The Diggers' (qv). British sculptor John Bunting created a statue of Madonna and Child for the museum in memory of Pte Joseph P. Bunting, killed 1 July 1916 on the Somme. It stands in a niche above the doorway.

A highly recommended visit, many new improvements, exhibits and audio-visual displays continue to be added by the current enthusiastic and welcoming owners, Niek and Ilse Benoot-Wateyne. Attached to the Museum, on the site of a former small school (built in 1922 and closed in 1974), is a pleasant modern **Café** with clean WCs. Excellent value, appetising soup/sandwich lunch.

Open: 1000-1800. Closed Mondays and January. Tel: + (0) 57 46 84 46. E-mail: info@hoogecrater. com Website: www.hoogecrater.com A small entrance fee is payable, with the option of a combined entry fee/lunch.

Beside the terrace, on the site of the toilet block of the old school, is **Entry Point East** of the Ypres Walking Circuit (qv). A fascinating film shows how this part of the front moved backwards and forward as the war progressed. Beside it are Information Panels describing the châteaux and castles in this area that were destroyed. The well-defined route, with its informative elm-tree stations (see description in In Flanders Fields entry, page 68) starts here, continues to the Château, to Bellewaerde Ridge, RE Grave and Memorials, returning to the starting point.

In August 2016 a beautifully restored cottage in the grounds was opened as a guest house, **The Cottage de Vinck** (after the Baron (qv)). Tel: + (0) 474771952, Email: cottagedevinck.be Website: www. cottagedevinck.be The 9 bedrooms can sleep

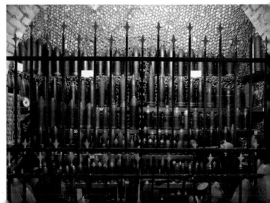

Dramatic display of shells,
Hooge Crater Museum

Hooge Crater Museum and Restaurant Terrace

Don't forget to look up, Hooge Crater Museum

18 in various combinations. 6 bathrooms, fully fitted kitchen. There is even stabling and pasture should you arrive by horse!

Walk carefully over the road to the cemetery.

• Hooge Crater CWGC Cemetery/10 minutes/Map I14

The Cemetery was begun during Third Ypres by the 7th Division's Burial Officer on land that had been heavily fought over in 1915 and 1916 and extended by concentration burials from the surrounding battlefields after the Armistice. Five thousand eight hundred and ninety two graves are registered here, including 513 Australians, 105 Canadians, 121 New Zealanders, 2 from the British West Indies and 45 Special Memorials. Over 60% are 'Known Unto God'. The Cemetery was designed by Sir Edwin Lutyens assisted by N.A. Rew.

Hooge Crater CWGC Cemetery with Hooge Crater Museum behind, from Canadalaan

The stone wall that encircles the Stone of Remembrance and which leads to the Cross of Sacrifice at the front of the cemetery is said to be reminiscent of the crater blown across the road on 19 July 1915.

Private Patrick Joseph Bugden, VC, of the 31st Battalion, AIF, who won the medal for his heroic actions at Polygon Wood on 26-27 September 1917, and who was killed on his fifth mission to rescue wounded men under intense fire, is buried here. In the area of the cemetery **2nd Lt Sidney Clayton Woodroffe** of the 8th Bn The Rifle Brigade won his **VC** on 30 July 1915, for gallantly defending his position against the German attack and for leading a counter-attack under intense fire, during which he was killed. His body was lost in subsequent fighting and Woodroffe is commemorated on the Menin Gate. The **VC** was gazetted on 6 August and on 8 August Woodroffe's friend, the poet Charles Sorley, wrote:

In Memorian S.C.W., VC
There is no fitter end than this.
No need is now to yearn nor sigh.
We know the glory that is his,
A glory that can never die.

Also buried here is **Lt Wilfrid Evelyn Littleboy** of the 16th Bn R Warwicks, killed on 7 October 1917, to whom there is a Plaque in Geluveld Church (qv).

Hooge Crater CWGC Cemetery showing symbolic Crater

Continue down the hill for 500m to the Canada Café on the left.

• Menin Road Museum/20.1 miles/15 minutes/Map I14c/GPS: 50.84693 2.93479

Behind the **Canada Café** is the small Museum owned by Gregory Florissoone. A typical private collection Museum, it has realistic dioramas, some interesting and unusual items such as displays of enlistment posters (including one on Exemption From Military Service) and old private memorial plaques. **Open** daily 1000-2200 for breakfast, lunch and dinner. **Closed** 24 Dec-2 Jan. Tel: + (0) 57 20 11 36. E-mail: info@menenroadmuseum.com. Small entry fee payable. Visitors' own food may be consumed here provided a drink is bought and the Museum visited.

Turn left up Canadalaan (Maple Avenue) to the cemetery on the right.

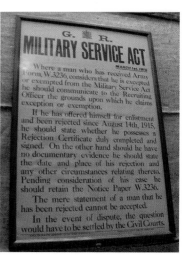

Exemption from Military Service Poster, Menin Road Museum

• Sanctuary Wood CWGC Cemetery, Lt Rae Memorial/21.0 miles/ 10minutes/Map I15/ GPS: 50.83838 2.94439

The Cemetery contains 102 UK, 41 Canadian and 1 German burial - the aviator, **Flieg Hauptmann Hans Roser, Iron Cross holder**, shot down by Lanoe Hawker on 25 July 1915, in the action that was to win him the first VC to be awarded for aerial combat. Hawker brought down two other planes in the same action. Here too is buried **Lt Gilbert Talbot** of the Rifle Brigade, after whom Talbot House (qv) was named. His grave stands apart from the main rows of headstones, much as does that of Gen Patton, who stands in front of his troops in Luxembourg American Cemetery.

Son of the Bishop of London and brother of the Rev Neville Talbot, Senior C of E Chaplain of 6th Division, Gilbert was educated at Winchester (where he became friendly with A. P. Herbert) and Christ Church, Oxford, where he was President of the Union and a brilliant debater. In the afternoon of 30 July 1915, he fell, near Zouave Wood, leading a counter-attack with what remained of his men after the brutal liquid fire attack of that morning. Near him as he was shot in the neck cutting the old British barbed wire was his servant, Rifleman Nash, who was shot through the finger as he lay Gilbert's body down. Later attempts by him to return with stretcher

Below: *'Solitary' Headstone of Lt Gilbert Talbot, Sanctuary Wood CWGC Cemetery*

Right: *Headstone of Flieg. Hauptmann Hans Roser, Sanctuary Wood CWGC Cemetery*

bearers to recover Gilbert's body failed, but Nash was later to receive the DCM for his 'devoted care and courage'. Neville Talbot crawled out through the dead of the Rifle Brigade two days later, first finding Woodroffe's body and then Gilbert's. He took his pocket book, prayer book, wrist watch and badge and gave his brother the benediction. A week later he brought the body in and buried it. Killed in the same attack, but whose body although buried and marked, could not be found after the war, was **2nd Lt the Hon G.W. ('Billy') Grenfell**, younger brother of Julian Grenfell (qv), the poet. Like Woodroffe, he is commemorated on the Menin Gate.

The Cemetery was designed by Sir Edwin Lutyens with N.A.Rew and in its fan-shaped layout is typical of Lutyens' originality.

Outside the Cemetery is a **Private Memorial to Lt Keith Rae**, also of the Rifle Brigade, killed on the same day. He was last seen at a spot near Hooge Crater in the Château grounds and after the war his family erected this memorial to him on that site. When the last member of the Vink family to own the Château felt that the Memorial could no longer be cared for, it was moved here and is maintained by the Commonwealth War Graves Commission.

Continue to Sanctuary Wood Museum car park.

Memorial to Lt Keith Rae, Rifle Bde, outside Sanctuary Wood CWGC Cemetery.

• *Sanctuary Wood Museum/Preserved Trenches/21.3 miles/30 minutes/RWC/ Map I17/GPS: GPS: 50.83698 2.94606*

The accepted story of how Sanctuary Wood got its name is that in October 1914, the area of the wood was under the command of Gen E. S. Bulfin of 2nd Infantry Brigade. At this stage it was a relatively quiet sector and Bulfin is said to have offered 'sanctuary here to stragglers until they could rejoin their units'. On 31 October the Germans had broken the Allied line at Geluveld and Sir Douglas Haig told the Grenadier Guards that he relied on them 'to save First Corps and possibly the Army!' The following morning Major the Lord Bernard Charles Gordon-Lennox (qv) of the 2nd Battalion described how his battalion was ordered to report to Gen Bulfin 'in a wood'. There was a mass of woods in the area and the Guards were doubtful of finding Bulfin's. Before they did, they discovered that Bulfin had been wounded and that his command was taken over by Major-General Frederic Rudolph Lambart, 10th Earl of Cavan. In the vicinity Gordon-Lennox met Major-General Thompson Capper, commanding 7th Division. 'I'm afraid your Division has had a bad time, Sir,' he remarked. 'Yes, so bad that there's no Division left, so that I'm a curiosity – a Divisional Commander without a Division,' replied the General. Capper was to be killed, leading a charge by a Worcestershire platoon at Loos on 26 September 1915, and is buried at Lillers Communal CWGC Cemetery and Gordon-Lennox was killed by a shell on 10 November 1914. He is buried in Zillebeke Churchyard (qv, Map N2). On Friday 13 November the Guards reported entering a 'wood, south of Hooge, known as Sanctuary Wood, as it had so far not been shelled'. But on 14 November, 'the wood was duly shelled.' The sanctuary was safe no longer.

By October 1917, James Halley (qv), a Sapper Officer, was writing in his diary, 'Of the terrible and horrible scenes I have seen in the war, Sanctuary Wood is the worst. Yet Sanctuary Wood in 1914 was a sanctuary, but today – Dante in his wildest imaginings never conceived a like'.

After the war the Schier family, who owned the wood, had the foresight to understand

Proprietor Rita Battiau & Assistant, Talitha, Sanctuary Wood Museum

Entrance to Trench System, Sanctuary Wood

that their battered piece of ground would one day be of interest to pilgrims and tourists. They enclosed the trench lines and dugouts, the splintered trees and the debris of war with a fence and added a small museum. During World War II they hid all the artefacts in the cellar and concreted it over. Visiting Germans (and the story goes that Goering was one of them) asked where all the exhibits were and were told, 'The British have stolen them'. The characterful and larger than life owner for many years, whose curatorial skills were sometimes questioned, Jacques Schier, who died in 2014, maintained the trenches, enlarged the museum and kept the superb 3-D pictures that give a graphic and sometimes horrifyingly real view of the war.

On Jacques' death the complex was inherited by his assistant, Rita Battiau and her daughter Cindy Bruycke. They have vastly improved the facilities, exhibits and cleanliness of the Museum and grounds, adding a new toilet block in 2015.

There is a book and souvenir stall and a **café**, with bar and limited snacks. Groups should reserve in advance. **Open** all year round during daylight hours. Entrance fee payable. Tel: + (0) 57 46 63 73.

Continue up Canadalaan. Some 300yd further on is

Chelsea Hospital In-Pensioner, Colour Sgt Denis Shiels, looking at 3D images, Sanctuary Wood Museum

• *The Canadian Memorial at Hill 62 (Mount Sorrel)/21.4 miles/5 minutes/Map N17/OP/GPS: 50.83515 2.94721*

This area is known as Hill 62, the name being taken from the height of its highest point above sea level in metres. Specific points, known as 'spot heights', are frequently marked on maps, together with their height in metres. Such is the case here, where the spot height 62 was marked on the British maps of the area. On this high point is the Canadian Memorial, clearly identified as being that for Mount Sorrel. Hill 62 (or 'Tor Top' as it was sometimes known) which is part of a high – above 50m - feature that runs like a closing bracket east from here, skirts the road Green Jacket Ride (qv) and curves back below the Canadian 15th Bn Memorial (qv) which stands on Observatory Ridge. Edmund Blunden (qv) in early 1917 described 'a reconnaissance of the trenches which we [the 11th Bn Royal Sussex Regt] were to hold ... They were those on a rising ground in Sanctuary Wood, near Hill 60, and were indifferently known as Tor Tops, Mount Sorrel and Observatory Ridge.'

The Canadians were early into the war. As the British ultimatum to Germany expired, the Canadian Government offered to raise 20,000 men for the fight. Barely two months later 33,000 Canadians in four brigades left for England and the training camps of Salisbury Plain. Most of them were new volunteers, with the notable exception of Princess Patricia's Canadian Light Infantry who were mainly old soldiers, either veterans of the South African War or reservists. The 'Pats' had actually left Montreal on *The Megantic* on 28 August but German activity in the Atlantic led to the cancellation of the sailing and they eventually left on *The Royal George* on 27 September, arriving in Salisbury on 18 October. Early in February 1915, the Canadians (less the 'Pats', who had been seconded to the British 27th Division in December and immediately went overseas arriving in France on the 21st. There they were involved in heavy fighting at St Eloi in the Salient and remained with the 27th until rejoining the 'Canadian Corps' on 27 November 1915) arrived in 'France' – actually Belgium – at Ploegsteert Wood. They were organised as a Division, the 1st, of three infantry brigades, the fourth formation that had sailed from Canada being left in England as a support force.

In March 1915 the 1st Division was in action at Neuve Chapelle and then moved to the area north of Ypres where it met the full onslaught of the German gas attack. At the same time a new Division, the 2nd, was on its way to Europe and the force left in England had been formed into a 'Training Division'. In January 1916 the 3rd Division was formed and joined the line in the Salient, thus completing the formation of the Canadian Corps.

In April the Canadians were again involved at St Eloi and Voormezeele, this time in vicious mine warfare, but it was in June of that year that the 3rd Division, occupying a position running from Sanctuary Wood, over Hill 62 and along Observatory Ridge, to Mount Sorrel where it joined up with the 2nd Canadian Division, was to take part in what was up to that time the greatest of all the Canadian battles - the 'Battle of Sanctuary Wood'.

Sir Max Aitken MP, later Lord Beaverbrook, in his Official History of the CEF in the early years of the war, takes over forty pages to describe the action whose German preliminary bombardment broke like a storm over the Canadians at 0830 on 2 June 1916, and killed the Divisional Commander, General Malcolm Smith-Mercer, MC, who is buried in Lijssenthoek CWGC Cemetery (qv).

The Canadian line ran from Hill 60 (Map N8) to Hill 62 (Map N17) where you are now, and then north to meet the Menin Road where Bellewaerde theme park is today. Sanctuary Wood thus lay just behind the Canadian front. The 1st Canadian Mounted Rifles were in trenches here and by 1315 they had suffered 367 casualties, while the 4th Mounted on their right down to Hill 60 lost 637 out of a strength of some 680. That afternoon the Princess Pats were overrun in communication trenches on the northern slopes of Hill 62, losing seventeen officers out of twenty-two and at one time were firing both forward and backwards, much as the Gloucesters did in Egypt in 1801, thus earning the right to wear their cap badges at the front and at the back. The Germans had won footholds on the high ground of Mount Sorrel, Observatory Ridge and Hill 62 and were poised to surge down through Sanctuary Wood towards Ypres. The Canadians rushed up reserves from Ypres, the KRRC from 60th Brigade taking over the positions on the Menin Road (Map I31, where their memorial is today) allowing the Canadians to shuffle their troops south to meet the German offensive.

At 1600 the Corps Commander, General Sir Julian Byng, decided to make a counter-

Canadian Memorial,
Hill 62

attack at dawn the following morning but, owing to the fact that many of the immediate reserves had already been thrown into the battle and much re-organisation was needed, the orders were not issued until 2145. The task of attacking Hill 62 was given to the Canadian 3rd Brigade who were way back in Corps Reserve (much as the 21st and 24th Divisions were too far to the rear at Loos in September 1915) and the task of moving up to be in position to attack at 0200 proved too much for them. There were delays all along the line and the artillery arrangements that had been timed for an attack at 0200 were in considerable disarray. Thus, when the attack did go in at 0710 (Lord Beaverbrook said

Spires of Ypres from Hill 62

'with those battalions that were ready'), the fire support was inadequate and two of the regiments that were supposed to move through Sanctuary Wood for the attack on Hill 62 had not arrived, having got lost in the mile-long communication trench leading to the wood. However, the 49th Battalion, new to battle, established defence lines in Sanctuary Wood and, while the counter-attack did not recover the old front line trenches, it did stabilise the contest and stop the German advance. At 0130 on 13 June, following a bombardment by over 200 guns through driving rain, under the cover of smoke and using gas in the north, the Canadians attacked again and recovered most of the ground lost. The front settled to that shown on the map as the position 12 months later, on 6 June 1917, just prior to the battle of Passchendaele.

The Monument that marks this fine Canadian achievement is the standard octagonal block of granite (cf Crest Farm, Map E3) approached by a flight of steps. Perpetuating the confusion between Tor Top/Hill 62 and Mount Sorrel, the Monument is actually inscribed 'Mount Sorrel'. Around it are direction signs to Menin, Wervicq, Comines, Messines, Hill 60, Kemmel, Zillebeke, Ypres, Hooge, Zonnebeek and Geluveld. Indeed this high point makes an excellent OP. There are three semi-circular stone walls, one to either side of the Memorial, one beyond it. From the right-hand platform the spires of Ypres can clearly be seen and the Cemetery straight ahead is **Maple Copse CWGC (Map N16, GPS: 50.83573 2.93909)** designed by Sir Edwin Lutyens with N.A. Rew). From the central platform Shrewsbury Forest can be seen ahead. The area is most beautifully landscaped and planted with a variety of ornamental and flowering shrubs and spring bulbs.

Return down Canadalaan to the Menin Road. Turn left towards Ypres.

• Menin Road

You are now driving along the most notorious section of that most notorious of roads, the Menin Road. Some of the desolate horror of that stretch of mangled highway was captured in Paul Nash's painting *The Menin Road*. Nash, born in 1889, was influenced by surrealism and *avant-garde* schools like the Vorticists. This reflects in his striking picture of this area, which hangs in the IWM. With his brother John, Paul was appointed one of the Official War Artists, and, ironically, his anti-war sentiments are strongly expressed in his World War I paintings, especially in *The Menin Road* and in *We are Making a New World*, a painting which has become an icon for the ghastliness of modern warfare. Paul Nash drew many other scenes in the Salient, including Sunset: Ruins of Hospice at Wytschaete, Mont St Eloi, The Field of Passchendaele, Gheluvelt

Village, Nightfall: Zillebeke, The Bluff and The Landscape: Hill 60. Nash felt that his duty as an Official War Artist and his experiences in the trenches made him a 'messenger', as well as an artist. 'Feeble, inarticulate will be my message, but it will have a bitter truth and may it burn their lousy souls.' Nash was chafing at the restrictions imposed on the war artists – 'I was not allowed to put dead men into my pictures because apparently they don't exist'. He ascribed later attacks of asthma to being gassed in 1917.

A poem, always thought to be anonymous, reflects the comradeship and indomitable spirit of the Tommies who slogged along this road from the Menin Gate:

Menin Gate

'What are you guarding, Man-at-Arms?
Why do you watch and wait?'
'I guard the graves', said the Man-at-Arms,
'I guard the graves by Flanders Farms,
Where the dead will rise at my call to arms,
And march to the Menin Gate.'
'When do they march then, Man-at-Arms?
Cold is the hour and late.'
'They march tonight,' said the Man-at-Arms,
'With the moon on the Menin Gate.
They march when the midnight bids them go,
With their rifles slung and their pipes aglow,
Along the roads - the roads they know,
The road to the Menin Gate.'
'What are they singing, Man-at-Arms
As they march to the Menin Gate?'
'The marching songs,' said the Man-at-Arms,
'That let them laugh at Fate;
No more will the night be cold for them,
For the last tattoo has rolled for them;
And their souls will sing as of old, for them,
As they march to the Menin Gate.'

Researcher Martin Passande informs us that it was actually by Eric Haydon, was set to music by Lowri Bowen and published by Boosey and Hawkes in 1930 for the Ypres League (qv).

Extra Visit to Birr Cross Roads CWGC Cemetery/Map I10/GPS: 50.84760 2.92866.

Round trip: 0.2 miles. Approximate time: 10 minutes

Continue some 300 yds to the cemetery on the left.

The Cemetery, designed by Sir Edwin Lutyens assisted by N.A.Rew, was originally christened by the 1st Leinsters in 1915 after their depot in Ireland. In it are buried 625 UK, 140 Australian, 12 New Zealand, 15 Canadian, 1 Newfoundland, 1 South African, 1 BWI, 11 unknown and 8 Special Memorials. Here is buried **Capt Harold Ackroyd, VC**, RAMC, attd 6th Bn the Berkshires killed on 11 August 1917. Between 31 July and 1 August, this dedicated medic worked continuously [between 'Clapham Junction' and Hooge], utterly regardless of danger, tending the wounded in the front line under heavy machine-gun, rifle and shell fire – true valour. After multiple recommendations

Headstone of 2nd Lt Raymond Lodge, Birr Cross Roads CWGC Cemetery

for the Victoria Cross, he was killed in action ten days later. The headstone of **De Wattine Camille L.E.** records that he was a *Sergent de 'Armée Belge Interprète á l'Armée britannique, mort pour la Belgique le 29 septembre 1918, Chevalier de l'Ordre de Léopold, Médaille de la Victoire, Médaille Commemorative de la Campaigne 1914-1918.* Also buried here is **2nd Lt Raymond Lodge**, attd 3rd Bn South Lancs Regt, killed on 14 September 1915, aged 25, son of Sir Oliver Lodge, the physicist and first principal of the University of Birmingham, whose interest in psychical research was heightened when Raymond was killed. He concluded that the mind survives death and wrote a book called *Raymond, or Life and Death* after his attempts to make contact with his son through the medium Mrs Osborne Leonard. The book was ridiculed by the *Daily Mail* which was campaigning to warn its readers against psychic fraud.

Turn round and pick up the main itinerary.

Continue towards Ypres for 150yds and take the first right along a small metalled road, Begijnenbosstraat. It is signed to RE Grave and Liverpool Scottish Stone. Follow signs to the memorial which is to the right off the road and park just before the barrier.

• RE Grave, Railway Wood/177th Tunnelling Coy Memorial/ Liverpool Scottish Stone/23.2 miles/10 minutes/Map I8, 9, 9a/GPS: 50.85357 2.93563

Here is a Memorial to an officer and eleven others under command of the 177th (Tunnelling) Company RE who were killed and lie buried somewhere in the tunnels below the Cross of Sacrifice. The original cross that marked the site is in the RE Museum in Chatham. The British front line ran through this area for almost two years and obvious craters remain, particularly in the wood

Beyond the Cross is the handsome **Memorial Stone to the Liverpool Scottish**, Bellewaarde 16-VI-1915. It was unveiled on 29 July 2000 (the Regiment's Centenary year) in the presence of a large contingent from the city of Liverpool, serving members of the Liverpool Scottish and their Officers' Association and Regimental Pipes and Drums, and the nephew of VC winner Noel Chavasse of the Regiment (qv), Capt E. F. J. Chavasse. The Stone, set in an attractive landscaped glade and with a seat opposite it and the Union flag flying beside it, was originally sited above the main entrance to the Regiment's HQ in Liverpool. It records that from a line 250m west (i.e. broadly from the direction of the Theme Park) of this point 23 officers and 519 other ranks of the 1/10th (Scottish) Bn, the King's (Liverpool) Regiment, TF, advanced east up the slope towards the German trenches on Bellewaarde Ridge (effectively where you are). Four officers and 75 other ranks were killed, 11 officers and 201 other ranks were wounded and 6 officers and 103 other ranks were missing (all the officers, and with very few exceptions, all the others were eventually reported killed). It has a brief history of the regiment in the war.

In this area of Railway Hill (which he christened 'the Little Hill of Death'), the poet Etonian **Capt the Hon Julian Henry Francis Grenfell DSO** was mortally wounded on 13 May 1915, a month after writing his most famous poem, *Into Battle*. His battalion, the 1st Royal Dragoons, had moved to second line trenches just north of Hooge on 12 May. The following day there was a heavy German bombardment, during which Julian was described by General Pulteney as 'strolling around as if he were on a river' in his capacity as observer. Grenfell was knocked out by a shell, but recovered to bring information to his OP about German movements around the Dragoons' flank. As he was reporting to the General another shell landed close by and a splinter from it lodged in Julian's skull. His first spoken reaction was, 'I think I'm done'. Grenfell was sent to base hospital at Boulogne, near Wimereux where his sister, Monica, was a VAD. Their parents, Lord and Lady Desborough, were sent for but Julian died on 26 May. He was buried two days later at Boulogne Eastern CWGC Cemetery. His famous poem ends:

The thundering line of battle stands,
And in the air Death moans and sings;
But Day shall clasp him with strong hands,
And Night shall fold him in soft wings.

On the same day that Grenfell was wounded, another aristocratic soldier poet, Etonian **Capt the Hon Colwyn Erasmus Arnold Philipps**, eldest son of Lord and Lady St Davids, serving with the Royal Horse Guards, was killed in this vicinity. Like Grenfell, Philipps was a professional soldier who wrote poetry before the war. Also like Grenfell he wrote vividly descriptive letters to a beloved mother once he arrived at the front (on 4 November 1914). The last recorded one is dated 29 April 1915, after the RHG had spent some time with the Canadians, who, wrote Philipps, 'have done a very fine thing which is most satisfactory, also they are becoming more disciplined. The other day one of them said: "Our chaps are all right, our rifle is a good one, the grub is first-rate, and our officers – oh, well we just take them along as mascots!"' This popular officer was killed leading his men in an attack on the German trenches, 'giving view-halloos as we advanced and shouting "Come on, Boys", and waving his cap', according to a fellow officer. In his kitbag found after his death were some lines of poetry which end,

Released from time and sense of great or small
Float on the pinions of the Night-Queen's wings;
Soar till the swift inevitable fall
Will drag you back into all the world's small things;
Yet for an hour be one with all escaped things.

Note the image of night's wings in both these final poems. Many poets have used similar phrases particularly Longfellow in 'The Day is Done'. Colwyn Philipps was mentioned in Despatches on 1 January 1916.

Coincidentally, a Trooper of the RHG, writing on 18 May 1915, and describing Philipps's last hours, makes several mentions of **Captain Bowlby**, Squadron Leader of the Life Guards, whose men 'were clean blown from the trenches and dug-outs without a semblance of cover.' Bowlby 'called the Life Guards together and they got back into the firing line.' Shortly afterwards 'the most awful shell fire that God has allowed' broke out, and at this stage 'Captain Philipps inquired where Captain Bowlby was, and I told him I had seen him climb over just previously.' This is the last mention of Bowlby, whose Private Memorial is visited next.

In his Despatches, Sir John French described the action of the Cavalry Brigade that day:

'On May 13, the various reliefs having been completed without incident, the heaviest bombardment yet experienced broke out at 4.30 A.M., and continued with little intermission throughout the day. At about 7.45 A.M. the Cavalry Brigade astride the railway [now the N37 road running north-east from Hellfire Corner], having suffered very severely, and their trenches having been obliterated, fell back about 800 yards. The North Somerset Yeomanry on the right of the Brigade, although also suffering severely, hung on to their trenches throughout the day, and actually advanced and attacked the enemy with the bayonet. The Brigade on its right also maintained its position; as did also the Cavalry Division, except the left squadron which, when reduced to sixteen men, fell back. The 2nd Essex Regiment, realising the situation, promptly charged and retook the trench, holding it till relieved by the Cavalry. Meanwhile a counter-attack by two Cavalry Brigades was launched at 2.30 P.M., and succeeded, in spite of very heavy shrapnel and rifle fire, in regaining the original line of trenches, turning out the Germans who had entered it, and in some cases pursuing them for some distance. But a

Remembrance Tree No, 73 on the Ypres Entry Route East, Railway Wood

Above: *RE Grave, Railway Wood*

Left: *Memorial to Liverpool Scottish, Railway Wood*

very heavy shell fire was again opened on them, and they were again compelled to retire to an irregular line in rear, principally the craters of shell holes. The enemy in their counter-attack suffered very severe losses.'

The site is on one of three designated and numbered walking routes (from 'Entry Points' – North, South and North) along the Front Lines. The Lines are marked by trees with coloured surrounds – blue for British and red for German - passing craters and remains of shelters and other points of interest. This Tree of Remembrance (qv), No 73, is on the British front line, on the Line from Entry Point-South at Hooge Crater (qv). It shows the situation of the others on the route. The App 'Ypres Salient' can be activated here. There are also standard Information Boards describing RE Grave and the story of the Liverpool Scottish near their Memorial.

Return to Begijnenbosstraat and continue.

On a clear day the 50th Northumbrian Memorial Obelisk in Oxford Road can be seen on the skyline ahead. The road crosses the route of the old railway line now the new N37 road.

Continue over the N37 to the two memorials on the right.

• Private Memorials to Captain Skrine and Captain Bowlby/23.6 miles/5 minutes/Map I7, 6/GPS: 50.85557 2.93029

The Memorials to these two Etonians have been moved together in one fenced and gravelled enclosure which is now maintained by the Belgian Army. **Capt Geoffrey Vaux Salvin Bowlby**, RHG, age 21, and whose brother is buried in Bedford House Cemetery (qv), was killed in the action described above, **Capt Henry Langton Skrine** of the 6th Bn the SLI was killed during the night of 25 September 1915, along with 2 other officers and 11 other ranks, by heavy enemy artillery fire. The Memorial was put up by his widow and his sister. Both men are commemorated on the Menin Gate.

Continue along what was known as Cambridge Road (see Holts' Battle Map).

The high ground to your right rear is that of the Bellewaerde Ridge. On 16 June 1915, 9th Inf Bde from their front line trenches parallel to this road and a few yards to the right, followed by 7th Inf Bde from the road itself, launched an attack on the Bellewaerde Ridge. Their object was to knock the enemy from that commanding position which gave them observation over the greater part of the Allied ground to the east of Ypres. The operation was planned with great care by Lt

Memorials to Capt Skrine (right) & Capt Bowlby

Gen Sir E. Allenby of V Corps to the extent that, should the telephone wires between HQ and forward formations be cut, a system of signalling and a pigeon service would take their place. The RFC sent out observation patrols but, according to the *Official History*, 'They could not help much ... as they were unable to distinguish friend from foe in the trenches'! A bombardment began at 0230 hours and lifted at 0415 when the German front line was assaulted and captured 'with little resistance'. Then things started to go wrong. In their enthusiasm at the initial success, the Royal Irish Rifles 'could not be restrained and rushed forward ... The spirit which prompted the movement was excellent, but the result was disastrous.' Their impetus pushed troops in front into our own artillery fire and men were jostled into a chaotic melee. Although the German second line trenches were briefly occupied, the enemy launched a counter-attack and the brigade was driven back to the first line, captured at the beginning of the attack. Repeated attempts were made throughout the afternoon to press on, but by 1800 hours, although the British front line had been pushed a little further forward, the Germans still sat on the Ridge and 3rd Division had lost 140 officers and 3,391 men. They took 157 prisoners and inflicted some 300 German casualties. Among 9th Bde's casualties was their Brigade Major, Archibald Percival Wavell. Returning to Bde HQ (some 400yd up the old Ypres-Roulers railway line, now the new road linking Hellfire Corner and the A19 — see the Battle Map) Wavell was hit in the head by a shell splinter and lost his left eye. Making light of his wound he insisted on walking back to the nearest CCS, but was soon sent home to the King Edward 7th Hospital. For his part in the attack on the Bellewaerde Ridge, Wavell was awarded the MC in the first list gazetted of this newly created decoration, constituted by Royal Warrant of 28 December 1914 by King George V. After a spell on the staff at GHQ, Wavell, a fluent Russian speaker, acted as liaison officer with the Russian Grand Duke Nicholas in the Caucasus. In July 1917 he was sent to Palestine to act as liaison officer between Allenby and Sir William Robertson, the CIGS. Wavell had immense admiration for Allenby (widely known as 'The Bull' for his great stature and quick temper) and later wrote his biography. Wavell played a prominent role in WW2 and evidenced a keen interest in poetry, publishing in 1944 his 'Other Men's Poetry' an anthology whose contents, is it said, he knew by heart. Oddly, another general, Tom Bridges, who lost a leg in this area in September 1917, also wrote an anthology published four years before Wavell's. It was called 'Word From England'.

At the T junction with the main road turn right towards Zonnebeke. Immediately on the right is a Cemetery.

The dramatic group of sculptures, French Cemetery, St Charles de Potyze

Individual graves

• French National Cemetery, St Charles de Potyze/24.2 miles/10 minutes/Map I4/GPS: 50.86352 2.92592

Here are concentrated both 3,748 individual graves and a mass grave (Ossuaire) for 600 unknown soldiers. Buried in grave 323 is **Lt Pierre Charles Léon Ginisty** of the 153rd Infantry Regt, Class of 1904. Ginisty was the son of the Director of the Théatre de l'Odéon and a playwright in his own right. Born in 1884, he was killed in the area of Poelcapelle on 24 December 1914. The graves are numbered from the front from right to left and on the second row from left to right and so on. They are marked by very small numbers in the top right hand corner of each concrete cross which also bears scant details of the man who lies beneath it, but always the phrase, *Mort Pour la Patrie*. An impressive dark group of sculptures is to the left of the entrance and the ossuary at the rear of the cemetery is approached through the symmetrical lines of crosses, interspersed occasionally by the headstone of a Colonial soldier. There is a box by the entrance which contains the Visitor's Book. The Cemetery was re-landscaped in 2010. Outside is an **Information Board**.

The area between here and the next cemetery was that of the front line prior to the opening of the Messines Phase of Third Ypres, although no offensive was launched in this area at that time. You will now be driving out of the British lines into the German.

Continue to the cemetery on the right.

• Aeroplane CWGC Cemetery/24.5 miles/Map I5/GPS: 50.86421 2.93093

Designed by Sir Reginald Blomfield, this was named after the wreck of an aeroplane which was for some years preserved in front of the Cross; 1,097 burials are recorded – 825 UK, 204 Australian, 47 Canadian, 1 Newfoundland, 17 New Zealand, 1 South African and 636 unknown, with 8 Special Memorials for casualties believed to be buried here. The area was part of no-man's-land until Third Ypres. On 26 July 1915, five men were executed on the ramparts of Ypres for desertion – one of the largest executions of the war – and buried near where they were shot. Three of them, **Pte Bert Hartells, Pte John Robinson and Pte Alfred Thompson**, were reburied here after the Armistice.

Continue over the motorway and stop at the memorial on the left on a slip road.

• The Scottish Monument in Flanders, Frezenberg/25.2 miles/10 minutes/Map I5a/GPS: 50.86765 2.94506

Inaugurated during the 'Scottish Weekend' of the 90th Anniversary of Passchendaele on 25 August 2007, in an impressive ceremony, this Monument in the style of a traditional Celtic or 'High' Cross of pink Scottish granite set on a plinth of original bunker stones, is the first to commemorate the contribution of all Scots who fought on the Western Front (including Canadian Scottish). It also pays tribute to the 1st S African Bde as they formed part of the 9th (Scottish) Division for most of the war and famously took the Bremen Redoubt (qv). Standing some 7.5 metres high, this imposing Monument was designed by Dirk Uytterschout of Halle and cost around £15,000. The money was raised by contributions from the Scottish Executive, Scottish regiments and businesses and the general public, supported by the Flemish Government and the commune of Zonnebeke, co-ordinated by Erwin and Mia Ureel-Vanhaverbeke.

A **Plaque** on the rear was donated by **Mrs Georgina van Daal Fyffe** of Stirling in memory of her family. Memorial Benches surround the Memorial, donated by the Mauchline Burns Club. The site was chosen as it was here that the 15th (Scottish) Division launched their bloody attack of 17 August 1917. It symbolises the departure line of Third Ypres and overlooks the important but often forgotten battlefield of Frezenberg, described in more detail on page 157, Itinerary Two.

Continue on the N332 and pass the Van Biervliet brickworks on the left.

At the rear of the brickworks is the huge underground **Bremen Redoubt**, part of the Bayern

The moment of unveiling of the Scottish Memorial, Frezenberg, 25 August 2007.

Stellung which stretched from Langemarck to Geluveld. The redoubt was taken by the South Africans on 20 September 1917. It was uncovered in the 1980s and renovated so that for some years it was visitable. Sadly it became dangerous and is now closed.

On 23 February 2007 the BBC News broke the story that Malcolm Weale of Geofizz Ltd (who works with the TV 'Time Watch' team) and Peter Barton (qv), underground warfare specialist, together with Kristof Jacobs of the ABAF, were given permission to make tentative archaeological explorations on an exciting new discovery beside the Bremen Redoubt, known as the Vampir. They had discovered it using trench maps together with cutting edge ground-penetrating radar technology. The dugout, named after a band of men who occupied it and who sallied forth at night to resupply the front line, comprises a British HQ which housed 50 men and was accessed by two 40ft deep stairwells. The original bores were started in the winter of 1917-18 and work began by 171st Tunnelling Coy in January 1918 with the assistance of 9th HLI. In April, 254th Tunnelling Coy completed the concreting of the floor and it is believed that it was later hugely extended by the Germans, after the British withdrew in April. In August 1918 it was retaken by the British.

Because it had lain untouched for some 90 years the team hoped that it would reveal a treasure trove of well-preserved artefacts. However they have reluctantly decided that further explorations would be extremely difficult and dangerous and the dugout was allowed to refill with the water that had preserved it for so many years. Like Bremen, it is therefore not visitable.

Continue to the roundabout, go straight over on the 332, signed to Zonnebeke, into the village. Turn right before the church onto Berten Pilstraat following signs to Paschendaele Memorial Museum.

• Zonnebeke
Zonnebeke came under fire as early as October 1914, the German gunners using the high steeple of the church as an aiming point to such effect that the British were forced to withdraw on the night of the 21st. Spy fever was at its height, one gunner officer even reporting that spies were signalling to the Germans using a windmill - 'The arms of a certain windmill were turning in an erratic manner ... We blew it up next day.'

• Passchendaele Memorial Museum/Sherwood Foresters Plaque/Tourist Office, Zonnebeke/27.1 miles/45 minutes/Map J11/GPS: 50.879619 2.988121
The Château was built in 1924 in the style of a country house in Normandy (where the then-owner, Emmanuel Iweins, stayed during the war). On 23 April 2004 a completely new Museum was opened here and changes and improvements are always ongoing as more of the beautiful grounds are acquired (including the old Manor House) and put to use and themed gardens are established.

Then a completely redesigned and much enlarged Euros 2 million Museum was opened in July 2013, in time for the 100th Anniversary commemorations.

Currently one enters onto a Reception desk in the main Château. To the left is Tourist Information with a book/souvenir stall. There are many helpful leaflets to pick up here, including the interesting 75km driving route 'Pioneer. The German Masters of Concrete in the Trenches' which starts and finishes at the Museum. There is also a booklet describing all the 2017 commemorative events planned in the area. To the right is a comfortable lounge with computer facilities. There are also interesting temporary exhibitions on the ground floor. Upstairs are the fine permanent exhibitions with dioramas, ephemera, photographs, uniforms, weapons, artefacts, gas masks etc, interspersed with videos in four languages.

The first rooms evoke pre-war Zonnebeke, completely destroyed during the conflict, ephemera of 1914 relating to mobilisation, the crucial events of October 1914 at Geluveld and the subsequent battles of First Ypres. In the third room is a reproduction of the famous painting by Mantania of the Green Howards at Kruiseik Crossroads (the original is in the Mess of the King's Division in York). Painted in 1925 it only portrays one man who survived the war. He is **Pte Henry Tandey** of the 5th Bn the Duke of Wellington's (W Riding) Regt. Tandey is shown carrying a wounded comrade. He went on to win the **VC** at Marcoing on 28 Sepember 1918. Tandey, who also won the **DCM and the MM** – thereby becoming the most-decorated private soldier of World War I – served as a Recruiting Officer in World War II and died in 1977. The odd story that Tandey had the opportunity to kill Corporal Adolf Hitler is told at www.firstworldwar.com. Room 4 portrays the Christmas Truce of 1914 and the gas attack of April 1915. Room 5 shows the years between Second Ypres to Third Ypres, which is depicted in Room 6. Room 7 concentrates on the German offensive of Spring 1918 – 'Fourth Ypres'.

This leads to **The Dugout Experience** which now extends underground into the wooded grounds. A running presentation of the 1917 battles is shown on a vast model of Passchendaele. There are three main themes:

1a.   The Landscape: The WW1 heritage research project has so far located 800 bunkers, 40 subterranean structures, old military cemeteries etc in Zonnebeke and Passchendaele alone.

1b.   The Nations and the International Dimension: Projections (in English with Dutch translation) with wartime footage and a series of exhibitions will give an atmosphere of the contribution of the Australians, Canadians, English, N Zealand, N & S Irish, Scots, Welsh… with testimony from the last veterans.

2.   The Artillery: featuring a private collection (the largest in existence).
       The Engineers: trench and light railway etc construction.

3.   Aerial, including many aerial photos.

The Trench Experience. Visitors will emerge into replicas of the different types of WW1 trenches, original dugouts and shelters (removed from their original sites in the surrounding area), including a rebuilt American 'Barrack', part of Herbert Hoover's 'Commission for the Relief of Belgium', which provided much-needed food and shelter. See: https://www.archives.gov/publications/prologue/1989/spring/hoover-belgium.html

Such supposedly temporary buildings were hastily constructed after the war to house a population returning to ruined dwellings. Many were known as 'King Albert' Barracks (see page 81). The pine example here was built in 1922 in Wevelgem by the Plets family, who lived in it until 1978. In 2013, the Memorial Museum reconstructed it to its original condition, restoring the façade and front room, which were destroyed by bombing during World War ll and furnishing it in period style.

Remembrance: 1919-Today. Further developments lead into an underground gallery which concentrates on the theme of Remembrance – the cemeteries, the iron harvest, veterans' memories etc. – a very moving experience finishing with effective *trompe l'oeil* image of the Memorial Wall at Tyne Cot Cemetery.

1. *Extraordinary Trompe l'Oeil, Dugout Experience, Passchendaele Museum*
2. *Trenches, Passchendaele Memorial Museum*
3. *Passchendaele Memorial Museum, Zonnebeke.*
4. *Interior, American Barrack, Passchendaele Memorial Museum*

Allow plenty of time for the 400 metre walk (there is also a disabled circuit).

This is an extremely well-conceived Museum, with sensitive use of modern technology – well worth a visit. Franky Bostyn, for many years the enthusiastic curator, and his dedicated team were also instrumental in the development of many WW1 sites in the region e.g. the Tyne Cot Information Centre, and with the ABAF, Bayernwald, Cryer Farm and 'The Road to Passchendaele', the physical link recently opened up between Zonnebeke and Tyne Cot along the old Ypres-Roulers railway (qv). Student programmes and guided battlefield visits with knowledgeable guides (several are GBG members) available, notably 'The Platoon Experience' (qv).

Many enterprising WW1-related events are organised throughout the year, including important ANZAC Day (25 April) commemorations. In 2017 the ceremonies will end with the planting of trees in the Peace Forest at Polygon Wood (qv).

One of the Museum's most ambitious projects is the **Passchendaele Archives** – the progressive recording of the data of men who fought at Passchendaele, complete with personal details and photographs, many used in the Tyne Cot Information Centre. Relatives are encouraged to contribute information. A large reference library of books and documents is being built up and **The Research Centre** is now housed in the former rectory, at Ieperstraat 1, near the Church in a modern building designed by architect Huib Hoste.

The Museum also works with the Belgian War Graves when human remains are discovered, especially when identifiable artefacts are involved.

Open: Every day except 16 December - 31 January: 0900-1800. Groups any time by appointment. Entrance fee payable. Tel: +(0) 51 77 04 41. E-mail: info@passchendaele.be Website: www.passchendaele.be

There is a lift for disabled people round the corner to the left of the Museum entrance and beside it is a fine Derbyshire Stone *bas relief* **Plaque**, presented to the Commune of Zonnebeke when the Sherwood Foresters Western Front Memorial (qv) was unveiled at Tyne Cot on 24 October 2009.

Return to the T junction with the 332, turn right, continue to the church and park. There is room behind.

• Canadian Artillery Memorial Plaque/'Archaeological Garden', Passendale Church/27.2 miles/5 minutes/Map J10, 10a/GPS: 50.87271 2.98683

On the outside right wall of the Church is a Memorial Plaque to the fallen of D21 Battery of the Canadian Field Artillery, erected by their comrades. The battery was stationed in the ruins of the church during Third Ypres, Oct-Nov 1917. The rebuilt church was the first church of modern design to be built in Belgium and at first it attracted some sharp criticism. The architect was Huib Hoste. It was built on the site of an old Abbey and excavations between 1987 and 1989 discovered not only medieval remains but also a 4 metre deep Australian dugout. The excavations have now been filled in but a symbolic 'Archaelogical Garden' on the ground at the side of the Church beside the Canadian Plaque, shows the various strata picked out in bricks and gravel. An explanatory board tells the story in four languages.

Continue to the local cemetery on the left.

• Flemish Memorial Crypt, Zonnebeke Local Cemetery/27.4 miles/10 minutes/ Map J9/GPS: 50.87431 2.99169

Walk up the central avenue and turn right at the intersection to the large concrete structure of the crypt.

Plaque to D21 Bty, Can Fd Arty, Zonnebeke Church

Steps lead down to a room where there are fifteen boxes containing the remains of Flemish soldiers, with their names, dates of birth and death and their photographs. On the roofs are some Joe English AVVVK Flemish headstones (qv).

Turn round and return past the turning to the Passchendaele Museum and take the second next turn to the left, following signs to Polygon Wood and other CWGC cemeteries and as the road bends sharp right before the wood, proceed along Lange Dreve. Park at the cemetery on the right.

Flemish Memorial Crypt,
Zonnebeke

• Polygon Wood CWGC Cemetery/Buttes New British Cemetery/ NZ Memorial/Australian 5th Division Memorial, Scott's Bunker/29.00 miles/25 minutes (add 25 mins to visit Scott's Bunker)/Map J12, 14, 15, 13/GPS: 50. 85703 2.99089

In 2007 Information Panels were installed here. On the right is the small Polygon Wood Cemetery containing mostly (57) New Zealand soldiers. There are 32 UK, 1 German and 28

unknown, with 17 UK Special Memorials and 13 New Zealand. In a tribute to the geometric name of the wood, this Cemetery is contained within an interesting pentagon-shaped wall. There used to be a German Cemetery beside it containing 347 graves, now all removed.

On the left is the replanted Polygon Wood. The original one, which had a trotting course inside it, was totally destroyed in the war. The high mound on which is the Memorial to the 5th Australian Division is an old rifle butte used for musketry training before 1870 and is full of tunnels.

Detail of Plaque

Below is the Buttes New British Cemetery made after the Armistice whose register records 1,317 UK burials, 564 Australian, 50 Canadian, 167 New Zealand, with 35 Special Memorials and 1,703 unknown – 81% of the total. As the area was a pre-war drill ground, the headstones are lined up like a battalion ready for inspection. Here the remains of five Unknown Australian soldiers were reburied on 4 October 2007. Also here is **Lt Col A.H. Scott**, DSO, 56th Bn AIF (qv), 1 October 1917, age 27 and **Lt-Col D.R. Turnbull**, CO 2nd Manchesters, age 22, both killed by the same sniper's bullet. The grave of 17 year old **Pte L.C. McMurdo**, 31st AIF, 26 September 1917, bears the inscription, 'Gave his life to bring in a wounded comrade. Deeply mourned.' A bunker in the wood has been named after Col Scott and can be visited – see below.

At the far end of the Cemetery is the New Zealand Memorial Wall, recording the names of 383 missing with no known graves. It was designed by Charles Holden who, after the 'big three' of Lutyens, Baker and Blomfield, was one of the Commission's most accomplished architects. Holden's style was more severe and minimalist than the Greek-influenced masters, as is demonstrated here (especially when it is somewhat stained and dark) and in his dramatic Artillery Memorial at Hyde Park (for which Jagger [qv] did the sculpture). Holden, who had served

Australian 5th Division Memorial, Polygon Wood

as a lieutenant on the Western Front, worked with the War Graves Registration Directorate from 1917, and went on to become one of London Underground's principal architects in the years between the wars.

On 4 October 1917, **Acting Captain Clement Robertson** of the Queens Royal West Surrey Regt, Special Reserve, Tank Corps, won a posthumous **VC** here as he led his tanks, on foot, into action under heavy shell, machine-gun and rifle fire after having spent the previous three nights going over the ground with his batman, taping the routes. Capt Robertson is buried in Oxford Road CWGC Cemetery (qv) and is thought to be the first member of the Tank Corps to win the award.

During the critical days of First Ypres in October 1914, when the Germans so nearly broke

Buttes New Brit CWGC Cemetery and New Zealand Memorial

through at Geluveld, Polygon Wood was an important tactical feature. On 24 October, during the Menin Road push, a battalion of 244th Reserve Regiment got into the eastern edge of the wood, overwhelming the 2nd Wiltshires to such an extent that they were reduced to the quartermaster, the Sergeant Major and 172 other ranks. General Capper reinforced them with the Northumberland Hussars and the 2nd Warwickshires who had lost their commanding officer, Lt Col Walter Latham Loring, the previous day: he is commemorated on the Menin Gate. (His two brothers were also killed early in the war and have no known graves: Major C. B. Loring, 37th Lancers Indian Army, killed on 21 December 1914, and commemorated on the Neuve-Chapelle Memorial, and Captain William Loring, Scottish Horse, killed on 24 October 1915, and commemorated on the Helles Memorial.) The Warwickshires cleared the wood, probably (according to the Official History) fighting the 'first serious engagement of any Territorial unit' (but see reference to the action of the London Scottish page 237). French cavalry from Zonnebeke came up in support but were not needed. Five days later, when the crisis was at its height, seven German battalions attacked again in an attempt to draw British and French forces away from the Menin Road. They did not succeed and suffered many casualties.

Polygon Wood was eventually given up following the German gas attack in April 1915, the 2nd King's Own, 3rd Monmouth and the 1st KOYLI withdrawing on the night of 3 May and it was two years before it was retaken. The Monmouths had dugouts in the mound of the Butte and not far away was 'Squeaking Pump' which it is thought inspired **Bruce Bairnsfather**'s cartoon, *The Fatalist – I'm sure they'll 'ear this damn thing squeakin'*.

In September 1917 the Australians were moved north to the Salient and took part in the 'Battle of Polygon Wood', an offensive launched north-east from Ypres on 26 September 1917, following a five-day bombardment. The 1st and 2nd Divisions, part of an overall force of eleven divisions, retook part of the wood and in continuing operations, 14th Brigade of the Australian 5th Division took the northern part of the wood on 26 September, including the Butte. Hence the position of the 5th Division Memorial.

The 2nd Royal Welch Fusiliers were on the right of the Australians during the 26 September attack and serving with them was **Private Frank Richards** (who later became famous as the author of *Old Soldiers Never Die*). It is sometimes difficult to relate the layout of the front line to the ground but stretcher-bearer Richards gives an excellent description. His front line was in Polygon Wood and his Casualty Clearing Station was at Clapham Junction (see the Battle Map), the route between the two was strewn with injured stretcher bearers and men who had been wounded on their way back. Following that route himself on 27 September he recalled seeing twenty tanks out of action. The mud was so thick that tanks became stuck and were then easy static targets for the enemy artillery. When the battalion was withdrawn it went to Dikkebus.

To visit **Scott's Bunker**, climb over the low wall behind the New Zealand Memorial and walk up the central track in the wood to 100 yards beyond the first cross junction. The Bunker is to the right, just off the track (**Map J15b, GPS: 50.85348 2.98750**). [Alternately it can now be reached from a track from Lange Dreve.] Lt-Col Allan Humphrey Scott, DSO (qv), was commanding officer of 56th Bn AIF, which advanced through to the Butte in the second wave on 26 September 1917. On the night of 30 September they were relieved by a British Battalion but Scott remained

Scott's Bunker, Polygon Wood

to brief the incoming commander. On 1 October he was shot through the head by a sniper. Craig Tibbitts of the AWM told us, "I could not find anything to indicate that Scott nor anyone in the 56th Bn had anything to do with the capture of this pillbox. According to my info the pillbox was in the 55th Bn's sector, slightly to the north of the 56th's. Scott's command posts during the Polygon Operation were initially back behind the jumping off point and then after the attack, at the Butte." Thus the naming of the bunker seems to be a courtesy to a popular commanding officer.

Continue skirting the wood along Lange Dreve. Stop by the café to the right at no. 16.

•Brothers-in-Arms Memorial Park/Wood of Peace/29.6 miles/35 minutes/GPS: 50.85401 2.97870

To the right is the **Café-Bar, De Dreve** (also known as ANZAC Rest). Tel: + (0) 47 55 87 58. E-mail: johanvandewalle531@hotmail.com. Website: www.dedreve.com. It is owned by the well-known archaeologist of WW1 underground in the Salient, Johan Vandewalle (qv), co-author with Peter Barton of *Beneath Flanders Fields* (qv) who has been associated with such projects as Beecham Dugout, Vampir etc. It is well-known for its choice of beers and provides light meals (even breakfast with prior notice). The café is full of WW1 items (especially Australian) and upstairs is an interesting and well-presented exhibition and video presentation of Johan's many archaeological finds and the touching story of the Brothers-in-Arms project. Of special note is the personal story of **Capt Oliver Holmes Woodward** of the 1st Australian Tunnelling Coy about his tunnelling experiences, particularly about Hill 60 (qv). It was written by his family and presented by them to Johan.

The project was inspired by Johan's discovery of 6 Australian bodies when a pipeline was being laid in Westhoek in 2006. The 6th body was buried in a most unusual way and when Johan uncovered the head the eyes seemed to him to be extraordinarily intact. Three of the bodies were identified by using DNA. The sixth proved to be John Hunter, who died in his brother Jim's arms. The experience made such an emotional impression on him that it has led to much research and the eventual construction of an ambitious Memorial Park, dedicated to 'Brothers in Arms'.

Personal story of Capt O.H. Woodward, 1st Australian Tunnelling Coy, Café de Dreve

L to R Johan Vandewalle, the Authors and Bert Degrauwe,
Café De Dreve

The Park is being constructed and landscaped in a field (a WW1 battle site which still contains the remains of German trenches) almost opposite the café, beside a

Brothers in Arms Memorial Medal

farm building which Johan is converting into a B & B. It will commemorate all brothers, of all nationalities who fought, and so often died, during WW1. It is designed by Andy Alengier and an avenue of trees border a 40m long plinth leading to a moving statue by Australian sculptor Louis Lauen depicting a soldier holding his dying brother in his arms and a stone plaque bearing a poem written by Jim Hunter.

A full description of this worthwhile concept can be seen at www.brothersinarmsmemorial. org and more information can be obtained from Bert Degrauwe (also a battlefield guide), one of the hard-working and tireless fund-raising and project development team, bert@ brothersinarmsmemorial.org. Donations are still being sought for this expensive concept and many fund-raising events are organised.

Incorporated in the Park is the **Wood of Peace** project. It involves planting, at each side of the park, avenues of trees, one for each soldier buried in the two Polygon Wood cemeteries. On ANZAC Day (25 April) 2017 a symbolic tree will be planted for every nation involved in the War and on 12 October 2017 will be 'Tree Planting Day' for the remainder.

Continue to the T junction and turn left along Lotegatstraat.

To the right of the road between here and up to Black Watch Corner, 5th Fd Coy RE of 2nd Div took part in continuous actions throughout 11 November 1914 while under fire from Germans in positions in Nonne Boschen on the other side of what is now the motorway. The Sappers had been working on defences in Polygon Wood when a German advance roughly along the line of the motorway threatened a breakthrough. In concert with elements of the Oxford Light Infantry, the HLI, the Connaught Rangers and the 5th Fd Coy, the Black Watch held the enemy advance. Seven DCMs were awarded to 5th Fd Coy that day, a record for a minor unit, adding to the Company's proud history in having as a former officer J.R. M. Chard VC of Rorke's Drift fame.

Continue and drive to the junction with the motorway. This is Black Watch Corner.

• Black Watch Corner & Black Watch Statue/30.00 miles/5 minutes/ OP/GPS: 50.84850 2.98175

On 11 November 1914 the fighting that involved the 5th Fd Coy RE was on the first day of the battle known as 'Nonne Boschen - Nun's Wood. Polygon Wood was at the northern edge of the German attack. Crown Prince Rupprecht ordered the Prussian Guard to take Polygon in co-operation with the 54th Reserve Division. Just after 0630 the German guns opened fire and at 0900 the assault began on a nine-mile front in mist and rain. The barrage had reduced the woods to a tangle of broken trees and undergrowth which impeded the German advance. On almost all of the front the attack faltered but at the southern end of Polygon Wood, between it and Nonne Boschen (where the motorway now is) was a gap in the British line for which the 3rd Foot Guard Regiment headed. At this south-west corner of the wood, the 23rd Field Company RE under Major C. Russell-Brown had completed a strong point just an hour before the assault, and in it were forty men of the Black Watch commanded by Lt F. Anderson. The position consisted only of a trench inside the hedges of a cottage garden, and a few strands of barbed wire, but it provided shelter from the artillery. Anderson's party opened such an effective fire on the Guards that they broke formation and were eventually stopped and beaten back by the guns of 2nd Division. In recognition of the role that the Black Watch played here the corner was named after them. It was during this period of fighting that Captain Brodie (qv) of the Cameron Highlanders was killed.

The Brigade formation which had taken the brunt of the attack was the 1st (Guards) Brigade under Brigadier-General Fitzclarence (qv) and, having stopped the German assault on 11 November, the Brigadier decided to mount a counter-attack to recover trenches lost to the Germans. While reconnoitring forward of Black Watch Corner he was mortally wounded by rifle fire. 'The wondrous spirit that had inspired the 1st Brigade and made its influence felt far beyond his own battalions was stilled for ever,' records the Official History. A farm to the south of the wood near Black Watch Corner was named FitzClarence Farm in honour of this popular old soldier who was affectionately known as 'GOC Menin Road'.

Just within the wood are a number of bunkers that can be explored with care.

OP. Stand with your back to the gateway to the corner of the wood and look along the motorway. Immediately behind the line of trees crossing your front ahead is the village of Geluveld, one mile away. It was from this corner, on 31 October 1914, at the height of the crisis of First Ypres, that Major Hankey led off the 2nd Worcesters in an advance that would end in their famous bayonet charge into the grounds of the Château. It was the church spire of Geluveld that they used as their marker for their objective.

Opposite is

Black Watch Statue

On 3 May 2014 this fine, larger than life (4.5 metres) bronze Statue of a kilted WW1 Black Watch soldier in fighting uniform on a plinth, set in a pleasant, small and well-tended park, was erected. It is by Edinburgh sculptor, Alan Herriot, and commemorates the more than 8,000 officers and men killed and 20,000 wounded in WW1. It is the only Black Watch specific Memorial of WW1. For more information, **Contact:** Maj Ronnie Proctor, Black Watch Association. Tel: 01738 623 214.

Black Watch Memorial,
Black Watch Corner

Extra Visits to Memorial to New Zealander Sgt H.J. Nicholas, VC, MM, 1891-1918 (Map J15a, GPS: 50.84841 2.99427) and Plaque to Capt Roberston, VC & Gnr Allen, DCM/ Tank Corps Flagpole, Restaurant Merlijn (Map J15d, GPS: 50.85010 3.00404)

Round trip: 2 miles. Approximate time: 20 minutes

Turn left along the side of the wood on Oude Kortrijkstraat to the memorial on the right.

The Memorial, unveiled on 14 September 2008, is near the site of the pillbox taken by the then **Pte Nicholas**, 1st Bn Canterbury Regt. A joint project by the Commune of Zonnebeke

and the NZ Embassy in Brussels, it was inaugurated by New Zealand Ambassador to Belgium, Peter Kennedy, in the presence of NZ military personnel and local dignitaries. Sgt Henry James Nicholas was the first soldier of the Canterbury Regt to be awarded the VC in Belgium and the third Kiwi winner. Memorials have also been raised to the first, L/Cpl Samuel Frickleton (qv) and the second, Leslie Andrew (qv). Nicholas singlehandedly, under heavy fire, destroyed a 16-man machinegun post in an advance on nearby Polderhoek Château which was in the woods across the field behind the Memorial. He was killed on 23 October 1918 near Le Quesnoy and is buried in Vertigneul Churchyard Cemetery, Romeries, some 13 miles due east of Cambrai.

Continue on Oude Kortrijkstraat to the next crossroads to the excellent Restaurant Merlijn on the left at No 70 (E-mail: info@restomerlijn.be. Website: www.restomerlijn.be/ Tel: + (0) 57 46 85 55. Closed Tues).

Memorial to H.J. Nicholas VC, Oude Kortrijkstraat.

On the wall of the Restaurant is a **Plaque to Capt Clement Robertson, VC, the Queens, Sp Res Tank Corps & Gunner Cyril Allen DCM**. It was inaugurated on 29 April 2015 in the presence of Lt-Gen A.D. Leakey (Hon Pres of Friends of the Tank Memorial and Black Rod), descendants Ian Robertson and John Allen and family members, the British Ambassador to Brussels, many local and UK dignitaries and friends. Robertson is buried in Oxford Road CWGC (qv) and Allen is commemorated on the Louverval Memorial, Cambrai.

After the ceremony a **Flagpole** was also dedicated to the **Tank Corps** in the garden.

A full story of Robertson VC is told in the Merlijn website.

Turn round and rejoin the main itinerary.

Plaque to Capt Robertson, VC & Gnr Allen, DCM, Merlijn Restaurant

Turn right over the motorway and continue, keeping to the right at the fork.

To the right is Glencorse Wood which is gradually being eroded by private houses.

Inauguration Party with Relatives. In centre, British Ambassador Alison Rose (with glasses), second to her left Lt-Gen A.D. Leakey (Black Rod) and behind him with Standard, Chris Lock (qv)

Extra Visit to the Private Memorial to Capt Brodie, Glencorse Wood (Map I28, GPS: 50.84802 2.97054)

Round trip: 0.2 miles. Approximate time: 10 minutes

Continue to the next small crossroads and turn right onto Sprookjesbosdreef.

Opposite the turning is an Information Panel describing Glencorse Wood, Nonnebossen, 11 November 1914, with a sketch map showing the site of FitzClarence Farm and the woods and copses.

Continue down the hill to the edge of the wood to a track to the right. The memorial is 100 yds on up a slope to the right.

Captain Ewen James Brodie of the 1st Bn the Cameron Highlanders was killed on 11 November 1914, near this spot, during the Battle of Nonne Boschen (Nuns' Wood), the adjoining wood to the north-east, held by the Prussian Guard. He was one of only three officers remaining from those who had left Edinburgh ten weeks before. On that same day his namesake, **Capt Walter Lorrain Brodie, MC**, of the 2nd Bn the HLI, won the **VC** for leading a charge against enemy trenches at Becelaere. Brodie went on to become a Lt Col but was killed at Moeuvres on 23 August 1918.

Return to pick up the main itinerary.

Memorial to Capt Brodie, Glencorse Wood

Continue to the junction with the Menin Road, turn left and immediately right at Clapham Junction along Pappotstraat.

To the right is the area of Stirling Castle named by the Argyll & Sutherland Highlanders after their garrison town and described in 1917 by Col Seton Hutchison (qv) as a 'treacherous heap of filth'. At 0800 hours on 25 September of that year the 2nd Bn the RWF marched round the corner of Zillebeke Lake ('a dirty pool now,' according to their MO, Capt J. C. Dunn), and through Sanctuary Wood to Stirling Castle. During the night the tired troops had to dig in as 'the battle was to be resumed in the morning.' In the early hours Stirling Castle and the RWF bivouacs were peppered with shells and there were some casualties. The Battalion deployed across the Menin Road at Clapham Junction and at 1005, with the object of establishing a new Brigade front some 1,400yd further to the east, attacked. 'When I, having been delayed by a badly wounded man, crossed the Menin road,' wrote Dunn, 'the Battalion was out of sight but for one individual, who, it was plain, did not mean to see it again if he could help'. (A week later the Calais police reported the arrest of this unidentified deserter there.) According to Robert Graves in *Goodbye to All That*, in the confusion that ensued the Battalion was effectively without a commanding officer and Dunn temporarily took command. Dunn does not mention the fact in his own account, but does say that 'the C.O. had gone on leave', that only inexperienced subalterns commanded A and B companies and that 'a shortage of maps caused some difficulty to begin with.' It was a day of little progress and high casualties.

Following this and after the right hand bend in the road, the rear of the Canadian Memorial at Hill 62 (Map N17) can be glimpsed to the right.

Continue to the first turning to the left.

Bunker, Shrewsbury Forest

N.B. By taking this turn to the left, Kranenburgstraat, **Shrewsbury Forest**, in which there are a number of Bunkers, may be reached. At the first corner there is an overgrown **Bunker** on the right (**GPS: 50.83153 2.95738**). The Wood was named by the 2nd King's Shropshire Light Infantry in March 1915 and after the war was one of the places where a landmark post was erected. Some forty posts were put up by the Ypres League (qv) at points of importance. They have not survived. In October 1914 the Germans took the Forest but were driven out on the 31st.

Continue on the road, which was known as Green Jacket Ride, to the Y junction.

N.B. Memorial to 15th Bn, Can 48th Highlanders, 3rd Bde CEF, Battle of Mount Sorrel, Observatory Ridge (GPS: 50.83289 2.93858). This may be reached by turning right and continuing to the brick Memorial on the left. It has a *bas relief* Map of the 2 June 1916 Battle and was unveiled on 22 October 2011 in an impressive ceremony with the Last Post Buglers and Pipers in attendance.

Memorial to 15th Bn, Can 48th Highlanders, Battle of Mount Sorrel, Observatory Ridge

At this junction is

•*Canadian Memorial to 4th Can Mounted Rifles and 3rd (Toronto) Regt, CEF, Battle of Mount Sorrel/32.4/miles/5 minutes /GPS: 50.83082 2.94798.*

On the ground are three black marble Canadian Plaques, similar to those near Passendale (qv). They commemorate the severe losses in the Battle of Mount Sorrel (of 22 officers and 68 men of the 4th CMR only 73 men answered the roll call and the 3rd Toronto suffered 16 officers and 412 ORs killed). They were inaugurated in June 2016.

Memorials to 4th Can Mounted Rifles & 3rd (Toronto) Regt CEF, Battle of Mount Sorrel

Continue straight on to the junction with the main road, Werviksestraat, turn right and then 600 yards later turn left following signs to Hill 60.

• Hill 60/Q Victoria Rifles, Aust 1st Tunnelling Coy & 14th Light Div Memorials/33.6 miles/30 minutes/RWC/Map N4, 5, 6, 7, 8/GPS: 50.82468 2.92975

'The place was practically a cemetery, and several hundred must have been buried on the ground, it proving impossible, when digging trenches, not to disturb some poor fellow in his last long sleep.' *(An officer who fought there.)*

The name indicates the height of this feature above sea level. It is artificial, being formed by the spoil taken from the cutting some 100m to the south when the railway was built and the resultant layers of soil, firm sand and quicksand made it a nightmare for the mining engineers – Australian, Canadian, French, German and British – during the war.

The Germans took the knoll from the French in December 1914 and when the British took over from the French following the race to the sea, it was decided that the feature must be retaken. Much of the fighting at Hill 60 was underground and it was probably here that the first British mine of the war was blown by **Lt White, RE** on 17 February 1915, in tunnels that had been started by the French. A major mining operation was then undertaken and the job was given to 173rd Tunnelling Company, RE. Work began early in March 1915 and three tunnels were started towards the German line about 50 yards away, a pit having first been dug some 16 feet deep. Almost immediately the miners came upon dead bodies and quicklime was brought up to cover them. The bodies were then dragged out, but many more were uncovered in the months ahead and the smell of quicklime hung over the hill for four years. Occasionally digging had to be done by 'clay-kicking', where a man lies on his back in the tunnel and pushes metal plates attached to his heels into the tunnel face ahead of him and then by bending his knees brings the soil towards him, a quiet though slow method which made it difficult for the Germans to hear what was going on. Although most tunnelling was carried out by traditional methods, it was all hot, strenuous, unpleasant and dangerous work. Apart from the constant threat that the tunnel would collapse and bury the miners alive, there was the possibility of poison gas (canaries and other small animals were taken below for early warning) and, not least, that the enemy might break into the tunnel or explode a mine of his own below it. By the time that the digging was finished the tunnels stretched more than 100yd and dragging the required ninety-four 100lb bags of gunpowder to the mineheads, winching them down the shafts and then manoeuvring them along the tunnels, was a Herculean task. On 15 April all the charges were ready and on 17 April at 1905 hours the mine was fired.

The explosion built up over 10 seconds, throwing volcano-like debris nearly 300ft high and for 300yd all around. Simultaneously, British, French and Belgian guns opened an artillery barrage and, encouraged by regimental buglers, the Royal West Kents fixed bayonets and charged the dazed Germans of the 172nd Infantry Regiment, killing about 150 for only seven casualties of their own. The hill was won.

Three days later **Lt Geoffrey Harold Woolley** won the **first Territorial Army VC** in resisting a German counter-attack. His citation reads, 'For most conspicuous bravery on Hill 60 during the night of 20th-21st April 1915. Although the only officer on the hill at the time, and with very few men, he successfully resisted all attacks to his trench and continued throwing bombs and encouraging his men till relieved. His trench during all the time was being heavily shelled and bombed, and was subjected to heavy machine-gun fire by the enemy.' Woolley was a member of the 9th London Regiment, Queen Victoria's Rifles, who had, with the Royal West Kents and King's Own Scottish Borderers, taken part in the initial assault on 17 April. He survived the war to be ordained and to serve as Chaplain to the Forces in N Africa in World War II. He was Vice-Chairman of the VC and GC Association during 1956-68.

On 20 April 1915 another famous **VC** was won here by **Corporal Edward Dwyer** of the 1st Bn the East Surrey Regiment. Dwyer was born in Fulham on 25 November 1895, so was only 19 when he won his country's highest award for gallantry (although he had been a soldier for three years already). It was gained for creeping out into the open to bandage wounded comrades and then climbing onto the parapet and 'dispersing the enemy by the effective use of hand-grenades' although subjected to a hail of bombs at close quarters. The young hero was brought back to the UK to receive his medal from the King and also to help the recruitment drive. Known as 'the Little Corporal' (a soubriquet first applied to Napoleon), he was at that time the youngest ever winner of the VC (this position was to be lost to 'the Boy' Cornwell, RN on 15 September 1916). Despite his youth, Dwyer was articulate and confident. He was marched through the streets, gave lectures at schools, spoke at rallies and, what sealed his notability, made a recording describing life on the Western Front and ending with a rendition of *Here We Are Again*. Dwyer's monologue was re-recorded on the 1980s by Pavilion Records *The Great War* (Gemm 3033/4) and it is haunting to hear this voice from the past. Dwyer married a nurse called Maude Freeman the following Christmas. In May 1916 he was back in France with his regiment and was killed on 3 September 1916, near Mametz Wood on the Somme. He is buried in Flatiron Copse CWGC Cemetery.

Yet another **VC** was won here on 15 April 1915. It was by **Lt George Rowland Patrick Roupell** also of the 1st Bn, the East Surreys. Roupell, despite being wounded, led his company in repelling a strong German attack, returning with reinforcements to hold the position through the night. He was also awarded the Croix de Guerre and the Russian Order of St George 4th Class. In World War II he commanded 36th Inf Bde and 105th Inf Bde. On 20/21April 1915, 2nd **Lt Benjamin Handley Geary** won the East Surrey's third **VC**. Geary, of the 4th Bn, led his men under heavy fire to join survivors in a crater, which he then held against repeated attacks and was himself severely wounded. Like Woolley, Geary went on to be a Chaplain to the Forces and served with the Canadian Army in World War II.

Underground warfare went on here for another ten months until the beginning of Third Ypres and many of the men who worked and fought in those black corridors in the clay died there and there they remain. Hill 60 is a cemetery.

Hill 60's **fifth VC. 2nd Lt Frederick Youens**, although wounded, on hearing of an imminent German attack, rallied a disorganised Lewis gun team when an enemy grenade fell on the position. Youens picked it up and hurled it over the parapet. Another grenade landed in the same place and again Youens picked it up. This time it exploded in his hand and he later died of his wounds. He is buried in Railway Dugouts CWGC Cemetery.

Another of the heroes of Hill 60 was the Australian, **Capt Oliver Woodward**. Trained as a mining engineer and metallurgist, he enlisted in August 1915 and arriving in Flanders worked with the 1st Australian Tunnelling Coy. He was awarded the MC at on 9-11 June 1916 for blowing up a sniper's post. Created Acting Captain on 23 October, he moved on to the Salient to work under Hill 60. He had been charged with maintaining the 2 of the 21 massive mines laid below the Messines ridge by the 3rd Canadian Tunnelling Coy until the signal came to blow them. On 9 June 1917 on the opening of the Battle of Messines he personally detonated the 53,000lb explosive mine under Hill 60, and the 70,000lb explosive mine under the Caterpillar Crater that the Australians had been protecting using listening posts and counter mines.

Woodward went on to win two Bars to his MC (at Bony on 29 September 1918 and near le Cateau on 4 November 1918). After the war he had a distinguished career in civil mining and metallurgy, becoming Pres of the Australian Mining and Metal Association 1952-1954. He died in 24 August 1966.

In 2010 an Australian film entitled *Below Hill 60* was released. It is based on Woodward's own account and is an extremely accurate, well-acted and moving story of the perilous existence of the underground miners.

After the war Hill 60 was acquired by the Queen Victoria's Rifles and the battle-scarred area fenced in. 'If a rough sea, in all its turbulence, could be solidified, the result would bear a marked resemblance to Hill 60 today,' wrote Capt H. A. Taylor in 1928, 'The ground is one mass

ON THIS SPOT WAS ERECTED IN 1923
A MEMORIAL TO ALL RANKS OF
QUEEN VICTORIA'S RIFLES
WHO GAVE THEIR LIVES FOR THEIR
COUNTRY IN THE FIRST WORLD WAR
1914 - 1918
THE MEMORIAL HAVING BEEN DESTROYED IN 1940 BY THE
GERMANS THIS PLAQUE HAS BEEN PLACED BY THE REGIMENT
ON SOME OF THE ORIGINAL STONES OF THE MEMORIAL TO
PERPETUATE THEIR MEMORY, AND IN GRATEFUL REMEMBRANCE
OF THOSE WHO GAVE THEIR LIVES IN THE SECOND WORLD WAR
1939 - 1945

Memorial to Queen Victoria' Rifles, Hill 60   *Detail of Plaque*

of hummocks and holes over which in summer Nature, as though a little ashamed of the sight, throws a rough cover of grass and weeds.' It was the focal point for many pilgrims, much as Sanctuary Wood and its trenches are today. Then the trenches were sand-bagged and kept clear and the underground chambers could be visited (in recent years there has been much talk about re-opening them, with no result so far) and postcards were sold showing them. Now the fenced in area is owned and maintained by the CWGC.

Many changes and investments have been made here in the years running up to the Centenary. Now it is the start point of Route 2 of the **Ypres Entry Point – South** (qv) and as one approaches, there is a generous car park to the left with Information Board before one enters a gate into the site. Raised duckboards wind their way through the enclosed site round the memorials, craters and bunkers to emerge, past signs on the ground indicating the German and Allied Front Lines, by the 14th Light Div Memorial. The hillock was created, as were the raised banks of Caterpillar Crater and the area known as The Dump, in c1854 when the Ypres-Kortrijk railway line was created.

Within the enclosed area is a **Memorial to the Queen Victoria's Rifles**. This was destroyed in 1940 by the Germans and later restored (see Detail of Plaque illus). By it is a marker to **'John Oliff, Veteran 40-45, 13.07.05/19.05.87'**, whose ashes were scattered here in 1987. (The ashes of many World War I veterans who wished to lie for their final sleep with their old comrades have been unofficially scattered on this site by relatives or friends.) At the back is a well-preserved concrete bunker. Peter Oldham, in his excellent book, *Pill Boxes on the Western Front*, shows a sketch of the bunker and explains that it was originally a German structure (that part now being almost below ground) but that the upper section was added in February 1918 by 4th Field Coy Australian Engineers. Despite that, the Germans captured it in April.

The **Memorial to 14th (Light) Division** was moved here from its original site in Railway Wood in 1978. Beyond it to the left is the

Memorial to 14th Light Division,
Hill 60

Memorial to the 1st Australian Tunnelling Company. It bears the marks of World War II bullets and has a large concrete platform in front of it. There is also a stone whose inscription is an excellent summary of the chequered actions that took place here – the German occupation from 10 December 1914 to 17 April 1915, their recapture of it on 5 May 1916, the British recapture during the Battle of Messines on 7 June 1917, when two mines were exploded, the German recapture during the Battles of the Lys in April 1918 and the final recapture by the British, then under the command of King Albert of the Belgians, on 28 September 1918.

Ypres is clearly visible from the hill to the left of the café (although a hard-fought battle with local developers and authorities was necessary to prevent construction which would obscure this exceptional, historical view). The area was run after the war by a veteran of the regiment who started a Museum. It was then taken over by a member of the Schier family who extended the museum and ran it for many years. In 2006 the café and museum were sold (the collection being bought jointly by In Flanders Fields Museum, Zonnebeke Passchendaele Museum with some funding by the Province, and some private collectors.) Today the smart **Hill 60 Tearoom/Restaurant** with its bright modern décor is run by the Comyn family. Snacks and a more substantial menu available. Tel: + (0) 57 20 88 60. It has its own car park for patrons and a pleasant terrace.

To the left of the railway bridge is a **Memorial**, erected in October 1969, **to two French members of the Resistance** who were killed on 2 September 1944 and on the bridge over the railway line are Boards with panoramic views of the wartime area – The Dump and Hill 60.

Memorial to Two French Resistance Members, Shot 2 September 1944, Hill 60.

Memorial to 1st Australian Tunnelling Company, Hill 60

N.B. Caterpillar Crater (GPS: 50.82242 2.92879). Beyond and parallel to the railway line, is the muddy path that leads to the 79.2m diameter Crater, named because of its shape, in what was Vierlingen Wood, but known as 'Battle Wood' to Tommy. It was created when an enormous mine was exploded 30.5m below in the lead up to 3rd Ypres. Today it is an area of great beauty and is also part of the **Ypres Entry Route South Walking Tour** (qv) which leads to the Palingbeek.

Caterpillar Crater – the water obscures the true depth– Hill 60

Continue over the railway line to the T junction.

Extra Visit to Entry Point South, Palingbeek (Map N7b, GPS at car park: 50.81383 2.92043) & The Bluff (Map N, GPS: 50.81339 2.93584), Indian Memorial, Hollebeke (Map N10a, GPS: 50.80465 2.92210).

Round trip: 6 miles. Approximate time: 50 minutes

Turn left on Komenstraat. Continue downhill to the first small road to the right signed to Palingbeek. Turn right and continue to the car park on the left. Stop.

Ahead on the right is the pleasant **Restaurant De Palingbeek**. Tel: + (0) 57 20 56 72. E-mail: restaurantdepalingbeek@hotmail.com Website: www.depalingbeek.be
Just before it is a turning to a path on the right.

Continue walking down the path to the Entry Point South Pavilion to the right.

Entry Point South Pavilion. In it is an excellent 15 min film telling the story of the war in this area and several Information Panels. It leads on to Walking Circuit 1 which continues to The Bluff. En route it describes the failure of the Ypres-Comines Canal, begun in 1864, but along which no barge ever travelled. It was finally abandoned after the collapse of the St Elooi Bridge in 1913.
The first stop on the route, which passes vestiges of craters, is at the Bluff (qv) and just beyond it is a raised viewing platform. In the field below it the **Installation** to house the 600,000 clay figures being made for the **CWRM project** (qv) will be constructed.

Return to Komenstraat and continue downhill.

The wood to your left is Battle Wood. At the bottom of the decline, in the thick bushes, and extremely difficult to spot, to the right under a street light some 100 yards up from the parking area at the bottom of the hill and 20m in, is a large bunker. The Bluff is now part of the Entry Point South Walking Tour (qv).

Stop in the parking area before the canal bridge and walk along the canal path.

You are now at **Lock No 6** and the path along which you are walking was known as 'Oaf Alley' – many of the other features in the area are also named 'Oaf'. As the ground rises steeply to the right you are entering the notorious feature, **'The Bluff'**, which changed hands many times and in and around which was much underground warfare. Traces of ruined bunkers and mine craters from 1915/1916, but also difficult to locate, may be discerned in the bank. As a prelude to their assault on Verdun in February 1916, the Germans launched a series of actions along the Allied front line. On 22 January they exploded a mine by the Bluff destroying defences occupied by 76th Bde and killing seventy men. Billy Congreve (qv) (who it was unanimously decided by his fellow officers was 'the leading spirit in the attack') described the affair in a letter to his father (Lt Gen Walter Norris Congreve, VC, commanding XIII Corps) thus:
'The mine destroyed the pride of my heart: the Bluff defences which we had just

Entry Point South, Palingbeek

completed. It's the hugest thing in the mine line I have ever seen – about four Hooge's rolled into one. It blew up 3,500 tons of earth. The crater is 60 feet deep (from the top of the Bluff) and 50 yards by 40 yards across. The actual depth from ground level is about 30 feet, and it blew off the end of the Bluff.'

On 14 February the Germans laid down a heavy bombardment on the sector, then held only by a platoon of the 10th Lancashire Fusiliers. All but three of them were buried by a small mine that exploded under the tunnel in the Bluff, where the men were sheltering and the Germans took the position. A major counter-attack was carefully planned by 76th Bde, reinforced by an RE Field Coy of 3rd Division and a Field Artillery Brigade. The Brigade-Major of the 76th, Billy Congreve (qv) was actively involved. In an unusual pattern of bombardment planned so as to deceive the enemy as to the precise moment of the attack, the heights were to be fired on in a series of two salvos at irregular intervals until Zero Hour: then just one salvo would be fired. The attack took place during the night of 1 March 1916 and achieved total surprise. Ironically, a large contingent of the enemy was discovered sheltering in the 22 January mine crater. A few days later Lt John Glubb (who later, as a Lt Gen, would be better known as 'Glubb Pasha', Commander of the Arab Legion) visited the Bluff. He was most impressed by Congreve who 'was famous as a brave man' and who 'had a great effect on the morale of his brigade'. (Glubb was also the son of a high ranking father: Major Gen Glubb was Chief Engineer of Second Army, based at Cassel.)

An interesting walk may be taken along the old Ypres-Commines Canal, through the pleasant Palingbeek Nature Reserve, passing Lock No 7 and the area of Spoilbank. The bank was made from spoil resulting from the construction of the canal. As you emerge from the Reserve and cross a road, **Spoilbank CWGC Cemetery**, designed by Sir Edwin Lutyens with W.H. Cowlishaw (Map M26) is passed on the right. Originally known as 'Gordon Terrace Cemetery', this has just over 500 burials and was used almost continuously from Feb 1915 to May 1918. In it are the graves of brothers **2nd Lt G. and 2nd Lt J. Keating**, both of the Cheshire Regt, who both died on 17 February 1915. Also buried here are **Lt-Col S. Binney, Maj E. Freeman and Capt W.F.Lyons**, all of the RWF and all killed by a shell burst on battalion HQ at Gordon Post (Lock No 7bis) on 3 March 1916. The walk will take you to the N365 Ieper-Mesen road where you will emerge at Lock No 8 by the Lankhof Demarcation Stone (Map M15). Allow about 45 minutes for the round trip if you take the walk.

Continue into the village of Hollebeke and where the main road goes sharply to the left take the road past the Church and War Memorial. Continue to the stone memorial on the left

The brick **Indian Memorial** was inaugurated on a rainy 3 April 1999 by Panj Piaras to commemorate all soldiers of the Indian Army who died in Belgium between 1914 and 1918. It reads 'On this spot on October 26 1914 troops of the Indian Army were deployed in World War One for the first time when they engaged in battle on the line Hollebeke-Wytschate-Mesen'.The inscription is in Hindi, Punjabi and Arabic.

Over the weekend of 2-4 April 1999 Sikhs from all over the world met in Ieper to pray for peace in the world. It was the 300th Anniversary of the founding of the Sikh Nation and they chose Ieper, where so many of their comrades died in 1914-18, as an appropriate venue for their commemorations. The Indian troops arrived in Wijtschate on 22 October 1914 and on the 26th the 129th Baluchis and the 57th Wilde's Rifles staged an attack to

Indian Memorial, Hollebeke

the south of Hollebeke. Over the next few months they were deployed near Festubert, Givenchy and Neuve Chapelle. On 25 April 1915 the Lahore Division was hurriedly brought up to Wieltje to support the Allies decimated by the Gas Attack. Three hundred and forty eight men of the 444 strong 47th Sikhs died in the action and between 24 April and 1 May the Division lost 3,889 men (about one-third of its total).

Turn round and rejoin the main itinerary.

Turn right towards Ypres and continue to the first junction to the right, signed to Larch Wood CWGC Cemetery.

N.B. Turning right here leads to a railway crossing, and over the crossing, is the brick entrance which leads down steps to a beautiful grass path with flowering shrubs on each sides, parallel to the railway line. This is **Larch Wood (Railway Cutting) CWGC Cemetery (Map N3, GPS: 50.82860 2.92218)**, designed by Sir Edwin Lutyens with W.H. Cowlishaw. On this site in October 1917 the **Rev Theodore Bayley Hardy** (qv) added the **MC to the DSO** he had won at Oosttaverne in August that year for bringing in wounded under 'an appalling bombardment'. 'Hardy's calm confidence was an inspiration', recorded the Rev Geoffrey Vallings, who was awarded the DSO in the same action. Hardy was a genuinely humble and unassuming man. 'His retiring nature made it almost a penance to wear those ribbons which most of us would give our right arm for,' wrote Lt Col Hitch commanding the 8th Lincolns, and others noticed that he would 'place his left arm across his breast to hide his decorations when he was speaking to a soldier who himself had no such decoration'.

Buried in the Cemetery are 614 UK, 35 Australian, 1 BWI, 86 Canadian and 354 unknown. There are 5 Special Memorials to men whose graves have been lost and 81 Special Memorials to those believed to be buried in the cemetery. Among the latter is **Rifleman Clarence E. Peel** of the KRRC, killed on 21 October 1917, the uncle of the author and playwright **Alan Bennett**. Bennett was the first member of his family to see the grave and the visit is described in his book, Writing Home, in his inimitable original, poignant and evocative style. It was also the subject of a Radio 4 programme. Also buried here is **Lt John ('Jack') Eden** of the 12th Lancers killed on 14 October 1914, during a patrol, brother of the future **Prime Minister Anthony Eden**

Train passing Larch Wood CWGC Cemetery

(qv). Jack was a pre-war professional soldier and had served with the regiment in India and S Africa. His sister, Lady Marjorie Brooke, made a generous donation in memory of her brother to the building of the church at Kruiseke on the outside of which there is Plaque recording the gratitude of the Commune. There is also a Merchant Navy man, **Chief Officer E. Woods,** of SS *Mascota* who died on 30 March 1917.

Continue towards Zillebeke and take the first turn right, passing the Zillebeke Demarcation Stone (see Itinerary 3). Continue towards Zillebeke over the railway line.

As you cross the railway line, the area of the buildings to the left was a major narrow gauge railway junction, known as Manor Halt, which linked rearwards to the complex of lines which surrounded Ypres.

Enter Zillebeke and turn left following signs to Menin before the church.

You will pass **Zillebeke Churchyard, Tuileries British CWGC and Perth (China Wall) CWGC Cemeteries** which are described in Itinerary 3 below. The large roundabout some 700yd later is on the site of **Hellfire Corner**.

Go round the roundabout and take the 4th (Menenpoort) exit. Stop at the first building on the right and walk back.

• Hellfire Corner Demarcation Stone/36.4 miles/5 minutes/Map H46/ GPS: 50.84893 2.91586

The intersection is with the Menin Road. It was an important route junction under constant observation by Germans on the high ground and anything that moved across it was shelled. Canvas screens were erected beside the road in an attempt to conceal movement.

By the roadside on Meenseweg is a Demarcation Stone (one of twelve surviving in the Salient) to mark the Germans' nearest point to Ypres. The metre-high stones, made from pink Alsace granite were designed by the sculptor Paul Moreau-Vauthier who had been seriously wounded while serving as a machine gunner at Verdun and who first conceived the idea for a stone at the *Salon des Artistes Decorateurs* in 1919. It was made by the stonemason Léon Telle and had three patterns: the Belgian, surmounted by a *Jass*'s casque, with, on its sides, a typical Belgian waterbottle and gasmask; the British, surmounted by a Tommy's tin helmet, with a British water bottle and small box respirator, and the French, surmounted by a *Poilu*'s casque, with on its sides a typical French water (or wine!) bottle and gasmask. Beneath the helmet was a laurel wreath. All bore inscriptions in the three languages: 'Here the invader was brought to a standstill 1918'; *'Hier werd de overweldiger tot staan gebrackt 1918'* and *'Ici fut arrêté l'envahisseur 1918'* (preferred to the original *'Ici fut brisé l'élan des Barbares'!* 'Here the thrust of the barbarian was broken') and the name of the appropriate sector. At each corner was a palm emerging from a hand grenade.

They were the inspiration of the Touring Club of France, supported by the Belgian Touring Club and the Ypres League (qv) and erected in the early 1920s, their sites having been decided by Marshal Pétain and his staff. They were to mark the length of the Front Line from the North Sea to the Vosges. Accounts vary wildly as to how many actually were erected - from 119 (Rose Coombs) to 280 (Swinton's *Twenty Years After*). There were probably 118 'official' stones. The history of the stones is being researched by Rik Scherpenberg (qv). Rik's website is currently in 'transition' and he is best found by searching through Google. Those remaining in the Salient are marked on the Battle Map as an orange dot.

At the end of September 1917 Wyndham Lewis (qv) served as a FOO with his battery of the RGA, 500yd south of Hellfire Corner in support of 1st ANZAC Corps' attack on Polygon Wood and Zonnebeke. The appalling conditions, exacerbated by heavy rain in October, reinforced Lewis's feelings about the futility and obscenity of war. On leave in November he applied to join Beaverbrook's Canadian War Memorial Scheme. On 1 January 1918 Lewis arrived at Canadian HQ, Vimy Ridge to start the powerful series of war pictures which were exhibited as *Guns* at the Coupil Gallery, London in February 1919. They showed a gunner's life from his arrival at the depot to his life in the line. Some are hum-drum scenes of everyday trench and battery life, others show the dangerous, hard labour of a gunner. They included *A Canadian Gun Pit, A Battery Shelled and Ypres Salient.*

In 1996 an original signboard that had marked Hellfire Corner was given to the National Army Museum. It had been brought home, complete with bullet holes, by Lt William Storie, and displayed in a shop window in Prince's Street, Edinburgh. Lost in family cupboards for some time it turned up again and came into the hands of Mr R. Arthur, whose wife was a niece of Storie's daughter, and he gave it to the museum, complete with photographs and other papers.

Continue towards Ypres.

After some 300yd, opposite the Opel dealership and garage and set back well back from the road on the right, was the site of:

• *White Château/36 miles*

On 20 October 1914, as 1BR Corps moved into action around Ypres, Sir Douglas Haig spent the night at Poperinghe. The next morning he left Pop at 0530 and set up his HQ in the Hotel Châtelaine in the centre of Ypres. By the 28th, the situation was becoming more desperate and Haig moved his Reporting Centre here to White Château, near the level crossing at Hellfire Corner. He also moved General Lomax from the 'small cottage of two rooms ... to make himself more comfortable in Hooge Château', thereby inadvertently causing Lomax's death when the Château (qv) was shelled three days later on the 31st. On 2 November White Château was heavily shelled, killing three men and crashing the large chandelier in Haig's office to the table. Haig accordingly moved back to Ypres to 'a fine old house with some good furniture in it'. There he dined well, 'with some good claret in spite of the shelling'. This house, too, received a direct hit the following day, when Colonel Marker, Haig's QMG, was mortally wounded, causing Haig to comment, 'Enemy had evidently some spies about to help him to direct his fire so accurately, this being the third time my Headquarters have been shelled in the last few days.' Col Richard John Marker, DSO, Légion d'Honneur, formerly of the Coldstream Guards, aged 47, died on 13 November 1914, and is buried in Gittisham Churchyard, Devon.

Hellfire Corner demarcation stone

Continue to the cemetery on the left.

• *Menin Road South Military Cemetery/36.9 miles/Map H35/GPS: 50.84995 2.90476*

First used in January 1916 by 85th S Staffs, 9th E Surreys and by Field Ambulances until 1918, this was amalgamated with the 'North' cemetery which once stood opposite. Designed by Sir Reginald Blomfield, it contains 1,051 UK, 263 Australian, 145 Canadian, 52 New Zealand, 3 British West Indies, 1 German, 119 unknown burials and 29 Special Memorials. Here is buried **A/Capt Thomas Riversdale Colyer-Fergusson, VC** of the 2nd Northants killed on 31 July 1917, capturing his second enemy machine-gun at Bellewaerde.

Continue to the T junction and turn left to Ieper Centrum.

Menin Road South
CWGC Cemetery

• Menin Gate: Last Post Ceremony, 2000 Hours/RB Australian Plaque/ Model of Menin Gate/Indian Memorial/37.8 miles/15 minutes/Map H47/GPS: 50.85217 2.89166

For information about the building and unveiling of the Memorial, see 'The Salient After the Great War' above and page 31.

Just before 2000 hours each night the police halt the traffic through the Menin Gate. The buglers then march into the middle of the road under the great arch, facing the spires of the Cloth Hall and play the Last Post (see 'Ypres Today' above for information about the Last Post Association). In its very simplicity, this is one of the most moving experiences imaginable. It is advisable to arrive early as there are frequently large groups at the ceremony and you may wish to climb up the steps each side to the ramparts, or look up names in the registers (in the bronze box in the left-hand column of the arch nearest to Ieper).

Among the 54,000 names (almost 20,000 more than the total inhabitants of modern Ieper) recorded on its panels – each important to those who mourn – are the **poets Lt John Collinson Hobson, MGC**, killed on 31 July 1917, **Lt Walter Scott Stuart Lyon** (qv), Royal Scots, killed on 8 May 1915, Etonian **Capt the Hon C. E. A. Philipps** (qv), RHG killed on 13 May 1915, and Etonian Lt Gerald George Samuel, RWK, killed on 7 June 1917. Also listed are **2nd Lt Henry Anthony Birrell-Anthony** (qv), 1st Bn the Monmouthshire Regt, killed on 8 May 1915, who is mentioned on the Monmouth Memorial (qv); **Capt Geoffrey Vaux Salvin Bowlby & Capt Henry Langton Skrine**, whose Private Memorials are side by side (see page 125); **Lt Aidan Chavasse** of the 17th King's Liverpool Regiment, missing in action on 4 July 1917 (youngest brother of Noel Chavasse, the Double VC winner); Etonian **Lt the Hon W. A. M. ('Bill') Eden**, KRRC, killed on

The Menin Gate in September 1918 with the ruins of the Cloth Hall behind. Note the light railway

3 March 1915, cousin of Anthony Eden (qv); Etonian **2nd Lt the Hon Gerald William ('Billy')
Grenfell**, Rifle Brigade, brother of the poet Julian Grenfell (qv); **Lt Alexis Helmer**, 1st Bde Field
Artillery, inspiration for John McCrae's poem In Flanders Fields, killed on 2 May 1915; Etonian
2nd Lt Arthur Oscar Hornung Attd 2nd Bn the Essex Regiment, killed on 6 July 1915, son of
E. W. Hornung, creator of Raffles, the 'Gentleman Burglar' and nephew of Conan Doyle; **L Cpl
Thomas** ('Pat') Rafferty of the R Warwicks, Bruce Bairnsfather's inspiration for 'Old Bill'; three
men who were **executed: Driver T. Moore**, of 24 Div Train ASC, shot on 26 February 1916, for
murder, **Cpl George Povey** of the Cheshire Regt, shot on 11 February 1915, **Pte W Scotton** of
the 4th Middlesex, shot on 3 February 1915, and **VCs L Cpl Frederick Fisher** of the Quebec Regt,
killed on 24 April 1915, Etonian **Brig Gen Charles FitzClarence** of the Irish Guards, killed on 12
November 1914, in Polygon Wood commanding the 1st Guards Brigade (a Boer War VC), **Sgt Maj
F. W. Hall** of the 8th Manitoba Regt, killed on 25 April 1915, **2nd Lt Dennis George Wyldbore
Hewitt** of the 14th Hampshires, killed on 31 July 1917, Lt Thomas Ernest Hulme-Lyon, RM Arty
Nav Seige Bty, 28 September 1917, Poet, **Capt John Franks Vallentin**, 1st S Staffs, killed on 7
November 1914, **Pte Edward Warner**, 1st Beds, killed on 2 May 1915, near Hill 60 and **2nd Lt
Sidney Woodroffe** of the Rifle Brigade, killed on 30 July 1915, friend of, and subject of a poem
by, the poet Charles Sorley (qv). Pte James Smith of the 1st Bn the Black Watch, killed on 31
October 1914, has the Regimental Number '1'. **Capt A. E. B O'Neill** of the 2nd Life Guards was
the first Member of Parliament (for Mid Antrim) to be killed in the war on 6 November 1914.
Brothers-in-law of the 1st Life Guards, Etonian **Capt Lord Hugh Grosvenor** (son of the Duke of
Westminster) and Etonian **Lt the Hon Gerald Ward**, MVO (son of the 1st Earl of Dudley) both
disappeared in the fighting of 30 October 1914, at Zantvoorde (qv).

Note that the UK names inscribed on the wall are for the period up to 15 August 1917, after
which date they were inscribed on the Memorial Wall at Tyne Cot (qv). The names of Australians,
Canadians, Indians and South Africans are for the entire duration of the war: they have no names
on the Tyne Cot Memorial.

*Name of L Cpl T.H. Rafferty (the
original 'Old Bill'?) on the Menin Gate*

*The Indian Memorial, Menin
Gate Ramparts*

Kiwanis' Model of the Menin Gate, Ramparts, 'Dedicated to the Relatives of the Soldiers who stood here from 1914–1918'

How To Find An Individual Name On The Menin Gate Memorial

Unless you know the regiment of the man you are looking for, this can be a complicated process. First you have to have established that the name you are looking for is on the memorial. The names and details are listed in alphabetical order in the thiry-seven registers. Registers 1 to 5 are soldiers from Canada, 6-9 are soldiers from Australia, 10 is soldiers from South Africa and the West Indies, 11 is soldiers from India, 12-36 are soldiers from the UK. No 37 lists additional names too late for inclusion in their proper order - so do not despair if you cannot find your name in the first thirty-six books! However, not printed in this alphabetical listing is the number of the panel on which the name is inscribed. To find this you must look up the regiment in the introduction to the memorial. These are listed in alphabetical order and by country. There are sixty panels on each side of the memorial. As you approach from the Cloth Hall side, the odd numbers are on your left, the even numbers are on the right. On the left Panels 1-15 and 15A are in the Main Hall, 17-33 are on the stairway and 35-59 are at the top of the stairs and in the Loggia. On the right, 2-16A are in the Main Hall, 18-34 are on the stairway and 36-60 are at the top of the stairs and in the Loggia.

On top of the embankment on the grass beside the right-hand loggia and near the Australian names is a **Ross Bastiaan bronze Australian tablet**, showing a bas relief map of the Salient. It was unveiled on 1 September 1993, by the Hon Bill Haydon, the Governor General of Australia.

On the opposite embankment is a 1.9m long, 1.05m wide bronze **Model of the Menin Gate**, standing on a Portland Stone socle with a Braille text in four languages. It was cast by Dirk de Groeve and funded by the local Kiwanis club (who also sponsored the Cloth Hall Model in the Grote Markt). It was unveiled on 20 September 2003 by the blind Belgian singer, Séverine Doré. Founded in 1915 in Detroit, the Kiwanis (originally all-male and business-orientated) are now an international philanthropic and idealistic, co-ed organisation.

Beyond it a white stone **Indian Monument** was unveiled on 10 November 2002 as part of the 'Flanders India 2002 Partnership Year' by Major-General A.J. Bajwa who had come all the way from India for the ceremony. It commemorated the 130,000 Indian troops who served in France and Belgium during WW1 (a landscape and culture totally alien to them). By the end of the war 1,100,000 Indians, all of them volunteers, had served overseas, earning 9,200 gallantry awards including 11 Victoria Crosses. Over 74,000 were killed, of which 447 are commemorated on the Menin Gate. On 12 March 2011 it was replaced, a little further along the Ramparts, by a splendid **new Memorial** depicting the lion emblems of King Ashoka, the symbol of Peace and Power. It lists the major battles of the Indian Forces, 9,000 of whom were killed in Flanders.

Drive on to the Grote Markt.

• *End of Itinerary One*

Invitation to the first six buglers to play under the Menin Gate at the inauguration on 24 July 1927. Courtesy of Jacky Plattieeuw

ITINERARY TWO

• **Itinerary Two** starts at the Menin Gate, heads north-east around the area of the Second Ypres gas attacks, runs along the Pilckem Ridge and the 1917 battle, goes on to the behind-the-lines areas *en route* to Poperinge and ends back in Ypres.

• **The Main Route:** Ypres – Ypres Town CWGC Cemetery and Extension; Potijze – Château Group of CWGC Cemeteries, Demarcation Stone; Frezenberg - 1st Monmouthshire Regt Memorial; Bridge House CWGC Cemetery; St Julien DS CWGC Cemetery; Poelkapelle – Guynemer & Tank Memorials and Poelcapelle CWGC Cemetery; Langemarck – Interpretative Centre, German Cemetery, Carlill & Lockley Plaque; 34th Division Memorial/Bunker, Chasseurs d'Afrique Memorial, 20th Light Div Memorial, Albertina Memorial, Harry Patch Memorial; Cement House CWGC Cemetery; Hagebos – Hedd Wyn Memorials & Welsh National Dragon Memorial; Ledwidge Memorial, Artillery Wood CWGC Cemetery; Breton Memorial, Carrefour de la Rose; Boezinge – Demarcation Stone, 'Little Bertha' Mortar; Steenstraat-Zuidschote – Gas Memorial, Belgian Memorials, Demarcation Stone; Talana Farm CWGC Cemetery; Bard Cottage CWGC Cemetery; Essex Farm CWGC Cemetery, McCrae Albertina Memorial, Dressing Station and Plaques, 49th (West Riding) Div Memorial; Duhallow CWGC Cemetery; Salvation Corner; Ypres Reservoir CWGC Cemetery; Goldfish Château; Vlamertinghe – Military CWGC Cemetery, Vlamertinghe Château, Blunden Info Board, Hop Store CWGC Cemetery; Brandhoek – Chavasse Memorial, *Gas Explosion Memorial*, Military CWGC Cemetery, New Military CWGC Cemetery No 3, New Military CWGC Cemetery; Red Farm CWGC Cemetery; Gwalia CWGC Cemetery; Poperinge – Walking Tour, including Execution Post, Skindles, Talbot House, Poperinghe New Mil Cemetery; Ypres.

• **Planned duration**, excluding stops for refreshments, Poperinge Walking Tour, Extra Visits and N.B.s: 6 hours. **Driving Time:** 1 hour 35 minutes.

• **Total distance:** 40 miles.

• **Extra Visits** are suggested to the 'Langemarck on the Run' Panels, Pte Dancox VC Memorial; Ivor Gurney Memorial; Pte T. Whitham, VC, Plaque; 38th Welsh Div Memorial, Gournier Farm & Minty Farm CWGC Cemetery; the Ziegler Group of bunkers; 'Entry Point North', Klein Zwaanhof; Colne Valley CWGC Cemetery; Yorkshire Trench archaeological site, Vlamertinghe New Military CWGC Cemetery; Château de Lovie, Dozinghem, Mendinghem, Bandaghem CWGC Cemeteries; Lijssenthoek CWGC Cemetery (if not seen on Approach One).

• **N.B.s** are suggested to Varlet Farm, Charles Dresse Memorial, Welsh Cemetery (Casesar's Nose); B17 Memorial; Jan Derynck Collection; St Sixtus Abbey.

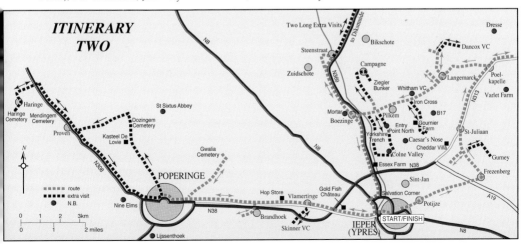

• *Menin Gate, Ypres/0 miles/RWC/Map H47*

From the far (eastern) side of the Menin Gate continue over the traffic lights along the N332 Zonnebeke Road. Stop at the sign by the entrance to the cemetery on the right.

• *Ypres Town CWGC Cemetery & Extension/0.3 miles/20 minutes/ Map H34 /GPS: 50.85439 2.89706*

The original Cemetery and Extension were started in October 1914 and enlarged after the Armistice. In the original plot are 142 UK, 49 I(or C)WGC workers, 1 Indian, and in the Extension 462 UK, 13 Australian, 15 Canadian, I Indian 2 German and 137 unknown, with 16 Special Memorials. The Cemetery also contains a large plot of World War II burials. It was designed by Sir Reginald Blomfield.

To the left of the path as one enters the Cemetery Extension is a short row containing the graves of several of 1BR Corps HQ staff, killed by a shell in Hooge Château on 31 October 1914: **Col Arthur Jex Blake Percival, DSO**, age 43 of 2 Div; Etonian Maj George Paley age 42 of 1st Div; **Col Frederic Walter Kerr, DSO**, age 47 (son of Admiral Lord Kerr) of 1st Div; **Maj Francis Maxwell Chevenix-French**, age 36 and **Capt Rupert Ommanney**, both of 2nd Div.

King George V visiting the grave of Prince Maurice in 1922

In the original plot (approached through the main Cemetery and then turning right into the local cemetery proper) is buried **Prince Maurice Victor Donald of Battenberg**, youngest grandson of Queen Victoria, son of Princess Beatrice, brother of Queen Ena of Spain, cousin of the Tsar of Russia and the Kaiser and nephew of Prince Louis of Battenberg. He was born at Balmoral on 3 October 1891, the first prince to be born in Scotland for nearly 300 years. A professional soldier, he was commissioned into the 1st Bn, KRRC in 1910. His battalion moved to France on 12 August 1914, and fought through Mons, the Retreat and the Aisne. By 12 October only 10 of the battalion's original officers remained. On the 13th Prince Maurice was Mentioned in Despatches. On 17 October the battalion arrived in the Salient and on 27 October the Prince was killed, leading his men, by a shell burst near Zonnebeke. His cousin, Prince Arthur of Connaught, who was serving as ADC to Sir John French at St Omer, rushed to the scene, but he was too late to be of any assistance. Maurice had died before reaching a field dressing station. He was 23. Lord Kitchener offered to have his body brought home, but his mother refused, knowing

Prince Maurice's grave today

that he would wish to be buried with his friends. The funeral was arranged by Prince Arthur on 30 October. A memorial service was held at the Chapel Royal, attended by King George V and Queen Mary, the Prime Minister and Lord Kitchener. The Prince of Wales (qv) reacted,

"Soon the dreaded casualty lists began to appear; and I found the names of my friends, including brother officers in the Brigade of Guards with whom I had trained only a few short weeks before. My equerry, Major Cadogan, was killed with the 10th Hussars; one of my cousins, Prince Maurice of Battenberg, and two of my father's equerries lost their lives about the same time, causing me to exclaim in my diary, 'I shan't have a friend left soon. Against the background of these incredible sacrifices my subsequent efforts to find an honourable place in the fighting were of small importance, except to me."

In 1922 the king visited his cousin's grave and Queen Elizabeth II visited it in 1966. Also serving in World War I were Prince Maurice's elder brothers, Prince Alexander (nicknamed 'Drino') and Prince Leopold. The former was invalided home with an injured knee, 'the result of a fall', and the latter, a platoon commander in the Grenadier Guards, was described during the retreat by his commanding officer, Maj the Lord Bernard Gordon-Lennox (qv) as 'not a heaven-born soldier'. On 17 September 1914, he was hospitalised with a chill and Gordon-Lennox asked the MO 'if he could get him sent home'. Dr Howell replied that he 'would be glad to get him away!'

Also reburied here is Etonian Lt Lord Charles Sackville Pelham Worsley of the RHG, aged 27, originally buried in Zandtvoorde (qv) on the site of the Household Cavalry Memorial on 30 October 1914. Beyond Prince Maurice's grave was a substantial plot of graves of Imperial (as it was originally known) or Commonwealth War Graves Commission workers. Among them is **Dick Collick** (qv) who taught the Last Post Buglers how to play in the British fashion, who died on 21 March 1986, age 95, and **'Billy' Dunn,** who died on 7 December 1987, age 88, who had served with the 1st Worcesters from 1917-1920. Also in the plot is his **Belgian wife Simone** (qv) who had vivid memories of the April 1915 gas attack and who died on 8 May 1995, age 92. **Sid Arnold**, 6 February 1995, age 79, and **Harry Fisher**, 29 September 1999, age 74, are also buried here. There are also several members of the **Brown family** (qv). It is interesting to note that the I & CWGC headstones are not consistent in their shape. In 2002 the original site of these graves was threatened as the Belgian authorities needed the ground for more local burials and subsequently most of them were moved to the main Cemetery and are now on the right as one enters.

A FASCINATING WW2 STORY: OPERATION CIRCUS 157

In the Cemetery are buried 3 RAF Pilots killed during *Operation Circus 157*, the codename for a 5 May 1942 bombing mission on the electricity power station at Lille. Six Boston-type Bombers were protected by 36 Supermarine Spitfires of 64th, 122nd & 313th Sqns as they took off from Swanton Morley, Fairlop and Hornchurch bases. The RAF pilots were made up of British, Czech, Canadian, Norwegian, Belgian, Rhodesian and Dutch pilots. Among them were Flt Sgt Stacey Jones (UK), Sgt Karel Pavlik (Czech), Flt Lt Baudouin de Hemptinne (Belgian) and Sgt Roland Joffre Ribout (Canadian). Due to cloud cover the Bostons were unable to drop their bombs and returned to their bases. The Spitfires, however, were attacked in a fierce dog fight by Focke-Wulfs of Luftwaffe Jagdeschwader 26 'Schlageter' over Heuvelland.

At 1535 hours 22 year old Stacey Jones was killed when brought down on Provensteenweg near Poperinge. He is buried in IV.A.44. At 1540 hours 27 year old Roland Ribout was hit, bailed out, but his parachute did not open and he was killed near Nieuwkerke. He is buried in IV.A.42 and a Memorial was unveiled to him in Ploegsteert in 2007 (see page 248). At 1545 hours 24 year old Karel Pavlik was shot through the head and his plane crashed on the side of Monteberg. His body and part of the plane were recoverd in May 1945 and the engine of the plane in 1997. He is buried in IV.A.41 and a Memorial was unveiled to him on 28 August 1999 near his crash site (see page 266). Also at 1545 33 year old Baudouin de Hemptinne was shot through the back and crashed his Spitfire on the De Wulf Farm near Dranouter. He was originally buried between his comrades in this cemetery but his body was moved to the Belgian Honorary Cemetery for Belgian Pilots at Evere in 1947. A Memorial to him was inaugurated in Dranouter on 5 May 1992 (see page 219).

On 5 May 2011 an important and emotional RAF Operation Circus 157 Commemoration Day, attended by dignitaries from the Czech Republic and Pavlik family members, the CWGC, RAF Fairfield Heritage Group, RAF/SAAF Assoc, Maple Leaf Legacy and WW2 RAF Veteran George Sutherland, was organised by Chris Lock and Milena Kolarikova, a distant relative of Pavlik. An impressive ceremony was also held in 2016. For more details see www.lestweforget.vpweb.be

Continue along the N332 signed to Roeselare and Zonnebeke, over the roundabout at which Potijze Burial Ground Cemetery is signed to the left, to the green sign to the CWGC Cemeteries on the left which are approached by a gravel path.

• *Potijze Château CWGC Cemeteries/Demarcation Stone/1.2 miles/15 minutes/Map H43, 44, 45, I3/ GPS: 50.86069 2.91572*

Potijze was in British hands for most of the war. During Charles Doudney's (qv) time with 18th Field Ambulance in 1915 it was used as a first aid post and he visited the château regularly. In July he sent a description of the place to the *Bath* and *Wilts Chronicle*:

'A year ago it was a charming villa set just back from the main road ... flanked by a small wood, a serpentine lake in the rear and grounds laid out in the French style, in which every point of view gives a finished picture. Inside everything showed the sign of culture, rare furniture, paintings and sculpture ... and now! The flowers are gone and their perfume is replaced by the all-pervading stench that one is even beginning to be accustomed to – of putrefaction fraught with chloride of lime ... it's the smell of a charnel house ... The garden is an area of mud or dust ... the shapely gate posts are rent and the iron gates gone ... the painted ceiling has fallen in ... all round the walls are tables … oaken bureau, and on them glisten the bright horrors of the surgeon. Bandages and dressings, splints of all sorts, blood stained stretchers litter the place. '

Here **Edmund Blunden** (qv) moved to trenches in January 1917 'in an Arcadian environment' by the *château*, which 'boasted a handsome cheval-glass and a harmonium, but not a satisfactory roof,' and which still housed a dressing station on the ground floor.

In **Potijze Wood** the 28 year old lawyer (reputed to be the first Scottish lawyer to fall in World War I and the first officer of his battalion) and poet, **Lt Walter Scott Stuart Lyon**, fell with the 9th Bn, Scots Guards on 8 May 1915. He is commemorated on the Menin Gate. Lyon was much moved by a grave he found in a trench on 16 April 1915, of an English soldier who was killed in Belgium and buried by a French soldier. It inspired his poem *On a Grave in a Trench Inscribed 'English Killed for the Patrie'*.

*Potijze Château CWGC Cemetery
with Potijze Château Wood Cemetery
Cross behind*

*Sign & paths leading to Potijze
Group of CWGC Cemeteries*

On the left are the following Cemeteries: **Potijze Burial Ground** (used April-October 1918 during the German offensive, containing 580 UK, 3 Australian, 1 Canadian, 21 unknown and 1 German burials); **Potijze Château Grounds** (formed in the Spring of 1915 but mostly used in May-September 1918, with further burials concentrated here after the Armistice, containing 304 UK, 23 Australian, 49 Canadian, 2 New Zealand, 1 South African, 195 unknown, 1 French and 1 German burials); **Potijze Lawn** (used May-December 1915 and July 1917-October 1918, containing 191 UK, 4 Australian, 22 Canadian, 9 South African, 29 unknown and 3 German burials) and **Potijze Château Wood** (used April 1915-June 1917, with 31,918 burials, containing 145 UK, 6 Canadian and 6 unknown burials). This long, triangular-shaped Cemetery is approached by an immaculate grass path from the back of Potijze Lawn and Château Cemeteries. There are **Information Boards** by the entrance to the path. In it lie, shoulder to shoulder, serried ranks of men of the Inniskillings and Hampshires - many killed by phosgene gas on 9 August 1916 - and French **Capt Raoul Johnston**, Liaison Officer with the British Army, 14.5.1915. As their names imply, all of the Cemeteries were built in the grounds of the ruined Château. They were designed by Sir Reginald Blomfield.

Continue and cross the Bellewaardebeek.

Potijze (Ypres) Demarcation Stone (Map I3, GPS: 50.86236 2.92176) is passed on the right, followed by the **French Cemetery (Map I4)** and **Aeroplane Cemetery (Map I5).**

Cross the motorway, passing the Scottish Monument and its slip road (Itinerary One, page 127) Note the windmills along the Ieper Canal in the distance to the left. Turn next left at the village of Frezenberg along Ieperstraat.

• *Frezenberg*

You are now driving over the Frezenberg Ridge, parallel to the Ypres Canal whose windmills can be seen to the left on the horizon. This is the site of the Battle of 8-13 May 1915. Following the German gas attack which opened Second Ypres, the British were forced back onto the Wieltje-Frezenberg Ridge, standing on the ground above the Zonnebeek (see Battle Map). This withdrawal shortened the front from 20,000 yards to 15,000 yards and helped to staunch further German attacks, many using gas. The stand was not without heavy loss. The 12th London Regiment, the

Rangers, was reduced to 53 men and no officers. It was, says the *Official History*, 'annihilated'. The Princess Patricia's Canadian Light Infantry, who were the first and only Canadian infantry regiment at war in 1914, were reduced to an effective strength of 154 men commanded by Lt H. W. Niven.

Turn left at T junction towards Ypres along Roeselarestraat.

Over this area the Liverpool Scottish advanced from their positions in Wieltje in the early morning of 31 July 1917, supported by two tanks, to take their objective of Capricorn Trench, beyond the Steenbeek behind you. The Medical Officer of the 10th Bn, **Capt Noel Chavasse** (qv), **VC**, set up his Regimental Aid Post in a captured German dugout near Setques Farm (close to this spot). It was dangerously near the front line.

Chavasse was hit in the head early in the attack and walked back to the main dressing station in Wieltje, returning, against protest, to his own dugout after treatment. It was inundated with wounded coming in for treatment and Noel coped as best he could with the aid of captured German medics. He was seriously wounded at least twice more, but refused to leave his post, despite the lack of sleep and food. Several times he went out under heavy fire to bring in the wounded. Eventually, on 2 August he was mortally wounded in the stomach by a shell that penetrated the dugout. He managed to crawl out and was picked up and taken back to CCS No 32 at Brandhoek (qv) which specialised in abdominal wounds.

Another medical officer, Robert Lindsay Mackay, serving with the 11th Bn Argyll and Sutherland Highlanders, wrote in his diary (to be found on the Internet at http://www.finsysgp. com/macbob/Text/Diary5.html) for that same day:

'Got to blockhouse on top of Frezenberg Ridge. Barrage closed down all around us. Sent off men in parties until I had only three left. Found at last, when no other of our men could be seen, a demented Boche. Felt like leaving the blighter, but could not. Got him on a stretcher. But men objected. Took an end of the stretcher myself. Then Boche turned a machine gun on us as our little party with the wounded Boche stumbled down the Roulers railway line. So much for civilised warfare! I fear that no prisoners will be taken by any of my men in the next show. '

Continue, and stop at the memorial on the left under the pylons.

• *1st Monmouthshire Regiment/Lt Birrell-Anthony Memorial/4.3 miles/5 minutes/Map I23/GPS: 50.87612 2.93022*

The Monmouth Regiment, a Territorial Bn made up of part-time volunteers, was mobilised on 10 August 1914 and was in Belgium in time to take part in the Christmas Truce at Plugstreet.

This Memorial (now maintained by the CWGC) commemorates **Lt H. A. Birrell-Anthony** and **Officers and Men of the 1st Bn** who were killed in the Battle of Frezenberg Ridge in Second Ypres on 8 May 1915, during which all three Battalions of the Regiment took part (in the 84th Brigade). Behind it is Von Heugel Farm…

The 1st Battalion found their right flank exposed as the 83rd Brigade covering it were forced to retire and the Monmouths were partly surrounded. They hung on desperately and when called upon to surrender, Captain Edwards shouted, "Surrender be damned".

The stirring event is immortalised by a painting, 'May the Eighth' by Fred Roe, held at Newport Art Gallery and Museum. (Later, on 22 December 1944 in the Battle of the Bulge, the American Commander, Brig-Gen Anthony McAuliffe, also asked to surrender, replied with one dismissive word, 'Nuts').

Eventually, by late afternoon they too were forced back into the support trenches.

The casualties of all three Battalions were so high that they were temporarily amalgamated into one until enough reinforcements could be found to reinstate them. Indeed by 9 May the six Battalions of the 84th Brigade numbered only 1,400. (An elemental *aide memoire* to British unit strength is that a battalion should have 1,000 men, a brigade four battalions and a division sixteen battalions, but the higher organisations varied wildly.) A telling and moving account of the casualties is that of Major Bridge of the 3rd Bn who took what remained of his troops to Poperinghe where '… they found piles of parcels from home which had not been possible to deliver during the

battle – most of them were addressed to men who could no longer receive them'.

Birrell-Anthony was one of the casualties on that fateful day. His body was lost and he is commemorated on Panel 50 of the Menin Gate. His father, Lt-Col Henry Birrell-Anthony, was commanding the 2/1st reserve battalion providing replacements in the field. He visited the land where his son was thought to have fallen, intending to build him a Memorial of Monmouth stone. He later decided to include the Officers and ORs of the Battalion killed that day in his inscription.

Later in the year the Monmouths then moved to the 29th, 46th and 49th Divisions - in the latter the 1st/3rd served, mainly in the Boesinghe area.

Memorial to Lt H.A. Birrell-Anthony & the Monmouths, Frezenberg

On 29th December 1915, prior to their move to the Somme, they paraded at nearby Elverdinghe Château where a long-range HE shell landed on the parade, killing over 35 men and wounding over 30.

Turn round, return along road and continue to the cemetery on the right.

• *Bridge House CWGC Cemetery/4.7 miles/5 minutes/Map I22/GPS: 50.87976 2.93681*

Named after the nearby farmhouse, this Cemetery, which contains 45 UK and 4 unknown burials, was begun at the end of September 1917 and mostly used by 59th (North Midland) Div after the battle of Polygon Wood of 26-28 September 1917. It was designed by A.J.S. Hutton. **Sjt F. Chymist** of the Tank Corps was killed on 26 September 1917 in the middle of the Third Battle of Ypres, and his burial here prompts the question why tanks were used in a year whose rains had turned the ground (low lying at best) into a quagmire. The Tank Corps had started out as the 'Heavy Branch of the Machine Gun Corps' which officially changed its name in July 1917 (and in 1923 it became the 'Royal Tank Corps').

The tanks proved largely ineffective, though training of the three Brigades totalling around 220 tanks had been done before the battle, and the messages brought back by the tanks' pigeons spoke often of being stuck in the mud.

Entrance to Bridge House CWGC Cemetery

Extra Visit to Ivor Gurney Memorial (MapI22a , GPS: 50.88006 2.95694)

Round trip: 2.00 miles Approximate time: 15 minutes

Continue along Roeselarestraat to the first turning to the right, Haezweidestraat. Turn along it and continue to the Memorial on the left.

Similar in design to those for Ledwidge (qv) and Chavasse (qv), the Memorial was unveiled on 12 September 2007, the initiative of Piet Chielens and Friends of the In Flanders Fields Museum. As the top Plaque, which bears a photo of Pte Ivor Gurney, 2nd/5th Gloucesters, describes, it is on the site where Gurney succumbed to mustard gas on 12 September 1917, near 'Hill 35', 'Gallipoli Farm'. Below is another Plaque bearing a poem. *Memory Let All Slip*, written during his hospitalisation in October 1917 subsequent to the attack and another, *The Battle*, written in Barnwood Mental Asylum in March 1925, where this troubled musical and poetic genius died on 26 December 1937. The Memorial is now on the, 'Writers' Path Trail' (qv).

Memorial to poet & musician, Ivor Gurney, Hill 35

Return to Bridge House and pick up the main itinerary.

Take the first left opposite the cemetery along Felixnaderstraat. Continue to the junction with the main road in St Juliaan. To the right is

• St Julien Dressing Station CWGC Cemetery/5.3 miles/5 minutes/ Map I19/GPS: 50.88783 2.93526

Designed by Sir Reginald Blomfield the Cemetery, attached to a Dressing Station, was started in September 1917, remaining in use until March 1918 when many of the graves were damaged by shellfire during the German offensive of 'Fourth Ypres'. After the Armistice graves from the surrounding battlefields were concentrated here. It contains 290 UK (including several RND), 10 Australian, 15 Canadian, 1 Newfoundland, 3 New Zealand, 3 South African, 96 unknown graves and 11 Special Memorials.

Turn right on the N313 and continue on the N313 direction Poelkapelle, past the Brooding Soldier Memorial on the right, which is described in Itinerary One.

The spires of Langemarck Church can be seen to the left. The road from Vancouver Corner to just short of Poelkapelle formed the eastern edge of the German advance following the Gas Attack of

St Julien Dressing Station CWGC Cemetery

Second Ypres. On entering Poelkapelle the Guynemer Memorial is straight ahead in the centre of the road.

Park on the right.

• *Guynemer & Tank Memorials/Poelkapelle/7.6 miles/10 minutes/Map D4/GPS: 50.91767 2.95708*

Capitaine Georges Guynemer was France's most popular air ace, with fifty-four kills to his credit. Guynemer had a personality that would probably now be described as 'charismatic'. Nervous, highly strung, frail looking, he nevertheless captured the imagination of the public and was lionised in the French press. In June 1917, with his score at 45, he was awarded the *Légion d'Honneur*. Guynemer saw almost continuous action for two years, which extracted a fearful toll on him. So shocked was his father by his haggard condition when Guynemer went home for a short leave that he begged his son to retire. But the driven pilot insisted on taking up his new appointment at St Pol sur Mer, with his squadron, christened *Les Cigognes* (the Storks), to help the RFC to clear the skies over Flanders during Third Ypres. Guynemer arrived to find his own favourite Spad aeroplane unserviceable and he was reduced to flying his missions in a series of second-class planes. Jamming guns, engine and structural failures followed one after another and had a disastrous effect on Guynemer's taut nerves. Word of his paranoic condition reached Paris and two distinguished emissaries were despatched to investigate: *Capitaine* Felix Brocard, the *Cigogne's* Commanding Officer, and Commandant Jean de Peuty, commander of the French Air Force Aviation Staff. They arrived at St Pol at 0900 hours on the morning of 11 September 1917. The sky was overcast. It was drizzling and the squadron was grounded – with the exception of Guynemer and a sub-lieutenant, Benjamin Bozon Verduraz, whom he had commanded to accompany him. While the Air Ministry delegation waited impatiently at St Pol, Guynemer and Bozon located an enemy over Poelcapelle. In the ensuing mêlée Bozon escaped but Guynemer was never seen again. A few days later Lt Kurt Wissemann was credited with the kill. There is a legend that after his death the storks on the fuselage of his squadron's Spads were painted black

in mourning for their hero and the stork on the memorial is said to be flying in the direction that Guynemer took on the day he died. The Memorial was unveiled in July 1923. There is also a Memorial to him in Guynemer's home town of Compiègne.

By the parking area just beyond it is the **Tank Memorial Ypres Salient (TMYS)**. Designed, constructed (with Dirk Vinck) and financed by Chris Lock (ex-R Tank Regt) and his wife Milena Kolarikova, it is on the site of the old 'Tank Cemetery'. The Plaque, of Indian black granite by local stonemasons, Timmerman, is mounted on locally produced black brick, symbolising the ruggedness of the Regiment. It was inaugurated with full military honours on 10 October 2009 by Maj-Gen Chris Deverell MBE with regimental and local dignitaries in attendance. A metal Register Box, constructed in Bovington ('spiritual home' of the Tank Corps

Tank Memorial with Guynemer Memorial behind, Poelkapelle

Miniature Tank, Poelkapelle

and Regiment). It contains a Visitor's Book and folder full of interesting information about the planning and construction of the Memorial and the grave sites of 244 soldiers commemorated locally. An original fragment of tank recovered from the battlefield is attached to the Memorial wall, on loan from Johan Vandewalle. In front of the Memorial is A 'Garden of Remembrance', designed by Milena, containing 243 personalised poppy crosses for the local casualties and a single WW2 R Tank Regt buried nearby.

On 13 April 2013 disaster struck when 3 local youths failed to negotiate the roundabout and crashed into the Memorial, knocking it off its base. Happily the rebuilding was covered by insurance and with the support of the Langemark-Poelkapelle Council it was completed in November that year.

The active TMYS Association and Friends' Organisation is run by Chris with Milena's support. They have their own standard and are represented at many local commemorative events, including an annual event at the Memorial. The Hon President of the Association is Lt-Gen David Leakey CMG, CBE, currently 'Black Rod'.

For more details see www.tankmemorial.vpweb.co.uk

By the Memorial is a small brick plinth with a replica miniature **Mk IV D29, Damon II WW1 tank**. It was erected by Ypres Technical School teacher, Johan Vanbeselaere, who for many years has had the aim of placing a full size tank in the village square, to replace the one that stood there until end of September 1941. The full story and how you can contribute, is told in http://www.worldofcrowdfunding.com/en/node/3240

> N.B. 1. **Varlet Farm** (GPS: 50.90575 2.98427). This may be reached by taking the N301, Wallemolenstraat, and continuing along the winding road to No 43. The original farm was renamed Varlet Farm by the Hood Bn of the RND who took it at 0730 on 26 October 1917. Rebuilt in 1920 it is now an immaculate and popular B & B for battlefield visitors who are given a warm welcome by knowledgeable owners Dirk Cardoen-Descamps and his daughter, Barbara. Tel: + (0) 470211654. E-mail: info@varletfar.com www.varletfarm.com. Can sleep up to 22. Advance booking essential for groups. An active farm, the family regularly unearth piles of 'Iron Harvest' and an exhibition of many WW1-related artefacts found in and around the Farm is in the barn opposite. On 2 March 2010 a **Plaque** was

Varlet Farm Memorials

Varlet Farm B & B near Poelkapelle

unveiled with the legend: '**Varlet Farm, Poelkapelle**. Captured by men of the 63rd Royal Naval Division 1917'. It is on the Memorial wall of a barn opposite the b &b which contains a variety of interemting exhibits and Information Boards.

Charles Dresse Memorial (GPS: 50.93805 2.97208). This may be reached by continuing past the church, taking the 2nd left on Bruggestraat, then turning left at the first crossroads, direction Staden, continuing and taking the right turn on Poperingestraaat, and continuing to the Memorial on the right, which is in a sad condition. It is surmounted by a Breton Calvary Cross between figures of Mary and Joseph and is in a walled enclosure with ornate wrought-iron gates. Beside it is an Information Board.

Dresse was born in Liège on 23 January 1897 to a wealthy family of industrialists. He volunteered in 1914 and was Aide-de-Camp (or Adjutant), 9th Inf Regt of Line. It stands on the spot where he was killed on 28 September 1918 and buried in a temporary grave. He is now interred in West-Vleteren Belgian Cemetery. The Monument was inaugurated on 28 September 1922. The 21-year old Dresse led his men during a strong German counter-attack after the 9th's successful assault at Madonna (district of Langemarck). He had taken command of his

Monument to Charles Dresse, 9th Belg Inf Regt, near Poelkapelle

dwindling group when all other officers had been killed or wounded and no orders were being received. They successfully stormed a machine-gun nest at nearby Davout Farm but Dresse was shot and killed in the attack. He was Mentioned in Despatches (**Citation à l'Ordre de l'Armèe**) for his gallantry, on 28 April 1919.

Continue in the same direction, past the church. On the right is a cemetery. Park in the layby on the left.

• Poelcapelle British CWGC Cemetery/8.4 miles/15 minutes/Map D5/ GPS: 50.92104 2.97202

This was formed after the Armistice by concentrating graves from the nearby areas including Langemarck and Sint Jan. Designed by Charles Holden it contains 6,541 UK, 117 Australian, 525 Canadian, 4 Channel Island, 8 Newfoundland, 237 New Zealand, 10 South African, 6,231 unknown burials (a huge percentage of the total) and 36 Special Memorials. One Special Memorial stone commemorates twenty-four UK soldiers and three Canadians who were buried by the enemy and whose graves could not later be found. The great majority of them are from the last five months of Third Ypres, especially October. Here is buried what was long considered to be the youngest British soldier to die in the war, at one month short of his 14th birthday. He is **Private J. Condon** of the Royal Irish Regiment, born in Trinity, Co Wexford and killed during Second Ypres on 24 May 1915. However extensive research by Aurel Sercu cast doubts on the age marked on the headstone, as well as the identity. See: http://www.irishcentral.com/roots/

history/Grave-of-Irelands-most-famous-WWI-soldier-may-
contain-other-remains.html Ironically Condon is buried next to
47-year-old **Thomas McCarthy** of the same regiment. There are
also seven men of the 48th Labour Coy, killed together when they
lit a fire to cook their meal while they were clearing the cemetery
after the war, thereby triggering an explosion of a war-time shell.
They are **Pvtes Bentham, Byrne, Eyre, Lloyd and Tilley, Sapper
Williams and Cpl Greaves**, buried side by side in Plot 17 Row
C. Also buried here is **2nd Lt Hugh Gordon Langton** of the 4th
Bn London Regt, killed on 26 October 1917, age 32, a talented
musician, who studied in Prague, Berlin and Russia.

> *Turn around, return to the road junction at the Guynemer Memorial
> and take the right-hand road to Langemarck. Continue to the cross
> roads with traffic lights.*

• Langemarck
The scene of heavy fighting in October and November 1914, the
village was captured by the Germans during the first gas attack in
April 1915 and retaken by the 20th (Light) Division on 16 August
1917, during Third Ypres. The Allied spring withdrawal in 1918 left
the village in German hands. It was finally taken by the Belgians
on 28 September 1918.

*Headstone marked Pte J. Condon,
age 14, Poelcapelle Brit /CWGC
Cemetery*

> *Turn right at the traffic lights and continue to the Church.*

Extra Visit to 'Langemarck on the Run' Information Panels, GPS: 50.91574 2.91776 Round trip: 1.3 miles

At the rear of the Church is an Information Panel about the 'Langemarck on the Run'
series of 16 numbered boards, the route shown on a sketch map. With the use of 'then and
now' photographs, picture postcards, letters, personal accounts etc, they tell – in Dutch
and English - the story of the pre-war commercially prosperous village. The tragic story
then unfolds as the village is variously gassed, occupied, bombarded and fought over
desperately and is gradually reduced to rubble. Most poignant is the plight of 'The Children
of the Yser' refugees, over 6,000 of whom were evacuated, first to Poperinghe, De Panne

Signboard showing all points on the 'Langemarck on the Run' Route, behind Langemarck Church

Mural of Harry Patch on Langemark Carrefour

and Dunkerke. Then, as the refugees obstructed troop movements, they were sent by train further into France and Switzerland. The Panels are the inspiration of Michel Gheeraert and Danny Vanacker. Michel's ancestor Sylveer, who went on to become Mayor of Langemarck, 1959-1971, was evacuated at the age of 7. His story is told at **Stops Nos 9 and 10**.

Stop No 15 is on the site of the magnificent 19th Century Château which was completely destroyed.

The route ends at Stop No 16 where the sometimes disappointing and emotionally difficult return of the refugees in 1919 is recounted

Nearby is the splendid Town Hall, with Plaques to each side of the door commemorating (a) the gas attack of 22 April 1915 and the 87th French DIT who had been here since 1914 and who were decimated by the attack and (b) The **Liberation of Langemark on 4 September 1944. (GPS: 50.91455 2.91782).**

'Langemarck on the Run' Panel No. 10

Here, at 1 Kasteelstraat, is the Langemark-Poelkapelle Tourist Office. Tel: + (0)57 49 09 41. E-mail: toerisme@langemark-poelkapelle.be. Website: www.langemark-poelkapelle.be. **Open**: Mon, Tues, Fri 0900-1200. Wed 0900-1200 & 1400-1600. Thurs 0900-1200 & 1400-1830.

On the nearby Carrefour supermarket is a **Mural of Harry Patch** (qv). It is part of an ongoing series of WW1 commemoration paintings by Moorslede artist, Philip Cardoen, 'The Westhoek Front Painting Tour'. On commercial buildings, the project for 60 pictures continues until 2018.

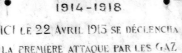

1914-1918

ICI LE 22 AVRIL 1915 SE DÉCLENCHA LA PREMIERE ATTAQUE PAR LES GAZ OU FUT DECIMEE LA 87ᵉ D.I.T. FRANCAISE QUI ARRETAIT EN CE LIEU L'INVASION ALLEMANDE DEPUIS OCTOBRE 1914

Plaque to The Gas Attack of 22 April 1915 & the 87th French DIT, Langemark Town Hall

Here on 31 July 1917, the Prince of Wales (qv), who had been commissioned into the 1st Bn, Grenadier Guards in August 1914 and who thereafter chafed to get into the thick of the action, got his wish:

> 'In an observation post atop the ruins of Langemarck church I had my closest call, being suddenly bracketed early one morning by two near misses and diving to safety as the third shell fell - a direct hit on the heap of rubble ... After seeing the great offensive begin with optimism and valour, then fizzle out into nothingness from sheer loss of life and human exhaustion, I in time shared the weariness and cynicism of the front line. The general disillusionment, the unending scenes of horror – not to mention several more narrow escapes of my own – had done their work.'

He wrote to his father,

> 'My dearest Papa ... I'm writing this in the office as I'm on watch or night-duty as they call it. It's very cold & damp still pouring in sheets the rain making a depressing pattering noise on the tin roof of the hut! ... But how thankful I am to think I am not living forward tonight ... one does appreciate this comfort when one has been forward & seen what it's like in the line now!! The nearest thing possible to hell whatever that is !!!! '

Bear to the right of the church and follow signs to Staden/Diksmuide to the Deutsche Soldaten Friedhof. Drive past the cemetery and park in the car park by the Interpretative Centre on the left.

• Langemarck German Interpretative Centre/Cemetery/Carlill & Lockley Plaque/11.5 miles/30 minutes/Map D2/WC/GPS: 50.92164 2.91675

The Cemetery offers free wifi which is found at the entrance. By downloading the available App to a smartphone it is possible to access seven stations around the Cemetery at which further details of the area and what happened here can be found.

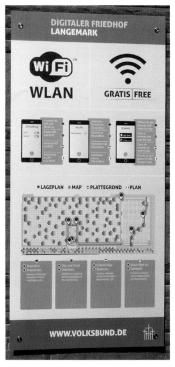

The Interpretative Centre and parking area was opened on 26 August 2006 on the land adjoining the Cemetery to the north - a joint initiative of West Flanders, the Commune of Langemarck and the *Kriegsgräberfürsorge*. In a black tunnel which is precisely the same length as the mass grave in the cemetery there are maps, photos, documentation and 3 video screens briefly explaining a) The First Battle of Ypres; b) The Gas Attack of April 1915; c) The history of the Cemetery and the work of the **Kriegsgräberfürsorge.** Slits on the opposite side look across to the bunkers in the cemetery wall.

Sadly there were no German veterans present at the unveiling. The last German WW1 veteran, Charles Kuentz, who fought on the Eastern and Western Fronts, died in April 2005, aged 108. In 2004 he made a pilgrimage to Passchendaele where he met the British veteran, Harry Patch (qv), then 106. Harry presented Kuentz with a bottle of the specially created 'Patch's Pride Cider'.

On 5 May 2011 the last Allied combat veteran of the Great War, Charles ('Chuckles') Choules died, age 110, the oldest man then living in Australia. Born in Pershore, Worcs in 1901, Charles lied about his age and joined the Royal Navy in 1915. He went on to view two momentous events of WW1: the surrender of the Imperial German Navy at the Firth of Forth on 21 November 1918 and the scuttling of the German Fleet at Scapa Flow on 21 June 1919. Charles served with the Royal Australian Navy between the two wars and served as their senior Demolition Officer in Western Australia during WW2.

Free Wifi sign, Langemarck Cemetery Car Park

Blacksmiths' Peace Monument, Langemark, specially photographed by Paul Foster

Peace Monument, Langemark. During 1-6 September 2016 there was an international gathering of hundreds of blacksmiths and farriers in Ieper, who assembled a monumental sculpture representing Peace, known as the 'WW1 Cenotaph'. Funded by crowd-funding (£100,000 has already been raised) the steel plate was supplied by Sigma. Standing 7m tall and weighing 12 tonnes, it consists of a tall column surmounted by a large poppy, with 2,016 steel poppies (forged during the event in Ieper) at its base, surrounded by 25 forged railings with WW1 representations, laid out in jig-jag trench formation. On 5 November 2016 the Monument was inaugurated in its new site next to the Information Centre of Langemarck German Cemetery in the presence of ambassadors and dignitaries from around the world. It is hoped that young people will make it a meeting point of reconciliation and reflection, with a Peace Register to sign.

The Cemetery. This is now approached by passing through the building and walking along the Cemetery wall to the main entrance.

It is maintained by the *Volksbund Deutsche Kriegsgräberfürsorge* – the German People's Organisation for the Care of War Graves – and is the only German cemetery in the actual Salient. When the war was over the German dead were all amalgamated into four cemeteries – Langemarck, Menin, Vladslo and Hooglede. As the bodies were exhumed, all those that could be identified were reburied in marked graves, sometimes several inscribed on one tombstone to symbolize comradeship in death. The unknowns were buried in a mass grave. Most of the landscaping work was completed between 1970 and 1972, much of it by international students working voluntarily during their vacations, although detailed work at Langemarck was not completed until the late 1980s.

Langemarck is one of the largest German cemeteries in Belgium, with 44,292 bodies, and has an impressive entrance with two chambers, one with the names of the missing carved in oak, and the other bearing a relief map showing the past and present German cemeteries in Belgium and containing the Visitors' book and Cemetery Register. The cemetery is planted with oak trees, the symbol of German strength, and in the communal grave rest the remains of 25,000 soldiers – half of whose names are known. Around the mass grave are the Regimental insignia of the student brigades who fought in this area.

In December 2004 a small bronze **Plaque** was attached to the end of the left hand column surrounding the mass grave. It commemorates **Pte A. Carlill**, Loyal North Lancs, 4 November 1918 and **Pte L.H. Lockley**, Seaforth Highlanders, 30 October 1918, both now known to be buried in the mass grave. Their names were located on the bronze panels (to be found by searching alphabetically, noting that Lockley is listed as 'Lookley') by researchers Michel Vansuyt and Michel Van den Bogaert. Carlill, sometimes recorded as 'Carhill' was originally recorded by the CWGC as being buried in Louvain Communal Cemetery, German Plot, and listed on the Loos Memorial, while Lockley was listed in Jemappes Communal Cemetery.

Correspondence between the Imperial War Graves Commission and the *Volksbund Deutsche Kriegsgräberfürsorge* [VDK] in July 1956 records that when the grave marked 'Carhil, Albert 1/4 Loyal North Lancashire Regt + 4.11.1918' was opened during work on the German Plot in Louvain Cemetery it was discovered that 'the "underground situation" of the graves did not conform to the inscriptions over the graves' and that therefore 'it was not possible, even to the British cemetery caretaker, to establish which are the remains of Albert Carhil amongst the German unknown casualties…For the above reasons the remains of the British casualty had to be transferred together with the 45 unknown German casualties to the German Military Cemetery at Langemarck'. The VDK promised that the cemetery register would list his name after the cemetery was completed. In August 1956 the Assistant Secretary of the IWGC wrote to the District Officer in Brussels wondering how a casualty with a recorded grave at Louvain could also be commemorated on the Loos Memorial in France and whether 'an appropriate individual memorial should not be erected in one of our cemeteries (perhaps Cement House)' or whether 'the lapse of time does not warrant any further action'. In fact the idea was agreed and a letter of 14 September 1956 gave the wording for a Kipling Memorial to Carlill in Cement House and requested that his name should be added to that cemetery's register. (The letter also explained that he was listed on the Loos Memorial as he 'Died prisoner of war'). This was implemented and his presence here remained un-noticed, as did Lockley's, until the two Michels rediscovered them in their researches and the present small Plaque was erected. Once that was done Carlill's Kipling Memorial and his name in the Report was removed from Cement House at the beginning of 2006.

In the north wall of the Cemetery are the remains of some massive German block-houses.

This area was captured by the British 20th (Light) Division on 16 August during the Third Ypres offensive of 1917. It had been defended by the French in 1914 and lost on 22 April 1915 (Second Ypres) during the gas attack. In continuing operations in October 1917 the 4th Bn Worcester Regiment were ordered to push further north from here. On the evening of 7 October the battalion had marched out from Ypres following the route you have driven, turned right at Boezinghe and along the Pilckem Ridge via duckboards to the front line at the northern end of the cemetery. They were in position by dawn on 8 October and spent the day preparing for their assault. In the engagement that followed the next day a famous VC was won by Private Frederick George Dancox (qv) a solid old soldier who captured a pillbox (qv) about a mile away to the north-east, part of the same defensive line as those in the cemetery.

Adolf Hitler, who claimed to have fought at Langemarck in 1914, visited the cemetery on 1 June 1940, in recognition of the debt he believed that Germany owed to those who fell there, so re-inforcing the 'Langemarck Myth' (qv). He toured the whole area from Poperinge to Courtrai and was photographed by Hoffman his personal photographer.

In May 2011 a meticulously researched book was published containing many hitherto unpublished facts and illustrations, entitled *De Duitse Begraafplaats in Langemark* – the Cemetery then known as 'Langemarck-Nord'. It is a joint work by respected historians Horst Howe of the *Volksbund Deutsche Kriegsgräbefürsorge*, Robert Missinne, local teacher and webmaster of the superb www.greatwar.be site and Col (Retd) Roger Beke, all of whom have helped us with our researches. Although written in Dutch (with short summaries in English and French), it is easy to extract much of the fascinating information about the number and character of the dozens of small German cemeteries that were concentrated into those remaining in and near the Salient today. The development of today's Langemarck Cemetery is charted, with many interesting and often poignant illustrations. Distinctive individual grave markers (some remain in a corner of the Vladslo German Cemetery (qv)) were replaced by standard crosses and then by the flat stones we see today, interspersed with groups of symbolic black basalt crosses. There are many personal stories (with photos) of those buried here. Among them is German Ace **Lt Verner Voss**, whose name appears on Panel 63 by the mass or 'Comrades' grave.

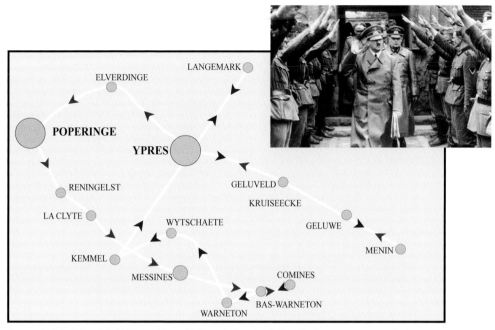

Route of Hitler's Battlefield Tour, 1 June 1940, and (inset) Adolf Hitler leaving Langemarck Cemetery

Voss, with 47 victories, was one of Germany's most charismatic 'Aces'. On 23 September 1917, commanding Jasta 10, he flew in the morning from Heule airfield (some dozen miles south-east of here) in his new Fokker FI 103/17, made another kill and, determined to increase his score to 50 before going on leave with his brothers Otto and Max, flew out again at 1806 hours in his triplane. Over the Frezenberg Ridge he ran into a group of seven experienced British pilots from No 26 Sqn RAF, led by the most-decorated member of the RFC, the famous Major James McCudden VC. After some incredible acrobatic evasion manoevres against the SE5s he was eventually shot and his plane brought down by A.P.F. Stuart-Wortley near 'Plum Farm' (50.87435 2.93927), Peperstraat [part of which has been renamed 'F. Nadarstraat'], St Julien. The British buried Voss in a mass grave near the site that was afterwards probably destroyed by subsequent fighting. McCudden commented, 'I shall never forget my admiration for that German pilot who single-handed fought seven of us for ten minutes and also put some bullets through our machines. His flying was wonderful, his courage magnificent and in my opinion he is the bravest German airman whom it has been my privilege to see fight.'

Detail of Mourning Soldiers

Mass Grave, Langemarck German Cemetery

Reverential re-interment of German Soldiers into Langemarck Cemetery Crypt

There is no real proof that there are any actual remains of Voss here in the Langemarck Comrades' Grave, but he is 'believed to be' buried here. The book is available from some local book and museum shops and directly from Robert (wo1@westhoek.be)

On 16 October 2015 an important ceremony took place to mark the **Re-opening of the renovated Cemetery**, now restored to its 1930s layout. The four impressive sculptures executed by Professor Emil Krieger have returned to their original place overlooking the mass grave. The ceremony featured the reverential **Burial of 10 German soldiers**, (all but one named) in the catacomb below the mass grave. The small cardboard coffins, draped with the German flag, were blessed and then passed down into the crypt by German soldiers. The German, Belgian, British and CWGC VIPs and dignitaries laid wreaths and bands and choirs (including local school children) played, sang and read poems. It was a memorable and moving occasion.

The entrance to the catacomb was resealed after the ceremony (it was below the Flandern Plaque) and the mass grave simply grassed over.

Return to your car, turn left out of the car park, continue to the Broenbeek and turn left along the north bank along Beekstraat. Stop on the right by a memorial and blockhouse.

Memorial to 34th Division & Bunker, Langemark

• 34th Division Memorial/Bunker/11.9 miles/5 minutes/Map C11, 10/ GPS: 50.92420 2.91335

The **Memorial to the Engineers and Royal Artillery of the 34th Division**, with its black and white checkerboard insignia, is in front of a large Bunker. The Bunker was captured in September 1918 and used as an ADS (Advanced Dressing Station) commanded by T. E. Lawrence's brother Robert. The 34th Division were in action here during the Battle of Passchendaele when on 22 October 1917 they attacked along the axis of the road you have driven up and then again in 1918. It was finally demobilised on 15 March 1919.

Continue some 0.2 miles further on and just past the first turning on the left a badly weathered stone memorial can be seen on the opposite bank of the Broenbeek.

• French Memorial/12.3 miles/5 minutes/Map C11a/GPS: 50.92471 2.90775

This is to **Emilien Girault and A. Malliavin** of the 2nd Chasseurs d'Afrique, killed in October 1917.

Memorial to E. Girault & A. Malliavin, Chasseurs d'Afrique, Langemark

Return to the main road.

Extra Visit to Pte Frederick Dancox, VC Memorial, Namur Crossing (Map D1a/GPS: 50.92747 2.93673).

Round trip: 2.00 miles. Approximate time: 15 minutes.

Turn left and continue some .7 mile to the small turning to the right along Klerkenstraat-Koekuitstraat by a 70km restriction sign. Continue some .6 mile, past a house on the right to the cycle path.

On 9 September 2006 a commemorative stainless steel Memorial Plaque to Dancox (qv) designed by Sam Eedle (ex-London Scottish) was unveiled by his grandson, also called Fred Dancox (whose son and grandson are also called 'Fred'). It was an initiative of the Worcestershire & Herefordshire WFA (notably Stephen Moorhouse), supported by the Dancox family, Worcester City Council, the Worcestershire Regt, the local commune and others. Representatives of all, including the authors, were present at the simple but moving inauguration ceremony at the 'Namur Crossing' on the disused railway line which is now a cycle path in the Langemark district of Madonna. The Memorial overlooks the site of the bunker – in a dip behind the bushy-topped tree – where Dancox's act of valour took place.

Inauguration of the Dancox VC Memorial, 9 September 2006. Members of his family and local dignitaries

Dancox had served with the 4th Bn, the Worcesters throughout the war. They assaulted near here at 0530 on 9 October 1917. *The Regimental History* tells us what happened:

'One of the concrete blockhouses in front of the line had not been struck by the shells, and its machine-gun swept the line of the labouring troops with burst after burst of fire. Officers and men were shot down or were driven to shelter in the shell-holes. Musketry was useless against the concrete walls, and messages were sent back for trench-mortars to deal with the blockhouse. But before the mortars could be brought up the fire of the machine-gun suddenly stopped. A minute later every man within sight was on his feet cheering and laughing, for stumbling through the mud towards the British line came a little crowd of enemy with hands raised in surrender, and behind them came a solitary British soldier, labouring along under the weight of a machine-gun – their machine-gun. The cheering grew as he was recognised: 'Dancox', the troops shouted, 'Good old Dancox!'

Return to the German Cemetery and pick up the main Itinerary.

Turn right and continue to the cross roads with traffic lights. Turn right and continue to the memorial on the right.

• *20th Light Division and Albertina Memorials/14.1 miles/10 minutes/ Map C12, 13/GPS: 50.90836 2.91564*

The Division was a New Army Division that had been formed in 1914 and arrived in France in 1915 where it fought at Loos and on the Somme. Here it was the 61st Bde of 20th Light Division that had the responsibility of taking Langemarck village. The divisional boundaries were the railway line and the Langemarck road (readily seen from the Battle Map) and the troops formed up on the night of 15 August 1917, in positions west of the Steenbeek. Engineers built bridges for the troops to cross over and the Brigade went in with the 7th KOYLI and 7th SLI leading. Blockhouses west of the village (probably part of the same set as those in the cemetery) held up the advance for a while and in clearing them Pte W. Edwards (qv) of the 7th KOYLI won the VC. Some 400 prisoners were taken, including the officer commanding the force that had held Langemarck. Following the successful attack the Army Commander, Gen Sir Hubert Gough, sent a message to the Division:

20th Light Division Memorial, Langemarck

'The Army Commander wishes to thank all ranks 20th Division for the part they have played in the Third Battle of Ypres. The Division may well be proud of the capture of Langemarck on August 16 ... '

A similar memorial on the Somme was so badly damaged that it was replaced in 1995 by a flat stone bearing only a bronze wreath (Somme Map Ref K33). Some 200yd along the road, on the Steenbeek, is an Albertina Memorial which marks the end of the Steenbeek Offensive on 28 September 1918.

Continue to the road junction ahead. Turn right and then right again along a track (just before the '100m/Cycle Path/Bend' sign) and continue to a rather difficult to spot low memorial to the left on the bank of the stream.

• *Memorial to Harry Patch, Steenbeek/14.6 miles/5 minutes/Map C14a/GPS: 50.90979 2.90864.*

In March 2008 the then-Poet Laureate Andrew Motion wrote a poem entitled, *The Five Acts of Harry Patch*, to honour Harry, the only surviving veteran of the Passchendaele battle and whose 110th birthday was on 17 June.

Later that year Harry decided to erect, at his own expense, this small Memorial. The inscription explains his desire:

> "Here at dawn on 16 August 1917 the 7th Bn DCLI 20th (Light) Division, crossed the Steenbeek prior to their successful assault on the village of Langemarck. This stone is erected to the memory of fallen comrades and to honour the courage, sacrifice and passing of The Great War Generation. It is the gift of former Private and Lewis Gunner, Harry Patch, No 29295, C Coy, 7th DCLI. The last surviving veteran to have served in the Trenches of the Western Front. September 2008."

Harry died on 25 July 2009, age 111 years, 1 month, 1 week, 1 day, then verified as the third oldest man in the world.

Return to the main road

The drive from here to Artillery Wood Cemetery is across the area captured by the Germans on 22 April 1915, as a result of the chlorine gas attack which drove the frightened French Colonial troops before it. You are travelling in the same direction as the gas cloud.

Continue to the cemetery on the left.

Harry Patch at the unveiling of 'his' Memorial at the Steenbeek, September 2008, with the Col and members of his Regt, now the 5th Bn, The Rifles

Harry Patch's Memorial, the Steenbeek & Langemarck Church beyond

Information Board with Photo of Harry Patch, Steenbeek

• *Cement House CWGC Cemetery/15.1 miles/10 minutes/Map C14/ GPS: 50.90500 2.90700*

Named after a fortified farm building which once stood nearby, the Cemetery was begun in August 1917 during Third Ypres for 231 soldiers of the UK, Newfoundland, Canada and Guernsey. These were later added to when burials from a small cemetery at Maisières (near Mons) were re-interred here, including **Capt J. E. Knowles** of the Middlesex Regt, one of the earliest casualties of the war, killed on **23 August 1914**. After the Armistice the Cemetery, designed by Sir Reginald Blomfield, was enlarged with remains from many small cemeteries in the vicinity. In March 2007 re-interments were made of soldiers discovered during the Boesinge archaelogical dig (qv). Today there are 3,592 burials here, 2,425 of them Unidentified. There are also 22 WWW2 burials.

Immediately after the Cemetery the spires of Ypres can be seen to the left. To their right, on the horizon, is Mont Kemmel.

Continue to the next small crossroads known as Iron Cross (Hagebos).

Extra Visit No 1 to Plaque to Pte Thomas Whitham, VC/GPS: 50.907222 2.899444

Round Trip: .75 miles Approx time: 15 minutes

Turn right onto Groenestraat and continue some 400yd later. Park and walk some 150 yd up the track signed Torhout/netwok of railways etc. to the Plaque to your left.

The VC's Plaque is situated overlooking the site where, on 31 July 1917, Pte Whitham of the 1st Bn, Coldstream Guards worked his way from shell hole to shell hole through our own barrage to rush an enemy machine gun which was enfilading the Battalion. He captured it, with its officer and two men, thus saving many lives and enabling the whole line to advance.

The Plaque, inaugurated on 12 September 2015 in a ceremony attended by some 100 people, was the initiative of the school named after Whitham and researcher Brian Hirst who located the site. The £2,000 required was raised by the school, the local E Lancs WFA Branch, the Whitham family and friends and supported by Langemarck Council. It contains interesting information, map and portrait.

Return to the main Itinerary.

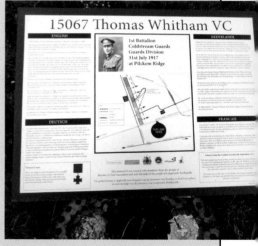

Plaque to Pte Whitham VC, Pilckem Ridge

Extra Visit No 2 to 38th (Welsh) Division Memorial, Gournier Farm Bunker, Map H38, 37/GPS: 50.89140 2.90427 & Minty Farm CWGC Cemetery, Map H39/GPS: 50.89063 2.90959.

Round trip: 3.5 miles. Approximate time: 25 minutes

Turn left (south) at the crossroads onto Groenestraat and then right at the T junction on Ieperstraat. (Note this junction).

To the left as you drive a large new pipeline was laid in 2016. During its construction, tons of 'Iron Harvest' were found and taken away for safe explosion by the Belgian military. The remains of several WW1 soldiers were also discovered and taken for examination for any DNA identification possibilities.

Continue 1 mile to the bunker on the right.

Gournier (often mis-spelled as Goumier, much as Pointe du Hoc was mis-spelt as Pointe du Hoe on Allied maps in the Normandy campaign and the mistake was perpetuated) Farm is to the right. Beside it is a large bunker with a **Memorial Plaque to the 38th Welsh Division**. This can be well-hidden at certain times of year by tall crops and tends to be overgrown. Permission from the farmer should be sought to visit the bunker, and enter it. The farm was in the area of 51st Division, rather than that of the 38th. It is said that the Plaque was placed by the local farmer. However, during the Welsh attack on the Pilckem Ridge on 31 July 1917, they met much resistance from the area of Rudolphe Farm (at the T junction below Iron Cross, Map C9). A platoon of the 15th Welsh was sent to help to deal with the enemy despite the fact that the farm was in the 51st Division area. It is likely that Gournier Farm – which is on the same road – was also involved and hence, perhaps, the Plaque. The blockhouse changed hands many times in the bitter fighting of end July 1917, and bears signs of strengthening by the Royal Engineers who built new walls to safeguard the rear entrance. The 51st Highland Division attacked in this area, and the garrison around this farm caused heavy casualties to the 6th Black Watch before they eventually captured it, taking two machine guns, a field gun and twenty prisoners. Then this battalion, together with soldiers of the 5th Gordons and a platoon of the 15th Welsh Regiment, took the nearby blockhouses at Rudolphe and François Farms.

Continue to the next junction and turn left and then turn left at the next T Junction. Continue for about half a mile.

Minty Farm CWGC Cemetery is up a track to the left just before the brick electricity station.

On 31 July 1917, the 6th Gordons took this fortified farm, used by the Germans as a blockhouse, within the first half hour of their attack. C Company advanced through it to within 250yd of the Steenbeek and dug in. Their company commander, Capt Hutcheson, noticed some enemy observation planes flying over their positions and when the planes had disappeared moved his forward position 100yd on and his rear 100 yards back. Soon the enemy artillery rained a heavy bombardment on the original position! The Gordons were then fired upon from across the stream by enemy machine-gun fire. **Pte George Macintosh** took off alone with revolver and 'bombs, rushed the machine-gun emplacement, killed two Germans and wounded one and hauled the machine guns back to his trench'. For this act of heroism and initiative he was awarded the **Victoria Cross.** Company headquarters was set up in Minty (then known as Minty's, a name probably adopted by the Wiltshires) Farm. The Cemetery, begun in October 1917, contains 188 UK, 4 unknown and 1 German burial. It was designed by W.H. Cowlishaw. One-third of them are of the RA.

Return to the previously Noted Junction.

N.B. Memorial to Crash Site of Flying Fortress, 08 February 1945. GPS: 50.90062 2.90859.

Continue straight on for some 200 yd to a small track to the right.

The Memorial commemorates **Flying Fortress B17 G** ('Lonesome Polecats') **8th USAAF, 457 Bomb Group** which left Glatton in the UK for bombing raid No 182 on Berlin on 3 February 1945. Miraculously, when the plane crashed here – on the farm of M Frans Deraedt - on its way back to Glatton, although the plane was a write-off, all the crew (including Pilot Lt Craig Greason and navigator Rudolph (Rudy) Haumann) survived. They returned to Glatton via Ypres and Merville, France.

For more information, see www.457thbombgroup.org/narratives/MA182.html

On 4 September 2001 a splendid commemoration took place here, attended by Rudy Haumann and his wife.

Memorial to Crash of B17G on 3 February 1945, Pilckem

Unveiling of Memorial to B17G. From l to r: Freddy Leclerk, Master of Ceremonies; Unknown; Dirk Decaeve, Alderman in 1945; Alain Weiffels, Burgomaster; Rudy Haumann, Navigator; Renaat Landuyt, Minister of Tourism

Return to Iron Cross and rejoin the main itinerary.

Stop immediately by the building on the left.

• *Hedd Wyn Memorials, Hagebos (Iron Cross)/15.4 miles/10 minutes/ Map C9/GPS: 50.90328 2.90097*

A Welsh slate Plaque (written in Welsh, Flemish and English) on the building at Hagebos crossroads marks the site of the first aid post where the Welsh poet, **Pte Ellis Humphrey Evans (Bardic pseudonym 'Hedd Wyn')** died on 31 July 1917. Below it is a photograph of Hedd Wyn and a black marble Plaque erected in 2011, with a version of B. Harris's poem, *In Passing*:

'To be born Welsh
Is to be born privileged.
Not with a silver spoon in your mouth,
But music in your blood
And poetry in your soul.

To the right is one of Hedd Wyn's poems in Welsh and a recent modern mural.

Born in the village of Trawsfynydd on 13 January 1887, this simple shepherd had always loved and written poetry, and won six bardic chairs before he joined the 15th Bn (the London Welsh) RWF in January 1917. He had been writing a long, bardic poem called *Yr Arwr ('The Hero')* since 1916 and was still working on it when the battalion arrived in France in mid July 1917. He posted it to enter the National Eisteddfod in Birkenhead under the pseudonym *Fleur de Lys*.

Hedd Wyn is on the Writers' Path (qv). His battalion was part of the 38th (Welsh) Division chosen to lead the attack on the Pilckem Ridge and Langemarck. It was seen as a chance to vindicate the unjustified poor reputation the Division had gained for their supposed tardiness in taking Mametz Wood on the Somme in July 1916.

Plaques to Hedd Wyn, Iron Cross

The Division was withdrawn from the line in June 1917 to St Hilaire to train for the battle. A replica of the trenches and strong points to be attacked was laid out and the brigades practiced their respective roles. They also practised machine-gun barrage. On 19/20 July the Division returned to the line to be subjected to heavy shellfire and attacks by the new and deadly mustard gas. On 27 July aeroplane reconnaissances reported that the Germans had evacuated their trenches and patrols were sent forward to check on the information. They discovered that the second line system was still strongly held. On the night of 30 July the Division went into their assembly positions. Their objectives were the village of Pilckem, the Pilckem Ridge to half-way between the village and the Steenbeek and finally the Steenbeek and its crossing (see the Battle Map).

As at Vimy, the objectives were denoted by coloured lines: Blue, Black and Green. At 0350 hours the 10th Welsh on the right, the 13th in the right centre, the 13th RWF in the left centre and the 16th RWF on the left moved forward. The Blue and Black lines were taken, but there was strong resistance on the Green Line at Rudolphe Farm (at the T junction just below Iron Cross, Map C9) and the 15th Welsh Regt were detailed to attack here. Near Iron Cross was a German RHQ and telephone exchange and some blockhouses which were strongly defended, leading to many casualties amongst the 14th Welsh Regiment. Many prisoners,

Modern Hedd Wyn Mural, Iron Cross

including 500 members of the Berlin Cockchafer (Guard Fusilier Regiment), were taken, but the 15th RWF lost every officer in the attack and Pte Evans was wounded in the chest by shrapnel from a shell. Welsh was his first language, the language of his poetry, but Hedd Wyn's last words, 'I am very happy', were spoken in English. He would have been happier had he lived to know that the name *Fleur de Lys* was called as the winner of the Bardic Chair at the Eisteddfod on 6 September. When it was discovered that the winner had been killed a few weeks before in Belgium, the bardic chair, ironically carved by a Belgian refugee, was blackened in mourning for him. Hedd Wyn would, thenceforward, always be known as 'the Black Bard'. He is buried in Artillery Wood CWGC Cemetery (see below).

Eventually all objectives were carried, but with heavy losses. On 26 November 1919, Field Marshal Sir Douglas Haig wrote, 'I do not think there is any Division which fought under my command in France which cannot point to at least one occasion when its actions reached the highest level of soldierly achievement ... One is the attack north of Ypres on the 31st July, 1917, when the 38th (Welsh) Division met and broke to pieces a German Guards Division.' Honour was restored.

Three Welsh VCs were won in the action: **Cpl James Lewellyn Davis**, 13th Bn RWF (buried in Canada Farm CWGC Cemetery); **Sgt Ivor Rees**, 11th SWB (survived); **Sgt Robert James Bye**, 1st Bn Welsh Guards (survived).

Continue some 100 yd and stop in the car park on the left.

•*Welsh National Memorial/15.5 miles/15 minutes/Map C9/GPS: 50.9029 2.90000*

This fine **Memorial** is not only to the 38th Welsh, but (as with the Scottish Memorial at Frezenburg), to all Welsh Forces who made the ultimate sacrifice during WW1 in the Salient.

Instigators of the Dragon, l to r, Mario Liva, Marc Decaestecker (the authors) and Erwin Ureel

As at Mametz it takes the form of a Welsh Dragon, but this time in bronze on a plinth made of blue Belgian limestone. It has been erected on land near the building which bears the Hedd Wyn Plaques and required some £44,000.

The idea was proposed by dedicated enthusiast **Marc Decaestecker,** owner of the Feestzaal Caracas and Sportsman Pub (Tel: + (0) 57 48 82 14) opposite, where he always has an interesting Welsh display, and his brother-in-law **Mario Liva**. Mario is a stone mason and made the Plaque opposite the restaurant. They are great supporters of the Welsh and on the first Monday of each month they raise the Welsh flag and hold a commemorative event with the Last Post being played. They have strong ties with various Welsh organisations who supported the project and with the Passchendaele Society. The main Belgian supporter was **Erwin Urweel**, Belgian co-ordinator (qv), and the Welsh Co-ordinator was **Peter Carter Jones**, supported by many Welsh official organisations and the Mayor of Langemark-Poelkapelle (who provided the ground). In 2013 the stones for the cromlech which supports the Dragon were provided by the Craig yr Hesq Quarry, Pontypridd. The chosen designer was Lee Odishaw (originally from Tenby). The bronze dragon was cast at Castle Fine Art Foundry, Llanrhaedt ym Mochnant in June 2014. The sculptor is Lee Odishaw.

The memorable and moving inauguration ceremony was held on 16 August 2014. Present were many Welsh, Belgian and British dignitaries and supporters, Welsh choirs, musicians, poets and local bands.

Now the site is surrounded by a pleasant **Memorial Garden,** maintained by local enthusiasts who fundraise by organising concerts etc. It contains a CWGC headstone, a wrought iron seat and detailed Information board. In the springtime 'a host of golden daffodils' erupts in the Memorial Park – one for every ten Welsh soldiers killed in the Great War.

The road you are travelling runs along the Pilckem Ridge.

Continue to the crossroads by the large buildings and turn right along Pozelstraat following signs right to Artillery Wood Cemetery to the memorial on the left.

• *Francis Ledwidge Memorial/16.7 miles/5 minutes/Map C5a/GPS: 50.89790 2.87396*

The enclosed Memorial with an Information Board beside it bears a photo of the poet and lines from his poem *Soliloquy*. Beside it the Irish flag flies and behind that an apple tree was planted in his memory on 27 March 2010. The signed 'Ledwidge Path' (on 'The Writers' Path') runs along the old railway line behind. Son of an Irish tenant farmer, the young Ledwidge was very early aware of the social and political problems in his country, and joined both his local Farmers Union and the Nationalist Irish Volunteers. As the First World War loomed the Volunteers were split about whether to support the hated British and Ledwidge was not popular when he joined the 5th Bn The Inniskilling Fusiliers in October 1914 and served in Gallipoli. Throughout all this time he had been writing poetry and he was published by Edward Marsh (qv) in 1915. L/Cpl Ledwidge was thought by many to have been a talent equal to the best. This Memorial is on the 'Writers' Path' (qv).

Beyond the Memorial on the right is a multilingual audio information machine.

Continue to the cemetery on the left.

Memorial to Irish Poet, Francis Ledwidge, Artillery Wood

• *Artillery Wood CWGC Cemetery/16.9 miles/10 minutes/Map C4/ GPS: 50.89967 2.87256*

The Wood was captured by the Guards Division during the Battle of Pilckem Ridge on 31 July 1917. The Cemetery was begun by the division after the battle and used as a front line cemetery until March 1918. After the Armistice it was greatly enlarged and now contains 1,243 UK, 5 Australian, 30 Canadian, 10 Newfoundland, 2 New Zealand, 1 South African and 510 unknown burials with 12 Special Memorials. It was designed by Sir Reginald Blomfield.

Headstone of Hedd Wyn (Pte Ellis Humphrey Evans), Artillery Wood CWGC Cemetery

In it are buried two of the war's most lyrical Celtic poets – **Ellis Humphrey Evans ('Hedd Wyn'** – see 'Iron Cross' above) and the Irish poet, **Francis Ledwidge**, both headstones bearing the date 31 July 1917. In fact it is believed that, although he was wounded on 31 July, Evans did not die until 4 August. His grave bears the inscription 'Yr Prfardd Hedd Wyn' (The Chief Bard). Hedd Wyn means 'Blessed Peace'.

Ledwidge was born on 19 August 1887, in Slane, County Meath. A maverick who flitted from job to job, Ledwidge was fascinated by Celtic folklore and myths and had a burning desire to write himself. His youthful work was seen by Lord Dunsany who became his patron. Although he joined the Irish Volunteers in the Spring of 1914, Dunsany persuaded him to join the 5th Bn the Royal Inniskilling Fusiliers in October. Ledwidge served in Gallipoli and Salonika before returning to the Western Front in December 1916 with the 1st Bn, eventually arriving in the Salient in June 1917. He was hit by a shell while laying duckboards over the muddy battlefield of the Pilckem Ridge and killed instantly. Francis Ledwidge had continued to write his delightful verses throughout his service, often in the most appalling conditions. The anthology, *Songs of the Field*, was published in 1915 to great critical acclaim, and Lord Dunsany believed he would 'have surpassed even Burns' had he lived. In *Soliloquy*, Ledwidge maintained,

> A keen-edged sword, a soldier's heart,
> Is greater than a poet's art.
> And greater than a poet's fame
> A little grave that has no name.

The last, uncomfortable, line of this poem, 'Whence honour turns away in shame', has been omitted in most anthologies. In 2016 much work was done by the CWGC to restore the entry porch.

Extra Visit to Ziegler Bunker/Map C3/GPS: 50.91013 2.87062

Round-trip: 3.3 miles. Approximate time: 10 minutes
The number of bunkers in the Salient is dwindling, which makes the remaining examples of even more interest.

> *Continue along the road to the T junction and follow the road to the right. Turn right at the next crossroads onto Sasstraat. Take the next right - easily missed - along Slaaktestraat (ignoring any 'dead end' sign). Continue to the bunker on the right.*

The important, two-storey Ziegler bunker, named after its engineer and constructed by the German Marine Corps, is in the field to the right. Because of its shape it is also known

The Ziegler Bunker

as the 'Viking Ship'. The pill box was captured by the French in July 1917 and it fell to the 554th Royal Engineers to convert it to Allied use. This consisted of virtually 'turning' the blockhouse, so that the entrance was shielded from German fire. So thick was the bunker, with its walls reinforced by steel rods, that they had to use high explosive to blow a doorway. There are more bunkers in the area. See the Battle Map C1, 2.

Return to the cemetery and rejoin the main itinerary.

Return to the crossroads. Stop at the memorial on the right.

• Breton Memorial, Carrefour de la Rose (Rose Crossroads)/17.1 miles/5 minutes/Map C5/GPS: 50.89724 2.87429

This Breton dolmen orientation table (which bears the French ORBAT of 22 April) and calvary are Memorials to the French 45th and 87th Divisions who were here during the gas attack of April 1915. The authentic Breton Calvary was brought here from Plouagat and the cromlech, weighing some eight tons, came from Henanhihen. On four of the eight great stones, also originating in Brittany, are carved the names of the regiments that fought here. The Breton soldiers in this area were older reservists, brought in to support the Belgians (much like the German 'Ear, Nose and Throat' soldiers of Army Group West garrisoning the coast line in Normandy in 1944). Nicknamed 'Les Pépères' (the Grand-dads), they expected a quiet life but were thrust into the horror of the gas attack and the subsequent carnage. After the war Boezinge became a place of regular pilgrimage for the Bretons and their families, hence this important Memorial.

Memorial to the French 45th and 87th Divisions, Carrefour de la Rose

Extra Visit to Ypres Salient Entry Point North, Klein Zwaanhof (Map H24a, GPS: 50.88944 2.87702)/Colne Valley CWGC Cemetery, (Map H24, GPS: 50.88468 2.87835)/Boezinge Archaeological Battlefield Site, Yorkshire Trench (Map H4a, GPS: 50.88778 2.87403).

Round trip: 4.5 miles. Approximate time: I hour.

Continue straight over the crossroads on Kleiner Poezelstraat following a group of green CWGC signs.

Pass a sign to Dragoon Camp Cemetery to the left up a small path.

[This is in the area captured by the 38th (Welsh) Division in July 1917 and contains 66 graves].

Continue to the first turn left onto Moortelweg.

[**N.B. The Welsh (Caesar's Nose) CWGC Cemetery (Map H25, GPS : 50.88666 2.88218). NOTE: By taking this N.B. you will miss the visits to Entry Point North and Colne Valley Cemetery.** To take it, turn left on Moortelweg and you will come to a pathway on the right. This is signed as a private road and normally there is a large descriptive sign at the turning and there is a wide CWGC grass verge to the right which goes as far as the final narrow grass path to the right to the Cemetery. On the site of 'Fortin 17' (qv), the Cemetery was begun in July 1917 by the 38th (Welsh) Division and it was used until November 1918. Its name derived from the sharp bend in a 1915 Front Line trench which was thought to resemble the shape of a Roman nose, which took it within 50 yards of the German Front Line. In it lie 23 men of the division, out of a total of 68 burials, mostly from the beginning of 3rd Ypres. The Cemetery was designed by A.J.S. Hutton. It is included in the walking tour which starts at Entry Point North (see below).

To rejoin the Extra Visit you will now have to continue to the crossroads with Pilckemseweg, turn right and rejoin it at the junction with Zwaanhofweg to the right.

Welsh (Caesar's Nose) CWGC Cemetery in the middle of a field, Boezinge

Continue to the farm building at No 6 with banners proclaiming

'**Entry Point North'.** This covers 'Fighting for every metre of high ground', the circular **walking tour** which follows the front line of 1915-17. It is marked with informative elm Remembrance Trees (qv). It begins here at the old Klein Zwaanhof (Little Swan Farm) and the unmanned information centre is **open:** 01/14-15/11 1000-1745; 16/11-31/03 1000-1645. There is an excellent introductory film, a reconstructed German bunker, Fortin 17 (qv), powerful images and exhibits.

Exterior, Entry Point North, Klein Zwaanhof

Continue to

Colne Valley CWGC Cemetery. It faces Colne Valley and contains 47 British soldiers, unusually many of them with no personal message. To the right of the Cemetery on facing it ran White Trench, the extension of Yorkshire Trench. [The Cemetery is on the walking tour which also follows the **'Writers' Path'**, tracing the sites where Ernst Jünger, Liam O'Flaherty, Hedd Wyn (qv), Francis Ledwidge (qv), David Jones and Edmund Blunden (qv) fought. It then visits Yorkshire trench (see below) before returning to Klein Zwaanhof].

The Cemetery suffered severe flooding in recent years as the development of the nearby industrial area raised the level of the ground around it. The Cemetery was occasionally completely under water and the tool shed washed away. Major reconstruction work was carried out in the winter of 2015/2016 to raise the level of the Cemetery itself, incorporating as many original elements as possible. It was a monumental task which epitomises the extent to which the Commission goes to maintain these precious Cemeteries. All headstones, the Cross and all structural features had to be dismantled and then re-assembled – stonework, brickwork, replanting to the original layout...

Colne Valley CWGC Cemetery under water

The reconstructed Colne Valley CWGC Cemetery

The Commission spent £150,000 on the project and the City of Ieper supplied a pumping station.

Continue, following the one-way system to the junction with Pilckemseweg. Turn right and continue to the junction with Zwaanhofweg. Turn right and continue to the 'T' junction with Oostkaai. Turn right and continue to the Biovita buildings with flags. Turn right on Bargiestraat and follow the road to the left to the site. It should be well-signed.

The 'Yorkshire Trench' site was first explored by the 'Diggers' in February 1992, but mostly excavated between 1998-2000, of an important trench and dugout system. The incredibly well-preserved 'A' frames and other original elements discovered in the retentive Flanders blue clay mud have been incorporated in a representation of the system in the In Flanders Fields Museum. At the site itself the Town of Ieper recreated the trench and entrance to the dugout, with realistic looking A-frames, duckboards and sandbags, and explanatory boards, inaugurated in May 2003. The duckboard path follows the trenchline alongside.

Return to Ooskaai, turn right, continue to Langemarkseweg, turn left and pick up the main itinerary.

Yorkshire Trench, Boezinge

Continue over the Ypres/Ijser Canal and the dual carriageway. Go into Boezinge.

This was the limit of the April 1915 gas cloud as it moved southwest.

Stop before the T junction.

• *Demarcation Stone, 'Little Bertha' Mortar, Boezinge/17.9 miles/5 minutes/Map H4/GPS: 50.89366 2.85926*

Facing you at the T junction, slightly to the right on the opposite side of the road, is a Demarcation Stone (qv) with a Belgian helmet. This is one of the best preserved of the remaining twelve in the Salient erected by the Ypres League. During World War II the Germans erased the words which had been on the stones, 'Here the Invader was brought to a standstill 1918'. Behind the privet hedge to the rear of the Demarcation Stone is an ivy-covered blockhouse, bearing a Plaque erected on 27 May 1967, commemorating the 1915 German gas attack. It is surmounted by a German mortar with the caption 'Klene Berta'.

Turn right at the T junction and continue through Boezinge, direction Veurne, to the N369 dual carriageway. Turn left direction Diksmuide and continue to a large cross on the left just before the Ieperlee stream. Stop.

Klene Berta Mortar,
Boezinge

• 1st Victims of Gas Memorial, Steenstraat/19.8 miles/5 minutes/Map B6/GPS: 50.91816 2.84107

This 15m-high Cross of Reconciliation commemorates the victims of the 22 April 1915 gas attack. It replaces the original 1929 memorial, erected through the efforts of the French 418th Infantry Regiment, which was blown up by the Germans on 8 May 1941 as they objected to the word 'barbarians'. The original memorial was sculpted by the famous sculptor Real del Sartre and showed a dramatic *bas relief* of soldiers suffering from gas standing in front of a cross. The present cross was erected by French and Belgians in 1961 in a desire for peace and reconciliation in the world. It was designed by the architects Paul Tournon and Pierre Devillers and is reminiscent of the De Gaulle Cross at Courseulles in Normandy. It bears the ORBAT of the French regiments involved. Note the *Lampe de Fraternité* in a small alcove on the base of the memorial, which resembles the Toc H lamp.

Memorial to the First Victims of Gas, Steenstraat

NOTE: At this stage the **Long Extra Visit** to the Belgian Cemetery at Houthulst; Diksmuide: the Trenches of Death and the Ijzer Tower; and an optional visit to Vladslo German Cemetery, may be made. See page 279.

> *Otherwise turn immediately left past the memorial onto Grenadierstraat and continue to the obelisk on the left.*

• Memorial to the Belgian Grenadiers/20.2 miles/5 minutes/MapB3/GPS: 50.92145 2.83514

This Memorial to the unyielding resistance of the Grenadiers killed in the gas attack of 22 April 1915, was unveiled by King Leopold III on 22 April 1934. In each corner of the enclosure is a 'Christmas tree' type fir, the Grenadiers cypher. A Plaque commemorates the **last Belgian War Veteran, Grenadier, Paul Oogher**, 17.05.1899 – 08.09.2001.

> *Continue to the crossroads. Turn left onto Gen Lotzstraat. Enter Zuidschote and continue to*

Memorial to Belgian Grenadiers,

• Carabiniers Plaque/20.7 miles/Map B4/GPS: 50.91633 2.83660

On house No 15, to the right near the crossroads, is a Memorial Plaque to the Carabiniers who withstood the gas attack of April 1915 erected by the 2nd and 4th Carabiniers Old Comrades.

Plaque to 2nd & 4th Belgian Carabiniers, Gen Lotz Street

Jan Derynck and part of his WW1 Collection, Lizerne

N.B. On the left at the corner of the crossroads is a house named LIZERNE at 69 Steenstraat. The windows are full of the most interesting WW1 items – trench art, maquettes, ephemera… They are part of the ongoing collection of Jan Derynck, whose grandfather fought in what was then known as 'The Battle of Lizerne' (not Steenstraat) and who is passionate about perpetuating the memory of this battle.
    Tel: 0032 495184513. janderynck8904@gmail.be

Continue over the crossroads.

• *Demarcation Stone/20.7 miles/Map B5/GPS: 50.91550 2.83733*

On the RH corner of the crossroads is the well-preserved Zuidschote Demarcation Stone.

Continue in the direction of Boezinge, to the main road and turn right along the dual carriageway, direction Ieper.

As you leave the village note how low and wet the ground is to your left. The trees on the bank indicate the course of the canal which for most of the war faced the German front line to the east. The banks were all fortified and concrete bunkers can be seen from time to time.

Continue past the turnings to Boezinge and note the green CWGC sign leading up a path to the right to

• *Talana Farm CWGC Cemetery/23.4 miles/Map H5/GPS: 50.88367 2.86610*

Used by both the French Colonials, the Zouaves (in April and May 1915) and the British (from June to December 1915 and again in autumn 1917) it contains 529 UK burials, 14 unknowns and 10 Special Memorials. The farm was obviously named by Boer War veterans after the 20 October 1899 Battle of Talana Hill. Nearby were other South African names for farms - Modder, Magenta, Colenso and Tugela. It was designed by Sir Reginald Blomfield.

Continue. On the right is

• Bard Cottage CWGC Cemetery/24.00 miles/Map H6/GPS: 50.87664 2.86906

This was begun by the 49th and other infantry divisions in June 1915. It contains 1,616 UK, 3 British West Indies, 9 Canadian, 6 Newfoundland, 2 South Africans and 3 German burials, with 3 Special Memorials. Bard Cottage was a small house near Bard's Causeway bridge over the Canal. The Cemetery was designed by Sir Reginald Blomfield.

> *Continue. On the left, before the road goes under the bridge which carries the Ypres ring road, is Essex Farm Cemetery. Pull over and stop.*

• Essex Farm CWGC Cemetery/Albertina Memorial/Dressing Station/49th (West Riding) Division Memorial/24.6 miles/20 minutes/ Map H9, 8, 7, 10/GPS: 50.87109 2.87276

Outside the Cemetery is an Albertina Memorial to the poet **John McCrae** (qv), unveiled on 15 November 1985 by the Governor of West Flanders and executed by the sculptor Pieter-Hein Boudens of Bruges. Unlike the other Albertina Memorials (qv), McCrae's bears a poppy instead of King Albert's Royal Cipher. To the left of the Cemetery is a commercial building and behind it some concrete dugouts. Between 1915 and 1917 these were used as a dressing station. The path to the canal leads to the site of the notorious 'Bridge 4'. Third Ypres casualties from the 51st (Highland) and 38th (Welsh) Divisions were treated here. A typically busy scene is encapsulated in a sketch done on 31 July 1917, by the 51st Division's official artist, Fred A. Farrell, who followed them through the Somme and the Salient. It shows an ambulance car crossing the bridge, with the dressing station bunkers to the left.

Canadian Medical Officer Colonel John McCrae, who had served with the Artillery in the Boer War, had written what is perhaps the war's best-known poem, *In Flanders Fields*, when he served in what was then a simple earthen dugout dressing station in the spring of 1915. On 24 April McCrae wrote home with one of the most vivid and moving accounts of the Second Battle of Ypres. He saw the 'asphyxiated French soldiers' and streams of civilian refugees – 'the very picture of debacle'. Afterwards, he wrote, 'For 36 hours we had not an infantryman between us and the Germans and this gap was 1,200 to 1,500 yards wide. God knows why the G[ermans] did not put in a big force to eat us up. We really expected to die.'

By 25 April the Canadians had lost 6,000 of their strength of 10,000. The shelling was unremitting and the small Cemetery beside the dressing station grew daily. On 2 May, one of McCrae's patients and a friend, **Lt Alexis Helmer,** was virtually blown to pieces by a direct hit by an 8in shell. McCrae was touched by the last words in Helmer's diary, 'It has quieted a little and I shall try to get a good sleep'. McCrae said the committal service over Helmer's body. 'A soldier's death,' he commented. A wooden cross was put over Helmer's grave and the Colonel was moved to write his famous lines,

> In Flanders fields the poppies blow
> Between the crosses, row on row,
> That mark our place and in the sky
> The larks, still bravely singing, fly
> Scarce heard amid the guns below.
> We are the Dead. Short days ago
> We lived, felt dawn, saw sunset glow,
> Loved and were loved, and now we lie,
> In Flanders fields.

> Take up our quarrel with the foe:
> To you from failing hands we throw
> The torch; be yours to hold it high.
> If ye break faith with us who die
> We shall not sleep, though poppies grow
> In Flanders fields.

The poem was published in *Punch* on 8 December 1915, and became an instant popular success. In 1918 Moira Michael, who worked with the YMCA in America, wrote a poem in response called *We shall keep the faith* and in it exhorted all who read it to wear a poppy 'in honour of our dead'.

The French Secretary of the YMCA, Mme Guérin, then had the idea of selling artificial poppies to raise funds for soldiers and their families. As a result the symbol of the poppy was taken by Earl Haig for the newly formed British Legion to represent remembrance of those who gave their lives in the Great War (and later subsequent conflicts) and as a means of raising money. The first 'Poppy Day' was held on 11 November 1921. 'Flanders Field' was chosen for the name of the American WW1 Cemetery in Belgium and 'In Flanders Fields' as the name of the major WW1 museum in Ieper.

Helmer's grave was lost in the subsequent fighting over the ground and he is commemorated on the Menin Gate.

In the early spring of 1995 extensive restoration began in the concrete bunkers of the dressing station at the joint initiative of the Ieper Town Council, Talbot House and local school children. It was completed in time for the eightieth anniversary of the writing of McCrae's poem on 3 May 1995, when an impressive ceremony was held.

Now the various chambers which housed the Officers' Mess, the wards for walking cases and stretcher cases, the latrines, the mess kitchen, the area for the wounded to be evacuated, the stores and offices – all built in 1916/17 - can once again clearly be seen. At the entrance are bronze plaques placed by the Historic Sites & Monuments Board of Canada with a brief summary of McCrae's career and his famous poem.

The sheer volume of visitors to this site was overwhelming it and in Spring 2003 extensive landscaping was undertaken, leading visitors on gravel paths to the 49th Div Memorial and to the canal bank, with Information Boards along the way.

The Cemetery contains 1,088 UK, 9 Canadian, 102 Unknown, 5 German prisoners and 19 Special Memorials. They include **15-year-old Private V. J. Strudwick** of 8th Bn the Rifle Brigade, killed on 14 January 1916, and **Pte Thomas Barratt, VC**, of the 7th Bn the S Staffs Regt who on 27 July 1917, acted as the scout to a successful patrol, killing two German snipers and covering the patrol's withdrawal, but was killed by a shell on his return. Also buried here is **Lt Frederick Leopold Pusch, DSO**, of the 1st Bn Irish Guards, age 20, killed on 27 June 1916. A silver memorial cup, inscribed to Lt Pusch - 'M. H. 1908-1910', was found by the authors in the shop at Delville Wood Museum on the Somme. His 19-year-old brother, 2nd Lt E. J. Pusch of the 11th Bn the Royal Warwickshires, was killed on 19 August 1916, and is buried in Flatiron Copse CWGC Cemetery on the Somme. **Lt Donald Campbell** of the Coldstream Guards, killed on 19 July 1916, and buried here is the son of Capt the Hon John B. Campbell, DSO, age 48, of the same regiment, who had been killed on 25 January 1915, and is commemorated on the Le Touret Memorial.

Behind the Cemetery on the canal bank is the *Memorial column to the 49th (West Riding) Division.* The 49th, a territorial division, came out early in 1915. It had the dubious distinctions of being, together with 6th Division, one of the first to face a phosgene attack when the two divisions suffered over 1,000 casualties from the gas alone and in the winter of 1915 having more than 400 cases of trench foot in just one battalion. Trench foot was the result of prolonged standing in water in flooded trenches. The feet swelled to football-sized proportions and became painfully sensitive to the extent that the sufferer found it virtually impossible to walk and hence became unfit for duty. The Memorial was inaugurated in 1924.

Walk to the canal bank.

The front lines between here and Ypres ran roughly parallel to, and beyond, the canal and at slightly varying distances according to how the battles were going, but here at the canal bank lived a unique community of men whose function was to support those in the line. In his diary Major J. M. Halley RE (qv) describes the scene at different times of the day and by reading aloud the following extract it is possible to get a remarkable sense of what it must have been like to have been here. He starts by describing the place to your right where the canal ends in Ypres:

'The warehouses are now the merest skeletons or are only a heap of bricks or twisted iron girders. Barges would find it very difficult to navigate these waters now, for a series of wooden or barrel bridges block the way. Troops have to be moved from one side of the canal to the other and dozens of little bridges span it ... On the canal bank a certain amount of coming and going is inevitable, orderlies with messages, a red-hat or two, but there is no aimless walking about because of aeroplanes ... Immediately the aeroplane sentry blows his whistle whatever life there was ceases, men take cover at once or freeze where they stand until the sentry signals 'all clear'... When the canal is being shelled you will never see a soul, everyone disappears as if by magic ... then you will hear the rush and crump of a high explosive shell, feel the frame of your dug-out tremble to its foundations. The fork in your hand with a piece of meat impaled on it stays motionless midway between your plate and your mouth. Something beyond your control keeps it poised there 'till you hear the concussion, then the hand continues its interrupted work .... Why does the Blighter always do it at meal times ? ... But the best time to see the canal is in the evening when both banks teem with life. Then there is no danger from observation from aeroplanes and the men come out to enjoy the remainder of daylight. You will wonder where so many soldiers came from, but if you look at the steep banks that rise on both sides of the water from the footpaths running along the edge of the

Headstone of 15-year-old Pte Strudwick, with student tributes, Essex Farm CWGC Cemetery.

canal you will see a series of small black holes ... these are 20th Century dwellings, the equivalent at the front of your villas and bijou residences. Some are detached, some only semi; they have their exits and their entrances; some have floors some have none ... Being human our houses are as inappropriately named as they are at, shall we say, Streatham Hill ... 'The Abode of Love' ... 'Leicester Lounge' ... 'Submarine Villa'... Most of the villas possess only one room so arranged that each of its inmates is in possession of two feet by six feet of floor space. This rectangle fulfills at once many functions, it is bedroom, dining room, drawing room, library ... For bathroom there is a share of a basin, perhaps ... It is more or less shell-proof (usually less) ... The men living on the canal bank are 'out of the trenches' for a few days' rest, but 'rest' is a comparative term. In this case they are 'in reserve' to their brothers in the line, fetching and carrying for them so that their nights are busy. They form ration parties, carrying parties, working parties. You must understand that the last stage of all transport to the line is done by men and at night ... You may see small parties of soldiers in single file struggling along muddy trenches, with petrol tins full of water, sandbags full of rations or loaded up with barbed wire, timber or hurdles. On a fine evening however, before it becomes dark, the soldiers come out and swarm about the canal bank. They wash themselves, they shave. You can see men sitting half naked, their bodies pink and fat .... like Japanese wrestlers .... picking vermin from their shirts. They make tea, they clean their rifles, they clean their little houses and they merely rest.'

Continue under the road bridge towards Ypres, whose spires are ahead. On the left is

Essex Farm Bunker Dressing Station.

McCrae Albertina marker, Essex Farm.

Memorial to 49th (West Riding) Division, Essex Farm.

• *Duhallow ADS CWGC Cemetery/25.2 miles/Map H11/GPS: 50.86378 2.87702*

This was started during the Battle of Pilckem Ridge during July 1917 and named after a South Irish Hunt. It contains 1,442 UK, 13 Australian, 26 Canadian, 12 Newfoundland, 6 New Zealand, 1 Belgian, 2 French, 52 German and 41 Special Memorials. The ADS, which then served 18th Division and to which the Cemetery was attached, was visited on 26 October 1917, by Dr Harvey Cushing, the distinguished American surgeon serving with the British (and a close friend of John McCrae [qv]). He found the conditions under which the RAMC were working quite appalling. The CO had 'erected his tents on a sea of mud and shell holes which had to be filled with whatever could be found. Indeed, more like the ancient lake dwellers in parts, for the Yperlee has expanded into a veritable lake, over which duckboards in many areas stand close together on piles.' The Cemetery was designed by Sir Reginald Blomfield.

Continue to the roundabout.

• *Salvation Corner/25.5 miles*

According to most sources, this was so named after the Salvation Army hut that stood here during the war, but according to H. A. Taylor in his *Goodbye to the Battlefields*, 'Here in the old days, much depended upon which way you turned. You might wheel and avoid the hazards of the shell-stricken city. Thus came the name. If you were unfortunate in your orders, you went on, skirting the city proper, to Hell Fire Corner.'

Turn right, following 'Andere Richtingen' signs. At next roundabout turn left following signs to Centrum on the N8. Take the first turn to the left after crossing the canal and stop at the cemetery on the right.

• *Ypres Reservoir CWGC Cemetery/26.4 miles/10 minutes/Map H12/ GPS: 50.85382 2.87762*

The Cemetery, whose stone gate posts bear bas relief wreaths with 1914 on the left and 1918 on the right, was started in October 1915, and was further laid out by the Town Major, Capt James Lee (qv) in 1916. It remained in use until the end of the war. Concentrations from nearby cemeteries then doubled the number of burials. There are now 2,248 UK, 142 Australian, 6 BWI, 151 Canadian, 2 Guernsey, 1 Indian, 28 New Zealand, 1,042 unknown and 1 German burials, with 12 Special Memorials. Here is buried (Plot IA.37) **Brig Gen Francis Aylmer Maxwell, VC, CSI, DSO & Bar** of the Indian Staff, attd Roberts' Light Horse, serving with the Middx Regt, who was shot by a sniper on 21 September 1917. Maxwell won his VC in the Boer War. The inscription on his grave reads, 'An ideal soldier and a very perfect gentleman, beloved by his men.' Also buried here is **Col Augustus David Geddes** of the 2nd Bn, the Buffs, of 'Geddes's Detachment' (qv), and Etonian **Major James Leadbetter Knott**, DSO, of the 10th West Yorks, killed on the Somme on 1 July age 33, whose body was moved here to be next to his brother, Etonian **Capt Henry Basil Knott** of the 9th Bn Northumberland Fusiliers, who died of wounds age 24 on 7 September 1915. Their father, Sir James Knott, paid for the tower in St George's Church as a memorial to his sons. A young American, 19 year old Wainwright Merrill of Bellevue, Massachusetts, then at Harvard, went to Canada to enlist. He served as **Gunner A. A. Stanley** with 6th Seige Bty Can Gar Arty, was killed on 6 November 1917, and is buried here. After his death Harvard granted him a BA for 'honorable service'. One of his ancestors was General Lewis Merrill who fought in the American Civil War.

There is an interesting story in the CWGC Cemetery summary that relates to **16 men of the 6th DCLI** buried here (in Plot VAA) who were killed on 12 August by shells from 'Ypres Express' firing from Houthulst Forest as they sheltered 'in the Cathedral Vaults'. Other reports state that they were sheltering in a cellar below the Cloth Hall. The survivors were rescued by the 11th King's Liverpools but the bodies of these men were not recovered until after the Armistice. Little

The Knott Brothers, Ypres Reservoir CWGC Cemetery, Ypres

else has been discovered by researchers in Ieper. Can any readers supply more about this incident?

Three of the tragic **'Shot at Dawn'** men who were executed for desertion lie in this cemetery: **Pte Thomas Lionel Moles**, 54th Bn Can Inf, 22 October 1917 (I.H.76); **Pte Ernest Lawrence**, 2nd Devons, 22 November, 1917, age 21 (I.I.145); **Pte Charles McColl**, 1/4th E Yorks, 28 December 1917 (IV.A.6).

Turn round and return to the N8 and turn left. At the next roundabout turn right onto the N308, signed to Station and then follow signs to Vlamertinge crossing over the railway line and passing 'Haig House' (qv) on the left.

At this point railway and road cross the canal at what was once known as Devil's Bridge. A few hundred metres further, on the right, is the Ypres Asylum, a large brick building. The original building was used as a forward dressing station and destroyed by shellfire. Graves in the grounds were moved to Bedford House Cemetery (Map M13). This road, leading to Poperinge, was the route up which the majority of supplies to the Salient were moved and was heavily shelled, frequently being under observation by the enemy from the Flanders Hills, which can be seen in the distance to the left. As the road crosses the railway for the second time the spire of St Martin's Cathedral can be seen behind at the end of the line in Ypres.

• *Goldfish Château/27.8 miles/GPS: 50.85115 2.85158*

Over the road to the right, in a copse, is a new building on the site of Rozelaar Château (nicknamed Goldfish after its fishpond) where many divisional HQs were sited. Divisional CWGC Cemetery, Dickebusch Road, about half a mile away (Map H2), served the HQs and was accordingly named.

Continue to Vlamertinge crossroads. Do not take the N38.

Extra Visit to Vlamertinghe New Military CWGC Cemetery (Map G9, GPS: 50.84841 2.81732). Round trip: 0.2 miles. Approximate time: 10 minutes.

Turn left, signed to the Cemetery, cross the N38 where the 'Agony' statue is and continue to the high cemetery sign on the right pointing to the left. The cemetery is up a small path.

Designed by Sir Reginald Blomfield, the Cemetery was started on 1 June 1917, in anticipation of needs during Third Ypres when Vlamertinghe Military Cemetery was full. Most of the burials - 1,609 UK, 44 Australian, 155 Canadian, 1 Guernsey, 1 New Zealand, 3 South African and 7 German – are from 1917, although the cemetery was used until the Armistice. The layout is pleasing, with the War Stone, the Cross of Sacrifice and pavilion higher than the graves.

Here is buried one of the most fascinating VCs of the war, **Acting CSM John Skinner, DCM,** of the 1st Bn KOSB. Skinner won his **VC** at Wijdendrift (on the Pilckem Ridge) on 18 August 1917, for working his way round the left flank of three blockhouses with six men and clearing them one by one, and taking sixty prisoners, three machine-guns and two trench mortars, despite being wounded in the head. This colourful character joined the army in 1900 at the age of 16 and Rose Coombs (qv) called Skinner's exploits, 'my favourite VC story'. She recounted how the wounded hero came to London for his

Headstone of CSM J. Skinner, DCM, VC, Vlamertinghe New Mil CWGC Cemetery

Investiture and 14 days' leave, which ended in a huge binge in Folkestone. He was then hospitalised and posted to a Reserve Battalion in Edinburgh. After two days, Skinner, who had his return warrant, got himself back to the Salient, thereby risking a Court Martial. The Regiment – even the Division (the 29th) - were delighted to have this popular and famous man back in their midst and no retribution ensued. Skinner had had a wager with his pal, QSM Ross: they had both been wounded eight times (three of Skinner's wounds were in the Boer War) and the bet was about who would get the ninth. Skinner unfortunately won. He was shot between the eyes on 17 March 1918, trying to rescue a wounded man. The funeral, held in pouring rain on 19 March was a unique and memorable occasion. It was delayed until six fellow VCs of 29th Division could be gathered together as pall bearers and his body was brought to Vlamertinghe on a gun carriage drawn by a magnificent team of horses. This incredible story was recounted to Rose (a great friend of ours) at the graveside by a veteran of the 29th who had been present at the original funeral.

The Guernsey Lt Infantry had been formed at the end of 1916 from the Guernsey Militia and had the word 'Royal' in its title to show its loyalty to the crown. In an odd coincidence the 29th Div Commander was Maj Gen Beauvoir de Lisle who came from Guernsey.

Return and pick up the main itinerary.

Headstone of Pte Richard le Page, Royal Guernsey Lt Inf, Vlamertinghe New Mil CWGC Cemetery

Continue and turn right after the church signed to Vlamertinghe Military Cemetery. Stop on the right.

• Vlamertinghe Military CWGC Cemetery/Mitford Memorial Gates/ Vlamertinghe Château/29.2 miles/15 minutes/Map G8,7/GPS: 50.85561 2.81995

There are 1,113 UK, 4 Australian, 52 Canadian, 2 Newfoundland and 2 South African burials in the cemetery, begun by the French in 1914 and used by the British fighting units and field ambulances until June 1917. Then further extension was forbidden and burials stopped when adjoining land was taken for the military railway being built. Where possible, men of the same unit were buried side by side and there is a high proportion of territorial units. In Plots IV, V and VI there are 250 men of the Lancashire Fusiliers. Etonian **Captain Francis Grenfell, VC** (cousin of the poet Julian Grenfell) is buried here and it is he and his twin, Riversdale, who are commemorated by a window in St George's Church (qv). There are 3 German graves and 4 WW2 from the Retreat to Dunkirk in May 1940.

The wrought iron gates are a Memorial to Etonian **Maj the Hon G. B. O. Mitford, DSO,** son of Lord Redesdale, of A Sqn 10th Hussars, killed in action on 13 May 1915, age 38. Mitford is buried in the cemetery.

The Mitford Memorial Gates

*Headstones to Pte A.
Rickman, 1st Bn Royal
Dublin Fusiliers shot at
dawn 15 September 1916,
Vlamertinghe CWGC
Military Cemetery*

*2nd Lt Harold Parry, KRRC, killed
6 May 1917, war poet, Vlamertinghe
CWGC Military Cemetery*

Also buried here is **Pte Noel Finucane** of the 1st/10th Bn the Kings Liverpool Regt, who died on 4 January 1917, having served on the *Lusitania* and the *Aquitania*, the latter until the evacuation of Gallipoli, and **Pte A. Rickman** of the 1st Bn the Royal Dublin Fusiliers, '**Shot at Dawn**' on 15 September 1916. Rickman volunteered when war broke out, fought through Gallipoli, saw comrades decimated on 1 July on the Somme and 'deserted' the following day. **Lt Frederick J. Christison** of the Argyll & Sutherland Highlanders, 4 December 1915, age 20, was the younger son of Surgeon General Sir Alexander Christison Bt. One of the authors' great-uncles, **Sjt H. Greenhalgh** of the 2nd Siege (R Anglesey) Coy, RA, killed on 12 March 1916, and a **war poet, 2nd Lt Harold Parry** of the KRRC, killed on 6 May 1917, also lie here. Parry was a twin, his brother serving in the Royal Navy survived the war. Although he gained a scholarship to Oxford he curtailed his studies in order to join the KOYLI in January 1916 and he fought with the KRRC on the Somme. Parry's poems were published privately after his death and his headstone carries a line from one of them.

Some 150m beyond the Cemetery, in the parkland to the right, is **Vlamertinghe Château (GPS: 50.85702 2.81872**) made famous by Edmund Blunden's (qv) poem *On Passing Vlamertinghe Château*, written in July 1917. The incongruity of the colourful flowers still blooming in the grounds, especially the vermilion poppies, ('Such a gay carpet! Poppies by the million') and the sacrificial blood of 'those who live with death and lice' struck the young poet forcibly. Miraculously the Château survived the war and is still in private hands. At the entrance is a perspex Information Board with a quotation from Blunden's poem.

Blunden's battalion, the 11th Royal Sussex, was 'camped in readiness among the familiar woods

*Vlamertinghe Château today –
no poppies to be seen*

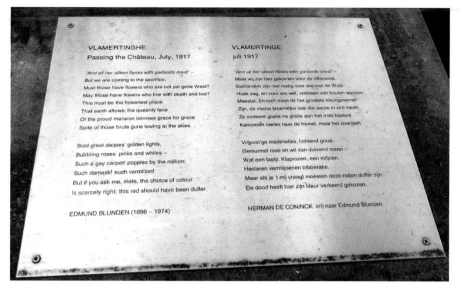

Poet Edmund Blunden Information Board, Vlamertinghe Château

west of Vlamertinghe' during the period of preparation for Third Ypres. In *Undertones of War* he maintained that 'The preparations for the new battle were perforce as obvious to the Germans, with their complete dominance in observation posts, as they were to us. All the available open space through the Ypres salient ... was crammed with men, animals, stores, guns and transports; from Poperinge forward the place was like a circus ground on the eve of a benefit. New roads and railways had changed the map so completely in a few weeks that one was a stranger here.' He was particularly impressed by the road from Poperinge, 'newly constructed of planks' (the 'Switch' Road) and at 'the new broad-gauge railway thrust ... into conspicuous open ground, and the trucks waiting on it.'

Return to the church junction, turn right and continue towards Poperinge.

• Hop Store & Hop Store CWGC Cemetery/30.00 miles/10 minutes/ Map G6/GPS: 50.85410 2.80890

In Vlamertinghe a notice erected in 1916 proclaimed: 'Tin hats must be worn from here onward'. The village (known as 'Vlam' to the Tommies) was marked only by piles of rubble and a battered church in 1918. However, the area of Hop Store Cemetery was just beyond the normal range of enemy medium artillery fire and the hop building here, although having recently been extensively restored, is basically original. It was owned by Mr Veys whose family, it is said, had enough sons to form a football team. Medical facilities were set up in the hop store, including an **Advanced Dressing Station of 18th Field Ambulance** in 1915, and casualties from the first gas attack were treated there. As well as being cared for by the medical staff, casualties were visited by priests - 'padres' in military terminology.

In 1914 there were about 100 Padres with the army and by 1918 there were 3,500. At first their duties were concerned mostly with visiting the sick and burying the dead, and one of those who fulfilled that duty here was the **Reverend Charles Edmund Doudney**. A much-loved parish priest in South Lyncombe, Bath, 'Charlie' volunteered to serve and came out to 'France' in April 1915. He was 44 years old. He quickly expanded the range of his duties to include visiting the men in the front lines and in holding services:

'These small voluntary services I make very informal. All sit down and sing some hymns – a few prayers, and then a very straight talk, the chaps' eyes riveted on one, and every now and then a broad smile and even a word from them as something goes home. These are the services I like best.'

He and the other padres of the 6th Division, the parent division of 18th Field Ambulance, held frequent policy meetings at which they discussed, among other things, the setting up of a rest house for soldiers and Charlie 'looted' (his word) a piano from Ypres for it. On the night of 13 October 1915, he was passing through Ypres on his way to a Regimental Aid Post to bury a soldier when he was mortally wounded by a shell splinter. He was evacuated to 10th Casualty Clearing Station alongside Abeele and died there two days later. He had been due to go home on leave on 14 October. He is buried in Lijssenthoek CWGC cemetery. Throughout his service 'Charlie' had kept in touch with his parishioners with regular letters home and so popular was he with the community in Bath, and with his comrades in the field, that his wife had over 200 messages of condolence. His replacement with the 6th Division was **'Tubby' Clayton** (Tubby called him the 'beloved Chaplain Doudney of 16th Infantry Brigade') and it could well be that Charlie and his piano were the inspiration for Talbot House. The full story has been sensitively told in a book written and published by his grandson, Jonathan Horne, entitled *The Best of Good Fellows*.

The Cemetery, approached by a tarmac track to the right, designed by Sir Reginald Blomfield, is on what was the safer side of the village and was opened in May 1915 and contains some 251 burials. Rest Camps were established on this 'safer side' of the village (on the opposite side of the track was Red Rose Camp). In one of them on 1 March 1916, the poet **R. E. Vernède** (qv) wrote two lines which he would incorporate into his poem *Before the Assault* in December of that year,

> Not in our time, not now, Lord, we beseech Thee
> To grant us peace. The sword has bit too deep.

Vernède, who had come to believe that what he regarded as the 'German abomination' had to be fought to the bitter end, would never live to see peace. On 9 April 1917 he was hit by a machine gun while leading his men in an advance on Havrincourt Wood. He is buried in Lebuquière CWGC Cemetery.

Please, make some time to spend a quiet period of reflection at this small, off-the-beaten-track Cemetery. Careful reading of the Cemetery Report yields poignant personal stories that bring home the sacrifice made by many families. The remarks in the Visitors' Book reveal how many people, moved by the stories, come to visit individual graves here. For instance, there is **Pte D.L.A. Berry**, 14 Oct '15, whose widow Leah's second husband, Robert Herring, also fell.

Hop Store CWGC Cemetery with Hop Store in background

> ESSEX England
> DAVID & LYNNE NEILL
> N. IRELAND
> DAVID & HELEN BUCKLAND
> EVESHAM
> Thank you for your sacrifice
> Remembering the 4 Lynn brothers killed in WW1
> VISITING GREAT UNCLE

Extract from Visitor's Book, Hopstore CWGC Cemetery

Here too is **Driver Robert Lynn,** RFA, 6 Aug '15, who had three brothers killed in the war – one in Belgium, one in France and one in Israel, and **Gnr Norman Sydney James**, RGA, 1 July '17, had two brothers killed. One can only imagine the grief of the remaining families.

Continue to Brandhoek Church on right.

• Chavasse Memorial/Ammunition Dump Explosion Memorial/30.8 miles/10 minutes/Map G2a/GPS: 50.85470 2.79018

On 29 August 1997 a Memorial (bearing a photo and brief history of Chavasse, and besides which the Union flag often flies) was unveiled outside the church to commemorate the 80th Anniversary of the death of the **double VC winner Capt Noel Chavasse** (qv) in the presence of a contingent from the Liverpool Scottish Territorials. The Memorial was initiated and funded by the Commune of Brandhoek.

Headstone of Driver R. Lynn, Hopstor CWGC Cemetery

In front of the Church is a **Memorial to those killed in ammunition dump explosion of 27 April 1918.** They include 6 members of one family (from 6 months-55 years old) and at least 50 British Servicemen, 20 of the 10th Bn Queen's Own West Kent, buried at Red Farm, Hagel Dump and Brandhoek CWGC Cemeteries.

Turn left following CWGC signs to the Brandhoek group of cemeteries, crossing the railway and dual carriageway (N38).

This behind-the-line area, thought to be out of the range of German artillery, was a **Field Ambulance/CCS** position throughout the war and hence a burial area too. On all sides were temporary huts and tents, supply dumps, horse lines, first-aid stations, fatigue parties, military police posts and forests of signs. On the left is

Chavasse VC Memorial, Brandhoek Church

Ammunition Dump Explosion Memorial, Brandhoek Church

Ontploffing munitiedepot Galgestraat, Brandhoek, 27 april 1918

Tijdens het Lenteoffensief van 1918, op 27 april, kwamen zes leden van de familie Deplaecie om bij een munitieontploffing in de Galgestraat: Henri (55 jaar), Jeanne (12 jaar), Irma (9 jaar), Marguerite (4 jaar), Julien (2 jaar) en Nera (6 maanden). Dit is de enige plaats waar ze in naam worden herdacht.

Minstens 50 Britse soldaten kwamen eveneens om. Er waren ook tientallen gewonden, burgers en soldaten. 20 Britse doden behoorden tot het Iode Bataljon Queen's Own Royal West Kent Regiment, die vlakbij hun rustkamp hadden. De slachtoffers liggen begraven op Red Farm Military Cemetery, Hagle Dump Cemetery en Brandhoek New Military Cemetery, No 3 in Brandhoek. Een aantal kreeg geen bekend graf.

Explosion of an Ammunition Dump at Galgestraat, Brandhoek, 27th April 1918

During the Spring Offensive of 1918, on 27th April, six members of the Deplaecie family of Brandhoek were killed: Henri (aged 55), Jeanne (aged 12), Irma (aged 9), Marguerite (aged 4), Julien (aged 2) and Nera (aged 6 months). This is the only spot where they are commemorated in name.

At least 50 British servicemen also died. There were also dozens of wounded, military as well as civilians. Twenty dead belonged to the 10th Battalion Queen's Own Royal West Kent Regiment, billeted in a nearby rest camp. The victims are buried on Red Farm Military Cemetery, Hagle Dump Cemetery and Brandhoek New Military Cemetery, No 3. Some have no known grave.

• Brandhoek Military CWGC Cemetery/30.9 miles/Map G3/GPS: 50.85309 2.79099

Begun in 1917 for the new Passchendaele Offensive beside a dressing station it was used until July 1917. There are 601 UK, 4 Australian, 2 Bermudan, 63 Canadian, and 2 German burials.

Turn right and drive to the cemetery on the left.

• Brandhoek New Military CWGC Cemetery No 3/31.1 miles/Map G1/ GPS: 50.85177 2.78792

This was opened when the New Military Cemetery became full and used until May 1918. The gates were presented by the father of **Lt Anthony Harold Strutt** of the 16th Sherwood Foresters, buried here and who died of wounds in the nearby CCS on 27 April 1918. In preparation for the new Allied Offensive 32nd, 3rd Aust and 44th CCSs were set up here. There are 849 UK, 46 Australian, 1 BWI, 46 Canadian, 18 New Zealand, 5 South African, and 1 Chinese Labour Corps graves. A quarter of the graves are of the Artillery as there were many gun positions in the vicinity. The Cemetery was designed by Sir Reginald Blomfield.

Walk back to the cemetery on the other side of the road.

• Brandhoek New Military CWGC Cemetery/31.00 miles/10 minutes/ Map G2/GPS: 50.85242 2.78826

This Cemetery, also designed by Sir Reginald Blomfield, was opened when Brandhoek Military Cemetery became full. Here is buried one of the truly brave heroes of the war – **Capt Noel Godfrey Chavasse, VC and Bar, MC,** RAMC. Noel was born in Oxford on 9 November 1884, the younger of twin brothers, to the Rev Francis Chavasse and his wife Edith. The identical twins were educated at Magdalen College School and then moved to Liverpool when their father

became Bishop of Liverpool where the whole family was renowned for its kindness and generosity to those less well off than themselves.

Noel and his twin Christopher attended Liverpool College where they became excellent athletes. They then went on to Trinity College Oxford in 1904 where they continued their sporting achievements. Noel gained a 'First' in Physiology in 1907 and then continued his studies in medicine and joined the Oxford OTC. In May 1910 he passed his MRCS exams (at the second attempt) and continued to study for a second MB, doing his hospital placement in Dublin. In 1912 he passed his final Medical Examinations and thus qualified as a doctor. He became House Surgeon at the Royal Southern Hospital in Liverpool and joined the Territorials – 10th Bn the King's (Liverpool) Regiment, the Liverpool Scottish.

On 2 August 1914 he left with them for annual camp - and never returned to civilian life. He volunteered for active service as a Doctor and his twin was accepted into the Army Chaplain's Department. The Liverpool Scottish left for France on 1 November 1914, and so began his extraordinary war.

Noel was posthumously awarded the bar to his VC, the only person to win both awards during World War I. His first VC was won for tending the wounded

Headstone of Capt Chavasse, VC and Bar, Brandhoek New Mil CWGC Cemetery

under fire on 9/10 August 1916, at Guillemont on the Somme, saving the lives of at least twenty wounded men. The news came through on 26 October 1916, after Chavasse had moved to the Salient, and his fellow officers laid on a celebratory dinner at Elverdinghe Château two days later. Mortally wounded near Wieltje (qv) on 2 August 1917, he was brought here to **CCS No 32** (which specialised in abdominal wounds) where he was operated upon. Although the operation was an apparent success, this gallant Medical Officer died on 4 August, on the third anniversary of the outbreak of the war.

CCS 32 was one of those set up and managed by **Head Sister, Kate Luard, RRC & Bar**. This most extraordinary woman - capable and efficient, compassionate, determined, brave, totally au fait with, and knowledgeable about, the military situation at all times, had served in the Boer War and went on to use her experience in most key battle areas of WW1. Her brilliant, informative letters to her family are reproduced in *Unknown Warriors*, republished by the History Press in 2014. It really is essential reading to understand the work of the brilliant medical teams who worked under the most appalling conditions to do all possible for the welfare of their patients, and of the stoicism and humour of the most terribly wounded men.

The Brandhoek CCSs were revolutionary in that they were nearer to the front line than previous CCSs and therefore could offer immediate treatment to the wounded. This concept was the brainchild of another exceptional Medical Officer, **Sir Anthony Bowlby**, who worked closely with Head Sister Luard as the CCSs came under direct fire by bomb and shell.

On 2 August 1917 Kate Luard writes:

"Yesterday morning Capt C.,VC and Bar, DSO, MC, RAMC was brought in – badly hit in the tummy and arm and had been going about for two days with a scalp wound till he got this. He was quickly x-rayed, operated on, shrapnel found, holes sewn up, salined and put to bed… He tries to live; he was going to be married".

She went on to describe the impressive funeral ceremony, with Chavasse's horse leading followed by pipers and "masses of kilted officers". A Piper played a lament at the graveside ("a large pit full of dead soldiers sewn up in canvas"). Then "his Colonel, who particularly loved him, stood and saluted in his grave. It was fine but horribly choky."

Buried near him is his servant, **Pte C. A. Rudd**, who died on 10 August. Chavasse's Bar to his VC was announced in the *London Gazette* on 14 September 1917.

In December 2009 Lord Ashcroft bought Chavasse's exceptional medals for a reported £1.5 million – a world record. They are now on display in the Lord Ashcroft Gallery (to which he donated £5 million) at the IWM with other famous VCs from his collection and some 50 VCs owned by the Museum.

Chavasse was distantly related by marriage to another double VC, Capt Charles Hazlitt Upham of the New Zealand Infantry, the third and last man to be awarded a bar to his VC, both won in WW2, in Crete and in the Western Desert.

The Cemetery also contains 514 UK, 11 Australian, 6 Canadian and 28 German graves.

Return to the dual carriageway, cross it and turn left on the N308 towards Poperinge. Continue. On the right, but not easy to stop at, is

• Red Farm CWGC Cemetery/31.8 miles/Map F8/GPS: 50.85456 2.78030

This tiny Cemetery is too small to contain Lutyens' (qv) powerful War Stone. When work got underway on the cemeteries in the early 1920s, keeping costs down soon became an important factor. The Stone of Remembrance, weighing 8 tons, cost £500 to make and install and it was also felt that it would dwarf the smaller cemeteries. Lutyens refused to reduce its proportions for these cemeteries and it was therefore decided to omit it, which, it is said, infuriated him. Blomfield, on the other hand, agreed to vary the size of his War Cross to suit the proportions of the cemeteries in which they were being installed. The Cemetery, enclosed by a brick wall, was attached to a Dressing Station and was begun during the German offensive of April and May 1918. It contains

46 UK burials, 17 unknown and 3 Belgian Civilians buried under one headstone. It was designed by A.J.S. Hutton.

Continue towards Poperinge to the roundabout with the R33 ring road. Turn right and then right again on the N333 following signs to Elverdinge and Gwalia CWGC Cemetery. Continue some 1.5 miles to a track to the left signed to the cemetery, which may be driven if dry.

• Gwalia CWGC Cemetery/35.2 miles/15 minutes/Map F5/GPS: 50.87623 2.76408

This interesting Cemetery (which is probably called after an old Welsh name for Wales, much used in Victorian times) designed by Sir Reginald Blomfield being so far off the beaten track, is little visited. From the road it is approached by a long (394 paces) beautifully maintained grass path, an example of the dedication and attention to detail of the CWGC. The Cemetery was begun in July 1917 in preparation for Third Ypres and set among the camps in this area. It was used by Infantry units, Artillery and Field Ambulances until September 1918. It contains 30 Royal Engineers, 30 Labour Corps, 4 Chinese Labour Corps, 444 soldiers and RM Gunners from the UK, 2 Australian, 14 BWI, 5 New Zealand, 1 South African and 3 German prisoners. The one American and one French grave were removed. In Plot I, Row H are **14 men of the 9th Lancs Fus** killed in the early morning of 4 September 1917, in a German air raid over nearby 'Dirty Bucket Camp' (qv). Here is buried **Lt Col Percy William Beresford, DSO, twice Mentioned in Despatches**, of the 2/3rd Bn the London Regt, killed in action on 26 October 1917, age 42, **Lt W D Reynolds-Parsons**, the Queen's, killed on 26 May 1918, buried with **8 Privates of the Queens, all killed the same day**, and the **Revd Cecil Langdon, Chaplain to the Forces** 4th Class, killed 31 October 1917, aged 35.

From July 1917 the whole of the flat area around Poperinghe was a seething mass of camps and stores and railways of various gauges. In his diary**, Edwin Campion Vaughan** (qv) who moved up to the Salient with his battalion, the 1st/8th Warwicks, arriving at Poperinghe station on 29 July 1917, recorded that they marched through countryside that 'was perfectly flat, devoid of trees or hedges and only relieved by compact, tangled hopfields ... to a tiny village around which were clustered numerous canvas camps.' (This was St Jan ter Brielen, about as far to the west of Poperinge as Gwalia is to the east. The scenery and conditions were identical to those at Gwalia.) After a short period of leave, Vaughan describes how 'a Boche plane came across and dropped a lot of bombs - fortunately in other camps. We were untouched but the night was rent with crashes, by the screams of archies and the frantic spluttering of Lewis guns.' On 11 August he was detailed to seek out the 'large-scale model of the front [that] had been fashioned somewhere near Pop' so that officers could be taken to examine it. As he 'foolishly did not ascertain where Divisional HQ was', Vaughan failed to locate it, despite wandering around the ruins of Vlamertinghe and 'Dirty Bucket Corner'. (Just over one mile due east of here.) Edmund Blunden (qv) obviously did manage to find the model, as he describes it in *Undertones of War* as 'an enormous model of the German systems ... open for inspection, whether from the ground or from step-ladders raised beside, and this was popular, though whether from its charm as a model or value as a military aid is uncertain.'

The next day Vaughan's battalion was moved nearer this point. 'We were part of the never-ending stream now,' he wrote, 'welling up into the great reservoir behind Ypres which was swelling and deepening until the dam should be loosed and all the men and guns and shells should pour out on to the enemy lines. Far above us little swarms of aeroplanes circled among the pretty pink shrapnel puffs, on either side were shattered poplars and barren fields, and meeting us were straggling lines of ambulances and tired troops.' Their new home was a 'nondescript camp consisting of bivouacs, tents, huts and tarpaulin shelters into which we stowed the troops as best as we could ... It was a baleful place for the shell-holes and shattered trees bore testimony to the attentions of the German gunners. Amongst the trees was a great concentration of tanks – and the name of the camp was Slaughter Wood!'

Return to the N308 and go straight over. Follow signs to 'Centrum' and park in the Grote Markt.
NOTE. Signs to this parking are not easy to follow - you will need to be patient!

In 2010, when re-cobbling the Square began, some important archaeological remains dating from medieval times were discovered, which required a long investigation.

• *Poperinge/38.2 miles/1 hour/RWC/GPS: 50.85573 2.72679*

Poperinge has been a settlement for over 2,000 years and, like Ypres, found its prosperity in the Middle Ages through cloth. The inability of the English traders to pronounce the 'R' in the name led to the description 'poplin' for material produced here. At the outbreak of World War I it had some 11,000 inhabitants. During the war the population of the town and the surrounding district fell to less than fifty as the inhabitants were evacuated or fled as refugees, then swelled to a quarter of a million as the Allied war machine and all the manpower it took to maintain it moved in and out of the area. As the war's most famous inhabitant, 'Tubby' Clayton, wrote:

'Alone free for years among Belgian towns, close enough to the line to be directly accessible to the principal sufferers and not so near as to be positively ruinous, it became metropolitan not by merit but by the logic of locality. In migrant and mobile times, its narrow and uneven streets filled and foamed with a tide-race of transport. Year in, year out, by night and by day, the fighting troops, with all the blunter forces behind that impel and sustain their operations, set east and west with that rhythm of fluctuation that stationary war induces. Until the great Switch Road [a by-pass round the northern edge of Poperinghe {PR12} built by the REs] was opened, and the railway track was doubled, every man and every mule (whether on four legs or closely packed in a blue tin) came up by one pair of rails or one narrow street. Moreover, before the camps were built, troops billeted in the town itself in huge number, prudently decreased as the thing called bombing grew in ease and frequency of performance.'

During this momentous time, much energy in 'Pops' was devoted to providing relaxation for the troops coming to and from the Salient. It was known as 'the last stop before Hell' and was the Town behind the lines of the BEF, to which all roads led. F. R. Barry, who served in the vicinity in 1917, wrote:

'The Town was always absolutely swarming with officers and men of all possible arms. There were mess presidents and mess cooks buying provisions on their lawful occasions. There were officers visiting the Field Cashier. There were people going on leave or coming back, with no objection to wasting a few days. There was a large (more or less permanent) garrison and nearly always at least a Division billeted. Besides this there was always a vast mass of people simply there for a 'day out'. The traffic passing through Poperinge would have made Oxford Street in June look sleepy, and every lorry, limber, car or tender from whatever direction it was coming shed a few people more into the mass. There was no lack of wonderful enjoyments. For the officers the magnificent club started originally by Neville Talbot, and the famous crowded restaurants such as Cyril's or La Poupée, known throughout the B.E.F. as 'Ginger's'. Or you could have your hair cut in a shop which warned its customers laconically, 'We do not work when the Germans are shelling'. You could buy all the things you had been needing for months – puttees and razors, shirts and studs and toothpaste. Expectant Subalterns could lay in an extra star. Colonels could get fresh supplies of ribbon. Other ranks knew well the best saloons for omelettes and vin blanc or fish and chips. 'Silk cards', too, you could buy, and passionate emblems of clasped hands and souvenirs innumerable. There were cinemas and 'shows' of various kinds besides the native picture-house and theatre. In a word the resources of civilisation left no dizzy joy to be desired.'

The YMCA was well represented in Pops (the best-known being in the Hotel De Kring on

Bertenplaats) as was the Church Army (established in the Market Square). Local cabarets sprang up, the most popular artists being the notorious trio nicknamed 'Chlorine', 'Vaseline' and 'Lanoline', later to be joined by 'Glycerine'. The town's brothels were strictly controlled by the MPs. Concert parties were a popular distraction, and on 30 July 1917 the 'Frolics' of the 61st Division put on a much-appreciated show. Christmas of that year saw several Divisional Variety Companies performing (the best being 'The Pedlars') and in the town, according to Captain Dunn (qv):

> 'The whole atmosphere has been Christmassy for days; nothing so like Christmas-tide at home has been known out here. The men have an extra pay-out and most appear to be getting postal orders from home. Christmas shopping is in full swing ... All the shops, and there are lots of them, are full of goods and buyers, doing a roaring trade .... There was any amount of liquor in the town.'

He dined off:

> '...hors-d'oeuvre, clear oxtail soup, fresh whiting, dressed cutlet and celery, stuffed turkey and trimmings, plum pudding, angels on horseback, dessert - apples, oranges, dates, walnuts: Veuve Cliquot, Kummel, coffee. The turkey, at 3s. 2d per lb., cost 30s. Everything was bought locally. I don't suppose any-thing like the dinner could be got at home. '

It certainly could not, and the Ministry of Food's recommended Christmas dinner 1917 was 'Rice soup; filleted haddock; roast fowl and plum pudding with caramel custard'. The home front was suffering severe food shortages, with long queues for sugar, butter and meat, with butchers often closed as they had no goods to sell. Supply was controlled by the Government, imported fruit was virtually unobtainable and rationing would be brought in in 1918.

Aerial activity over Poperinge was intense and by 1917 the air war had become sophisticated, with machine guns replacing the hand weapons that opponents had fired at each other in the early days. One of the most extraordinary aerial combats of the war ended at Poperinge. In August during the early days of Third Ypres, Capt Mc. A. M. Pender in a Sopwith 11/2 strutter was attacked by German Albatros scouts. Pioneer W. T. Smith, Pender's observer, fired a double drum of ammunition at one Albatros which then went down, but before it did so one of its bullets went through both the main petrol tanks of the Sopwith and seriously wounded the pilot in the back. Capt Pender fainted and his aircraft went into a spin. Pioneer Smith, sitting behind Pender, was unable to make Pender hear him and so he climbed out of his cockpit and worked his way along the outside of the falling aircraft to the pilot. There he found the control lever wedged between Pender's legs. Smith managed to pull Pender back and to push the lever forward and the machine came out of its spin. At that point Pender revived, took control and landed at Poperinge with Smith still standing on the outside of the aircraft. Observers on the ground heard Smith encouraging his pilot, particularly when they were about to crash into some hop poles, 'Pull her up sir!' shouted Smith - or words to that effect!

Today 'Pop' makes a good base for touring the Salient. There are some pleasant small hotels and excellent restaurants in or near the Square. Face the **Café de la Paix** from the centre of the square. This is 12 o'clock. Beyond, up Gasthuisstraat, is **Talbot House** (Toc H). At 5 o'clock is the attractively furnished 3-star **Hotel Amfora**, Tel 57 33 88 66, with seven en-suite bedrooms. At 6 o'clock is the Stadhuis (Town Hall) with its church-like tower. At 7 o'clock is the War Memorial and St Bertin's Church and at 10 o'clock at No 16 is the **Café De Ranke** (qv) which makes a good lunch or tea break and specialises in sinful cream and chocolate cakes.

From the square you have Three Options

1. A short **Walking Tour**, followed by a choice of the two options below.
2. To take the **Special Visits to St Sixtus Abbey and Dozinghem, Mendinghem and Bandaghem CWGC Cemeteries** and then pick up the main Itinerary
3. **To continue on with the Main Itinerary**

Option 1. The Walking Tour. The town is best seen on a short walking tour, in which the points of interest are numbered 'WT1' etc. All the main points of World War I interest have been marked on the map that accompanies local historian Piet Chielens's (qv) **'POP Route'** {PR} Flemish language booklet and bear commemorative markers – see the illustration below. The book is available from the Tourist Office.

Start at the Stadhuis.

• WT1. Stadhuis (Hotel de Ville/Town Hall)

This neo-Gothic structure was built in 1911. It was used as a Divisional HQ for the forces in the line around Ypres. It was damaged by the German shelling of Poperinge which began in April 1915. During the war a huge black notice board indicated whether the wind was 'SAFE' or 'DANGEROUS' (for gas). At the top of the steps leading to the entrance is a bronze Plaque in memory of the **Polish Armoured Division** who liberated Poperinge on 6 September 1944.

A **Tourist Information Office** is situated in the basement, its door to the right of the steps. Town maps, guides and information about events are available. Of course the famous Poperinge Beer and the Hop Museum feature strongly. Perhaps the most interesting events planned for the Centenary in 2017 will be held in July-September 2017, concentrating on **The Chinese in Poperinge**. It begins on 1 July with a photographic exhibition in the Hospital Chapel; a Chinese Shadow Theatre will be repeated several times during the period and on 1 September begins a 'Chinks Back in Town' Festival throughout the town. See also Busseboom in Approach Two, page 64. Tel: + (0) 57 34 66 76. E-mail: tourisme@poperinge.be. Website: www.toerismepoperinge.be

Turn right out of the office and right again on Guido Gezell. Continue to the large gateway on the right.

• WT2. Condemned Cells and Execution Post {PR21}

The Town Hall courtyard in which allied soldiers were executed, the Execution Post (beside which is a moving poem by Erwin Mort with bird footprints on the cobblestones, representing the fragility of man) and the rooms used as prisons for the condemned men were renovated in 2012. There are instructive Information Panels.

It is thought that at least 17 men were shot here, **including Chinese Labourer Wang Ch'un Ch'ih** who was executed for murder on 8 May 1919. The last sentence was carried out on 19 May. Four of them, **Albert Botfield**, **William Symons** and

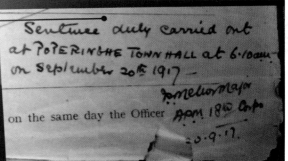

Confirmation of Herbert Morris's Execution, Condemned Cell, Poperinge

Execution Post Memorial Poperinge

Herbert Morris are buried in Poperinghe Mil Cemetery (qv), as is as **2nd Lt Eric Poole**, the first officer to be executed.

In the bare cells is Paul Renière's artwork, S*hot at Dawn* and an audio presentation which gives a shockingly realistic and disturbing sound picture of a condemned soldier's last hours. The tone of some of the graffiti that can still be made out on the walls is defiantly disrespectful – the cells were also used to lock up boisterous and drunken soldiers.

Open: Daily from 0600-2200.

On this sensitive subject of 'Shot at Dawn', artist Anno Dijkstra has created a dramatic sculpture with that name. It will be exhibited in various forms in Poperinge and Watou before the final bronze takes its place near the Poperinge Market Place in 2018. An interesting leaflet available in the **Tourist Office** features executions not only in the British Army but in the French, German, Italian, American and Belgian Armies. See also www.poperinge14-18.be

Cross the square to No 16.

• *WT3.* **Café de Ranke**/*RWC*

The lozenge-shaped **Pop Route plaque** {PR11} is to the left of the entrance (difficult to spot in warm weather as outside tables obscure it). It commemorates the fame of the café (especially of the precocious Ginger) and the next door, **Café de l'Espérance** (known as 'What 'Opes') during the war. The façade of the café 'A la Fabrique', is exactly as it was during the war.

'Pop Route' commemorative plaque No 11 on the wall of the Café de Ranke ('Gingers'), Poperinge

The De Ranke was the café known as 'Ginger's' or 'A la Poupée', run by Madame Cossey and her three red-haired daughters, Marie-Louise, Marthe and Eliane (Ginger). In this officers' haven it was said that more champagne corks popped during the war than anywhere else in France or Belgium. Certainly rumours of troop movements and imminent attacks abounded.

One typical habitué of this seductive hostelry was the young Royal Warwickshire Captain, Edwin Stephen Campion Vaughan (qv). In his diary (published later as *Some Desperate Glory*) Vaughan described his first visit when he was served by

> "A sweet little sixteen-year-old girl ... I fell a victim at once to her long red hair and flashing smile. When I asked her her name, she replied 'Gingair' in such a glib way that we both gave a burst of laughter. We had a splendid dinner, with several bottles of bubbly, and Ginger hovered delightfully above us. Over our cigars and liqueurs I offered her my heart, which she gravely accepted."

On 11 August Vaughan paid another visit to La Poupée where 'Ginger told us (in strict confidence) that there would be a big advance in less than a week. This, by the way, is the first rumour we have had'. As usual, she was right. The Warwickshires were to take part in the Battle of Langemarck on 16 August. A vivid, and harrowing account of their losses on 27 August appears in Vaughan's diary when he was the only officer left in his company.

Edmund Blunden, who described Poperinge as 'one of the seven wonders of the world' for its bustling life, recalled in *Undertones of War* that Ginger 'was daily attending school in Hazebrouck, a courageous feat'.

After the war Ginger, it is said, moved to England as did her elder sister, Marie-Louise, who married Captain Jack Reynolds.

Walk up Gasthuisstraat. On the left is

• WT4. No 12 Gasthuisstraat - 'Skindles'

The wartime café on this site (now a pharmacy) was originally called *Café à la Bourse du Houblon* (Hop Market Café) but the name was too difficult for its British officer patrons and a member of the Rifle Brigade nicknamed it 'Skindles' after the riverside hotel at Maidenhead. Skindles was run by Madame Bentin and her daughers Maria, Zoe and Lea. After the war the hotel moved to its present site (qv). The family also opened a temporary hotel named Skindles near Ypres Railway Station. A Sapper Officer, James Halley (qv), described in great detail his first visit there, when he, like Captain Dunn, had a sumptuous meal which would have been totally unavailable at home. 'Skindles was not always a café,' wrote Halley who had been a distinguished architect in civilian life, 'for although it has the air of never having been anything but what it is now, there are crucifixes still affixed over doorways and on the fireplaces, which are most agreeably profaned by a superabundance of champagne bottles, the delightful shape of which reminds me so forcibly of 18th Century women in crinolines, little groups of plaster statuary of saints and such like. So it is probable that once upon a time the shop appealed to higher appetites than were eating and drinking.' At the next table were 'Five Padres', who in their obvious enjoyment of the delectable meal 'did not talk shop' and whom one would never have known were padres!

Skindles was used as an extension of Talbot House from June 1916 when it became known as 'The Officers' Club' and was run by the Rev Neville Talbot, one of the founders of Talbot House and the father of Gilbert Talbot (qv). It was later taken over by the Expeditionary Force Canteens and closed down in April 1918. General Plumer stayed in Skindles from 7 June 1917, the opening of the Messines Offensive.

Continue up the road to No 26.

• WT5. No 26 Gasthuisstraat – 'Hotel Cyrille' ('Cyril's')

No longer an hotel, this original officers-only establishment was run by Monsieur Cyrille Vermeulen and his wife, who were refugees from Ypres. During the final offensive in March 1918 the enemy totally destroyed the building by a direct hit. The Vermeulens and their four maids were killed, Cyrille being decapitated and blown right across the road.

Cross the road and continue to No 43 on the right.

NOTE that the entrance to Talbot House is round the corner in Potterstraat, where there is minimal parking. The Extra Visits described under Option 3 actually start from that point.

• WT6. No 43 Gasthuisstraat – Talbot House (Toc H)/Map F1/RWC/ GPS: 50.85593 2.72288

Still hanging outside the elegant building, where **Padre Philip Byard (Tubby) Clayton** started a rest house which inspired the movement which is now world-wide, is a sign which states, 'Talbot House 1915-? Every Man's Club'. This extraordinary club was named after Gilbert Talbot, son of the Bishop of Winchester, who was killed in the Salient and is buried in Sanctuary Wood Cemetery (qv). Tommy shortened the name in Army signallers' language to 'Toc H'. It had the atmosphere of a home, where the men, weary and frightened from a spell in the trenches of the Salient, could come, whatever their rank, and be refreshed physically and spiritually.

Talbot House was officially opened on 11 December 1915, in the empty house of the banker and hop merchant, Maurice Coevoet, rented from him for a nominal amount. It operated on 'the Robin Hood principle of taking from the rich to give to the poor', maintained Tubby, another of whose occasional nicknames was 'Boniface' (after the innkeeper in George Farquhar's *The Beaux Stratagem*). Tubby had a marvellous knack of wheedling supplies, furniture and other domestic items from all and sundry. According to *Tales from Talbot House*, for 5 francs officers arriving from the leave train at one a.m. secured cocoa and Oliver biscuits or before departure at 5 a.m. a cold meat breakfast. Other ranks did not pay until June 1916 when the officers were 'thrown out' to Skindles (see above). Until then they (but never other ranks) could get a bed. The 'General's bedroom' had a bed with real sheets. Otherwise stretcher beds and blankets were the norm. A cup of tea cost 1 penny and The House became self-supporting from the profits of the tea-bar, the dry canteen and the small grocery stall which sold 150 different items of such necessities as cigarettes, biscuits and toothpaste. It was used by some 5,000 men each week and on one particularly busy day in September 1917 4,000 teas were served. The library was much appreciated by men starved of intellectual stimulation and for the same reason the lively debates that frequently took place were highly popular, as were the convivial concerts – although the house was 'dry'. It has been jokingly (but very exaggeratedly) said that Talbot House was the only house in Poperinge during the war that was not a brothel!

Only one soldier was killed in Talbot House during the war. He was Sgt G.J.M. Pegg, ASC CEF, who was mortally wounded by a shell that hit the side of The House on 28 May 1916. He is buried in Poperinghe New Mil Cemetery (qv).

From April 1918 the Germans pressed ever closer to Ypres, Kemmel fell, defensive lines were hastily built around Poperinge, great expanses of countryside between Dunkirk and St Omer were flooded. Poperinge was evacuated of civilians; cinemas, shops and other entertainments closed down. Alone Toc H remained open. But it was heavily shelled and eventually 'imperative orders to leave at once' were received. It closed on Whit Tuesday, 21 May to re-open on 30 September at the end of Fourth Ypres. It finally closed in December 1918.

Tubby moved to Knutsford after the war where in the prison he ran a Service Candidates' School for the many men who found spiritual solace in Talbot House and who had vowed that should they be spared they would offer their lives to the Ministry. It was Tubby's dream to recreate The House and its camaraderie in London and so the Toc H movement was founded in 1919. Then in 1929 Lord Wakefield of Hythe, at the instigation of Major Paul Slessor (who gave his name, to the 'Slessorium' – originally a bath house for post-war pilgrims – built in the garden in 1930 and to whom there is a memorial plaque in the hall), put up sufficient funds to buy the Old House. He also bought the 'Pool of Peace' or Spanbroekmolen crater at Wijtschate (qv) for Toc H. Lord Wakefield, who owned 'Wakefield Oil' which was to become known as Castrol, was Lord Mayor of London in 1915 and a prolific benefactor, especially of military causes.

During the 1930s when the Imperial War Graves Commission's workers were experiencing loneliness and isolation as their numbers declined and, as much of their work was in remote cemeteries, the Committee of Talbot House allowed the Commission's personnel to use the house as a club.

During World War II the Germans occupied Poperinge on 29 May 1940. One report, as yet unconfirmed, says they requisitioned Talbot House on 13 July and in 1943 used it as billets for the Kriegsmarine. On 6 September 1944, Polish troops liberated the town and all the precious contents, whisked away by local sympathisers as the Germans moved in, were soon restored. On 10 September the house re-opened, with its original purpose to act as a rest house for British soldiers.

Many original artefacts, pictures and signs remain to be seen, witness of Tubby's relaxed attitude and the sense of humour which made him so special. 'All rank abandon ye who enter here' was his motto, inscribed over his, the Chaplain's, room and other signs read 'To pessimists, way out', with an arrow pointing towards the front door; 'No Amy Robsart stunts down these stairs' (after the neck-breaking accident which befell the wife of Queen Elizabeth I's favourite, Essex); 'The waste-paper baskets are purely ornamental...'

Portraits by one of the ninety-odd

Chapel, Talbot House

official war artists, Eric Kennington, hang on the walls. Kennington enlisted with the 1/13th Bn the London Regiment on 6 August 1914, serving as a private soldier in France and Flanders before he was discharged unfit in January 1915 and was appointed an Official War Artist in 1916. Born in 1888, Kennington was a contemporary of Bernard Law Montgomery at St Paul's School. After the war he was art editor for T. E. Lawrence's *Seven Pillars of Wisdom* and, a sculptor as well as an artist, he executed the group of figures before the British War Memorial at Soissons and the 24th Division Memorial in Battersea Park. Some striking examples of his work hang in the Imperial War Museum.

The Chapel on the top floor, with its carpenter's bench which served as an altar, looks much the same as in the days when over 20,000 officers and soldiers received the Sacrament there before going into the trenches. In 1922 Barclay Baron, a founder member of Talbot House, suggested that the form of an early Christian lamp should become the symbol of Toc H ('as dim as a Toc H lamp' was a popular post-war phrase). The lamp was first lit by the Prince of Wales in 1923. In the well-tended, tranquil garden, which gave rest to many a man from the shattered landscape of the Salient, is an obelisk-shaped Mié Tabé Peace Post (qv) inaugurated on 24 September 1988. Mié is a Japanese artist who comes from Hiroshima (destroyed on 6 August 1945 by the first atomic bomb) and she has erected these pleas for world peace in some 70 countries. There are reputed to be thousands of them in Japan. The old Slessorium was converted into a Visitors' Centre for lectures and orientation talks.

During the war Tubby 'liberated' a hop store adjacent to the garden of Talbot House. 'I need that,' he said, and made a hole in the wall, only asking for permission from Poperinge Town Hall after the event. The hop store was then used as a Chapel and a theatre/lecture room – a sort of socio-cultural centre, where the many eminent intellectuals who simply became humble elements of the British fighting force rediscovered their civilian expertise and gave some fascinating talks. Oxbridge professors spoke on 'The Economic Position of Women', or 'The Drink Problem'. As Toc H grew in popularity the Upper Room was sometimes too small to house the large congregations who sought solace there. Then the hop store was used for services, with Godfrey Gardner, organist of the Royal Philarmonic Society, playing the 'old groan box'. The Welsh Guards sang hymns in their inimitable way. Lt Gen the Earl of Cavan (Commander of XIV Corps and a cousin of Tubby) often attended the services. Chess tournaments and whist drives were held, as were St Nicholas parties for local children and film shows of Charlie Chaplin's latest exploits. In the spring of 1917 when Poperinge was buzzing and overflowing with the build-up to Third Ypres regimental bands, music hall artists, concert parties, opera companies – all performed here, as did the resident house band and drama group. Lord Plumer was a regular attender, sitting in the front row.

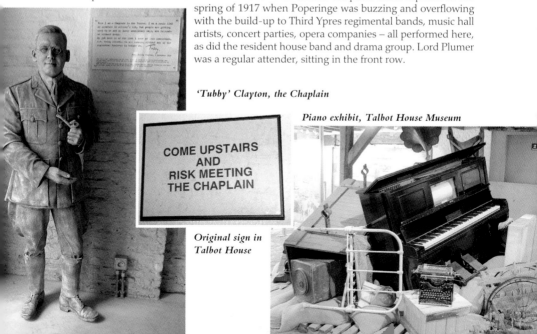

'Tubby' Clayton, the Chaplain

Piano exhibit, Talbot House Museum

COME UPSTAIRS
AND
RISK MEETING
THE CHAPLAIN

*Original sign in
Talbot House*

Talbot House, Poperinge

On 24 October 1996, the Talbot House Association finally succeeded in purchasing the old hop store, sold by the original owner, Georges Lebbe, in 1919. Once more it forms an integral part of the Old House. The Association also owns and runs The House and provides guides and members of staff to look after it. Their Chief Executive is Mrs Annelies Vermeulen, e-mail talbot.house@skynet.be Tel: + (0) 57 33 32 28.

The House has had a succession of wardens and guides. For many years the most knowledgeable and enthusiastic guide was the popular Jacques Ryckebosch (qv). Much research has been done by The Secretary, Mr Jan Louagie and his wife, authors of Talbot House – Poperinge, *'First Stop After Hell'*.

Talbot House provides clean and comfortable self-catering accommodation at a reasonable price. It makes an excellent base for touring the Salient. It is extremely popular – there is something very special about staying in this Club, so redolent of the Great War and the men who peopled it – and booking well in advance is advised. The bedrooms are gradually being redecorated in 'period' style and the ground floor toilets have been refurbished.

Until 2003 the House was entered by the imposing front door in Gasthuisstraat. However on 15 May 2004 the entrance was moved to Pottestraat (first right after the building). It leads into a reception and exhibition area with shop and toilets in the old Hop Store, which has been renovated and reinforced for the purpose. The shop is well stocked with books, maps and souvenirs, including a lovely, illustrated (with modern pictures of the House) version of Tubby Clayton's *10 Tales of Talbot House* and an amusing mock edition of **The Talbot Times.** The exhibition is based on 'Life Behind the Front' – e.g. medical facilities, traffic, entertainment and punishment etc. A new glass extension gives access to the first and second floor of The House and the garden has some informative plaques. The Slessorium houses audio-visual presentations on Talbot House itself and Little Talbot House (qv) and Skindles. It includes a recreation of Tubby's original 'hut' (located at Proven in 'Dingley Dell'). The small stream (once part of a tanner's workshop) has been opened up. On the first floor of the Hop Store the Concert Hall has been recreated with a lively audio-visual representation of a wartime concert (leaving intact the historic space used for drying hops). The second floor houses a documentation and archives area and is not part of the regular visitor circuit.

At first these changes created much controversy with regular and faithful visitors to Talbot House who had appreciated the delight of entering through the beautiful old front door to become immediately bathed in the warm glow of welcome created by Tubby in 1915 and which lingers still. Conscious of this, the Association gave them careful consideration but concluded that the changes had to be made for the very preservation of The House (a listed 18th Century building with a frail structure) itself. Such is the volume of visitors in recent years that the pressure has become too great for Talbot House to support and the Belgian Monumental Care Department seemed likely to insist on the measures. The changes are also designed to improve the quality of staying in The House. **Closed** Monday. **Open:** daily 1000-1730. Tel + (0) 57 33 32 28 e-mail: talbot.house@skynet.be website: info@talbothouse.be Consult this for Centenary events and exhibitions (which will include 'The Pool of Peace and Talbot House' and 'The Zenith of Talbot House').

Continue up the road to No 57 on the right

• WT7. No 57 Gasthuisstraat - 'Skindles' No 2

This was used extensively by pilgrims when it was opened after the war (still with the same owner, the widow Emma Bentin) taking the name of the original Skindles Hotel at No 12. The visitors' book contained many famous names, such as Field Marshal Haig and Lord Plumer and, during World War II, Joseph Goebbels and Field Marshal Montgomery. It ceased to be a hotel long ago.

Continue walking to the roundabout, and turn left following signs to Ypres to the T junction on Boeschepestraat.

•WT8. 'The Savoy Restaurant'.

At No 11, 125 yards to the right is the site of The Savoy. This was an officers' hotel run by Francois Herman. Despite the camaraderie of the trench lines a few miles away beyond Ypres, 'officers' and 'other ranks' establishments were clearly defined. The only significant exception was Talbot House, but this too became 'other ranks' when Skindles opened as an Officers' Club.

Turn left and continue along the road keeping to the right of St Bertin's Church into the Grote Markt.

On the left as you enter the Grote Markt is the local War Memorial which commemorates the dead of both wars. On the wall behind are memorial plaques.

Return to your car in the Grote Markt.

Option 2. The Special Visits

Extra Visits to the CWGC Cemeteries of Dozinghem (Westvleteren) Map T2, GPS: 50.89206 2.69904; Mendinghem (Proven) GPS: 50.89843 2.64414; and Bandaghem (Roesbrugge-Haringhe) GPS: 50.90170 2.61486, with three Albert Medal Winners.

Round trip: 15 miles. Approximate time: 1 hour 15 minutes

These three cemeteries, based on casualty clearing stations for the Passchendaele offensive, were named with typical Tommy's humour to sound like the many local names which bear the suffix 'hem', meaning settlement (e.g. Wulverghem, Houthem). Somewhat off the beaten track and not often visited, you may have difficulty in 'findinghem'. Following the appointment of Maj-Gen Skinner DMS as Surgeon-General each CCS was assigned a specific medical assignment. Dozinghem was for infected wounds, NYD (Not Yet Defined) gas cases and self-inflicted wounds; Mendinghem was for head wounds and tear gas cases and Bandaghem for 'back area' casualties and NYDN (Not Yet Defined Neurotic) conditions.

Continue by car on Pottestraat past the entrance to Talbot House museum and bear left on the road signed to Krombeke and continue on this road over roundabouts and cross roads to De Lovie on the left.

The old **Château at De Lovie (GPS: 50.87916 2.70327)**, now a home for mentally handicapped boys, was Fifth Army HQ during Third Ypres and King George V stayed here during his tour of the front in July 1917. It had been taken over in May 1915 by VI Corps who were followed by XIV Corps in February 1916 and by VIII Corps in July. II Corps took over from Fifth Army after Passchendaele. During the German offensive of April 1918, 34th, 41st and 49th Divisions all made their HQ here at one time or another, II Corps returning in August 1918. There was an aerodrome at what was then known as La Lovie.

General Gough had his HQ in the Château in June 1917 and he remembered it as

"…A large pretentious, ugly square building… A Belgian Count and his family was still in residence…There were sinister stories of their secret influence with the Germans, which was supposed to account for the Château having been spared from all bombardments."

Pass De Lovie and continue to the sign to St Sixtus Abbey to the right.

[N.B. St Sixtus Trappist Abbey (Map T1, GPS: 50.89554 2.72114)

This may be reached by turning right opposite a restaurant called

T'Jagershof Restaurant. Tel: + (0) 57 33 55 25. E-mail: info@hetjagershof.be Website: www.hetjagershof.be The restaurant has an interesting menu, pleasant terrace with games and has added an interesting WW1 Museum concentrating on the action nearby. **Open**: 1130-1800, Sun 0930-1200 and 1400-1800. Small entrance fee.

Field Gun outside Museum,
Jagershof Restaurant

Continue following signs to the Abbey, just over a mile away, through woods on Nonnenstraat,.

The monks are of the Cistercian or Trappist order and are committed to a life of seclusion, prayer and manual labour. They brew their powerful, dark beer and there is a sales office, Tel: + (0) 70 21 00 45. Over the road is an Information Centre/**Café/Shop 'In de Vrede'**, Tel: + (0)57 40 03 77, which has an audio visual historical presentation of the Abbey's history. There is some car parking which is shared between the Abbey and the restaurant.

During the war there were further CCS and other military establishments here. As many as 400,000 Allied soldiers lived in and around the Abbey during the war years, as well as hundreds of refugees. Here, too, as identified by Putkowski and Sykes in *Shot at Dawn*, was carried out the execution of Pte Herbert Chase of the 2nd Lancashire Fusiliers. Chase deserted shortly after he joined up, was arrested in October 1914, escaped and was not recaptured until December. In January 1915 he was sentenced to three years' imprisonment, a sentence that was suspended in May. On 23 May Chase went missing during a gas attack, was later found and declared to be showing no signs of having been gassed. He was executed on 12 May 1915. The bullet marks on the wall against which he was shot are still visible in the cloisters of the Abbey, one of the monks' private areas. They respect these marks and often say a prayer for Chase as they pass. The marks and the wall are featured in the audio-visual presentation. Chase was buried nearby, but his body was re-interred in White House CWGC Cemetery (qv) after the war.

A somewhat bizarre, but fully corroborated (to the authors by one of the monks) story links Gen Montgomery (who had served in Flanders with the R Warwicks in 1914) to the Abbey. During the retreat to Dunkirk in May 1940, Monty had his HQ at the Abbey and on leaving it he entrusted the Prior (or Deputy Abbot) with a trunk full of his possessions. The monks hid the trunk from the occupying Germans who were aware of its existence and were anxious to find it - eventually burying it. When his own shoes wore out, the Prior dug up the trunk and purloined Monty's, which were recognised as such by an Officer of the SD [German Security Police] in Ghent when the monk had to pay him a visit. The Prior was sometimes accused of collaborating with the Germans and it is thought that he had hoped to disprove this by openly wearing Monty's shoes. On 16 September 1944, after the liberation of the area, Monty wrote to the 'Père Abbé', to 'give you my very best thanks for helping me' in keeping the possessions and concealing them from the Germans.

Return to the main road.

Entrance to St Sixtus Abbey

Continue as the road goes through woods on each side until you see on the right the green CWGC sign to **Dozinghem CWGC Cemetery***. (Note that parking is difficult.)*

This is approached by a long rough track, driveable with some reversing on the way back. Here were situated 4th, 47th, 61st, 62nd and 63rd CCS, and the burial ground set up to serve them was in use until March 1918. It is a significant cemetery which contains 3,021 UK burials, 6 Australian, 34 BWI, 61 Canadian, 19 Newfoundland, 14 New Zealand, 15 South African, 3 Chinese Labour Corps, 65 Germans and a plot of 73 World War II burials from the withdrawal to Dunkirk in May 1940. 118 Belgians who were originally interred here have been removed. In it is buried **2nd Lt Edward Revere Osler** of A Battery 59th Bde RFA, age 21, killed on 30 August 1917. He was the son of Sir William Osler and a great-great grandson of Paul Revere, the American silversmith and patriot, leading light in the Boston tea party of 1773, who rode through the night of 18 April 1775, to Lexington to warn the colonists of Massachusetts of the approach of British troops and was the subject of Longfellow's poem, *The Midnight Ride of Paul Revere*. John McCrae (qv) had studied under the charismatic Osler at the Johns Hopkins Hospital in Baltimore. Osler, who was Regius Professor of Medicine at Oxford 1904-19, took an active interest in the Canadian Army Medical Corps during the war. McCrae visited him at Oxford whilst on leave in June 1917 and was to share his grief at the young Edward's death two months later. He had been seriously wounded in the chest, stomach and thigh near St Julien and rushed to the 47th CCS at Dozinghem. Several distinguished American surgeons (Harvey Cushing (qv), Eisenbrey, Darrach and Brewer) tried desperately to save this son of a famous physician, but without success. He was buried, wrapped in an army blanket covered by a British flag (how would his great-great grandfather have reacted to that?) in the adjoining cemetery where 'the new ditches half full of water [were] being dug by Chinese coolies wearing tin helmets'. Here too is buried **Pte Dominic Foaley** who died on 23 August 1917. His headstone reads, 'A native of Moscow Russia enlisted in Newfoundland Regt 24/11/15.'

Also buried in this Cemetery is **Flight Sub-Lieutenant G. L. Trapp** from British Columbia. Flying with 10th Squadron RNAS he had scored five victories when, diving on an enemy aircraft, his Camel broke up and he crashed to his death. His brother Stanley was killed with 8th Squadron RNAS in December 1916 and his brother Donovan with 85th Sqn RAF in July 1918. Ray Collishaw, who had commanded B Flight of 10th Squadron in 1917 and went on to become one of the top aces, wrote an account of his war in his book *Air Command* and married one of George Trapp's sisters.

Buried here too is **Commander Walter Sterndale-Bennett, DSO & Bar**, who was appointed Adjutant of Drake Bn, the RND, after Gallipoli. He was awarded the DSO for

Headstone of 2nd Lt E.R. Osler, Dozinghem Cemetery

Memorial Plaque to US Nurse Helen Fairchild, Dozinghem

**U.S. Army Reserve Nurse Helen Fair[ ]
(21.11.1884 -18.01.1918)**

From Pennsylvania Base Hospital 10, (Br. 16), Le Trepo[ ]
volunteered 22, July, 1917, as a surgical nurse for the [ ]
here in these Dozinghem fields at CCS No. 4. Sufferin[ ]
bombardment on 17 August, she was evacuated to Base H[ ]
10. Her chaplain wrote, "She died from her work at the [ ]
She lies buried in Somme American Military Cemetery, [ ]

Deze Amerikaanse verpleegster behoorde tot de Penns[ ]
Hospital Unit 10. Vanaf 22 juli 1917 werkte ze als opera[ ]
pleegster in Dozinghem CCS No.4 dat in de omliggende [ ]
stond. Na het nachtelijk luchtbombardement van 17 au[ ]
werd ze geëvacueerd naar Base Hospital 10 in Le Trépo[ ]
aalmoezenier schreef: "Ze stierf als gevolg van haar we[ ]
het front." Ze ligt begraven op Somme American Cen[ ]
Frankrijk.

Photo by courtesy of Women in Military Service for America Memorial Foundation,

his services to the battalion before and during the Battle of the Ancre in November 1916. He again used commendable initiative and leadership during the attack on Gavrelle on 22-25 April 1917, by which time he had been appointed Commander of Drake Bn. Sterndale-Bennett was mortally wounded on 4 November 1917, in an attack on Sourd Farm, in the area of Passchendaele New CWGC Cemetery, and died at the dressing station here on the 7th.

'Sterndale-Bennett possessed in rare degree the qualities, so seldom associated, of energy and judgement, and his death was a great loss,' wrote Douglas Jerrold in his *History of the Royal Naval Division*. He had a Bar to his DSO.

On 7 August 2010 a **Memorial Plaque to American Nurse Helen Fairchild**, who served as a surgical nurse at CCS No 4 from July 1917, was unveiled here. After the bombardment of 17 August she was evacuated to Base Hospital No 11 at Le Tréport, was exposed to mustard gas in November 1917, developed a gastric ulcer and died on 18 January 1918. She is buried in the American Cemetery at Bony on the Somme. Helen wrote many letters home which were collected by her niece, Nurse Nelle Fairchild-Rote, who was present at the ceremony. As the memorial is not standard, it could not remain in the cemetery but will be re-sited in the vicinity.

Continue to the next crossroads at the Café Leeuwerk and turn left direction Proven. Continue to the T junction and turn left. Continue to the village and turn right on the N308.

Proven was a busy rail centre for the BEF and the site of an aerodrome.

Continue some 500m to a green CWGC sign to the left.

Up a track is **Mendinghem British CWGC Cemetery** built to serve Nos 12, 46, 61 (staffed by Americans, who sometimes thought that 'Endinghem would have been a more appropriate name') and 64 CCS. No 46 was particularly active during Third Ypres, increasing its beds from 200 to 1,300. It contains 2,272 UK, 15 Australian, 26 British West Indies, 28 Canadian, 3 Newfoundland, 12 New Zealand, 33 South African, 8 Chinese Labour Corps and 51 Germans. As with many cemeteries attached to hospitals or CCSs, there are no unknown burials. It was designed by Sir Reginald Blomfield. In the Cemetery is the grave of **Captain (acting Lt Col) Bertram Best-Dunkley**, commanding 2/5th Bn the Lancashire Fusiliers, who was awarded the VC for his heroic leading of his men against heavy machine-gun and rifle fire until all their objectives had been taken on 31 July 1917, at Wieltje. He died here of his wounds on 5 August. Beside him lies **Lt the Hon Esmond Elliot**, CO 'G' Coy, 2nd Bn Scots Guards, age 22, died 6 August 1917, the younger son of the 44th Earl of Minto. Also buried here is **Maj C. M. B. Chapman, MC**, of 29 Sqn who was killed on 1 October 1917. Six days later his brother, Lt W. W. 'Bill' Chapman, was shot down by Lt Hans -Gottfried von Haebler of Jasta 36, Haebler's first victory. There are also three tragic graves of **executed British soldiers**: **Pte Charles Britton** of 1/5th Warwicks, 12 September 1917, for desertion, **Pte David Gibson** of 12 Royal Scots on 4 September 1918, for failing to return from leave and **Pte John Hyde** of the 10th KRRC on 5 September 1917, for desertion.

The American surgeon Dr Harvey Cushing (qv) described his wartime experiences in the book, *From a Surgeon's Journal* 1915-1918. In May 1917 he became Director of Base Hospital No 5 and was detached here with No 46 CCS from the end of July 1917 for the Messines and Passchendaele Battles. Then the RAMC personnel lived in canvas Armstrong huts and tents around the garden and tennis court that still existed and in Nissen huts in a pear orchard. Adjoining No 46 was No 12 and No 64 was 'just across a track.' No 46 was equipped to take in 1,000 mustard-gas cases. 'Poor devils', wrote Dr Cushing, 'I've seen too many of them since - new ones - their eyes bandaged, led along by a man with a string,

Headstone of Lt-Col Bertram Best-Dunkley, VC, Mendinghem CWGC Cemetery

while they try to keep to the duckboards. Some of the after-effects are as extraordinary as they are horrible ... They had about twenty fatalities out of the first 1,000 cases, chiefly from bronchial troubles. Fortunately vision does not appear to be often lost.' Cushing's words exactly describe John Singer Sargeant's powerful painting, *Gassed*, which hangs in the Imperial War Museum. Although an American citizen, Sargeant settled in London in 1885 and joined the ranks of British war artists during the war. He had already painted General Sir Ian Hamilton in 1898 and in 1922 painted *Some General Officers of the Great War.*

There was even 'secondhand' danger from the mustard gas. The evacuation officer, Telfer, 'did a lot of handling of patients himself and to-night has a bad cough, swollen and lachrymating eyes – like the men themselves.'

When Third Ypres opened on 2 August, Cushing reported that it was 'pouring cats and dogs all day – also pouring cold and shivering wounded, covered with mud and blood ... The pre-operation room is still crowded – one can't possibly keep up with them. Operating from 8.30 a.m. one day till 2 a.m. the next; standing in a pair of rubber boots and periodically full of tea as a stimulant, is not healthy. It's an awful business, probably the worst possible training in surgery for a young man ... Something over 2,000 wounded have passed, so far, through this one C.C.S. There are fifteen similar stations behind the battle front.'

The artist Professor Henry Tonks who had qualified in medicine and who was 52 when war broke out, often accompanied Sargeant (of whom he drew an amusing portrait in action on the Western Front) around the battlefields. His own painting *An Advanced Dressing-Station in France, 1918* (also in the IWM) illustrates the hell that Cushing wrote about in Belgium in 1917, while C. R. W. Nevinson's *The Harvest of Battle* (another IWM possession) depicts the pathetic stream of wounded towards the rear.

Continue to the village of Roesbrugge and turn left direction Haringhe. Follow CWGC signs to the southern outskirts of the village.

Haringhe (Bandaghem) British CWGC Cemetery. This Cemetery is listed on CWGC maps as 'Haringhe' and therefore often not located by those who are looking for 'Bandaghem'. Like Dozinghem and Mendinghem it was opened to serve the CCSs set up here in anticipation of casualties from Third Ypres. Here were Nos 62 and 63. No 62 CCS dealt with nervous cases and received 5,000 casualties during the battle. No 36 CCS was set up here in 1918 and operated until October of that year. The Cemetery, with its densely serried rows of headstones, now contains 732 UK, 2 Australian, 1 Bermuda, 4 BWI, 1 Canadian, 5 Newfoundland, 11 New Zealand, 4 Chinese Labour Corps, 1 French civilian and 39 German (other German, French, American and Belgian graves having been removed after the war). The cemetery was designed by Sir Reginald Blomfield.

One of the most unusual groupings of headstones – three recipients of the rare Albert Medal, side by side in Bandaghem Cemetery

A unique trio of headstones is to be seen here: **three Albert Medal winners** of 29th, 12th and 21st Lt Railway Operating Coy RE, buried side by side. They are **CSM A. H. Furlonger, DCM, and Sappers J. C. Farren and G. E. Johnston.** Their medals were awarded for an act of heroism on 30 April 1918, when they were manning an ammunition train as it arrived at a refilling point. They had just uncoupled the engine when the second truck suddenly burst into flames. Furlonger immediately ordered the driver, L/ Cpl J. E. Bigland (also awarded the AM) to move the engine back to pull away the two trucks nearest the engine. Without hesitation Bigland did so. Furlonger coupled the engine himself and Sapper J. H. Woodman (the fifth winner of the AM in this incident) uncoupled the burning truck from the remainder of the train. The two trucks were drawn clear of the ammunition dump but the ammunition in the burning truck exploded, completely wrecking the engine and both trucks, killing Furlonger, Farren and Johnston and seriously wounding Bigland. 'Had it not been for the courageous action of these men, whereby three of them lost their lives and one was seriously injured, there is not the slightest doubt that the whole dump would have been destroyed and many lives lost', reads the citation in the *London Gazette.*

The rare Albert Medal (only 45 of the higher class and 290 of the lower class have been awarded) was instituted by a Royal Warrant (named after Prince Albert) dated 7 March 1866, for acts of gallantry at sea. In 1877 it was extended to the land. There were two classes of the medal - 1st: Gold and 2nd: Bronze. The standards of gallantry required to win this award have always been extremely high. The criterion is that 'the recipient's risk of death has to be greater than his chances of survival'. In the case of the Gold Medal the risk has to be 'exceptional'. In 1971 the Albert Medal ceased and living recipients were invited to exchange their medals for the George Cross.

Return to the N308 and hence Poperinge and pick up the main itinerary.

Option 3. Continue with the Main Itinerary

Poperinge seems to change the one-way system frequently and so the following directions are more general than we would like but should work. From the square take the N308 in the Ieper direction. En-route you will pass -

• Poperinge Railway Station/39.1 miles/GPS: 50.85478 2.73572

This is on the right {PR13}. As a centre of military comings and goings it was a registered target for the enemy's long-range artillery and a very hot and unpopular spot. Opposite was an Officers' Club – 'a most inviting and comfortable place with a verandah in front where we lounged in deck chairs and drank whisky whilst watching the chains of vehicles crawling past towards Ypres,' reported Campion Vaughan (qv).

Continue using the right fork ahead on Ieperstraat. At the roundabout junction with the R33 ring road turn right signed to Abele.
Continue over the railway line to the CWGC sign at the next roundabout and turn right to Centrum. Continue to the cemetery on the right.

• Poperinghe New Military Cemetery/40.5 miles/10 minutes/Map F4/ GPS: 50.84738 2.73305

Here lie more (**17**) **executed soldiers** than in any other Western Front Cemetery: **Pte J. H. Wilson** 9.7.16; **Pte C. LaLiberte** 4.8.16; **Pte J. Bennett** 28.8.16; **Pte A. Botfield** 18.10.16; **Pte R. Stevenson** 28.10.16; **Pte B. McGeehan** 2.11.16; **Pte R.T. Tite** 25.11.16; **Pte W.H. Simmonds** 1.12.16; **2nd Lt E.S. Poole** 10.12.16 (one of only three officers executed on the Western Front); **Pte J. Crampton** 4.2.17; **Pte J.W. Fryer** 14.6.17; **Pte J.S. Michael** 24.8.17; **Pte J. Stedman** 5.9.17; **Sgt J.T. Wall** 6.9.17; **Pte G. Everill** 14.9.17; **Pte W. H. Morris** 20.9.17 and **Pte F.C. Gore** 16.10.17.

Poperinghe New Mil Cemetery

Crocheted poppy tributes, Poperinghe New Mil Cemetery

After years of campaigning by the descendants of soldiers 'shot at dawn', in August 2006 the British Government announced a group pardon for the 306 men executed during the war. The New Zealand Government had already pardoned its executed soldiers in 2005. Although there was immense sympathy for the families who have lived under a cloud of stigma for nearly a hundred years, and there are indubitably some horrendous miscarriages of justice in the trials and sentencing of men, often poorly represented and/or suffering from shell-shock and other nervous conditions, there was not universal approval for the action. Historian Corelli Barnett, for example, warned of the danger of applying modern morals and ethical values to the past and the fact that a blanket pardon would include cases of real criminality, dereliction of duty etc. The graves of several other executed soldiers are visited on the itineraries in this book – consult the Index.

Also buried here is **16 year old Rfn Alfred Robert Halford**, 8th KRRC, 5 August 1915 and **Pte G. Ryan,** 2nd Hants, age 22, 9 August 1916. His brother, Pte H. Ryan, was killed on the same day. He is buried in Potijze Burial Ground CWGC Cemetery.

There is a large French plot to the left containing 271 graves including two Belgian civilian women: **Martha Declerq** (died 14 July 1917) and **Euphrasie Vanneste**, buried under French grave markers. Ten Belgian soldiers originally buried here were transferred to Westvleteren Belgian Cemetery or returned to their families. The Cemetery was first established in June 1915 and was designed by Sir Reginald Blomfield.

Return to Ypres.

• End of Itinerary Two

ITINERARY THREE

- **Itinerary Three** starts in Ypres, and concentrates on the southern part of the Salient, the mining activities of Third Ypres around Mesen, the Fourth Ypres loss of Kemmel Hill and returns to Ypres via Dikkebus.
- **The Main Route:** Ypres – Little Toc H, Lille Gate, Rose Coombs Memorial, Ramparts CWGC Cemetery, Shrapnel Corner; Bedford House CWGC Cemetery; Lankhof Farm Bunkers and Demarcation Stone; St Eloi – Tunnellers' Memorial, Craters; 19th (Western) Div Memorial; Oosttaverne Wood CWGC Cemetery, Bunkers; Somer Farm CWGC Cemetery; Wytschaete - Military British Cemetery/16th (Irish) Div Memorial, 36th (Ulster) Div and 16th (Irish) Div Memorials; Spanbroekmolen, Lone Tree CWGC Cemetery; Kruisstraat Craters; Messines Ridge British CWGC Cemetery, New Zealand Memorial; Mesen – New Zealand Soldier Statue, Info Centre, Christmas Truce Statue, RB Plaque, Peace Post, Church, Frickleton VC Memorial, New Zealand Memorial Park & Bunkers; Island of Ireland Peace Tower and Park; Ploegsteert – Hyde Park Corner/Royal Berks CWGC Cemeteries, Plugstreet Memorial, Plugstreet '14-'18 Interpretation Centre, Bunkers, Strand Military CWGC Cemetery, Churchill Memorial; Lancashire Cottage CWGC Cemetery, Le Gheer; Le Pélérin Mine; Pte Wilkinson Cross, Bairnsfather's Billet and Plaque, Khaki Chums Christmas Truce Cross, Prowse Point Christmas Truce Memorial & Military CWGC Cemetery, Mud Corner CWGC Cemetery, Toronto Ave CWGC Cemetery, Ploegsteert Wood Military CWGC Cemetery, Rifle House CWGC Cemetery; Underhill Farm CWGC Cemetery; Neuve Eglise (Nieuwkerke) Churchyard, Capt Crowe VC Info Board; Kemmel Château Military CWGC Cemetery; Kemmel Hill and Belvedere, French Memorial and Cemetery; Lettenberg Bunkers; La Laiterie CWGC Cemetery; American Monument; Vierstraat Demarcation Stone; Suffolk CWGC Cemetery; Godezonne Farm CWGC Cemetery; French 32nd Division Memorial; Kemmel No 1 French CWGC Cemetery; Klein Vierstraat British CWGC Cemetery; 'American Bridge' Dickebusch New Military CWGC Cemetery Extension, Dickebusch New Military CWGC Cemetery, Dickebusch Old Military CWGC Cemetery, Dikkebus Lake; Belgian Battery Corner CWGC Cemetery; Railway Dugouts Burial Ground CWGC Cemetery; Blauwepoort Farm CWGC Cemetery; Zillebeke Demarcation Stone, Church Memorial & Churchyard Cemetery; Tuileries British CWGC Cemetery; Perth (China Wall) British CWGC Cemetery; Ypres.
- **Planned duration**, excluding stops for refreshments, Extra Visits and N.B.s: 9 hours 15 minutes. **Driving Time**: I hour 15 minutes.
- **Total distance**: 42 miles.
- **Extra Visits** are suggested to: Bus House CWGC Cemetery, Voormezele Enclosure CWGC Cemeteries 1, 2, 3, Bunker; Croonaert – Croonaert Chapel CWGC Cem, Fr Chass à Pied Mem, Bayern Wood, Hitler's Sunken Road picture site; Irish House CWGC Cemetery; Mesen – London Scottish Memorial; St Yvon – Craters; Locre – No 10 CWGC Cemetery, Demarcation Stone Locre South, Churchyard Cemetery and French Memorial Plaques, Hospice CWGC Cemetery, Private Memorial to Maj Redmond; Dranoutre Mil CWGC & Dranouter Churchyard Cemeteries, Lindenhoek Chalet Mil Cemetery.
- **N.B.s** are suggested to; Peckham Farm Crater; Sgt Ribout Memorial, Ploegsteert; Sgt K. Pavlik Memorial, Dranouter.

• *Ypres/0 miles/RWC*

Leave the Grote Markt along Rijselstraat at the N336 Regina Hotel corner.

No 83 on the left is the site of Little Toc H (GPS: 50.84781 2.88802) which opened on 13 November 1917, and lasted for three months until the withdrawal from Passchendaele during Fourth Ypres, when it matched the facilities of the senior house in Poperinghe. There is a commemorative Plaque

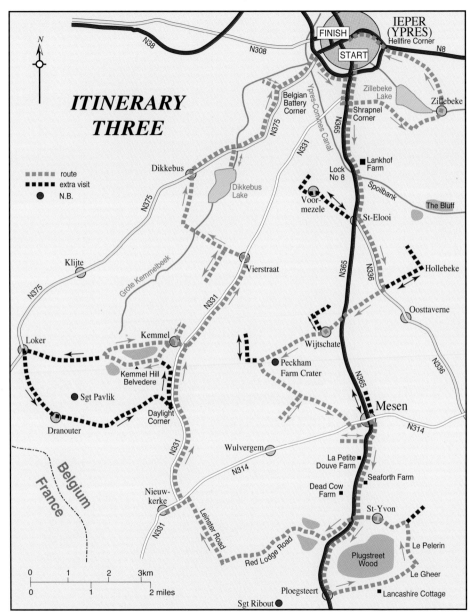

on the wall. The Town Major of Ypres from 1916 to 1918, Captain James Lee, DSO (qv), was one of the leading lights in setting up the facility. On 17 April 1918, Capt Lee claimed to be 'the oldest present inhabitant of Yper during the War'. The previous night 'the two rooms used by the Town Major, which had remained intact from the beginning of the siege … were smashed in by two heavy shells' and 'nearly all the noteworthy buildings have now disappeared'. Lee, who had enlisted in the Argyll & Sutherland Highlanders in 1891 had served in India, volunteered again in 1914, age 42. He went on to become Town Major of Hazebrouck in 1918 when he was promoted to Lt Col. He was awarded the Order of Leopold and the Belgian *Croix de Guerre* and the silver *Médaille Reconnaissance Française*. He was twice mentioned in Despatches and died aged 87 in 1959.

Plaque on Little Talbot House, 83 Rijselstraat

Continue past St Peter's Church to the town gate. Park before it on the right.

Just before the Gate on the right is the **'T Kleine Rijsel pub**. No longer a museum but a popular pub with excellent beer. Irregular opening times. Tel: + (0) 57 20 02 36.

• *Lille Gate/0.6 miles/GPS: 50.84461 2.89030*

The towers of the gate date from 1395 and the ramparts were revamped by Vauban. Most British troops entered the Salient through here as the Menin Gate was particularly exposed to enemy observation. On the left under the arch is a doorway which once led to a small museum and previously to dugouts, with which all the ramparts were riddled. This one was used at one time as an HQ for the Canadian Tunnelling Companies. Canada was the first of the Dominions to provide such specialist units.

Under the arch are some original IWGC signs to local cemeteries.

Lille Gate with, inset, original IWGC Cemetery signs

Walk up the ramparts to the right.

• Rose Coombs Memorial Walk/Ramparts CWGC Cemetery/10 minutes/Map H 22, 23

The path to Ramparts Cemetery is dedicated to Rose Coombs of the IWM whom we knew well and whose book *Before Endeavours Fade* revived interest in the World War I battlefields when it was published in 1976. Rose deliberately chose that title so that the initial letters gave BEF. This hauntingly beautiful cemetery, running down to the moat, is one of Ypres' smallest and was begun by the French in November 1914 and used by the British from February 1915 to 1918.

Burials recorded here are 153 UK, 11 Australian, 10 Canadian, 14 New Zealand and 5 unknown. Rose Coombs' ashes were buried here on 4 May 1991, (she died on 7 January), marked only by a rosebush.

Cross to the other side of the Gate and walk a short way along the restored ramparts towards the Menin Gate.

Note the remains of old shelters and machine-gun emplacements which mark the line of a trench which once ran all along the top of the ramparts.

Return to your car and leave Ypres from the Lille Gate following signs to Armentières on the N336.

In 1918, to strengthen the Ypres defences, the British destroyed the sluice gates at Zillebeke Lake and flooded the ground to the left from Ypres up to the railway crossing.

Continue straight over the roundabout to the railway line. This is:

Ramparts CWGC Cemetery, Ieper

• Shrapnel Corner/1.1 miles

This crossroads was a regular target for German guns. As at Hellfire Corner much traffic passed this way, particularly at night when ammunition and rations were taken to the line. During the day it was normal to gallop across.

Continue towards Armentières and stop at the cemetery on the left.

• Bedford House CWGC Cemetery/1.8 miles/20 minutes/Map M13/ GPS: 50.82705 2.88803

'Bedford House' (original name Château Rosendal) was a moated château whose remains are still (but difficult to discern) in front of the Cemetery. It was used by nearby British Field Ambulances and Dressing Stations from the early days of the war as a burial ground. It was hardly touched until January 1917 when it was used as an HQ by 55 Brigade and severely damaged by 8in shells. In one day during Third Ypres more than 500 gas shells were dropped in the area. In this large Cemetery with five different enclosures are 3,951 UK, 201 Australian, 6 BWI, 3 Guernsey, 20 Indian, 30 New Zealand, 1 Russian, 335 South African and 501 unknown burials, with 47 Special Memorials. It

Bedford House CWGC Cemetery

was designed by W C von Berg. It contains the grave of **Temp 2nd Lt Rupert Price Hallowes VC** of the 4th Bn the Middlesex Regt, who for five days inspired his men with no thought for his own safety until he was killed himself on 30 September 1915, at Hooge. Also buried in Enclosure No 2 **is Lt Philip Comfort Starr** of 154th Field Coy, RE, killed on a night reconnaissance before Ypres on 20 February 1918, age 28. Comfort, 'One of Harvard's Vanguard', was from Chicago and went to Canada to volunteer in 1916. In 1919, a street in Winnetka where he grew up, was named after him. In Enclosure No 4 is the Jewish headstone of **Pte Harry Reidler** of the Russian Labour Corps killed on 17 July 1919. It is believed that his real first name was Isaac and that his family were immigrant Jews who lived in Britain from whose community two labour battalions were formed and sent to France in 1918.

Buried in the Cemetery is **Lt Lionel Henry Salvin Bowlby**, age 24, R Scots Greys, 4 June 1916, brother of **Capt Geoffrey Vaux Bowlby** (qv).

On a cold, wet and windy 10 November 2002, following the unveiling of their new memorial at the Menin Gate (qv), an Indian ceremony of remembrance, led by Major-General A.S. Bajwa and at which two Gurkha Pipers played a lament, was held in the Cemetery where there are several Indian graves. The inclement weather was a reminder of how these volunteer soldiers from hot climes suffered in the cold winter of 1914 in Flanders. The General had arrived in Summer uniform (the authors were heavily wrapped) and despite the awful conditions showed no signs of discomfort.

Continue to the large farm on the left with bunkers in front of it.

• *Lankhof Farm Bunkers/Demarcation Stone/2.1 miles/Map M14,15/ GPS: 50.82234 2.88916*

The farm, originally surrounded by a moat, was extensively used by artillery and infantry units during the war. Known as the Lankhof Battery, 36th Bty RFA provided support for 23rd Division at Hill 60 in April 1917 and a bombardment on the Messines Ridge prior to the attack in June. In November 1917, at the end of the Passchendaele Battles, the shell-proof concrete shelters were started by 153rd Coy RE and completed by 4th Field Coy of the Australian Engineers who took over in January 1918. On 25 April 1918 the 18th Reserve Corps of the German 7th Division reached Lankhof in their major assault on Ypres. The bunkers were then strengthened by the 6th Bn of the Leicesters, who were nevertheless surrounded on 27 April and forced out. A platoon of 8th Bn attempted to recapture them, but were also beaten off, as was a company of the 7th Bn. On 30 August 1918, following the German withdrawal after the failure of their Lys Campaign, the area became the responsibility of the 30th US Division which successfully withstood a German attack here on 2 September.

The Bunkers can clearly be seen (other than when maize is planted around them), but are on private property, on a small island to the left. As the road rises to cross the canal at Lock No 8 about 100m on from Lankhof, there is a **Demarcation Stone** on the right (**GPS: 50.82095 2.89035**).

Continue on the N365 until the road forks at the roundabout in St Eloi.

The Lankhof Farm Bunkers

Extra Visit to Bus House CWGC Cemetery (Map M16/GPS: 50.81290 2.88735) & Voormezeele Enclosure CWGC Cemeteries 1 and 2 & 3 (and grave of original 'Peter Pan') (Map M8, 7/GPS: 50.81776 2.87411/50.81843 2.87371) & Bunker (Map M6)

Round trip: 2 miles. Approximate time: 15 minutes.

Turn sharp right, signed Voormezele, to Bus House CWGC Cemetery (easily missed), on the left.

This small Cemetery (109 UK burials, 10 Australian, 1 British West Indies, 2 Canadian and 12 unknown) was started, like so many of the cemeteries in this area, in June 1917. It was named for the nearby estaminet, so-called, according to Rose Coombs, because one of the London Transport B-type ('Ole [sic] Bill') omnibuses used at the beginning of the war to transport troops to the front (an example of which can be seen in the IWM) was used here by the 1/14th London Scottish to take them to Wijtschate. There they became the first Territorial Battalion to take part in the War. In this area **Acting Sgt Louis McGuffie** of the 1/5th Bn KOSB won the **VC** on 28 September 1918, for entering enemy dugouts and single-handedly taking many prisoners. He was killed on 4 October and is buried in Zantvoorde British CWGC Cemetery (qv).

There are also 79 British and 2 French burials from the withdrawal to Dunkirk in May 1940. The Cemetery was designed by C.W. Cowlishaw

Bus House CWGC Cemetery, Voormezeele

The hill behind the Cemetery is Mont Kemmel.

Continue to the church at Voormezeele.

In front of it is a **Mié Tabé Peace Post** (qv) (GPS: 50.81668 2.87677) and in the churchyard is a **Special Memorial** to **Lt Edwin Robinson**, 5th (Royal Irish) Lancers, killed on 25 October 1914 and whose grave was destroyed by shellfire.

Continue to the T junction. Turn right and continue to Voormezeele Enclosures 1 and 2 CWGC Cemeteries on the left.

This Cemetery, which contains 502 UK, 17 Australian, 53 Canadian, 2 New Zealand, 43 unknown and 5 German burials, was begun in March 1915. Originally there were two separate Regimental plots which are now undivided. The Germans used the cemetery during their occupation of the village in mid-1918. There are fifteen Special Memorials and here is buried **CSM Henry Gerald Weston**, 8th Bn, Queen's Own R West Kent Regt, 17 November 1915. Weston, a public school boy from a good family, was a pre-1914 professional soldier who had a somewhat lurid and louche career in India with the RWF which is described in amusing detail by Frank Richards (qv) in *Old Soldier Sahib*, with explanatory annotations by Dr. H.J. Krijnen (qv). Weston later served in both the Australian and NZ Forces and after this picaresque career returned to the UK to enlist in 1915.

Special Memorial to Lt E.W. Robinson, Voormezeele Churchyard

Continue to Voormezeele Enclosure No 3 CWGC Cemetery, whose entrance is on the right.

This was started by Princess Patricia's Canadian Light Infantry in February 1915. After the Armistice over 1,200 bodies were moved here and now there are 1,481 UK, 8 Australian, 100 Canadian, 2 New Zealand, 3 South African and 612 unknown burials with 20 Special Memorials. In it is buried **2nd Lt George Llewelyn Davies**, 6th Bn KRRC, attd 4th Rifle Bde, killed on 15 March 1915. In 1897 the playwright J. M. Barrie befriended George, his brothers Jack and baby Peter (and later two more brothers, Michael and Nicholas) as they were walked in Kensington Gardens by their nanny. The boys' father died in 1907, their mother in 1910 and Barrie became their benevolent guardian. After Eton, George went to Cambridge where he became a member of the OTC and in 1914 volunteered. He was commissioned in the Special Reserve of the 60th Rifles. In September Barrie travelled to New York with A. E. W. Mason and there was interviewed by the *New York Herald*:

Worn Headstone of 'The real Peter Pan', 2nd Lt George Llewelyn Davies, Vormezeele Enclosure No 3 CWGC Cemetery

'It's funny that **the real Peter Pan** [George] – I called him that – is off to the war now. He grew tired of the stories I told him, and his younger brother [Jack, who joined the Navy after attending Naval College, Dartford] became interested. It was such fun telling those two about themselves. I would say, 'Then you came along and killed the pirate' and they would accept every word as truth. That's how Peter Pan came to be written. It is made up of a few stories I told them.'

George corresponded regularly with 'Uncle Jim' until in the early hours of 15 March his battalion advanced on St Eloi in an attempt to drive out the Germans. A fellow officer, Aubrey Tennyson, described George's premonition of death as they advanced and his desire to be buried where he might fall. He was shot through the head during a briefing by his Colonel and died almost immediately. It was simply not practical to carry out his wish to bury him on the spot and the body was taken back here to Voormezele and the grave planted with violets. A letter from him to Barrie, dated 14 March, and exhorting him to keep up his courage was delivered the following morning. According to Peter Davies, Barrie was 'shaken to the core' by George's death coming at the end of a series of personal tragedies. George's uncle, Guy du Maurier (qv) had been killed only six days earlier at Kemmel and is buried in Kemmel Château Military CWGC Cemetery (qv).

The Voormezeele Cemeteries were designed by Sir Edwin Lutyens with W.C. Von Berg.

Continue to the farm ahead on the right.

Just before the entrance is a large Bunker, which may be obscured by maize.

Turn round and return to pick up the main itinerary.

Continue straight over the roundabout onto Rijselseweg (the third exit), the N336, and stop immediately on the right.

• Monument to the St Eloi Tunnellers/1916 & 1917 Craters/3.0 miles/15 minutes/Map16a, 17/GPS: 50.81002 2.89206/50.80910 2.89348

The brick Memorial, erected on 11 November 2001, bears transparent Plaques with details of the mining activities by 172nd Tunnelling Coy 3rd Br Div, 2nd Can Div and 7th Belg Fld Arty. **T.E. Hulme** (qv) served in the trenches at St Eloi in the spring of 1915 and wrote a poem *Trenches: St Eloi* which expresses the mind-numbing emptiness and apparent futility of trench warfare:

....Behind the line, cannon, hidden, lying back miles.
Before the line, chaos:
My mind is a corridor. The minds about me are corridors.
Nothing suggests itself. There is nothing to do but keep on.

Hulme was wounded in the arm here on 14 April 1915 with a 'Blighty one'. An extract from his poem is inscribed on the Memorial.

The British flag flies beside it and in 2003 the gun was added.

Two of the Craters blown here on 27 March 1916 and 7 June 1917 are now visitable, one on each side of the road. On the right after some 50 yards is an Information Board about the 7 June 1917 mine and a wooden path through a locked gate leads to the impressive water-filled Crater where there is a seat and more Information Boards. A trail round the Crater leads to a well-preserved Bunker. **Note**: Access is available from 1 April-15 Nov from 1000-1700. To enter you must pick up the code from the Tourist Office in Ieper before you leave the town or ring them on +(0) 57 23 92 20 from the entry gate, giving your name and mobile phone no. Well worth the effort.

Walk over the road to the small road to the left, keeping left by the telephone exchange tower to the second crater.

This Crater was created by one of six mines blown astride the old German front line at 0415 hours on 27 March 1916. Shafts dug to position the mines were up to 55ft deep and took more than 8 months to prepare. The mines were blown as part of an assault by 9th Brigade, after which most of the 4th Royal Fusiliers' objectives were still in enemy hands. Casualties were forty officers and 809 other ranks. On 3 April, 76th Brigade was brought in to reinforce a new attack. During the assault the Brigade Major, Etonian Capt Billy Congreve (qv), reached the rim of one of the craters. He wrote in his diary:

Memorial to St Eloi Tunnellers with Krupp Kanon

'Imagine my surprise and horror when I saw a whole crowd of armed Boches! I stood there for a moment feeling a bit sort of shy, and then I levelled my revolver at the nearest Boche and shouted, 'Hands up, all the lot of you!' A few went up at once, then a few more and then the lot; and I felt the proudest fellow in the world as I cursed them. '

Crater at St Eloi, 27 March 1916

Bunker near St Eloi crater, and crater, St Eloi, June 1917

Congreve brought in four officers and sixty-eight men – though other accounts make it five officers and seventy-seven men – for which he was recommended for the VC (which he was not to receive until July 1916 and then posthumously after further acts of bravery on the Somme) and awarded the DSO.

Today the water-filled crater is stocked with fish.

Beyond the Crater was the artificial hill known as 'The Mound', made from spoil from a nearby brickworks. It was about 10m high and 100m across and featured in many accounts of the fighting of March 1915. On the 14th the Germans mounted an attack on St Eloi, blowing two mines and capturing the Mound. The 2nd Royal Irish Fusiliers sustained many casualties in the action and their gallant bayonet charge was recorded by the *Graphic's* war artist, Charles Payne (known as 'Snaffles'). Prints of the picture were sold with the caption by Rudyard Kipling, 'There were lads from Galway, Louth and Meath Who went to their death with a joke in their teeth.'

In April the Worcesters took over the trenches opposite the Mound which was still held by the Germans, and described it as 'a particularly unpleasant area of activity' (much of it underground by both sides).

One of the Royal Army Chaplains' Department's three World War I VCs was won here, the others being the Rev Theodore Bayley Hardy, DSO, MC (qv), who won his on the Somme and

Rev William Robert Fountaine Addison who won his in Mesopotamia. The third and first was Capt the Rev T/Chaplain Edward Noel Mellish, MC, whoever the period 27-29 March 1916, 'went backwards and forwards under continuous and very heavy shell and machine-gun fire between our original trenches and those captured from the enemy, in order to tend and rescue wounded men. He brought in ten badly wounded men on the first day from ground swept by machine-gun fire. He went back on the second day and brought in twelve more and on the night of the third day he took charge of a party of volunteers and once more returned to the trenches to rescue the remaining wounded.'

The 1917 mining activity in this area is covered on page 141.

Continue on the N336.

After some 750yds the **Diependaalhoek Bunker** (Map M18/GPS: 50.80291 2.89726) can be seen to the left.

Continue to the next crossroads, on the left is (but difficult to stop by)

• *Memorial Cross to the 19th (Western 'Butterfly') Div/Oosttaverne Wood CWGC Cemetery/Bunkers/4.3 miles/10 minutes/Map M19, 20, 21/GPS: 50.79469 2.90110/50.79400 2.90238*

The Memorial marks the area of one of the greatest successes of the 19th Division in which they used a barrage of massed machine guns for the first time. The 19th was in the opening battle of Messines on 7 June 1917, when 19 mines were blown at 0310 in the morning. The battle line is shown on the Holts' map and from there the objective lines were Red, Blue, Green and finally Black. The Black line at this crossroads was reached in just 5 hours and 57th Brigade of the Division took Oosttaverne village just ahead. By noon the Division had taken 1,253 prisoners and lost 51 officers and 1,358 other ranks killed, wounded or missing. The Memorial is similar to the one at la Boisselle on the Somme.

Memorial to 19th Division, Oosttaverne

Continue to the cemetery on the right.

Oosttaverne Wood Cemetery was opened in June 1917 and after the Armistice graves from the surrounding battlefield were concentrated here, including Germans. It contains 923 UK burials, 43 Australian, 133 Canadian, 19 New Zealand, 1 French, an unknown number of Germans and one **Special Memorial**. It was designed by Sir Edwin Lutyens with N.A. Rew.

Behind it are two **German Bunkers**.

In this area on 3 August 1917, the **Rev Theodore Bayley Hardy** (qv) was awarded the **DSO** for having stayed 'between 36 and 48 hours' through pouring rain with a man slowly dying as he was being sucked into the mud. Though suffering himself from a broken wrist that was in splints and from complete exhaustion, this 53 year old Padre remained with the soldier, offering him food and drink on a long pole, and comfort and support, until all efforts to save him failed and he died.

Bayley Hardy went on to win the **MC** at Larch Wood (qv) in October 1917 and the **VC** at Bucquoy near Gommecourt for acts of gallantry on 5, 25, 26 and 27 April 1918. King George V presented the award to this modest man, whose catch-phrase, as he frequently crept out under fire in No Man's Land, was, 'It's only me, boys'. In 1967 the ceremony

German Bunker, Oosttaverne
Wood – 'with house on top'!

was recorded in an oil painting by Terence Cuneo who died in 1996. It hangs in the newly formed Armed Forces Chaplaincy Centre in Amport House, Netheravon. Bayley Hardy died of wounds at Rouen on 18 October, the most-decorated non-combatant of World War I. He is buried in St Sever Cemetery Extension, Rouen.

Return to the crossroads. Turn left towards Wijtschate. Continue to the cemetery on the left,

• Somer Farm CWGC Cemetery/5.1 miles/10 minutes/Map M32/GPS 50.79047 2.88965

Also started during the Battle of Messines, this small Cemetery now contains 64 UK, 22 Australian, 1 Unknown burial and **5 Special Memorials**. The area was the scene of heavy fighting on 31 October 1914, when the London Scottish rushed to fill a gap in the line, suffering heavy casualties, then again in 1917 during the Messines Battle, and finally during the Fourth Battle of Ypres. On 26 May 1996, Peter Wallace Jones, an Australian Vietnam veteran from New South Wales, proudly attended a ceremony in this cemetery which was the culmination of an inspiring 20-year-long crusade to add inscriptions to two headstones. Jones had been researching the service of his grandfather, L Cpl Wallace Alfred Jones of the 53rd Australian Battalion, killed nearby on 17 March 1918, and buried here. By examining old photographs he found that four men had been buried in two graves. The CWGC headstones had recorded only two burials – **Pte G. R. G. Hill** in one grave and **L/Cpl J. F. K Comb** in the other. Jones, using the Regimental records of the 53rd Bn, deduced that the two missing men, whom he identified as **Pte R. Pendleton** and **Pte S. I. Mears** (who were commemorated on the Menin Gate), were actually buried with Hill and Comb and that all four of them had been killed together by a shell. Peter Jones was

Headstones of Pte G. Hill and L/Cpl J.F. Comb, with added names of Ptes R. Pendleton and S. Mears, Somer Farm CWGC Cemetery

determined to get the omission rectified and contacted the Australian War Graves Commission. He also contacted the relatives of twenty of the twenty-two Australians buried in Somer Farm and discovered that Pendleton's father had tried in vain to locate his son's grave and that, ironically, Mears, one of four brothers who had volunteered, (only two of whom were to survive – one shell-shocked and the other suffering from being gassed), wrote home to his sister telling her 'not to let any more belonging to [her] get over there' as he saw 'his mistake now' – i.e. in volunteering.

The CWGC agreed with Jones's theory and he determined to witness the headstones being changed in person. His State RSL and the Department of Veteran Affairs declined to help, but thanks to sub-branches of the Vietnam Veterans, Cathay Pacific and Europ Net, plus personal fundraising he and his wife made the trip. Also present was Malcolm Mears, grand-nephew of Stan Mears. Peter Jones was also gratified to get his grandfather's age on his headstone corrected from 27 to 25 and Mears' and Pendleton's names removed from the Menin Gate. Note that there is no Latin Cross on the headstones now because room was needed for the extra names.

Continue to the crossroads.

• Wijtschate

Nicknamed 'Whitesheet' by the Tommies, fighting began around here in the first year of the war.

The Germans held this area of high ground despite efforts by both the British and the French to take it. In the first, Messines, phase of the Third Battle of Ypres, the village was taken by the 36th (Ulster) Division and the 16th (South of Ireland) Division. On 3 July 1917 General Plumer presented King Albert of the Belgians with the bell of the church which had been dug out of the ruins. Serving near Wijtschate from 6 June 1917 with 224th Siege Battery RGA was the vorticist artist, writer and philosopher, Wyndham Lewis. Lewis was born on 18 November 1882, of an American father and a British mother. Deserted by his father, he was brought up in England by his mother, attending Rugby and the Slade School of Art, where he was taught by Henry Tonks (qv). On 20 June 1914 he launched the Vorticists group and their avant-garde magazine *Blast*. In March 1916 Lewis volunteered with the RGA, being commissioned at the end of the year. On 24 May 1917 he arrived on the Western Front with 330 Siege Battery RGA before the move to Wijtschate in time for Plumer's successful assault on the Messines Ridge. Lewis acted as an observer and on 14 June he wrote to Ezra Pound, using his artistic sense of observation as well as his gunner's eye:

> 'Imagine a stretch of land one mile in depth sloping up from the old German first-line to the top of a ridge, stretching to right and left as far as you can see. It looks very large, never-ending and empty. There are only occasional little groups of men around a bomb-dump, or building a light railway: two men pushing a small truck on which a man is being brought back lying on his stomach, his head hanging over the side. The edge of the ridge is where you are bound for, at the corner of a demolished wood. The place is either loathesomely hot, or chilly according to the time of day at which you cross it. It is a reddish colour, and all pits, ditches & chasms, & black stakes, several hundred, here & there, marking the map-position of a wood.'

Later in June Lewis contracted trench fever and was hospitalised in Boulogne.

Continue over the crossroads into the square.

Extra Visit to Miner Statue (GPS: 50.78594 2.88240), Fr 1st Chass à Pied Mem (Map M9a), Croonaert Chapel Cem (Map M9, GPS: 50.80150 2.87510) Bayernwald [Bavarian Wood] Trenchlines, Site of Hitler's Sunken Road Painting.

Round trip: 4 miles. Approximate time: 15 minutes

Turn right direction De Croonaert.

Immediately on the right is a **Statue of a Miner** by Jan Diensaert, inaugurated on 31 October 2008 and **Information Boards** on the Battle for Wijtschaete/Bayernwald & Tunnelling.

Continue to a right turn signed to Croonaert Chapel Cem. Continue to parking area on the left, with Bayernwald to the right. Park. The path to the cemetery is some 100 yds straight ahead and leads left.

Note that as you walk the Flanders Hills (Kemmel, Rodeberg and Mont Noir) are visible to the left. To the right are the windmills on the Canal and Spires of Ieper.

At the start of the path there is a grey stone **Memorial to Lt Lasmer,** 11 *'Sous Officiers',* 174 *Caporals & Chasseurs* of the **1st Bn Chasseurs à Pied**

Miner Statue, Wijtschate

Sign to Croonaert Chapel Cemetery, with Memorial to Lt Lasmer & 1st Bn CAP and a Cross to Alphonse Bourges, Kemmel in background

who fell here in the defence of Belgium and France in the fighting of 3-15 November 1914. It was unveiled on 9 June 1935 when 90 veterans of the regiment came from all corners of France to pay homage to their old comrades with their old commanding officer, General Somon. To the left of the Memorial is a small **Cross to Alphonse Nicolas Edmond Bourges** of 1st CAP, killed on 14 December 1914 during the taking of Bois Quarante (Bayernwald). The Cross was inaugurated exactly 100 years later by his granddaughter, Edith Hugnot.

In **Croonaert Chapel Cemetery** there are 75 burials, seven of which are unknown. After the Armistice 51 German graves from 1917 were removed. The grave of **Chang Chi Hsuen** of the Chinese Labour Corps, 23 January 1919 lies in a separate plot just within the entrance. The Cemetery, which was designed by W. C. Von Berg, was begun in June 1917 by 19 Division and used until the following November. Two later burials were made in April 1918 and January 1919.

It is on the site of the original chapel painted by Adolf Hitler who fought in this area in the 16th BRIR.

Turn round, take the first turning left to Bayernwald.

As one turns on the left there are Panels with information about the 4th S Lancs in front of Bayernwald and to the left a Panorama describing points on the battlefield.

Continue to the entrance to Bayernwald.

Standing with one's back to it one is overlooking the British lines under which tunnelling to lay mines in preparation for the Messines assault of 1917 took place. The Germans saw evidence of this work and within the area of the wood constructed sophisticated underground listening posts with special equipment to

Croonaert Chapel CWGC Cemetery with Kemmel Hill on the horizon

Bayenwald reconstructed trenches showing plank and wattles

Wartime German trench showing wattle construction.

track the progress of the British tunnels with the aim of intercepting them with even deeper mines.

The **Bayernwald,** also known as Bois Quarante, was owned for many years by M. Becquaert (Senior) who operated an idiosyncratic museum here. After his death the site was left to deteriorate but it has now been sold and the present owner granted permission to the ABAF (qv) to excavate the interesting network of trenches, dugouts and the Bertha 4 and 5 mineshafts. Together with the Commune of Heuvelland they have restored 4 exceptional concrete bunkers made of pre-cast blocks, 2 deep German counter-mine shafts constructed to listen for British workings, about 100m of the trench system from the main German line of resistance 1916-17, recreating with A-frames and wickerwork, 320m of trenches and constructing a wooden shelter with Information Boards. This is a superb site for being able to get the feel of a true German WW1 trenchline. Unfortunately in March 2007 the water level became such a persistent problem, causing the recreated trenches to crumble (an all too realistic WW1 situation), that the site had to be temporarily closed to put in a new drainage system. Entry is controlled by combination-lock gates and to make a visit, contact the **Heuvelland Tourist Office** (qv) for tickets. There is an entrance fee of 4.00 (Student/Group concessions).

Return to the T junction then turn first right along Vierstraat.

Some 250m to the right are the **Hollandseschuur Craters** (see also illustration pages 302) **(Map M9b, GPS: 50.79772 2.86842)**.

Turn round and continue to the farm on the right. Pull in at the end of the farm buildings. Ahead in the meadow to the right is a distinct dip leading up to 5 tall poplar-like trees.

This is the site of the Sunken Road painted by Adolf Hitler in 1914 (qv) and where the comparative photo shown here was taken.

Return to Wijtschate Square and rejoin the main itinerary.

The Sunken Road at Cronaert today. The current road is on high ground to the left

Adolf Hitler's picture of the 'Hohlweg bei Wytschaete' [the Sunken Road], 1914

Keeping right past the bandstand follow signs to Kemmel. On the right is

• Wytschaete Military CWGC Cemetery/16th Irish Div Memorial/5.8 miles/10 minutes/Map M10/GPS: 50.78452 2.87673

Containing 486 UK, 31 Australian, 19 Canadian, 7 New Zealand, 11 South African, 1 German, 25 Special Memorials and 673 unknown burials, the Cemetery was created after the Armistice by concentration of graves from the surrounding battlefields. It contains the graves of **Drummer James Etak McKay**, 1st/4th Gordon Highlanders, 19 March 1915 age 20 and **2nd Lt John Victor Ariel Gleed**, 45th Sqn RFC, age 20 who 'Died of wounds received in aerial combat 7 July 1916'. Gleed's commission had been announced in the *London Gazette* barely 6 weeks earlier on 20 May. The Cemetery was designed by Sir Edwin Lutyens with W.H. Cowlishaw.

Memorial to 16th (Irish) Division unveiled 10 June 2007

16th Irish Division Memorial with Wytschaete Mil Cemetery behind

Just beyond it is the Memorial to the 16th Irish Division who captured Wijtschate on 7 June 1917. It carries the words *'Do chum Gloire De Agus Onora na hEiraan'*, 'To the Glory of God and the Honour of Ireland and was inaugurated on 21 August 1926. There is a similar monument to the Division at Guillemont on the Somme and one in Salonika to the 10th Division. All three, each weighing around 4 tons, were produced as a result of a decision in 1925 of the Irish National War Memorial Committee and were made from granite carved in Ireland.

Continue to the memorials on either side of the road

• 16th (Irish) & 36th (Ulster) Div Memorial Stones/6.3 miles/5 minutes/Map M11/GPS: 50.78196 2.86568

On 10 June 2007 as part of the 90th Anniversary of Passchendaele Commemorations, two new Irish Memorials were inaugurated to the 36th (Ulster) Division on the left (bearing the 'Red Hand of Ulster' symbol) and to the 16th (Irish) Division on the right (bearing the traditional 'Shamrock' symbol), on the spot where the mainly Protestant 36th Division and the mainly Catholic 16th Division fought side by side for the first time Map M4b, 4c. Erected on the initiative of the Municipality of Heuvelland, they are similar in format to the stone slab memorials in the Island of Ireland Peace Park (qv). Kemmel Hill is visible on the horizon ahead.

Continue to a green CWGC sign to the left to Spanbroekmolen Cemetery.

Memorial to 36th (Ulster) Division.

N.B. A short distance up the road to the left (and only visible from that road) is the large water-filled **Peckham Farm Crater** (Map M4, GPS 50.77967 2.86301). At the start of the Messines offensive the German front line here ran broadly from Bayernwald (from where you have just come) over Peckham crater, Spanbroekmolen (the next visit) and then to the Kruisstraat craters. (See also page 302.)

Peckham Farm Crater

Continue along the road (which was known as Suicide Road) to the CWGC sign to Lone Tree Cemetery to the left.

Extra Visit to Irish House CWGC Cemetery (Map M3/GPS: 50.78421 2.85223)

Round trip: 1 mile. Approximate time: 15 minutes

Continue to the next small crossroads and turn right signed to Irish House CWGC Cemetery (easily missed).

As you drive along on the skyline to the right the spires of Ypres and the windmills along the Ypres Canal may be seen. After a turning to the right immediately past the farm buildings is the path leading to Irish House CWGC Cemetery. This was opened in June 1917 by the 16th (Irish) Division, next to a CCS. It contains 103 UK burials, 13 Australian, 40 unknown and 4 German, with a **Special Memorial** to an Australian soldier who is one of the Unknown. In Row A are **33 men of the 1st Gordon Highlanders** who were reburied here when the Cemetery was opened. They were killed in the attack on Wijtschate of December 1914.

The CCS was visited by the American **Dr Harvey Cushing** (qv) on 26 October 1917, who wrote of it,

They are to receive casualties from the 18th Corps, where are the 63rd - the Naval Division - on the right, and the 58th on the left, to which Division the C.O. belongs. In his outfit are four M.O.s, fifty-six bearers, and thirty temporarily attached people. At a similar place during the last – i.e. Monday's – battle they passed on 1,745 wounded and 246 walking-sick in twelve hours ... A toy of a narrow-gauge Decauville [railway] with its little gasoline engine pulls into the camp with a load ... from some forward area ... a large slug of an observation balloon begins to rear its carcass up from wrecked copse just behind the camp.'

Return to the sign to Lone Tree Cem and pick up the main itinerary.

Turn left along Kruisstraat. Stop on the left at the entrance to the Spanbroekmolen crater.

• *Spanbroekmolen (Pool of Peace)/7.00 miles/15 minutes/Map R1/GPS: 50.77658 2.86124/OP*

Named for the windmill that stood here for three centuries until it was destroyed by the Germans on 1 November 1914, this is the site of what was probably the largest mine explosion of the nineteen blown on 7 June 1917, at the start of the Messines phase of the Third Battle of Ypres. In order to start a tunnel the tunnellers look for some cover under which to dig a vertical shaft from which the tunnel, or gallery, can be driven forward towards the enemy lines. Here the start point was in the area of a small wood some 300 yards beyond, and on a line from here to the cemetery ahead. In December 1915, 250th Tunnelling Coy dug a 60ft shaft and then handed over the work to 3rd Canadian Tunnelling Coy in January 1916. Other operating changes occurred until finally 171st Tunnelling Coy took over and extended the work to here, having driven the tunnel forward by 1,717ft (171 Coy had done that in seven months, a curious coincidence of numbers).

In February 1917 German mining damaged the main tunnel and a new drive was started from a different point which after 1,172ft cut into the original. Mining was greatly hampered by gas, several miners being overcome by fumes, but eventually – and only a few hours before zero hour – the charge of 91,000lb of ammonal was in place and secured by 400ft of tamping and a primer charge of 1,000lb of dynamite.

Following a seven-day bombardment the battle opened with nine divisions of infantry advancing on a 9-mile front. They had been told to advance at zero hour, 0310, whether the mines had blown or not. Spanbroekmolen went up 15 seconds late, killing a number of our own soldiers from the 36th Ulster Division, some of whom are buried in the cemetery ahead. The war diary of the 3rd Bn Worcester Regiment, that attacked a little south of here, records for that day, 'Battalion casualties were heavy and difficult to account for – a fair proportion must have been caused by our own barrage'.

Sir Philip Gibbs (qv), the war correspondent, described the scene thus:

'Suddenly at dawn, as a signal for all of our guns to open fire, there rose out of the dark ridge of Messines and 'Whitesheet' and that ill-famed Hill 60, enormous volumes of scarlet flame from nineteen separate mines, throwing up high towers of earth and smoke all lighted by the flame, spilling over into fountains of fierce colour, so that many of our soldiers waiting for the assault were thrown to the ground. The German troops were stunned, dazed and horror-stricken if they were not killed outright. Many of them lay dead in the great craters opened by the mines.'

An attack on the mill, then in German hands, was used by the British as a diversionary action during the Neuve Chapelle Battle of March 1915 as a means of drawing away enemy reserves. On 12 March the 1st Wiltshires and 3rd Worcesters achieved little but incurred heavy losses.

In September 1929 Tubby Clayton wrote to *The Times* to point out that the last of the big craters at St Eloi, now 'a pool of rare perfection', was in danger of being lost in plans to extend the village. One major crater, however, still remains visible in the village today (qv). Tubby's letter prompted discussions which led to Lord Wakefield buying the Spanbroekmolen Crater (purchasing the land for a total of 53,436 Belgian Francs from eight different owners). He then sold it to the Talbot House Association for a token One Belgian Franc. It was renamed 'The Pool of Peace' and then left untouched as a memorial. On 22 April 1985 (the seventieth anniversary of the inauguration of Talbot House) Princess Alexandra visited the Pool and planted two mountain ash trees. She was due to be accompanied by her husband, the Hon Angus Ogilvy, who was Patron of Toc H, but he was ill and could not travel. Nevertheless he is mentioned on the commemorative **Plaque** that was erected at the time at the entrance. However on 2 June 1992 the site was listed as an area 'of outstanding natural beauty' and therefore subject to the attendant rules and regulations. This included the removal of this Plaque. After the listing a new wooden gate and fence were erected

Spanbroekmolen Crater (Pool of Peace)

and the perimeter cleared. There is an **Information Board** outside the entrance.

On 14 November 2014 a **Cross** was inaugurated by a French delegation (see also pages 228 & 229), dedicated to **Antoine Justin Norton**, killed at that spot on 2 November 1914 during a German night attack.

Visitors can walk all the way round the original borders, now reclaimed from gradual encroachment of the surrounding fields, which affords some wonderful views over Mesen and Wijtschate. It is forbidden to walk around the pool but there is now a small 'amphitheatre' for viewing the crater.

Continue a few yards to the concrete path on the right to the cemetery and park on the left.

O.P. From this point a superb view over the Messines battlefield can be seen. Looking back down the road the bulk of Kemmel Hill is clearly visible. To the left on the skyline is Wijtschate Church and looking forward along the road Messines Church can be seen on the Ridge and to its right the Irish Tower.

• *Lone Tree CWGC Cemetery/Map R2*

The Cemetery contains 88 UK burials and 6 unknown, many of them of the RIR Rifles (36th) Division, killed on 7 June 1917, the first day of the Messines Offensive, some by our own mine. **Rfn S. Matier** was probably one of them.

Continue, to the next crossroads and turn right along Wulvergemstraat (once known as Pill Road). On the crest of the hill, before the house on the right are some large craters. Stop.

• *Kruisstraat Craters/7.7 miles/10 minutes/ Map R33, 34/GPS: 50.77014 2.86491/OP*

You are now standing on the German front line at the beginning (7 June 1917) Messines Phase, of Third Ypres. The attack came from the direction of Kemmel Hill (which can be seen just beyond the craters) passed over the area where you now are, (and have just crossed) down into the valley and up onto the Messines Ridge where the distinctive shape of Messines Church can be seen.

These two craters are legacies of the mines blown at the start of Third Ypres. The digging was begun by 250th Tunnelling Coy in December 1915, handed over to 182nd Company at the beginning of January 1916, and to 3rd Canadian at the end of the month. In April, 175th Tunnelling Coy briefly took charge and when the

Headstone of Rfn S. Matier, RIR killed on 7 June 1917, age 21, Lone Tree CWGC Cemetery

gallery reached 1,051ft it was handed over to 171st Company who were also responsible for Spanbroekmolen. See also 'War Underground', page 298.

At 1,605ft a charge of 30,000lb of ammonal was laid and at the end of a small branch of 166ft to the right a second charge of 30,000lb was placed under the German front line. This completed

Kruisstraat Crater

the original plan, but it was decided to extend the mining to a position under the German third line. Despite meeting clay and being inundated with water underground which necessitated the digging of a sump, in just two months a gallery stretching almost half a mile from the shaft was completed and a further charge of 30,000lb of ammonal placed. This tunnel was the longest of any of the Third Ypres mines. In February 1917 enemy countermeasures necessitated some repair to one of the chambers and the opportunity was taken to place a further charge of 19,500lb making a total of four mines all of which were ready by 9 May 1917.

The two craters that remain, probably the first two charges, are favourite fishing spots for licence holders.

Return to the crossroads and turn right towards Mesen (Messines). At the next T junction is

• Messines Ridge British CWGC Cemetery/New Zealand Memorial/9.1 miles/15 minutes/Map R9, 8/GPS: 50.76532 2.89085

Created after the Armistice, the Cemetery contains 986 UK, 332 Australian, 1 Canadian, 115 New Zealand, 56 South African, 954 unknown and a large number of Special Memorials. At the entrance to the Cemetery is the **New Zealand Memorial,** listing 840 men killed in the Salient and who have no known graves, following their policy not to list their missing on the Menin Gate. New Zealand Memorials are all in cemeteries chosen as appropriate to the fighting in which the men died. This Cemetery and Memorial were designed by Charles Holden (who also designed the New Zealand Memorial at Polygon Wood).

On 7 June 1917, during the Messines action which was the prelude to Third Ypres, one of the war's most beloved Padres was awarded the Military Cross for his work on the Messines Ridge. The citation which was published in the *London Gazette* of 16 August reads:

'For conspicuous gallantry and devotion to duty. He showed the greatest courage and disregard of his own safety in attending wounded under heavy fire. He searched shell holes for our own and enemy wounded, assisting them to the dressing station, and his cheerfulness and endurance had a splendid effect upon all ranks, whom he constantly visited.'

This brave Padre was the **Rev Geoffrey Anketell Studdert Kennedy**, Chaplain to the Forces, then serving with 17th Bde of 24th Division and better known as 'Woodbine Willie'.

> They gave me this name like their nature
> Compacted of laughter and tears,
> A sweet that was born of the bitter,
> A joke that was torn from the tears.

This unconventional Padre endeared himself to the men for his habit of doling out Woodbine cigarettes, for using their own strong language when he felt it necessary, and because he questioned his own faith when confronted by the cruel carnage around him. His *Rough Rhymes of a Padre* expressed his love for his fellow soldiers and his understanding of their love of each other, as exemplified in the poem, *His Mate,* which describes the burial of a soldier and whose last verse is,

> There are many kinds of sorrow
> In this world of Love and Hate,
> But there is no sterner sorrow
> Than a soldier's for his mate.

The New Zealand Memorial, Messines Ridge Brit Cemetery

Studdert Kennedy was not so popular with the Establishment. General Plumer walked out half-way through one of his sermons in ire and had Woodbine Willie removed from the Second Army. After the war Studdert Kennedy continued his tireless ministry, speaking on many themes that were then considered to be avant-garde - divorce, contraception and abortion. At his funeral in 1929, the two-mile cortège from Worcester Cathedral to the cemetery was lined by crowds of his old comrades and the coffin was showered with packets of Woodbines. On the 75th Anniversary of his death a silver statue of Studdert-Kennedy by Ben Twiston was unveiled by the Chaplain General, the Ven J. Blackburn QHC in the Armed Forces Chaplaincy Centre at Amport House near Andover, Tel: 01624 773144.

Buried here is **Usko Leonard Salonen** 'of Finland' serving with the 39th AIF, killed 8 June 1917 aged 29. From the top of the cemetery the Island of Ireland Tower can be seen.

Turn left along Nieuwkerkestraat.

On the right is the entrance to the **Messines Peace Village** (qv). Attractively laid out student accommodation (for up to 165 in 43 studios) and study centre with restaurant, bar and access for wheel chairs. The first stone was laid by Irish Prime Minister, Bertie Ahern, in June 2006. Tel: +(0) 57 22 60 40 e-mail: info@ peacevillage.be Website: www.peacevillage.be

The Village also caters for Sports Club (inside and outside games) with a 'Flanders Peace Field' with facilities for football, basketball, netball etc.

By the entrance is a **Memorial to the Christmas Truce of December 1914** and on the wall to the left a **Plaque to the 1st, 2nd & 4th Chasseurs d'Afrique**, Messines 1914.

Christmas Truce Memorial, Peace Village, Mesen

Continue to the crossroads with the N365.

Extra Visit to the London Scottish Memorial (Map R7, GPS: 50.77256 2.89303)

Round trip: 1.5 miles. Approximate time: 5 minutes

Turn left and continue to the memorial on the right.

The inscription on the grey granite Celtic Cross records how near this spot on Hallowe'en 1914 the London Scottish came into action, being the first territorial Battalion to engage the enemy. The battalion lost 394 of their 700 strength in the action. It was erected to the memory of all the Officers, NCOs and men of the Regiment who fell in the Great War, 1914-1919 and shows its Battle Honours year by year. It was unveiled by King Albert 1 in May 1924. The film star, Ronald Colman, who served with this regiment was wounded in the battle.

Turn round and return to Nieuwkerkestraat and pick up the main itinerary.

London Scottish Memorial, Messines

Turn right at the crossroads along the N365 into Mesen and first left following signs to Bethleem Farm CWGC Cemetery. Park near the bandstand in the square.

• Messines (Mesen)/New Zealand Soldier Statue/Museum & Tourist Info/Christmas Truce Statue/Peace Post/Ross Bastiaan & N Zealand & Frickleton VC Memorials/Ross Bastiaan Plaque/Church/9.7 miles/25 minutes/Map R36, R37/GPS: 50.76541 2.89808

As one turns left there is a fine **Statue of a New Zealand Sergeant** to the right, facing the main road. It is a Memorial to all the soldiers of the New Zealand Division who took part in the Battle of Messines Ridge (7 June 1917) and was sculpted by Jan Dieusaert. The New Zealand Ambassador comes to Messines each year to celebrate ANZAC Day and Messines is associated with the New

Interior of Mesen Tourist Info Point, showing models of Mesen Church, the Irish Peace Tower and the NZ Obelisk

Memorial Statue to New Zealanders who fought at Messines, Mesen

Zealand town of Featherston, where some 8,000 NZ soldiers trained before coming to the Western Front.

On the left, on the site of the old Town Hall (now in the fine building opposite) and Museum is a smart new unmanned Museum. In it is a TIP **(Tourist Information Point)** which tells the story of Messines in WW1 and its general history. **Open** daily: 0830-1730. Tel: + (0) 32 057 22 17 14. E-mail: info@mesen. be/toerisme@mesen.be. www.mesen.be.

Upstairs is a theme room, visitable by reservation, as are guided tours. **Open**: Mon-Thurs: 0900-1200, 1330-1700 and Fri pm until 1600.

Outside is the moving, life-sized statue by artist Andy Edwards depicting a German and British soldier meeting in No Man's Land during the Christmas Truce of 1914. It was unveiled on 22 December 2015. For more information see www.christmastrucestatue. co.uk

To the right is a small group of memorials including a **Ross Bastiaan Australian bronze relief Memorial Tablet** and a **Japanese International Peace Post** (qv) unveiled on 17 September 1989 by the artist, Miss Mié Tabé, and given to Messines by the Japanese Peace Movement. Its message says 'May Peace Rule the World'.

Turn right to the church.

This was rebuilt after the war. The mother of Queen Matilda (William the Conqueror's wife) was buried in the church. **Cpl Adolf Hitler** is purported to have been treated in the

Germans in Messines

Christmas Truce Statue, Mesen

crypt, which served as a German Field Hospital, when he was wounded in the arm, shortly after being promoted to Corporal. He was stationed at Bethlehem Farm nearby (50.76057 2.90961) and at Croenaert (Hill 40) near Wijtschate, serving in the area from November 1914 to March 1915 with the 16th Bavarian Reserve Infantry Regiment. He had volunteered in August 1914 and joined his regiment in Munich. It was sent to Ypres and joined the 6th Bavarian Division of Prince Rupprecht's Sixth Army in time to take part in the First Battle of Ypres. Hitler proved to be a brave soldier and was twice recommended for the Iron Cross Second Class, actually receiving the award on 2 December 1914. Twice more he served in the Salient: in July 1917 during Third Ypres and in the autumn of 1918 during Fourth Ypres when he was temporarily blinded during a gas attack on the night of 14 October near Wervick after having won the Iron Cross First Class. Seven days later he was back in Germany. In *Mein Kampf* he tells a little of his experiences in Flanders and anyone who has been out and about early on a winter's morning around Ypres can visualise the scene that Hitler describes as he marched into war in 1914:

Ross Bastiaan Australian memorial, Messines Square

Mié Tabé Peace Post, Messines

The distinctive outline of Messines Church

'And then came a damp, cold night in Flanders, through which we marched in silence, and when the day began to emerge from the mists, suddenly an iron greeting came whizzing at us over our heads, and with a sharp report sent the little pellets flying between our ranks, ripping up the wet ground; but even before the little cloud had passed, from two hundred throats the first hurrah rose to meet the first messenger of death. Then a crackling and a roaring, a singing and a howling began, and with feverish eyes each one of us was drawn forward, faster and faster, until suddenly past turnip fields and hedges the fight began, the fight of man against man. And from the distance the strains of a song reached our ears, coming closer and closer, leaping from company to company, and just as Death plunged a busy hand into our ranks the song reached us too and we passed it along: *Deutschland, Deutschland über Alles, über alles in der Welt*'.

During his time at the front Hitler continued to draw and to paint. He was certainly more than the 'house painter' that Allied propaganda presented him as during World War II. In his early days he had sold his watercolours to earn his keep and in 1936 *Esquire* magazine ran a major article about him, reproducing his works in colour. Heinrich Hoffmann, his photographer, published a collection of his watercolours, including some of those done around Messines and the painting of the Sunken Road at Croonaert reproduced above.

In June 1967 a German veteran called Otto Meyer who had fought nearby presented the church with a copper chandelier, known as the 'Rose of Messines', as a symbol of peace. Then came the idea to install a carillon of bells which would also symbolise peace. The church's original carillon of fifteen bells, erected in 1703 had been taken by French revolutionaries in 1793 and melted down to make

Memorial to Samuel Frickleton, VC, outside Messines Church.

canons. When it became known that Pope John Paul II would visit the church on 17 May 1985, tremendous efforts were made to raise enough money to install the fifteen new bells in time for his visit. Other bells have since been added and it has now reached its full complement of 61 bells. The names of all those who subscribed more than 20,000 Belgian Francs are inscribed on the bells. They include Toc H, the WFA, the London Scottish and their then-Colonel-in-Chief, the Queen, the Governments of Great Britain, Australia, Canada, Germany, Italy, the Netherlands, New Zealand and Poland, as well as many local contributors.

On 7 June 2007, as part of the Messines commemorations of the 90th Anniversary of Passchendaele, a Memorial was unveiled to the left of the church door to L/Cpl (later Captain) **Samuel Frickleton, VC,** of the 3rd NZ (Rifle) Bde in the presence of two of his grandchildren and his great-grandson. The bronze Plaque bears his photo. Frickleton, of Scottish and Irish stock, had moved to Blackball, N Zealand in 1913. Five Frickleton brothers enlisted when war broke out, two being wounded at Gallipoli. Samuel contracted TB on arrival in Egypt and was discharged. He re-enlisted and sailed for England, becoming a Rifleman with the 3rd Bn the NZ Rifle Bde. He served in France (where his brother William was killed on the Somme and is buried in Flatiron Copse Cemetery). Moving to Flanders he was involved on the right hand flank of the NZ attack of 7 June 1917, pinned down by intensive machine-gun fire. Frickleton, although wounded in the arm, rallied his section and advanced through his own Allied artillery barrage to attack one of the machine-gun emplacements, killing several of the enemy by throwing a Mills bomb and using his bayonet as well as taking several prisoners. He then destroyed a second machine-gun post and was again wounded and later evacuated, badly gassed. He returned to France in July 1917 but had once more to be evacuated because of the effect of the gas. Promoted to Sergeant he attended an Officer Cadet Training Course at Cambridge where, despite his damaged lungs, he won a boxing contest. He was eventually commissioned in October 1919 and was finally retired in April 1927. He volunteered again for overseas service in 1939 but was rejected on medical grounds. He died on 6 September 1971 at the age of 80. His was one of the 9 VCs stolen from the NZ Waiouru Museum in December 2007 which were recovered in February 2008, due to award money donated by Lord Ashcroft and others (see Andrew, VC, page 294).

Ross Bastiaan plans to erect another of his bronze Plaques here in 2018 to **Capt Robert Cuthbert Grieve, 37th (Victoria) Bn AIF, VC,** and the Australian participation around Mesen. He was the nephew of Sgt-Maj J. Grieve who also won a VC (at Balaclava).

Messines is twinned with Featherston in New Zealand where 8,000 soldiers trained, after which town the Square is named. Near Messines the first Australian casualties of the war were killed on 17 June 2016. They are **Ptes James Jack Mollison and Beaumont James Philpott.** Commemorative ceremonies were held on 17 June 2016 in both Flanders and Australia. Their full story is told in the Last Post Association Newsletter of June 2016.

The high ground on which the village stands is a continuation of the ridge which sweeps north-east to Passchendaele. The Germans gained the area in November 1914 and were driven out by the New Zealand Division in June 1917. The Germans recaptured it for a few hours on 10 April 1918, were repulsed by the South African Brigade of the 9th (Scottish) Division and took it back on 11 April. The Germans were finally ejected by the 30th Division on 28 September 1918.

Return to the N365 opposite the church. Continue. Turn right as the main road takes a sharp bend to the left, following signs to the New Zealand Memorial. Park at the entrance.

• New Zealand Memorial and Park/Bunkers/10.2 miles/15 minutes/ Map R11, 12, 13/GPS: 50.76076 2.89098/OP

This Memorial is identical to that at 's-Graventafel (qv). It was unveiled on 1 August 1924 by King Albert I of the Belgians and overlooks a memorial park at the foot of which are two large, well-preserved German pill boxes.

It was well known that the Germans were constructing numbers of pill boxes on the Messines Ridge and prior to the opening of Third Ypres frequent patrols were made into German lines in order to find out more about the defences. The New Zealanders maintained daily intelligence summaries on the current state of the defences and their engineers blew up concrete dugouts half a mile south of here at Petite Douve Farm (qv) barely two days before the offensive opened. These two pill boxes appear identical, but the one on the left was made in situ while the other was put together with concrete blocks, probably to a pre-fabricated design.

On 7 June the attack here was led by the 3rd New Zealand Rifle Brigade advancing broadly from the direction of Nieuwkerke and the bunkers were taken in the first hour.

Bunker and Obelisk, New Zealand Memorial Park

Panorama, with Mont Kemmel extreme right, New Zealand Memorial Park

From the seat between the bunkers a good view of the Messines battlefield can be had provided trees do not obscure the view. There is a **Panorama Panel** describing the points of interest ahead. The front lines here were about 700yd away. Take straight ahead as 12 o'clock. At 1 o'clock the church on the skyline is Nieuwkerke. At 11 o'clock on the horizon are the spires of Armentiéres and at 10 o'clock in the middle distance is Ploegsteert Wood Military CWGC Cemetery (Map R26). A duckboard path from the adjacent football pitch links the NZ Park with the Irish Park.

O.P. Standing outside the park, with one's back to the entrance, look straight towards the hills ahead and take that as 12 o' clock. At 10 o'clock in the middle distance is the spire of Wulvergem Church roughly 1,500 yards away. Moving clockwise, next is the tall wireless mast of Mont des Cats at 12 o' clock, then Mont Noir and next to it, the tallest hill, Kemmel, with a smaller radio mast. At 12 o'clock on the horizon are the bushes which surround Spanbroekmolen.

Return to the N365 and follow signs to Ploegsteert and Armentières. Continue to the large tower to the right.

• Island of Ireland Peace Park and Tower/10.6 miles/15 minutes/Map R14a /GPS: 50.75979 2.89572

For many years following the Armistice, during the turbulent period leading to the formation of the Irish Free State, men from Southern Ireland who fought with the British in the Great War were often considered as 'traitors' and their sacrifice deliberately forgotten. This imposing grey stone tower is dedicated to the memory of all those from the Island of Ireland who fought and died in the First World War in an overdue gesture of remembrance and reconciliation between nationalists and unionists. The Tower was the brainchild of Catholic Nationalist MP Paddy Harte and Protestant Unionist Glen Barr who visited the area together in 1996 and conceived the project as 'A Journey of Reconciliation'.

It was unveiled on 11 November 1998 by President Mary McAlease and Queen Elizabeth II in the presence of the King and Queen of the Belgians. The process of reconciliation was furthered by HM Queen Elizabeth's historic visit to Ireland in May 2011 (the first for a British monarch for 100 years) during which she visited the Irish National Memorial Gardens where the 50,000 Irishmen who gave their lives in the Great War are honoured.

This site was chosen as it stands on the Messines Ridge where men from the north and the south of the Island fought almost shoulder to shoulder in June 1917. The Town of Messines

Irish Peace Tower, Messines

'Quotation Stone' to Francis Ledwidge

Memorials to the three Irish Divisions, the 36th, the 16th and the 10th

supported the project and facilitated the purchase of the appropriate land. Young Irish people were involved in the construction, working with Irish and local masons. The stone was brought from Mullingar in Ireland where an old almshouse dating back to the Famine of 1845-8 had recently been demolished. The first VC of the War (at Mons), Lt Maurice Dease, was born in Mullingar.

As one passes through the entrance in the grey stone walls there are polished granite information plaques in Belgian, French, English and Gaelic leading up to the tower itself. They include some moving quotations from the poets **Francis Ledwidge** (qv) and **Tom Kettle**, from the Official War Artist, **Sir William Orpen** (qv), **Chaplain Francis Gleeson** of the R Munster Fusiliers and others who served with Irish Regiments. Other plaques salute the memory of the 10th (Irish) Division which lost 9,363 men, the 16th (Irish) Division) which lost 28,398 and the 36th (Ulster Division) which lost 32,186. Another reproduces 'The Peace Pledge' made by both Catholics and Protestants and the names of all the Provinces from Antrim to Wicklow. Bronze *bas relief* Plaques show maps of the Ypres Salient, June-December 1917 and the Battle of Messines, June 7 1917.

In the room at the base of the slim Tower, a traditional Irish form which has been built in Ireland since the 8th Century, are beautiful bronze boxes which contain the names of the Irish casualties and a Visitor's Book. The park surrounding the tower includes four gardens for the four Provinces with four different types of tree representing the Irish soldiers marching towards the tower. Owing to financial difficulties experienced by the originators, the park is now maintained by the Commonwealth War Graves Commission.

A well-constructed duckboard path links the park to the football pitch beside the New Zealand Memorial Park.

Continue downhill.

Just before the bottom on the right hand side is **La Petite Douve Farm**. Under this farm, many experts believe, is one of the powerful remaining unexploded mines set to fire on 7 June 1917. Walk softly! The farm was enclosed by a German trench system known as 'ULNA' and would have been a natural target for a mining operation. Also at this point was a junction on the narrow gauge railway system which ran from the forward areas beyond Messines to the rear areas around Nieuwkerke.

Continue as the road rises to a crest where, pointing left, are signs to Ploegsteert Wood ('Plugstreet' to Tommy) and other cemeteries and to the Bairnsfather Plaque visited later on the Itinerary.

NOTE: This is a French-speaking (Walloon) area of Belgium, the only such area occupied by the Germans.

On the slope opposite is broken ground and the remains of the old **Château du Mont de la Hutte, on Hill 63** (now under further development, there is a walking tour which covers this and the catacombs - qv Tourist Office), under which the British built large subterranean shelters.

Continue and stop near the Memorial on the right.

Opposite is a Comines-Warneton signed walking route along what was once 'Mud Lane Duck Walk', a communication track to Mud Corner. It leads to the cemetery of that name. At one time a trench called 'Look Slippy Lane' then led to the Bairnsfather Cottage.

• *Ploegsteert Memorial/Berkshire CWGC Cemetery Extension/Hyde Park Corner CWGC Cemetery/Plugstreet '14'18 Interpretative Centre/ Last Post/12.4 miles/1 hour/RWC/Map R16, 15, 17/GPS 50.73772 2.88234*

Here, since June 1999, the Last Post has been played on the first Friday of the month at 1900 hours by local buglers. The event is organised by the *Comité du Mémorial de Ploegsteert* and the Committee HQ is at the **café/restaurant Auberge** opposite. Special ceremonies may be

Ploegsteet Memorial & Berkshire CWGC Cemetery Extension

requested. Tel: +(0) 56 58 84 41. E-mail: restaurant@auberge-ploegsteert.be/ Website: auberge-ploegsteert.be It is owned by Claude and Nelly Verhaeghe, (see Tourist Information for details). It contains some fascinating plaques and memorabilia and is very handy for a lunchtime snack or meal.

Claude, who is an Administrator of the Comines-Warneton Tourist Office (qv), was responsible, with author Ted Smith (qv) and the Comines-Warneton Historical Society, for the research for the splendid new Comines-Warneton Information Panels (see above). He runs excellent battlefield tours.

From this point you will begin to see examples of the 19 well-researched and illustrated three-language **Information Panels** outside the war cemeteries, memorials and remaining sites of WW1 interest in this area. They have been erected by the Commune of Comines-Warneton. In this vicinity are: 1. The Ploegsteert Memorial; 2. The Last Post; 3. The Catacombs of Hyde Park Corner; 4. The Château de la Hutte; 16. Mud Lane from Hyde Park Corner, Hyde Park Corner. A leaflet describing a route is available at local Tourist Offices/Town Halls.

Guarded by two lions, one baring his teeth, the other looking benign, designed by Sir Gilbert Ledward (who was to do work in the World War II Reichswald Cemetery on the Dutch-German border) is the **Berkshire Cemetery Extension** which was begun in June 1916. The rotunda structure is the **Ploegsteert Memorial to the Missing** bearing the names of 11,370 officers and men from nearby battles for every year of the war and has its own registers, separate to those for the adjoining Cemetery.

There are three **VCs** commemorated on it: **Sapper William Hackett** (qv) of 254th Tunnelling Coy, RE, for helping to rescue men entombed with him in a mine after an enemy explosion on 22/23 June 1916, at Givenchy, and who was killed four days later; **Pte James Mackenzie** of the 2nd Bn Scots Guards for on 19 December 1914, at Rouges Bancs rescuing a severely wounded man under very heavy fire and who was killed later that day attempting the same act; **Capt Thomas Tannatt Pryce** of the 4th Bn Grenadier Guards for on 11/12 April 1918, at Vieux Berquin leading an attack on the village, beating off 4 counter-attacks and driving off a fifth with a bayonet charge, who was last seen, with only 17 men and no ammunition, leading another bayonet charge. The Report for the Memorial shows the continuing work of the Commission. Several entries have been amended as men whose names are inscribed on the memorial have been identified in Cemeteries, e.g. **Serjt J. B. Coutts**, now in Tournai Cemetery, and **Pte T. Gordie** buried in Le Grand Beaumont British Cemetery

The Memorial was originally planned to stand in Lille, but the French were becoming 'disquieted by the number and scale of the Memorials which the Commission proposed to erect' and when the number of Imperial Memorials in France was reduced from the planned twelve to four (Soissons, La Ferté, Neuve-Chapelle and the Somme) extra land was acquired from the Belgians here at Ploegsteert. The names of the missing destined to be inscribed on other cancelled memorials were inscribed on memorial walls built inside the land assigned to a cemetery, e.g. Vis-en-Artois and Pozières. The disappointed architects of the aborted memorials were given other assignments. Thus Charlton Bradshaw, who had won competitions for his designs for Lille and Cambrai (another memorial which was cancelled) was allotted Ploegsteert and Louverval. This explains why the memorial commemorates the Missing of the Battles of Armentières, 1914, Aubers Ridge, Loos and Fromelles, 1915, Estaires, 1916 and Hazebrouck, Scherpenberg and Outtersteene, 1918. It was inaugurated on 7 June 1931, by the Duke of Brabant.

In the **Berkshire Cemetery Extension** are 295 UK, 51 Australian, 3 Canadian and 45 New Zealand burials, among them **Anthony Eden's Platoon Sergeant, 'Reg' Park** – see below.

Over the road is **Hyde Park Corner** (originally known as **Royal Berkshire**) CWGC Cemetery which was begun during Second Ypres by the 1st/4th Royal Berkshires, remained in use until November 1917 and contains the grave of **16-year-old Pte Albert Edward French**, the subject of a BBC Radio 4 documentary in 1983. His story came to light when his letters home to his sister Mabel were found after her death in 1975. Albert had been an apprentice engineer at Wolverton railway works in Buckinghamshire when he left to enlist in October 1915. His father found out what had happened and tried to stop him, but Albert had already taken the King's Shilling. He was killed on 15 June 1916, a week before his seventeenth birthday. Apparently the War Office refused the family a war pension as Albert had lied about his age on joining up and was under the official enlistment age when he was killed. The local Member of Parliament took up the case and eventually Albert's father received 5s a week. His brother George spoke the words that gave the title to the radio programme about Albert, *He shouldn't have been there, should he?* On the programme George remarked that when he visited the grave he found it one of the few he had seen not to mention the age of death on it. That has since been rectified by the CWGC and the grave now bears the legend, 'aged 16 years'.

Headstone of Lt. Max Seller, Hyde Park Corner CWGC Cemetery

The Cemetery contains 83 Commonwealth burials and 4 Germans, including Jewish soldier, Lt. Seller, age 26, who had joined up in August 1914. He had previously been wounded and returned to the front before being killed on 24 June 1915.

The two Cemeteries were designed by C. Charlton Bradshaw.

Beyond the Cemetery to the left is Ploegsteert ('Plugstreet') Wood where **Lt Bruce Bairnsfather** (qv) of the Royal Warwickshires drew his first war cartoons and 'Old Bill' was born. Also serving in the 1st Bn was **Lt A. A. Milne**, creator of Christopher Robin and the famous bear Pooh. When Bairnsfather wrote a play called *The Better 'Ole* in 1917, he named one of his characters Captain Milne. The Wood is about 2,000 yards wide, east to west, and about 1,000yd, north to south. Critical fighting for possession of it took place in 1914, between mid-October and the beginning of November - known as the Battle of Armentières. It ran, therefore, concurrently with First Ypres and this point, Ploegsteert, marks the bottom end of the Salient. A fine bayonet charge by the 1st Somersets (their '1st in France', as the Regimental History puts it - although they were in fact in Belgium) stopped one German attack on the village of le Gheer at the south-east corner of the wood. Conditions in the wood were abominable. The Somerset History records:

> 'On 25 October ... the trenches were absolute quagmires ... the water and mud were ankle deep in the front lines; by the beginning of November the trenches were knee-deep in slime and filth. The stench from dead bodies often partially buried in the soggy, slimy ground, just as they had fallen, was awful. Unwashed, caked with mud, clothes sodden... aching with rheumatism and the early symptoms of trench feet, verminous and generally in a deplorable condition [the Somersets] held the line with a degree of staunchness, determination and cheerfulness of spirit never surpassed in the whole glorious history of the Army.'

Although they made excursions into the eastern edge, the Germans never took the wood.

Continue past the Berkshire Cemetery to the entrance and parking area on the right to:

The Plugstreet '14-'18 Experience (Interpretative Centre)

Inaugurated on 9 November 2013 in an important international ceremony, the reception area of the Centre, which is below ground, lies beneath a glass pyramid (the original designer was Comines-Warneton architect, Isabelle Delforge).

On that day a *bas relief* **Memorial to the Australian Mining Corps** 1916-1919 was unveiled by donator Ross J Thomas, the sculptor Michael Meszaros and the popular and charistmatic then-

Field Gun & Figures, Centre Grounds

Burgomaser Gilbert Deleu. Another version of the Memorial is in Townsville in Australia. The Centre is near the site of the Catacombs where the Australian forces took shelter in 1917 after suffering badly:

The Australian historian, C.W. Bean, in his Australian Official History describes,

'The … battalions …were meeting with steady gas–shelling, and on their entering Ploegsteert Wood, in whose stagnant air the gas lay densely, the difficulties increased. Long stoppages occurred, intervals of tense anxiety for all ranks. The Germans were shelling the wood more heavily, using high–explosive and incendiary shells as well. One of these exploded a dump near the track of the northernmost column … checking the march for a moment … A high–explosive shell burst in the leading platoon of the 39th Battalion as it reached 'Ploegsteert Corner'. Here and there officers and men were hit direct by gas–shell. Wherever the slowly–moving columns were locally dislocated by such incidents, and excitement or haste occurred, men tended to be gassed by the steady shower of shell, and fell out by the way, retching and collapsed.'

Australia now has many ties with the Commune, as does New Zealand. ANZAC day (25 April) is always commemorated here.

The funds for this Centre were provided by the Commune, together with the *Région Wallonne* and the *Commissariat Général au Tourisme,* Deulys (an association of 7 nearby cities) and some 20 other partners (including, principally, the Australians and the CWGC). It is part of a European project 'The Great War Remembered', with a budget of nearly Euros 3million. It shows the human face of the War, how the local population lived throughout it in relation to the various armed forces who occupied their region (co-operation, evacuation, destruction and rebuilding after the War – including that of the Ploegsteert Memorial - etc). Contemporary newspaper accounts,

Miniature diorama of New Zealander Miners, Plugstreet Centre

Entrance to the Plugstreet Centre on Inauguration Day

photos, postcards, personal accounts etc, illustrate these facets. The visitor is encouraged to enter a war-time character's 'living space'. There is an excellent video which clearly charts the progress of the war in the area.

Temporary exhibitions have featured Bairnsfather's Old Bill in the story line and the postcards from the authors' book covering the First World War, *Till the Boys Come Home*. The nearby Christmas Truce is also well-covered.

Many 'involving' experiences and events for student and family participation are now being organised.

In April 2016, twenty five years after a visit by his father, Winston Spencer Churchill to the area, Winston Churchill's great grandson, Randolph, with his 7 years old son, John Winston, inaugurated the **'Churchill Route'** The Centre has produced displays in the Foyer and a leaflet outlining the clearly signed route in the area, with a map. Point No 1 starts at the school at Le Gheer (also known as 'the Covent') used as an advanced observation post. No. 2 is the site of Laurence Farm (where Churchill painted one of his famous watercolours); No 3 is the Nunnery Hospice, where Churchill had a room; No 4 is London Support Farm near Brigade HQ; No 5 is London Rifle Brigade Cemetery; No 6 is Soyer Farm where Churchill took refuge and No 7 the Churchill Plaque (qv) in Ploegsteert.

Contact: Tel: +(0) 56 48 40 00. E-mail: info@rememberplugstreet.com Website: www. plugstreet1418.com **Opening times**: 1 April- 30 Sept: Mon, Tues, Thurs, Fri: 1000-1700. Wed: 1300-1700. W/E 1000-1800. **1 Oct-31 March**: Daily 1000-1700 (Wed 1300-1700). Last Post Fri (1st of the month) 1000-1900. **Closed:** 25 Dec-20 Jan.

Continue towards Ploegsteert village.

On the left, behind a house some 300yds on, is a group of three well-preserved **British Bunkers** (GPS: **50.73460 2.88099**). They were part of the Dressing Station known as Charing Cross following the series of central London names used by the soldiers in this area. They are on private land but permission from the owner may give you the opportunity to discover the etched outline of an 'Old Bill' look-alike spotted on the exterior of one of the bunkers.

Continue. On the left is

'Charing Cross' bunkers, Ploegsteert

• *Strand Military CWGC Cemetery/12.7 miles/5 minutes/Map R19/ GPS: 50.73268 2.88024*

This early Cemetery was begun in October 1914 to serve the Dressing Station at the end of 'The Strand', a trench which led into Plugstreet Wood. (Another trench in the wood was called Regent Street and there were junctions called Oxford Circus and Piccadilly Circus). It was used again in 1917 and was enlarged by concentration from nearby battlefields after the Armistice and designed by Charles Holden. The Cemetery contains 725 UK, 284 Australian, 26 Canadian, 87 New Zealand, 1 South African, 356 unknown, and 11 Germans, with 19 Special Memorials and 8 WW2 graves from the withdrawal to Dunkirk in May 1940. On the grave of Pte Thomas Cordner, 1st RIR, died 9 November 1914, is a personal plaque stating that he died trying to save a wounded friend. It was placed by his sister who died in 1933. There is a Comines-Warneton Information Panel No 15 here.

Continue to Ploegsteert crossroads and park by the splendid war memorial with a triumphant soldier. To the left of the entrance to the Mairie is

• *Memorial Plaque to Winston Churchill/13.2 miles/5 minutes/Map R38/GPS: 50.72617 2.87991*

The white stone *bas relief* Plaque shows Sir Winston, in his habitual World War II homburg, with his trademark cigar, in the World War I trenches! It was unveiled by his grandson, Winston Churchill MP (who died on 2 March 2010) on 11 November 1991. In 1915 Churchill had lost his post as First Lord of the Admiralty and his daring plan to take Constantinople through the Dardanelles had failed. He opted for the cathartic experience of serving in the trenches. After a spell of initiation in front line trenches before Ypres, he commanded the 6th Royal Scots Fusiliers here at Plugstreet Wood, serving during the winter of 1915/1916 as a Lt Col. The prospect of 'so famous and so controversial a figure was awaited with a certain

Winston Churchill Plaque, Ploegsteert Mairie

trepidation', records the Regimental History. The fears were soon dispelled. A fellow officer, Maj A. D. Gibbs, wrote:

> 'I speak with all possible affection of him as the friend of his officers. He took endless trouble; he borrowed motor cars and scoured France, interviewing Generals and staff officers great and small in his efforts to do something to help those who had served under him ... No man was ever kinder to his subordinates, and no commanding officer I have ever known was half so kind ... We came to realize his tremendous ability. He came to be looked on as really a possession of our own, and one of which we were intensely proud.'

Local literature describes Churchill as 'always a little eccentric, he chose to wear a French "Adrian" tin helmet, a gift from General Fayolle of the French Army'. Considered to be a fussy, mistrusting and quick-tempered man by the local population, he was not much liked, although the troops thought otherwise. Inside the *Mairie* is a framed copy of the Bairnsfather Plaque at St Yvon (qv). Comines-Warneton Information Plaque No 14 is here.

To the left of the church is a path leading to the churchyard with nine British graves. To the right of the *Mairie* is the conveniently sited **Hostellerie de la Place**, Tel: + (0) 56 58 86 77. Good for a quick lunch.

N.B. Memorial to Sgt Roland Joffre Ribout (GPS: 50.71534 2.87077). By continuing on the N365 towards Armentières and turning right on the rue de l'Oosthove and right again at the T junction along rue Sainte-Marie for 400 yards, the Memorial may be seen in a field. The Canadian RAF pilot was shot down by two Focke-Wulfs in *Operation Circus 157* (see page 128). Ribaut was seen to bail out but his parachute failed to open. The Memorial, inaugurated in 2007, is topped by a plane tail made by the students of St Joseph School, Komen. It was repainted in March 2011 by enthusiast Joseph Dupont. Beside it is an Information Board with photo and text in 3 languages. His crash site is at GPS: 50.72179 2.84514.

Memorial to Sgt R.J. Ribout RAF, Ploegsteert

Return to the crossroads and turn right, signed Lancashire Cottage CWGC Cemetery. Continue to the cemetery on the right.

• Lancashire Cottage CWGC Cemetery/14.1 miles/5 minutes/Map R31/ GPS: 50.72918 2.89774

The Cemetery, which has splendid wrought iron gates, was named by the 1st E Lancs in November 1914, when they started it with the 1st Hampshire. The E Lancs have 84 (mostly buried to the left of the path) and the Hampshires 56 of the 265 UK burials here. There are also 23 Australian, 2 Canadian, 5 unknown burials, 13 Germans and 2 Special Memorials. Here is buried Bugler Morgan Dudley, 15th Can Inf, 15 September 1915, age 17. It is interesting to note that there are several groups of three headstones, the centre of which is simply a cross, the other two bearing two names and no cross. The Cemetery was in German hands from 10 April to 29 September 1918. It was designed by Charles Holden.

Continue to the entry to the wood to the left beside a house. Stop if desired in the car park by the building.

'**Plugstreet Wood**' (GPS: 50.73122 2.90611). If you wish to walk into the wood please ask permission at the house, as game is raised in the wood and cannot be disturbed at certain times of year. It is also very overgrown if you leave the main path, Hunter's Avenue, to which this is the entry point. However, the determined and hardy may be rewarded by finding well-preserved British machine-gun posts and bunkers, notably the First Aid Post, 'Blighty Hole', along a small track to the left some 100m into the wood. At the roadside is Comines-Warneton Information Panel No 12, including photos of Eden, Leighton, Churchill, Bairnsfather and Williamson.

A much easier entry to the wood is from Prowse Point Memorial Park, visited later.

In April 1916, when in reserve, the young Anthony Eden, known as 'the Boy' by officers of his Yeoman's Battalion of the KRRC, 'lived in Hunter's Avenue, a series of unimpressive forts offering no protection. As they were far back in the wood, however, the trees sheltered us to some extent ... The Rats were a plague in the trenches … they were much resented, not least by

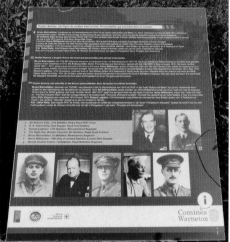

Info Panel showing personalities who served in Plugstreet Wood

Reg Park' – Eden's staunch Platoon Sergeant. Park decided 'to go after them' with traps. While he was out in Hunter's Avenue on his rat hunting mission a 5.9 inch shell hit the fort and Reg was killed instantly. 'We buried him in a little cemetery behind the wood and I lost a friend I have never forgotten', wrote Eden. Sgt John Reginald Park, 21st Bn KRRC, age 22, was killed on 20 July 1916, and is buried in the Berks Cemetery Extension. It is an extraordinary concidence that the future World War II Prime Minister, Winston Churchill, and his Foreign Secretary, Anthony Eden, should have been serving in exactly the same area during World War I, a fact that must have forged a rapport between them.

Continue

Some 250yd to the south was **Laurence Farm**, painted by Winston Churchill, a keen amateur artist, during his stay in the area. It is another curious coincidence that some 2 miles up the road in the area around Mesen and Wijtschate, his World War II opponent Adolf Hitler was also painting local landscapes (qv).

Continue to the crossroads.

• *Le Gheer Crossroads/13.7 miles*

Here is Comines-Warneton Information Panel No 11. At this point on the night of 1 November 1914, **Drummer Spencer John Bent of the 1st E Lancs won the VC** when he took command of his platoon, his officer and platoon sergeant having been struck down, and 'with great presence of mind and coolness succeeded in holding the position'. Bent had already won the MM for bringing up ammunition under fire on 22/23 October and on 3 November bringing in some wounded under enemy fire. He went on to become RSM and died in 1977.

> *Turn left to Le Pélerin, following the road round to the right.*
> *Continue to the sharp bend to the left.*

Memorial Cross to Pte Wilkinson whose body was found at St Yvon in 2000

Here there is Comines-Warneton Information Panel No 10 about the 24 mines laid in preparation for the Messines Battle. Some 200yd up the road straight ahead is the site now filled in, on the right, of the Mine which exploded on 17 June 1955 when lightning hit a power cable (Map R32).

> *Continue to the left.*

On the left hand side are **Memorial Markers** (GPS: 50.73939 2.91082), including one to **Pte Harry Wilkinson**, 2nd Lancs Fus, (Map R25a) whose remains were discovered here in 2000 and who was re-interred in Prowse Point Cemetery in 2001, visited later. In March 2006 the remains of three more British soldiers were found by local archaeologists including Frederic Seynave. One of them bore an identification disc, 8372 Pte Richard Lancaster of the Lancashire Fusiliers, together with his scabbard, cap badge, ammunition pouch, toothbrush, razor, fork and spoon. His identification was announced in the press before MOD PS(4) could make their formal identification and announcement. Lancaster, a regular soldier, enlisted on 1 March 1901 at Bury at the age of 18. In the Reserves for 12 years he was recalled for active service on 1 August 1914. He went into battle with the 2nd Lancs Fusiliers about 1100 on 9 November 1914 in a night attack on Ploegsteert Wood in support of the Argyle & Sutherland Highlanders and was then unaccounted for. Lancaster was commemorated on the Plugstreet Memorial as having died on 11 November 1914, age 32. His remains were reburied with full military honours and in the presence of family members (he had 4 children) at Prowse Point Cemetery on 3 July 2007.

> *Continue to a turning to the right.*

Here is Comines-Warneton Information Panel No 9 re Factory Farm and Ultimo Craters.

Extra Visit to St Yvon Craters (Map R25, 24, GPS: 50.74294 2.91210)

Round trip: 400 yds. Approximate time: 20 minutes (to include some time to explore)

> *Turn right and continue some 200 yards to the trees on the left.*

These surround the Factory Farm Crater (Map R25). The crater to the right is Ultimo or Trench 122. This is occasionally opened for visits in the summer. See also pages 302. They were among the nineteen mines placed in a huge arc from Sanctuary Wood in the north via

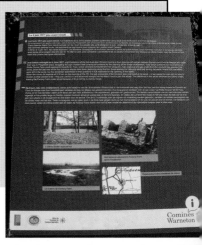

Comines-Warneton Information Panel No 9,
''Le 6 juin peu avant minuit…''

Spanbroekmolen in the west and down below Ploegsteert in the south. They were fired on 7 June 1917 to open the Battle of Messines. Two (at least) failed to blow – one at Le Pélerin (see above), but the site of the remaining unexploded mine is still unknown. In the opinion of the authors the missing mine is probably in the area of La Petite Douve Farm (qv) beside the N365.

Turn round and return to the Main Itinerary.

Continue. Turn left along the Chemin du Mont de la Hutte. Continue to the houses on the left. Stop near Number 12.

• *Commemorative Plaque to Capt Bruce Bairnsfather on House No 12, Chemin du Mont de la Hutte, St Yvon/15.8 miles/5 minutes/Map R28a/ GPS: 50.74298 2.90404*

You are now in the village of St Yvon. Here in the cellar of a cottage (Comines-Warneton Information Panel No 8) the cartoonist Capt Bruce Bairnsfather (qv) (then a Lieutenant) was billeted and created his immortal character, 'Old Bill'. Bairnsfather, a trained artist who had previously served in the Royal Warwickshires before the war, rejoined the colours in August 1914

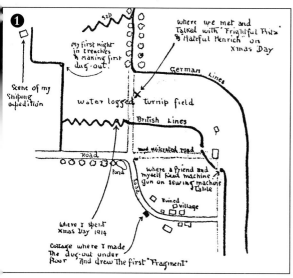

1. *Bairnsfather's Sketch Map of the area.*

2. *Bairnsfather's original cottage, St Yvon 1915*

3. *House on site of 'Bairnsfather's' Cottage, with enlargement of Plaque inset, St Yvon*

4. *The road from the pond to Bairnsfather's cottage today*

and by November was with the 1st Battalion in the trenches at Plugstreet Wood. Possessed with sharp powers of observation and a quick pencil he began to draw cartoons to amuse his men - on anything that was to hand, from ammunition boxes to walls. Just behind the regiment's lines in this village he and a fellow officer called Hudson took over a cottage as living quarters which they used for each four or five day period when they came up into the trenches. That cottage was on the site of house No 12, Chemin du Mont de la Hutte to your left.

On 13 December 2003 the authors unveiled a bronze Plaque on the cottage wall to commemorate the birth of Bairnsfather's unique cartoons and the seeds of his extraordinary career. It bears the cartoon 'They've evidently seen me' (see below). The ceremony took place on a wet and windy day in the presence of the Mayor and dignitaries of Warneton, Chaplain Ray Jones, the local band and standard bearers, members of the Khaki Chums, readers of the Old Bill Newsletter, many WFA, RBL and Holt family members and friends from Warneton, Ieper, Poperinge, the UK and Holland. In a situation that Bairnsfather himself would have appreciated a large group that had travelled from England for the ceremony was delayed by enthusiastic local police, who were controlling security, and missed the ceremony. Undeterred, the band was recalled, the Khaki Chums marched again, the bugles were blown and Padre Ray blessed the plaque a second time and the ceremony was repeated!

On one occasion when Bairnsfather and several of his comrades were in the cottage, the Germans began to shell the village and, knowing that the enemy would have ranged his guns on the buildings, they dashed outside and took cover in a nearby ditch. At last when the shelling seemed to be over they went back into the cottage and just as they did so a heavy shell landed close by and to a man they rushed to the broken doorway and with one voice exclaimed, 'Where did that one go to?' Bairnsfather turned the situation into a cartoon of that title. It was an action that was to lead to a lifetime career which included the immortal character 'Old Bill' that emerged from his cartoons, collectively called *Fragments from France*, stage plays with C. B. Cochran, requests from France, Italy and America for him to draw for them, films with Alexander Korda and even to his appointment as Official Cartoonist to the American 8th Air Force in World War II. [It is a story that we examine in our biography *In Search of the Better 'Ole, The Life, the Works and the Collectables of Bruce Bairnsfather.*]

At about the same time Bairnsfather decided to try his hand at sniping, considered an 'officer's sport', and climbed onto the roof of another cottage. He had hardly done so when another German barrage began and he had to beat a hasty retreat, an experience that he turned into the cartoon, *They've evidently seen me*, which shows a startled soldier clinging to a chimney as a huge shell whistles by. The precise sites of each of the cottages are easy to find – see the sketch map on previous page.

It was in this area that men participated in that curious phenomenon, 'The Christmas Truce' on 24/25 December 1914. On 7 December 1914, *The Times* reported that the Pope was endeavouring to arrange a truce to take place at Christmas. Nothing official ever materialised but on part of the British front around Ypres fighting stopped on 25 December. In the days leading up to Christmas the commanders of each side were concerned that the other would take advantage of any truce to mount an attack, and orders were issued to be vigilant. Despite these misgivings the Germans started a cease-fire by singing *Stille Nacht*, by placing fir trees on the parapets of their trenches on Christmas Eve, and later that night by burning candles. The British responded, and in some places initiated meetings in no-man's-land when drinks, cigars and souvenirs were exchanged. Some reports said that football was played but they have proved difficult to substantiate. What is certain, however, is that the 1st Battalion the Warwickshire Regiment in Plugstreet Wood took part in the truce and 2nd Lt Bruce Bairnsfather, in his book, *Bullets and Billets* gives a full and humourous account of what happened. After singing and shouting 'a complete Boche figure suddenly appeared on the parapet and looked about itself. This complaint became infectious. It didn't take Our Bert long to be up on the skyline. This was the signal for more Boche anatomy to be disclosed and this was replied to by all our Alfs and Bills until in less time than it takes to tell, half a dozen or so of each of the belligerents were outside their trenches and advancing towards

COIFFURE IN THE TRENCHES
" Keep yer 'ead still, or I'll 'ave yer blinkin' ear off."

Bairnsfather cartoon, inspired by the Christmas Truce

each other in no-man's-land.' He goes on to describe how he joined in the fraternisation and how eventually everyone returned to their trenches. 'The last I saw of this little affair was a vision of one of my machine gunners, who was a bit of an amateur hairdresser in civil life, cutting the unnaturally long hair of a docile Boche who was patiently kneeling on the ground whilst the automatic clippers crept up the back of his neck'. The experience may well have led to one of his *Fragments* cartoons entitled *Coiffure in the Trenches* where a soldier (either Alf or Bert) is having his hair cut by Old Bill as a large shell sails by. Bill is saying 'Keep yer 'ead still or I'll 'ave yer blinkin' ear off'.

In one of the ironies of the war, Sgt Frank Collins of the 2nd Bn the Monmouthshire Regiment, Mentioned in Despatches, age 39, was killed during the period of the truce on 25 December 1914. The Monmouths had responded to the Germans' initiative by cautiously displaying copies of the *Cardiff Times* on the ends of their rifles. Then both sides met in no-man's-land exchanging gifts with the 7th Bavarians. Sgt Collins visited the German trenches to hand out more gifts of tobacco. On his way back to his own lines a shot rang out from the enemy trenches and he fell dead. The informal truce came to an abrupt end in this sector. Collins is buried in Calvaire CWGC Cemetery to the south of Ploegsteert, where 16-year-old Pte Shaw, also of the Monmouths, is buried.

Sir John French reacted quickly to the news of the truce. Units that had participated were moved out of the lines and hostilities immediately recommenced.

Christmas Day 1914 was not without its official pleasures, however. Every officer and soldier in the field was given two gifts. The King and Queen sent a postcard bearing pictures of themselves, the King in service dress, and on the reverse in a facsimile of the King's hand the message, 'With our best wishes for Christmas 1914. May God protect you and bring you home safe. Mary R. George R'. Princess Mary, following a tradition that Queen Victoria had begun in the Boer War, sent an embossed brass tin containing a mixture of cigarettes, pipe tobacco and chocolate together with a small folded card wishing the recipient a Happy Christmas. The arrangements for getting the boxes to everyone on time were very complex and the delivery vans were securely locked with special locks that needed a code-word dialled into them in order to open the doors. At one distribution point there was a near disaster when the receiving officer forgot, or had not been given, the secret word, and the lock had to be wrenched off using another lorry. It says little for imaginative security or officer intelligence that the 'code' word was 'Noel'.

The 2nd Bn the Grenadier Guards, who had recently moved from the Salient to Le Touret did not share the Warwicks' festive spirit. Their commanding officer, Lt Col Wilfred Robert Abel Smith, complained that 'the rations of the Army are to be held up for twenty-four hours to enable the Princess Mary's presents to come up and I have had reams of orders as to their distribution. I do not know what I am not responsible for in connection with this present. It was the longest order I have had since I have been out, and it seems rather ridiculous to make such a tremendous business of it when, after all, our first business is to beat the Germans.' On 25 December he reported, 'At daybreak a few Germans put their heads up and shouted, 'Merry Xmas'. Our men, after yesterday, were not feeling that way, and shot at them. They at once replied and a sniping match went on all day.' The next day Lt Col Abel Smith wrote, 'I am sending home my Christmas card, and shall send my Christmas present from Princess Mary. Bless her – she has been a nuisance!'

Continue.

Note, on the left at the bend, the pond that featured in Bairnsfather's sketch.

Continue some 50m, passing, just before the radio mast, on the right hand bank

• Khaki Chums' Christmas Truce Cross/16.00 miles/5 minutes/Map R26a/GPS: 50.744438 2.90257

The simple wooden Cross was erected by the Khaki Chums (the Association of Military Remembrance) when they spent a cold Christmas in the area to commemorate the 85th Anniversary of the Truce. The site was visited on 20 March 2002 by Bruce Bairnsfather's daughter, Barbara Littlejohn, her daughter, by Rudolf Zehmisch, a German soldier who had also taken part in the Christmas Truce and his daughter. Together they laid a poppy wreath to commemorate the meeting. On 13 December 2003 a more substantial Cross replaced the original. It now seems to

be the custom to leave a football as a tribute. Beside the Cross is Comines-Warneton Information Panel No 7.

Continue to the track to the left leading to a group of cemeteries and park in the large car park.

From this point you will have to walk if you wish to visit the **cemeteries which are in Plugstreet Wood** itself. If you do, allow an extra hour.

Follow the track to **Mud Corner CWGC Cemetery** (Map R27). This was used from 7 June (when the NZ Division captured Messines) to December 1917 and contains 53 New Zealand (all without personal messages on their headstones, as is always the case), 31 Australian and 1 UK burial. Mud Lane (qv) met Look Slippy Lane at this point.

Khaki Chums' Christmas Truce Cross, St Yvon

Continue along the track into the wood to **Toronto Ave CWGC Cemetery** (Map R28).

This was begun by 3rd Australian Div during the Battle of Messines, 7-10 June 1917. It contains 78 Australian burials.

Continue to **Ploegsteert Wood Military CWGC Cemetery** (Map R29).

This Cemetery concentrates several small regimental burial grounds and contains 117 UK, 1 Australian, 28 Canadian, 18 New Zealand, and 1 unknown burial.

Continue to **Rifle House CWGC Cemetery** (Map R30).

This contains 229 UK burials, including **15-year-old Rifleman R. Barnett** of the 1st Bn the Rifle Bde, killed on 19 December 1914, and 1 Canadian burial.

Return to the car park.

• Prowse Point Christmas Truce Memorial Area/16.1 miles/15 minutes/ GPS: 50.74427 2.89883.

Inaugurated on 11 December 2014 by UEFA President Michel Platini, a large Memorial area has been constructed here. It includes a Truce Memorial which has become a shrine to football, recreated trench lines and bunker and the entry to the 1.5km path which leads to the Plugstreet Experience.

Christmas Truce Memorial Area, Prowse Point

• *Prowse Point Military CWGC Cemetery/16.2 miles/10 minutes/Map R26*

Beside the Cemetery is **Comines-Warneton Information Panel No 6**. Designed by W.K.Cowlishaw, this attractive Cemetery with an unusual irregular layout was named after **Brig-Gen C B ('Bertie') Prowse, DSO**, who fell on 1 July 1916, and is buried at Louvencourt on the Somme. It was begun by the Dublin Fusiliers and the 1st Warwicks and was used from as early as November 1914 until April 1918 and contains 159 UK, 42 New Zealand, 13 Australian, 1 Canadian and 12 German prisoner burials. At the front of the Cemetery is a rectangular pond with water lilies.

Also buried in Louvencourt CWGC Cemetery is the poet, **Lt Roland Aubrey Leighton**, probably best known for being the fiancé of Vera Brittain, author of *Testament of Youth*. On 12 April 1915, Leighton's battalion, the 7th Worcesters, reached trenches in Plugstreet Wood. Here he wrote the poem to Vera entitled *Villanelle*,

Violets from Plug Street Wood,

Sweet, I send you oversea.

(*Violets from Oversea*, the first line of the last verse, gave us the title of the first edition of our book on twenty-five poets of World War I.) Leighton was killed on 23 December 1916.

Another poet was **Charles Sorley** (qv) of the 7th Suffolk Regt serving to the south of the wood in July 1915. In his letters Sorley describes a bombing raid on a 'redoubt of some kind' the Germans were making and upon which the battalion did not have enough shells to fire. Although some bombs (grenades) were thrown, the Germans soon raked the ground 'with an absolute hail of rifle and machine-gun fire'. Many of the raiding Suffolks were wounded. Nevertheless the officer leading the raid, described only as 'C' by Sorley, was noticed the next day on trench patrol, 'dressed in summer get-up; gum boot, breeches, shirt-sleeves, Sam Browne belt and pistol. He had a bandage round his head, but only a very slight scratch from a fragment of bomb. He was walking along, reading from his German pocket edition of *Faust*.'

In the Cemetery, on 31 October 2001 was buried, with full military honours, the body of **Private Harry Wilkinson**, of the Lancashire Fusiliers, killed on 10 November 1914, discovered at the archaeological site at Boezinge (qv). Present at the funeral were three generations of the family, including his grand-daughter, great grand-daughter and great, great grandson, who wore Private Wilkinson's medals.

On 22 July 2010 **Pte A.J. Mather**, 33rd Bn AIF, died 8 June 1917 age 37, was also buried here, his remains having been found in Ploegsteert Wood in August 2008. He was identified through painstaking DNA

The beautiful cemetery at Prowse Point with headstone of newly-interred Pte A.J. Mather, 22 July 2010

matching (using his tooth enamel) with a 97-year-old cousin. He was buried with full military honours in the presence of 7 family members and Lt-Gen Ken J. Gillespie, chief of the Australian Army.

Continue to the main road.

This is the area known as La Hutte. Up the small road to the right are Comines-Warneton Information Panels Nos 4 and 5.

Turn left.

On the left was a position known as 'Straffer's Nest'.

Drive downhill towards the Ploegsteert Memorial. Just before the Memorial is a right turn, signed Neuve Eglise/ Nieuwkerke. Turn right and continue.

Bunker, Hill 63, near entrance to the Catacombs

The high ground to the right, which peaks at Hill 63 some 500 yards north of here, was riddled with trenches and tunnels. On the right on the edge of the road is a clearly visible **Bunker** (GPS 50.74115 2.87417) which is close by where an entrance to the tunnel system called the 'Catacombs' used to be.

The defensive system was constructed by the 1st Australian Tunnelling Company early in 1917 and its tunnels and chambers could sleep well over 1,000 men. So proud were the Aussies of their work that they held an 'official' opening with a band and a considerable number of visitors including several General Officers in attendance. To finish off the occasion the entrance path was named Plumer Road, decorated with coloured bunting and was given another name – Wallangarra. Clearly this was a jump-off area for the Messines offensive. If the direction of your travel is taken as 12 o'clock, Messines is just short of 2 miles away at 1 o'clock on the centre line of the advance of the NZ Division on 7 June 1917.

7th Fld Coy, Australian Engineers at the entrance to the Catacombs. January 1918

Continue to the cemetery on the right

• Underhill Farm CWGC Cemetery/17.6 miles/5 minutes/Map R6/ GPS: 50.74103 2.87015.

Started in June 1917 during the Battle of Messines and used until 1918, this Cemetery at the foot of Hill 63 (Rossignol, or Nightingale, Heights) contains 102 UK, 47 Australian, 1 Canadian, 39 New Zealand, 1 unknown burial and 5 Special Memorials. It was designed by G. H. Goldsmith and contains the grave of **Sjt T.E. Adcock**, 12th Norfolks, age 24, whose service spanned almost the entire war. He enlisted on 3 August 1914 and was killed on 11 October 1918. The ruined Château de la Hutte on the heights was defended by the 19th Hussars and 1st Dorsets in 1914. In 1918, 25th Division held the position. Here was Comines-Warneton **Information Panel No 19** re Under Hill Farm and the Château de Rosenberg, absent in 2016.

Continue along Red Lodge Road to the T junction and turn right along Leinster Road (Zuidlindestraat). Approaching Nieuwkerke (Neuve Eglise), turn left at the T junction(in 1918 there was a camp here known as 'Emu') and continue to the church. Park in the square opposite the War Memorial.

Underhill Farm CWGC Cemetery, Hill 63 behind

• Neuve Eglise Churchyard, Nieuwkerke/20.4 miles/5 minutes/Map Q1/GPS: 50.74567 2.82554

At the entrance to the Churchyard is an impressive local War Memorial. The CWGC plot, with its Cross of Sacrifice, contains 69 UK, 5 Australian, 1 Canadian, 1 Indian, 1 New Zealand, 1 unknown and a World War II plot of 11 UK and 4 French burials from 1914, 1915 and 1918. Here is buried **Pte James Jacobs**, 2nd King's Own R Lancasters, age 26, 25 June 1915, 'the son of a Crimean Veteran'.

On the morning of 13 April 1918, the Germans pushed the tiring troops of 34th Division back towards Neuve Eglise [see 'Fourth Battle of Ypres' above] and, in response to their pleas for help, 100th Brigade sent forward their 'Battle Reserve', the 2nd Worcesters. By late afternoon the Worcesters were forced northwards up the N331 into the village, the CO, Colonel Stoney, losing contact with A, C and D Companies. He set up his HQ in the *Mairie* and with help from two rifle platoons of B Company barricaded the windows, made improvised loopholes and prepared the area for defence. (The *Mairie* has been rebuilt opposite the church where you are now. At the time of the action described, it was on the RH side 200 yards up the Dranouter Road where Capt Crowe's Memorial now is.)

Continue to the immediate T Junction, turn left on the N331 and then first right on the Dranouter Road, N322. Continue to the Memorial on the right (opposite the fire station).

• Capt Crowe VC Plaque, Nieuwkerke/20.7 miles/MapQ1b/5 minutes/ GPS: 50.74662 2.82223

The Chaplain, the Reverend Tanner, set up a first aid post in the cellar here. That night the Germans entered the village and a contest began between enemy machine guns, and rifle grenades which the Worcesters had found in the cellars of the *Mairie*. At dawn the *Mairie* was surrounded and mortar shells were falling on it, causing many casualties. Machine guns were firing at it on three sides, from the church where you now are, from the crossroads to the south and from the open high ground to the west. Something drastic had to be done. The 26-year-old 2nd Lt Anthony Johnson, who in the previous two days had carried messages between the companies, volunteered to set out for help, but was killed, winning a bar to his MC for his bravery. He is buried in Kandahar Farm CWGC Cemetery (Map Q5).

The adjutant, Captain J. J. Crowe, then asked for volunteers to go with him in an attempt to silence the enemy machine guns on the high ground and with CQMS Trotman and nine others rushed to a nearby cowshed. Then with two picked men he crawled to the crossroads and left along the Dranouter Road to a position behind two machine guns that were firing at the *Mairie*. The three men jumped to their feet and ran at the enemy, firing as they went, the Germans bolting. Captain Crowe signalled for the rest of his party at the cowshed to join him and consolidated the position. Enemy reinforcements continued to enter the village and the ammunition at the *Mairie* was running out so, at about 1330 Colonel Stoney gave the order to withdraw and, covered by Captain Crowe's party and Private F. R. Bough who continued firing his Lewis gun from a window until the very last moment, they withdrew from the *Mairie* and the whole force retired safely along the Dranouter Road (though three badly wounded men had to be left in the cellar). For this action Private Bough and CQMS Trotman were awarded the DCM, Lt Colonel Stoney the DSO and Captain Crowe the VC.

On 16 April 2011 in the presence of many members of his family and representatives of the Mercian Regiment, the Information Plaque in a wooden frame was erected on the white Hospice Wall on the right to commemorate Capt Crowe's bravery. It describes Crowe's action in detail, complete with photo, clear sketch map and text in English, French, Dutch and German. **Capt Crowe,** age 41, was awarded his **VC** by King George V in the field on 6 August 1918. He died, age 88, in 1965, when the Rev Tanner (see above) assisted at his funeral.

While this was going on, the other companies of the Worcesters were engaged in isolated

Plaque to Capt J.J. Crowe VC, Nieuwkerke Hospice

actions with the enemy. Just beyond Neuve Eglise to the north east, about half a mile on the road past the church, **Lt C. S. Jagger** (qv) rallied the remnants of D Company and held up the German advance from the east. Gathering stragglers of other regiments he set up defensive positions in the buildings at La Trompe Cabaret (now called Trompe) and held on until relieved. As they were moving back, Jagger was badly wounded, but survived, both to receive the MC and to become a famous sculptor. Charles Sergeant Jagger, ARA, who had learnt silver-engraving with Mappin & Webb and studied at the Sheffield School of Art and the Royal College of Art, went on to create some of the most powerful war memorials of World War I, notably the Royal Artillery Memorial at Hyde Park, the British Memorial to Belgium in Brussels and the *bas reliefs* panels on the Cambrai Memorial at Louverval.

Return to the area of the church, keeping left of it on the N331, direction Kemmel and take the next left to Kemmelberg on the N331 signed to Ieper.

At the second junction to the right with Makkestraat was where, on the left, **'Better 'Ole Farm'**, and on the right, **'Better 'Ole Camp'** were sited. (**GPS: 50.751954 2.826880**). Between here and Kemmel village, to a first approximation, in July 1918 the British front line ran between 150-300 yards parallel to this road to the right with the German lines barely 100 yds beyond it.

Continue uphill past the sign left to Lindenhoek Chalet Military CWGC Cemetery (Map L6, visited at the end of the next Extra Visit) and then downhill to Kemmel village roundabout. Turn left following signs to Kemmelberg and Ossuaire Française. Continue to the church on the left.

In **Kemmel Churchyard** are 22 British graves of winter 1914, only 3 of them identified. The others have Special Memorials.

Note that the new **Heuvelland Tourist Office** will be in the old Vicarage beside the church here in 2017. See page 329.

Turn right and continue to the Cemetery on the right.

• *Kemmel Château Military CWGC Cemetery/24.1 miles/10 minutes Map L17/GPS: 50.78667 2.82888*

An early Cemetery, begun in December 1914 in the grounds of the château which would be destroyed in 1918, it was used until the German offensive of March 1918 and again from September of that year when the village was retaken. The present Cemetery contains 1,030 UK, 24 Australian, 80 Canadian, 1 New Zealand, 21 Unknown and 21 World War II burials from May 1940. It was designed by Sir Edwin Lutyens. Many men from the Sherwood Foresters and from Irish Regiments lie here. Also buried in the Cemetery is **Lt Col Guy Louis Busson du Maurier, DSO**, of the 3rd Bn the Royal Fusiliers, killed on 9 March 1915, brother of the novelist Gerald du Maurier. A professional soldier, who had fought in the Boer War, (where, so sensitive a man was he that his hair had turned white when the man next to him had been killed) du Maurier went out to the front in January 1915. He wrote graphic and rather depressing letters to his wife, Gwen, of the horrors of the war around him. Two hundred of his men were hospitalised in one day, many with frostbite, and the dead of the Highlanders, killed the previous December, and Frenchmen still lay rotting in and around their trenches. Guy was the uncle of **George Llewelyn Davies** (qv, the original **'Peter Pan'**) also newly out. 'When we've done our four days I'll try and go over and see George,' he wrote, 'who I think is only two miles off.' George's youngest brother Nicholas ('Nico') wrote to his brother 'Uncle Guy is having an awful time I believe. He went out with 900 men. He has only 230 left. The other 700 are laid up with their toes nearly off.' Both Guy and George wrote home about the château after which the cemetery is named. Guy described it as 'a lone and much-shelled château, looking picturesque in the rising moonlight'. A month later his nephew George wrote of it to James Barrie: 'It was all white with four great pillars in front, one of them broken. I walked up to it feeling, in spite of mud & dirt, like a Roman Emperor. It is the best sight I've seen yet.' Nothing of the château, which was badly damaged in August 1918, now remains. George heard of his uncle's death from Barrie and commented on it in the last letter he wrote, dated 14 March 1915.

Headstone of Lt-Col G.L. Busson du Maurier, DSO, Kemmel Château CWGC Cemetery

Also buried here is **Pte J.H. Smith,** one of 12 soldiers all killed on 10 June 1916 and buried together in a row. All were tunnellers, working 27m under the Petit Bois in a very small tunnel 1.2m high and 90cm wide which was collapsed by a German countermine. Only one Sapper survived when, after six and half days of frantic tunnelling by their comrades, the men were reached. He was Sapper William Bedson.

Return to the main road, turn left and first right and follow signs to Kemmelberg keeping to the right of the bandstand (which was used by British bands to entertain the troops in quiet periods) and then left following Kemmelberg signs up the hill. At the crest opposite a car park turn sharp right up a cobbled road signed to the Hostellerie Kemmelberg.

Just before the Belvedere is a concrete and brick **Memorial** on the bank to the left, to **a French Regiment**.

• Kemmel Hill and Belvedere/25.2 miles/10 minutes/RWC/OP/GPS: 50.77923 2.81571

Currently (July 2016) closed and awaiting sale, the Tower (which is a rebuilt and different version of the original which was destroyed during the war) was for many years open from the end of April to the end of September and could be climbed for a small fee. On a clear day, and provided the trees do not obscure it, it provides superb views over the Salient to Ypres and beyond, as well as south to Armentières. The original Tower had been used as an OP, particularly by observers for the heavy artillery. The adjoining **Belvedere Restaurant** had a bar and an attractive restaurant and made an ideal lunch stop. Enquire at the **Heuvelland Tourist office** (qv) for up-to-date news.

The hill was in Allied hands until Fourth Ypres. The French had taken it over on 17/18 April 1918, by which time the Germans had stormed through Armentières and pushed the front to a line running from Dranouter to Wijtschate. On 25 April, preceded by a savage artillery barrage of high explosives and gas that one French soldier described as 'worse ... than anything at

Kemmel Hill Belvedere Complex

Owners Philippe and Kristine Vercoutter, in the elegant Hostellerie Kemmelberg

Verdun', three and a half German divisions attacked the six French regiments holding the hill. By 0710, the Alpine Corps, leading the assault, reached the summit taking 800 prisoners. Before 0730 Kemmel village fell to the 56th Division which took 1,600 prisoners. French infantry tumbled in confusion down the far side of the hill, their failure to hold the height adding to the distrust that was growing between the Allied politicians as to what each others' true priorities were – Paris or the Channel Ports. The German assault, the last victory of 'Georgette', was filmed in great detail by the official cameraman Franz Zeldte, as Malins had filmed the Somme in 1916. Zeldte told the story of how he and his team followed the attack in his 1933 book, *Through a Lens Darkly.*

German faith in victory and determination to carry on had reached their zenith and commanders and soldiers began to lose heart. Early in August there were rearward movements in the south and the Allies kept up a constant pressure so that, on the night of 29 August, withdrawal began along the whole front, the British 34th Division retaking Kemmel on 31 August.

Continue up the hill.

On the left is the upmarket **** **Hostellerie Kemmelberg** (qv) with 21 bedrooms/suites, a gastronomic restaurant and fantastic panoramic views from its terrace. They stretch over a calm and tranquil agricultural plain some 40k straight ahead to the Loos Double Crassier and Vimy Ridge, and to Lille towards the left.

Completely renovated (with lift) and beautifully designed throughout by new owners, Kristine and Philippe Vercoutter in 2012. Restaurant closed for non-residents, Mon & Tues night. Annual closing 4 Jan-11 Feb. Tel: + (0) 57 45 21 60. E-mail: info@kemmelberg.belg Website: www.kemmelberg.be

During the War the building on this site was known as *Belle View Cabaret.*

Continue to the tall column of the French memorial. Stop.

• Memorial to French Soldiers 1918/25.5 miles/5 minutes/Map L4/GPS: 50.77820 2.81064

This 60ft high column with its winged figure of the Greek Goddess of victory, Nike, commemorates those who fell in the battles on the Flanders Hills during the German assault of April 1918. It was inaugurated on 18 September 1932 in the presence of General Pétain. Until 1970, when it was struck by lightning, the column was capped with a French casque. It was unveiled by General Pétain in 1932. The French plaque on the Cloth Hall commemorates in general the French who fell in the Salient. This Monument commemorates the units who fought in this sector and whose names are inscribed around the column. The Monument had fallen into a poor state of repair but, taken over by the Westhoek Province, it has been beautifully restored.

Detail of Figure on French Memorial, Kemmelberg

Continue down the hill some 200m to the cemetery.

• French National Cemetery, Kemmel/25.6 miles/10 minutes/Map L3/ GPS: 50.77883 2.80838

The cockerel (emblem of France) standing on an elongated pyramid marks the ossuary where 5,294 officers and soldiers lie buried, most of whom fell in the April 1918 battle of Mount Kemmel. Of these only fifty-seven have been identified. The bodies were concentrated here between 1920 and 1925. On the right of the pyramid are inscribed the French units which fought in Belgium and on the left the names of their commanders. There is also a **Plaque to the 30th RIF** who defended Kemmel. Outside the Cemetery are **Information Panels** with some interesting contemporary photos.

Continue.

As you drive down the road (weather permitting) the flashing wireless aerial of Mont des Cats can be seen at 11 o'clock on the horizon. To the right of it the abbey is visible in the dip between Mont Noir to the left and Mont Rouge to the right.

Continue to the next small crossroads.

French National Cemetery Kemmelberg

Extra Visit to Locre Hospice CWGC Cemetery (Map K12) & Private Memorial to Major Redmond (Map K11), Loker Churchyard Cemetery (Map K7, GPS: 50.77959 2.78096), Plaques to 2nd Fr Cav Bde, 4th/12th Fr Dragoons, 23rd Fr Inf Regt, (Map K 8, 9, 10, GPS: 50.78179 2.77234), Locre South Demarcation Stone (Map K13, GPS: 50.77597 2.77497), Locre No 10 CWGC Cemetery (Map P7, GPS: 50.77178 2.77698); Dranoutre Military CWGC Cemetery (Map P4, GPS: 50.76749 2.78025) & Dranouter Churchyard Cemetery (Map P5, GPS: 50.76603 2.78340); Lindenhoek Chalet Mil Cemetery (Map L6, GPS: 50.77642 2.82369).

Round trip: 6.1 miles. Approximate time: 35 minutes.

Turn sharp left onto a very small road signed to Monteberg, follow the road right towards Loker on Gockschalkstraat and stop on the left by House No 34 at the grass path to the cemetery.

Locre Hospice CWGC Cemetery was opened in June 1917 (during the Battle of Messines) and used until April 1918 when the Germans attacked. It lies near the Hospice, now also a school and a convent, and was the scene of fierce battles in 1918. The Germans took the area in April and the French counter-attacked on 20 May 1918. They failed to retake the position, which was only regained in July.

Entrance to Locre Hospice CWGC Cemetery

The Cemetery contains 238 UK burials, amongst them 28 year old **Pte Denis Jetson Blakemore of the 8th N Staffs**, who was arrested in Boulogne 18 days after he deserted whilst already serving a suspended sentence for the same offence. He was **shot** on Mount Kemmel on 9 July 1917, and his grave bears the inscription, 'Thy will be done'. Also buried here is **Pte William Jones** of the 9th RWF, a stretcher bearer who absconded whilst taking a wounded man to a dressing station on 15 June 1917. Jones gave himself up to the assistant Provost-Marshal at Bristol on 4 September and was shot on Kemmel Hill on 25 October. He, too, was already under a suspended sentence for desertion. Who now can blame these men for reaching the end of their tether under unspeakably horrific conditions? Tragically their supposed 'crimes' were committed in an age when there was little understanding of the reasons why. Here is also buried Etonian **Brigadier General Ronald Campbell Maclachlan, DSO**, CO 112th Inf Bde, Rifle Bde, 11 August 1917 age 45. There are also 2 Australian, 1 British West Indies, 1 Canadian, 1 New Zealand and 2 German burials with 12 Unknown and 14 burials from May 1940.

Private Memorial to Maj W.H.K Redmond

To the right of the Cemetery entrance a path leads to the **Private Memorial grave of Major William (known as 'Willie') Hoey Kearney Redmond**. Redmond was the Irish Nationalist MP for Wexford, then for North Fermanagh and finally for East Clare. Born in 1861 he was a fervent Irish nationalist and was imprisoned as a nationalist 'suspect' in 1881. With his brother John, the MP for Waterford, who was Charles Parnell's successor as leader of the Nationalist Party 1890-1916, he went on a political mission to Australia and America in 1883. He joined the Royal Irish Rifles and was a well-loved officer. Col Rowland Feilding called him 'a charming fellow, with a gentle and very taking manner' after they had dined together in Locre Convent [Hospice] on 17 January 1917 (where the food appeared to have been hearty and the champagne flowed). Coincidentally another Irish MP, Peter Kerr-Smiley the member for North Antrim, was also present at the dinner. Redmond met yet another, Capt J. L. Esmonde, the member for North Tipperary who, according to Col Feilding 'looks about nineteen', in Bailleul on 4 May 1917. Redmond was wounded at Wijtschate on 6 June 1917, leading his men in the attack on the Messines Ridge. 'Aged fifty-four', wrote Feilding [he was actually 56], 'he asked to be allowed to go over with his regiment. He should not have been there at all. His duties latterly were far from the fighting line. But, as I say, he asked and was allowed to go - on the condition that he came back directly the first objective was reached; and Fate has decreed that he should come back on a stretcher.' Redmond had received several anonymous letters from Ireland 'accusing him of staying behind because he was afraid'. For this reason he was determined to prove himself in the great attack on Messines. His company were the first to go over and Redmond was immediately hit in the hand as he crossed the parapet and again in the leg as he reached the German wire. Though neither wound was apparently serious, and a younger man would probably have survived, Redmond's injuries proved fatal. He was taken to the 36th (Ulster) Div Dressing Station at Dranouter where he subsequently died. His body was originally buried in the Nuns' garden, a spot near the grotto of Our Lady of Lourdes personally chosen by Col Feilding for his own grave should he himself be killed. On 20 October the Mayor of Wexford, accompanied by 'a red-hot Sinn Feiner', came from Dublin with special passes to visit the grave.

There has been much discussion on social media as to whether Redmond's body was moved at any time. The consensus by reliable researchers is that after the war Redmond's widow paid for the cross which still surmounts the grave. She was adamant that his body should not be moved into the Military Cemetery being built beside it. Although the grave was neglected for a period it was finally bought by the Belgian Ministry and then donated to the CWGC to maintain. On 19 December 2013 the Irish Taoiseach, Enda Kenny, and UK Prime Minister, David Cameron, lay wreaths on the grave.

Continue to the T junction at Loker Church and park near the local memorial.

In the churchyard are the two plots, one either side of the church, of **Locre Churchyard Cemetery**. Here are 184 UK burials, including (in the left hand plot, which contains the cemetery Report and Visitor's Book) the sad graves, side by side, of two young **Privates of the 1st Royal Scots: Andrew Evans and Joseph Byers** (the first Kitchener Volunteer to be executed and who was not represented at his trial). **Both were shot** at Locre on 16 February 1915, for 'attempting to desert'. In the next row lies 20-year-old **Pte George Collins** of the 1st Lincolns, shot on 15 February for desertion – also undefended at his trial. Here too are buried **Pte F. Eke**, 1st Devons, 28 March 1915, **age 16** and **Lt C. Hawdon,** Yorks Regt, age 20, 27 June 1916. His two **brothers** also fell. 'In death they are not divided.' The brothers were Capt R.A. Hawdon, RFA, age 24, who was killed on 4 November 1918 and is buried in Ruesnes Comm Cemetery and Chaplain 4th Class Noel Hawdon, who died 16 November 1918 and is buried in Terlincthun Brit Cemetery. One can only imagine the grief of the parents who, as the war drew to a close, would have believed that only one of three of their sons had been taken from them.

There are 31 Canadian and 2 unknown burials and in the church a beautiful SGW.

In the Church on Sunday 17 December 1916, Col Rowland Feilding, commanding the 6th Connaught Rangers, arranged a special Church Parade and High Mass for his Irish troops. The men marched through the village with pipes and drums and three priests officiated. 'All was very impressive,' wrote Col Feilding to his wife, 'and, considering that they are only out of the trenches

Headstone of Pte J. Byers, Locre Churchyard CWGC Plot.

Free-standing Register Box, Locre Churchyard Cemetery

for a few days' rest, the smart and soldierly appearance of the men was very remarkable.' Rowland Feilding was the very best kind of Regimental officer. He had a genuine love of and respect for his men and commanded the same in return. In a typical gesture, Feilding got his wife to obtain miniature crucifixes, have them blessed by the Pope and brought back from Rome by a Cardinal. They were presented to the men (each of whom kissed the crucifix as he received it) at another splendid Church Parade on 22 April 1917. The Mass was conducted by Father O'Connell 'for Mrs. Feilding's intention'. 'I may admit that the devout reverence of these soldiers, redolent of the trenches, as they filed towards the altar, affected me, too, very deeply,' reported the Colonel.

By the playground beyond the Church is an **Information Board to Major Redmond,** including a moving picture of the Nuns by his original grave. Beyond the bus stop are **Plaques to three French units** who succeeded in repulsing the Germans from the village in April 1918: the **17th/18th Light Cav of 2nd Bde, the 4th/12th Dragoons and the 23rd Inf Regt.**

> *Turn left direction Dranouter. Continue, following signs to Dranouter on the N322.*

On the right, on leaving Loker, is the **Locre South (Kemmel) Demarcation Stone.**

> *Continue. On the right is*

Locre No 10 CWGC Cemetery/OP, originally started by the French during the German offensive of April 1918. After the Armistice the French graves were removed (probably to the Kemmel Ossuary) and British and German dead were reburied here from the surrounding battlefield. There are 55 UK burials, mostly of the 2nd London Scottish and the 2nd S Lancs, and 75 Germans in mass graves under two different types of headstones, only 3 of whom are identified. There are 14

Information Board re Major Redmond, Loker

Plaque to French 23rd Inf Regt, Loker   *Plaque French 17th & 18th Light Cavalry, Loker*

Locre South (Kemmel) Demarcation Stone

German Headstones over 2 Mass Graves, with individual burial behind, Locre No 10 CWGC Cemetery

Unknowns, including 3 'Kipling' headstones and one grave has 'Five soldiers of the Great War'. There is no Cemetery Register box here.

Stand to the right of the Cross and look over the brick wall.

At 1 o' clock is the wireless mast of Mont des Cats. Just to its immediate right is Mont Noir. Just before 3 o' clock is Mont Rouge, also with a wireless mast, and at 6 o' clock Mont Kemmel - all the Flanders Hills.

Continue to Dranouter, passing on the right

Dranoutre Military CWGC Cemetery, approached by a track that passes the local timber yard. The Cemetery was in use from July 1915 until the German assault of March 1918. There are 421 UK, 17 Australian, 19 Canadian, 1 New Zealand, 3 unknown and 1 German burials. Many of those from April-June 1916 were of the 72nd Bde of 24th Division. It was designed by Charles Holden. Buried here is a member of the Australian YMCA, the **Rev Thomas George Trueman**, attd 5th Bn Australian Inf, killed on 22 March 1918, age 30, and **Pte Frederick Broadrick** of the Royal Warwickshires who deserted from his billets in Locre on 1 July. He was arrested in Calais five days later and, as he was already serving a suspended death sentence for a previous desertion, was executed on 1 August at Dranouter.

Headstone of 2nd Lt G. Staniland, Dranoutre Churchyard CWGC Plot

The village was captured by the Germans under the Crown Prince of Bavaria on 25 April 1918. The depth of the German advance in this area during Fourth Ypres was formidable and can be readily seen by using a pencil to join the marker stones K13, L1, L5 and L13 on the Holts' Map.

Continue to the church in the centre of the village.

Beside it is **Dranouter Churchyard Cemetery.** 19 UK burials and 2 unknowns still lie in this small plot, 19 graves having been moved in 1923 to the nearby Military Cemetery.

Memorial to Kapt-Vlieger B. De Hemptinne, Dranouter Churchyard, with Belgian War Memorial behind

The Churchyard was used for burial by the British from October 1914 until the Military Cemetery was opened in July 1915. In the left-hand British plot is the grave of **Norbert D'Huysser**, age 9, an innocent victim of the war. His headstone is non-standard.

Just inside the hedge on the right is a long row of 1915 headstones in single file. At the front is the grave of **2nd Lt Geoffrey Staniland**, Lincolnshire Regt, 13 April 1915, age 34. Three months later the body of his brother, **Capt Meaburn Staniland**, of the same Regt, 29 July 1915, age 35, was brought here for burial in the nearest space – the third from the end of the row. The remarkable story of the brothers is told by Martin Middlebrook in *Captain's Staniland's Journey*.

In the left front corner is a **WW1 Memorial** in the form of a Belgian soldier, erected by the Flemish Old Soldiers' Association with the Joe English 'AVVVK' (qv) insignia. Beside it is a **World War II Memorial** in the shape of an aeroplane tail to Belgian **Capt Flyer B. de Hemptinne**, 5 May 1942, inaugurated in May 1992. Hemptinne was shot down in his Spitfire in the *Circus 157 Operation* (see page 265).

N.B. Memorial to Sgt Karel Pavlik, RAF (GPS: 50.770236 2.792804). By turning down Lettingstraat past the Hemptinne Memorial and continuing for approximately half a mile the Memorial will be reached at the edge of the road to the left. It was inaugurated on 5 May 1992. Beside it is an **Information Board.** The Czech pilot was shot down near the site on 5 May 1942 in *Operation Circus 157*. His body was still in the plane when it was recovered three years later (see page 155).

Memorial to Sgt Pavlik, RAF, brought down here 5 May 1942

Continue and turn left past the church on the N322 signed Nieuwkerke and fork left signed to Wulvergem on Kruisabelestraat. Continue over the next crossroads to the T Junction with the N331 and turn left towards Kemmel (signed to Ieper). Continue uphill and turn left at the crossroads on the crest on a narrow, easily missed road, signed to Lindenhoek Chalet Mil Cem. Continue to the cemetery on the right.

Lindenhoek Chalet Mil Cemetery. The first burials here were in March 1915 and it was in use by fighting units and field ambulances until October 1917. Enlarged after the Armistice and designed by Charles Holden, it contains 315 burials, 67 unidentified, with 6 Special Memorials. There are 9 Australian, 15 Canadian and 7 New Zealanders here. Buried here is **Capt William Walbeoffe-Wilson**, 3rd Monmouths, died 2 August 1915, age 33, whose father was a JP in Abergavenny and whose mother lived in Cap d'Antibes. His promotion to Captain had been gazetted on 16 October 1914.

Continue keeping left to the T junction and turn right and immediately left, uphill to Kemmelberg. Continue past the Belvedere to the French Ossuary and pick up the main itinerary.

Turn right and after some .6 miles on the left is a small parking area and the

• Lettenberg Bunkers/26.7 miles/20 minutes/Map L3a/GPS: 50.78231 2.81681

The Lettenberg is a smaller (79m high) outcrop of Kemmelberg. Towards the end of 1916 British Engineers and Tunnellers started excavating an underground HQ and troop accommodation beneath what was their most important OP from 1914 and for the Messines campaign of 1917.

From here British Officers viewed the mine explosions of June 1917. Between 4 April and end May 1917 175th Tunnelling Coy built five shelters. They were constructed with reinforced concrete poured in rough gravel on corrugated plates, known as 'elephant plates', each with an entrance and a window opening to the west. During their Offensive of April 1918 the Germans took the area and created a medical facility in one of the shelters. A faded red cross is still visible today.

In 2004 the ABAF (qv) cleared the debris that had clogged up the shelters in the post-war years to make them accessible to the public. They were opened on 17 April 2005. **Information Panels** were erected at the site and paths leading to them and to the top of the hill (where there are excellent views and an Orientation Table).

Some of the Bunkers have been modified to provide ideal hibernation habitat for big-eared

One of the four Lettenberg Bunkers

bats, and so keen are the local authorities to preserve the natural ecology that the Bunkers have now become overgrown again.

Continue following signs to Kemmel and go left past the bandstand.

Around the Square is a variety of useful shops, **restaurants and cafés.**

Continue down Polenlaan towards the T junction.

On the left at No 7 is the pleasant **Casino Restaurant** (on the site of the old Casino Hotel/ Casino), Tel: + (0) 57 85 98 30, Website: www.casino-kemmel.be

Beyond it on the wall is an imposing **Belgian Memorial Plaque: The Village of Kemmel 1914-1918.** It lists the names of twelve fallen soldiers, 6 on the left and 6 on the right and then Civilian Casualties in alphabetical order.

Currently the helpful and informative **Heuvelland/ Kemel Tourist Office**, manned by Ingried Tierson, is at Polenlaan 1, but it is due to move by February 2017 to the old Vicarage by the Church Sint-Laurentiusplein 1. (**GPS: 50.7842382.826360**).

There will be several interesting exhibitions, both temporary and permanent in the office and in the Church (e.g. Mines; The Irish in Flanders and Archaeology of a Battle). Tel: +(0) 57 45 04 55. E-mail: Toerism@heuvelland.

Kemmel WW1 War Memorial

be Website: www.tourismheuvelland.be Apply here for a ticket to the Bayernwald (qv) and for a ticket to the fascinating and well-preserved 1963 **Cold War Command Bunker** which is at 64 Lettingstraat, Kemmel (**GPS: 50.77612 2.816856**). It is important to reserve in advance as only small parties are permitted at set times: 1000; 1145; 1330; 1515. Allow 90 minutes. **Open:** Tues & Sat.

Turn right to the Kemmel roundabout and at the roundabout turn left.

Except for a short period during Fourth Ypres these were all rear areas criss-crossed by narrow gauge railways and studded with training and rest camps. To the right here were White, Gibraltar and Ramilies Camps and to the left Kemmel, Rossignol and La Polka Camps.

Turn left in the direction of Ypres on the N331. Continue. On the left is

La Laiterie CWGC Cemetery

• *La Laiterie CWGC Cemetery/28.1 miles/10 minutes/Map L16/GPS: 50.79123 2.84207*

The Cemetery, named for the Dairy Farm here, was begun in November 1914 and the plots were treated as regimental burial grounds (e.g. Canadians are in Plots II and III and 5th Northumberland Fusiliers in X). The Cemetery fell into German hands on 25 April 1918 but was retaken in early September. It contains 468 UK, 7 Australian, 197 Canadian, 1 Newfoundland and 78 Unknown burials. It was enlarged with concentrations after the Armistice and designed by Sir Edwin Lutyens assisted by G. H. Goldsmith. Here are buried **Lt Gerald Davies Blackwell**, 6th Northumberland Fusiliers, attd MGC, age 23, 7 June 1917 'entered in the records of the Irish Division for gallant conduct and devotion to duty', and **2nd Lt Hugh Vaughan Charlton** of the same regiment, age 32, 24 June 1916 whose brother Capt J.M. Charlton of the 21st Tyneside Scottish was killed at la Boisselle on 1 July 1916 and his name is on the Thiepval Memorial. Several headstones in the Cemetery bear the inscription 'Death divides but memory clings'. The epitaph, 'Death divides, fond memory clings' is universally found over the centuries and around the world but the source has proved elusive. The headstone of Lt Robert Lightbourn (pictured) carries a heart-felt message from his parents in Bermuda.

Continue to the memorial on the right.

Headstone of Lt R. Lightbourn, La Laiterie CWGC Cemetery, with moving personal message.

• *American 27th and 30th Divisions Monument/28.7 miles/5 minutes/Map L19/GPS: 50.79763 2.84908*

When the war began America was firmly neutral, but the activities of the belligerents at sea began to interfere with American maritime trade and when, on 4 February 1915, Germany declared that she would regard the waters around Great Britain and Ireland as part of the war zone in which even neutral vessels could be targeted, America protested. The stories of German atrocities in Belgium (many, if not all, the products of the Allied propaganda machine), their use of poison gas which was considered an 'evil' weapon, and patently false German propaganda being produced by the Washington embassy, contributed to an atmosphere in which America became sympathetic to the Allied cause. The event that more than any other prompted American entry into the war was the torpedoing of the liner *Lusitania* on 7 May 1915, with the loss of 1,100 lives, some American, (see

Vlamertinghe Cemetery entry, Itinerary Two for the fate of a survivor of the *Lusitania*), although it was two years before war was declared – on 6 April 1917.

Urged on by the Allies, whose armies were hard pressed and anxious for fresh troops, the Americans created the 1st Division from existing formations and sent it to France, the first units landing at the end of July 1917 at St Nazaire. (After the war the 1st Division erected a magnificent memorial depicting a Doughboy overcoming a German eagle which was destroyed by the Germans on 13 December 1941, much as they damaged a similar statue at Compiègne. A maquette of the St Nazaire statue is held in the St Nazaire *Mairie* and in 1989 a 21m-high replica of the Memorial was unveiled.)

General Pershing established his HQ at Chaumont on the Marne and was soon visited by Clemenceau, the French Prime Minister, who as a schoolmaster had been in Richmond, Virginia, during the American Civil War when General US Grant marched into the city. Clemenceau wanted the Americans to be under the total command of the Allies. Pershing would have none of it.

Nevertheless, to accustom the Americans to the 'new' European type of war, some were attached to different Allied formations, the first deaths occurring on 3 November 1917, while serving with the French. The three men killed, near Bathelemont on the German border west of Strasbourg, are commemorated by a Memorial erected there by the French.

Monument to the American 27th & 30th Divisions, Vierstraat

The divisions commemorated here, the 27th and 30th, arrived in Europe in May 1918 and served with the British until the Armistice, initially as small units and finally as divisions. In August 1918 the 27th Division took over the sector from, but excluding, Kemmel (Map L4) to here, and the 30th Division from here to the area of Lankhof (Map M14), the front lines being roughly parallel to this road and 700yd west of it (i.e. to the left of the road - the memorial area was behind the German lines). On 31 August 27th Division attacked towards where you are now standing and the following day the 30th followed suit. Both the villages up ahead, Vierstraat and Voormezele, were taken with advances of up to 2,000 yards. Some of the American casualties from the operations here are buried in the Flanders Field Cemetery near Wareghem (qv). By the time that the two Divisions were relieved three days later the 27th had suffered nearly 1,300 and the 30th some 800 casualties.

The Memorial is a rectangular white block with a soldier's helmet in front resting on a wreath. The architect was George Howe of Philadelphia and it was unveiled on 8 August 1937, the same day as In Flanders Field US Cemetery (qv) was inaugurated. To the left is an Information Board with a detailed Map.

Taking your direction of travel as 12 o'clock, Mont Kemmel and its Belvedere (which you have recently visited) are on the horizon at 7 o'clock. Broadly speaking the Germans held the ground containing this road and the Americans attacked from your left at 9 o'clock.

Continue to the large Goudezeune Prefab buildings on the left and a group of CWGC signs on the right. Immediately turn left at the crossroads along Vierstraat. Continue to the next small crossroads. Just before it on the left is

• *The Vierstraat Demarcation Stone/29.3 miles/Map L13/GPS: 50.80359 2.84607*

This Stone once stood alongside the Kemmel No 1 French CWGC Cemetery (qv) and was moved beside the American Memorial when it was damaged, then to this site. There are continuing disputes as to its rightful location.

Turn left following CWGC signs to

• Suffolk CWGC Cemetery/29.4 miles/5 minutes/Map L14/GPS: 50.80310 2.84509; Godezonne Farm CWGC Cemetery/29.8 miles/5 minutes/Map L15/GPS: 50.80059 2.84036; French 32nd Division Memorial/30.1 miles/5 minutes/Map L15a/GPS: 50.79853 2.83447

The tiny **Suffolk Cemetery,** approached by a grassy path, contains 47 UK and 8 unknown burials and was begun by the 2nd Suffolks in March 1915. There are many York & Lancs burials from April 1918. Originally it was called the Cheapside Cemetery and was designed by J.R. Truelove.

Continue along the road (once also known as 'Cheapside') to

Godezonne Farm Cemetery with mostly Suffolks and York & Lancs burials. Designed by W.H. Cowlishaw and was named after the farm on the site and was made between February and May 1915 by the 2nd R Scots and the 4th Middx. It contains 79 burials, 44 Unidentified and in the back row is a row of graves from April/May 1918. Buried here is Etonian **Capt the Hon Douglas Arthur Kinnaird**, Scots Guards, age 35, 21 October 1914. His brother, Lt the Hon A.M. Kinnaird, was buried in Ruyaulcourt Mil Cemetery, Pas de Calais.

Suffolk CWGC Cemetery.

Continue to the obelisk on the right, just beyond a turning to the left.

This is to the **French 32nd Division** Wytschaete 1914, Kemmel 1918 and from the Canal de Charleroi to Dunkerque 1940. The Ieper architect was August Taurel. Its insignia is in the form of a bunch of grapes, a reminder of the wine-producing area of the Division in Perpignan. Inaugurated on 8 September 1919 it was partially dismantled during WW2 by the Germans for its metal content. It was re-inaugurated on 15 July 1963 at the instigation of Dr Canapeel (qv), and further restored in 2014, The Centenary. Then a delegation from Loupia (who came to pay homage to three soldiers from the village, killed in this area), the

French 32nd Div Memorial, Vierstraat, with 2014 Plaque

French Consul General and local Burgomaster, unveiled a Plaque to the three.

Return to Vierstraat, turn left and continue following signs to Dikkebus. On the left is

The 'fortress-like' corner of Klein Vierstraat Brit CWGC Cemetery, seen from Kemmel No 1 French Cemetery

• Kemmel No 1 French and Klein Vierstraat British CWGC Cemeteries/31.00 miles/15 minutes/Map L12,11/GPS: 50.80546 2.84079

Originally started by the French, who later removed their burials to the Ossuary at Kemmel or the French National Cemetery at St Charles de Potijze, the Kemmel No 1 French Plot was taken over by the British. It contains 277 UK, 12 Australian, 3 Canadian, 3 New Zealand, approximately 89 German in a mass grave and 5 named and 1 unknown burial. It is approached by an imposing, but fairly steep, flight of stairs. In it is buried **Pte Richard Sawdon** of 'Y' Coy 8th NF, killed on Kemmel Hill on 28 May 1917, age 41, who served with the Imperial Yeomanry in the SA Campaign.

Behind it is **Klein Vierstraat Cemetery** which contains 777 UK, 8 Australian, 1 British West Indies, 8 Canadian, 7 New Zealand, 1 South African, and 1 Chinese Labour Corps burials. It was begun in January 1917. All of this area was involved in the fierce fighting during the German April 1918 assault of Fourth Ypres. Both Cemeteries were designed by Sir Edwin Lutyens assisted by W.H. Cowlishaw. The impressive entrance and sympathetic use of different levels are typical of Lutyens' original conception.

The Cemeteries are right on the front line of the American Divisions as they attacked towards you in August 1918.

Continue downhill to a small bridge over the Kemmelbeek (known by the Germans as the 'Bardenbrug').

• "American Bridge", Vierstraat/ 31.4 miles/10 minutes/GPS: 50.80792 2.83379

'American Bridge', Vierstraat

The bridge is thought to have been built by the Americans in 1918, hence its local name. However the retaining walls are built from British precast concrete slabs, made for bunker construction. There is a small Plaque in one of the coping stones on the left-hand wall stating '245-GT-AT-RE–7 Aug 1918', most probably 245th Army Troop Coy, RE. This unit of XIX Corps specialised in bridging. The bridge played a major part in the transport of troops and supplies during the August 1918 Offensive when the road you are on was the centre lines of the American 27th Division as it drove uphill towards Vierstraat.

Continue and at the next junction keep right up Kerkstraat towards the church to the cemeteries. Stop on the left between the first two.

• The Dickebusch Group of CWGC Cemeteries/32.2 miles/20 minutes/ Map L8, 9, 10/GPS: 50.81833 2.83240

The group of cemeteries was designed by Sir Edwin Lutyens. In these two, on the left is a Cross of sacrifice and on the right is a War Stone. *On the left is*

• Dickebusch New Military Cemetery Extension Cemetery

This was begun in May 1917 in succession to the other Dickebusch cemeteries and used until January 1918. It contains 520 UK, 24 Australian, 2 Canadian, 1 South African and 1 German burials. It contains **Driver W.E. Evans RFA**, 28 May 1917 whose headstone is also in memory of **Cpl J.L. Evans**, Middx Regt, I July 1916 whose grave is unknown. This Cemetery (and the following) was designed by Sir Edwin Lutyens, assisted by W.C. Von Berg.

On the right is

• Dickebusch New Military Cemetery

This contains 528 UK, 11 Australian and 84 Canadian burials, including the poet and classic scholar Lt R. W. Sterling of the 1st Royal Scots Fusiliers. He was killed on 23 April 1915, after holding a trench all day with fifteen men in the Second Battle of Ypres in 'the storm and bitter glory of red war', to quote from one of his short poems, *Lines Written in the Trenches, 1915.* Here are buried 5 men of the 354 listed on the Newton-le-Willows & Earlestown WW1 Memorial: **Baddley, Ball, Hamblett, Hunter and Reeves** of the 4th S Lancs, April/May 1915 (research by pupils of St Aelred's Catholic School, June 2002). Here too is **Pte Horace Hill**, 24th Can (Quebec) Inf Regt, age 22, 30 April 1916. Beside him is his **brother, Pte Cyril Charles**, age 19 who died on

Headstones of the Hill Brothers, who both died on 30 April 1916. Dickebusch New Mil CWGC Cemetery

the same day. Their service numbers are sequential – they obviously joined up together and both bear the same private message, 'Lest We Forget'.

Beside the church is

• Dickebusch Old Military Cemetery

A front-line Cemetery from January to March 1915, it contains 41 UK, 2 Canadian and 1 German burials. There are 10 burials from 1940.

Continue to the N375 'T'junction

Some 2.5 miles down the N375 to the left is Klijte (La Clytte), where the future Prime Minister **Anthony Eden** served during the winter of 1916/17 as Adjutant of 21st Bn, KRRC. His older brother 'Jack' had been killed in the Salient in October 1914 (qv), his cousin 'Bill' (the Hon WAM) Eden (qv), also of the KRRC, had been killed on 3 March, 1915 and his younger brother, Nicholas, was killed as a 16 year old Midshipman when the *Indefatigable* went down in the Battle of Jutland and is commemorated on the Plymouth Naval Memorial. Anthony's sister, Marjorie, served on a hospital train in France. 'When Winston Churchill and I were colleagues in the Second World War', wrote Eden, 'he often spoke to me of seeing Marjorie standing at the door of that hospital train at Poperinghe during the battle of Ypres. In her nurse's uniform, "She looked beautiful as an angel", he would say.' To complete this aristocratic family's contribution to the war, Eden's maternal Uncle, Robin Grey, a pilot with the RFC, was shot down, taken prisoner and suffered solitary confinement as he was a cousin of the Foreign Secretary, Sir Edward Grey. The family seat, Windlestone, in County Durham, was used as a war-time VAD hospital and as a prisoner of war camp in WW2. In the late 1950s it was acquired by the local council and then sold to a private individual in 2011 who was later jailed for fraud in the raising of the money to complete the purchase.

Turn right and after approx 0.6 mile right again following signs to Dikkebus Vijver/Etang (Lake). Stop in the car park.

• Dikkebus (Dickebusch) Lake/33.5 miles/10 minutes/RWC/GPS: 50.82188 2.84752

The name Dickebusch means 'thick forest' and dates from the era when this area was dense woodland. On the right of the path leading from the car park to the lakeside café (closed Monday and winter weekdays), which has a bar and offers snacks, is an old Vauban watchtower and from it around the edge of the water are ramparts dating from 1678 which may be walked. The lake has been artificially enlarged and is a leisure resort for fishing and boating. The patio railings posts are shells and behind them over the water is Kemmelberg.

Dikkebus Lake

Neither the village nor the lake were ever taken by the Germans, although in the May 1918 fighting they reached the edge of the water. Rest camps of temporary huts and tent lines were set up here and **T. E. Hulme** (qv), serving with the 1st Bn, the HAC, was billeted here in March/April 1915. The Liverpool Scottish were also here and stayed through May. In 'the Black Hut' in Dickebusch their **MO, Noel Chavasse**, held his sick parade and he sent home for sweet pea, nasturtium and other seeds to brighten up the huts area (Ann Clayton *Chavasse Double VC*).

Overlooking the lake is

The **Tea Room/Brasserie Dikkebus Lake** with a large terrace. Opening times are flexible! During the Summer **Open**: 1100- 1800 if not raining! During the Winter – fine weekends. Tel: +(0) 47 54 56 66.

Return to the main road and turn right following signs to Ypres.

At the first crossroads on the left was **Matawi Camp** and on the right the camps of **Café Belge, Maida, Nelson, Vauban** and **ANZAC**. Running along with the road, switching from one side to the other, was a narrow gauge railway.

After some 1.5miles the sign to Belgian Battery Corner Cemetery is to the left.

Turn left and then right to the cemetery on the right

Several narrow gauge railway lines met at this junction.

Entrance to Belgian Battery Corner CWGC Cemetery

• Belgian Battery Corner CWGC Cemetery/35.3 miles/5 minutes/ Map H3/GPS: 50.83930 2.86146

This was begun by 8th Division in June 1917 and contains 430 UK, 123 Australian, 8 New Zealand, 7 Canadian, 2 Indian, 9 unknown burials (including one American) and 2 special Australian memorials. It was named after the Belgian Artillery group stationed here in 1915 and was designed by Sir Edwin Lutyens assisted by J.R. Truelove. Here is buried **Lt-Col A.J.E. Sunderland**, 2nd Devons, age 32, 31 July 1917, three times **MiD**.

Return to the main road, turn left and continue over the railway line to the Ieper Ring Road and turn right direction Menen. Turn right at the roundabout direction Armentières. Turn left immediately before the railway line signed Zillebeke.

This is **Shrapnel Corner**. After approximately 0.6 mile the **Railway Dugouts Bunker** is passed on the left (Map H36). *Stop on the right by the large cemetery opposite.*

• Railway Dugouts Burial Ground CWGC Cemetery/38.1 miles/15 minutes/Map M24/GPS: 50.83549 2.90303

This spacious Cemetery, designed by Sir Edwin Lutyens assisted by J.R. Truelove, with an interesting irregular layout, was begun in April 1915 on a site known as Transport Farm. It continued to be used throughout 1916 and 1917 when Advanced Dressing Stations were placed on the nearby dugouts. Many of the graves were obliterated by shell fire before they could be

Circle of Special Memorials, Railway Dugouts CWGC Cemetery

marked. At the time of the Armistice it contained 1,705 known and marked graves. Then more graves were concentrated here from nearby small cemeteries and the surrounding battlefield. Today it contains some 2,500 burials including almost 700 Canadians, over 150 Australians and Special Memorials, arranged in a circle, to 258 men whose original graves were destroyed by artillery fire. There are 4 Indian and 4 German burials.

Buried here is **Temp 2nd Lt Frederick Youens, VC** of the 13th Bn DLI who won his VC at Hill 60 (qv) on 7 July 1917 and who died two days later. Two **brothers** of the 43rd Bn Can Inf (the Manitoba Regt) were killed on the same day – 21 August 1916 – and lie here: **Pte Reginald Wild, age 22 and Pte Frederick George Wild**, age 27. **Pte V.K. Merchant**, 58th Bn Can Inf, 6 June 1916, age 16 was 'the only child of aged parents' – one can only imagine the grief. In developing a regimental 'family' spirit it was not unusual for brothers to serve together, but because of the appalling effect upon those at home if both brothers were killed, such service was later discouraged. Nevertheless in the Canadian Second World War Cemetery at Bény-sur-Mer in Normandy there are nine pairs of brothers and the film *Saving Private Ryan* is centered on the theme of preventing a similar disaster as the loss of that of the Sullivan and Nilands (full stories in our *D-Day Normandy Landing Beaches Guide Book*).

Also buried here is **Lt Albert Service** of 52nd Bn, Canadian Infantry (Manitoba Regiment), 18 August 1916. He is the brother of the popular poet and author, Robert Service, author of *The Shooting of Dan McGrew* and many other poems and tales of the frozen north. Service served with the Red Cross during the Great War (after having worked as a correspondent for the *Toronto Star* during the 1912-13 Balkan wars. He wrote an anthology called *Rhymes of a Red-Cross Man*, dedicated to his brother which was published in 1916. Service was born in Preston, Lancs in 1874 and emigrated to Canada in 1894. He died in Lancieux,

Poignant message on headstone of 16 year old Pte V.K. Merchant – 'The Only Child of Aged Parents'

France in 1958. He was known as 'The Canadian Kipling'. Kipling would have approved of the audio alliteration.

Across the road from the Cemetery is the path leading to Zillebeke Vijver (Lake). Like Dikkebus this was created in the 13th century to serve Ypres with water and also has a restaurant. A path, in places overgrown, encircles the lake. Throughout the war the area was fiercely bombarded (a fixed target for German guns) and its banks were heavily defended. In October 1917 **Herbert Read**, then a Company Commander with the 7th Green Howards, (and holder of the Military Cross for his part in a raid in the Arras sector in July of that year) held the right support position in the Line near the Lake. Of the action, Read wrote, 'We have had a terrible time, the worst I have experienced and I'm getting quite an old soldier now. Life has never been quite so cheap nor nature so mutilated.' An incident during this five days of hell inspired him to write *Kneeshaw Goes to War*, in which a man sinks in the mud, cries for help, and despite the efforts of his comrades to dig him out sinks in deeper and deeper, terror-stricken,

'Eventually,
An officer shot him through the head;
Not a neat job - the revolver
Was too close.'

Continue over the railway line. On the right is the path to

• Blauwepoort Farm CWGC Cemetery/38.5 miles/5 minutes/Map M33/GPS: 50.83147 2.91025

With just 83 UK and 7 unknown burials, this was started by the *Chasseurs Alpins* in November 1914 and used by the British from February 1915 to February 1916. The French graves have been removed.

Turn left at the next junction passing the

• Zillebeke Demarcation Stone/38.6 miles/Map M27/GPS: 50.83095 2.91211

This was erected by the Touring Club of Belgium and the Ypres League (qv).

Continue over the railway line, turn left and following signs to Menin continue towards the Church at Zillebeke.

Zillebeke Demarcation Stone

• Zillebeke Church Memorials and Churchyard Cemetery/39.2 miles/15 minutes/Map N1, 2/GPS: 50.83559 2.92222

This is one of the most fascinating burial grounds in the Salient, known locally as 'The Aristocrats' Cemetery'. In it are some of the earliest burials in the Salient, many of them Old Etonians. The majority of them are Upper Class officers, Sandhurst graduates, professional soldiers and sportsmen, brought up to respect the ideal of the Edwardian officer. They were inspiring leaders.

The Church (which may be locked) contains **Memorials to members of the De Marq Family, to Captain Mortas** and a stained glass window to Etonian **Lt Howard Avenel Bligh St George**, age 19, of the 1st Life Guards killed on 15 November 1914, and buried in the churchyard.

Buried here is 51-year-old Etonian **Lt Col Gordon Chesney Wilson, MVO** of the RHG (the 'Blues'), a Boer War veteran who was killed on 6 November 1914. His headstone bears the unusual inscription, 'Life is a city of crooked streets, death is the market place where all men meet', which is thought to have originated in a Warwickshire saying of the 1800s. Also buried here is Etonian Major the **Lord Bernard Charles Gordon-Lennox** of the 2nd Coy 2nd Bn the Grenadier Guards, age 36, the third son of the 7th Duke of Richmond and Gordon, killed on 10 November 1914 (qv). Before the Graves Registration Commission was established in 1915 by Major Fabian Ware (qv) there had been no official organisation responsible for the recording of graves, and certainly no standardisation in marking them. Wealthy families were still able to bring their loved one's body home, or to mark it with an expensive, custom-designed stone. The less well-off casualties had their graves marked with a simple wooden cross, which was often lost as the war ebbed and flowed backwards and forwards over the same stretch of earth, hence the high proportion of unidentified burials after the war when the bodies were reinterred in the official IWGC Cemeteries under the standard headstone. At this stage the vast majority of still existing private markers were changed, for ease of maintenance, to the chosen standard marker and today few of them remain in the Salient (notably those of Bowlby, Brodie, Rea, Skrine, and Redmond (qv), now all maintained by the CWGC or the Belgian Army). Unusually, the original privately placed headstones remain in this churchyard for **2nd Lt Alexis G. de Gunzburg**, 11th Prince Albert's Own Hussars, attd RGA, killed on 5 November 1914, son of Baroness de Gunzburg of St Germain, Paris, and 19 years old Etonian **Lt John H. G. Lee Steere**, 2nd Bn Grenadier Guards killed on 17 November 1914. On that morning in Kleine Zillebeke Wood, Lee Steere took command of No 2 Company when his commander, **Capt Cholmeley Symes-Thompson**, was killed. He, too, is buried here. The enemy had attacked at 1300 hours and were repulsed with heavy losses on both sides. Lee Steere sent a message back to say that he was running short of ammunition, but when reserve platoons of the

Above: *Grave of Lt John H. G. Lee Steere with private tribute*

Top Right: *Private tribute on grave of Major the Lord Bernard Charles Gordon-Lennox, Zillebeke Churchyard*

Right: *Memorial SGW to Lt Howard Avenel Bligh St George, Zillebeke Church*

Grenadiers reached the company, Lee Steere was already dead. 'A very good boy, who had only lately come out,' commented the battalion's CO, Lt Col W. Smith.

Lee Steere also has a Memorial Plaque in the church porch, as does **Petrus Joseph Chambard**, killed in 1915 at Hooge, **Amedée Rabusseau**, killed March 1915 at Zillebeke and **Lt Alfred Schuster**, 4th Queen's Own Hussars, killed at Hooge, November 1914.

Other aristocratic burials are Etonian **Lt Henry B. F. Parnell**, 5th Baron Congleton, age 24, of the Grenadier Guards killed on 10 November 1914, and Etonian **Lt the Hon Wm Reg Wyndham** age 38 of the 1st Lifeguards (who had previously served as a Capt with the 17th Lancers), killed on 6 November 1914.

In the autumn of 2016 there were private tributes on all the Old Etonian graves - was there a visit from the School or from the Old Etonian Assoc?

Altogether there are 22 UK burials, 10 Canadian and 2 Special Memorials in the Cemetery which was designed by W.H. Cowlishaw.

Continue towards Hellfire Corner to the sign to the cemetery on the left.

• *Tuileries British CWGC Cemetery/39.5 miles/Map I12/GPS: 50.84019 2.92115*

Approached by a beautiful grass path bordered by flowering shrubs, this was begun in 1915 on the old tile works, totally destroyed by shellfire and reconstructed after the Armistice. It originally contained 106 UK and 3 French burials, but most of the graves were lost in the shellfire. Only twenty-six were able to be identified, twenty-seven headstones are unidentified, a Special Memorial commemorates sixty-nine and the French are commemorated by their own single cross. There is a large open lawn around the Cross of Sacrifice. It was designed by W. C. Von Berg who also designed Bedford House Cemetery. He served in the London Rifles during the war.

Continue to the next cemetery on the right.

• *Perth (China Wall) British CWGC Cemetery/39.8 miles/15 minutes/ Map I11/GPS: 50.84184 2.92087*

The Cemetery takes its name from a communication trench that led from here to the Menin Road which was shielded by a wall of sandbags and became known as 'The Great Wall of China'. It was initiated by the French in November 1914. Taken over by the British in June 1917, it was used as a front line Cemetery until October 1917. It contains seven of the tragic graves of British soldiers who were executed during the war. They are: **Pte T. Docherty, KOSB; Pte E. Fellows, Worcs; Pte E. Fraser, 19 R Scots; Pte T. Harris, 21 RWK; Cpl F. Ives, Worcs; Pte L. R. Phillips, 23 SLI and Pte G. E. Roe, 19 KOYLI.** Ives and Fellows were executed with three others (see Aeroplane Cemetery above) on the Ramparts on 26 July 1915. It also contains 2,360 UK, 134 Australian, 129 Canadian, 22 New Zealand, 7 South African and 1,371 - 50 per cent – unknown. The graves in the original French plot have now been removed. There are also 135 Special Memorials and the grave of **2nd Lt Frederick Birks** of 6th Bn, AIF, **VC**, who on 20 September 1917 rushed an enemy machine-gun post at Glencorse Wood and single-handedly took it, killing its defenders. Later he successfully led a party attacking another strong point only to be killed whilst rescuing some of his men buried by a shell. Another **VC** is **Capt William Henry Johnston** (qv) of 59th Coy RE who, on 14 September 1914, repeatedly worked a raft over the River Aisne with his hands, ferrying ammunition in one direction and the wounded in the other under heavy fire. He was killed in Ypres on 8 June 1915. Also buried here is **Lt Richard William Laurence Anderson**, 1 Sqn RFC, killed 12 June 1917. Three days previously he had survived a dogfight during which Oberleutnant Kurt-Bertram van Doring had shot down another of 1 Sqn's aces, Lt Frank Sharp, who was taken prisoner. Kurt-Bertram was to become a Lt General in the Luftwaffe. On 22 August 1918 Capt Dennis Latimer of 20 Sqn, credited with twenty-eight kills, was shot down by Lt Willi Nebgen of Jasta 7 and also became a POW. His main observer, Etonian **Lt Thomas C. Noel, MC and Bar**, credited with twenty-four kills, killed in the crash, is buried here.

Here, too, is **Lt S. F. Cody**, son of the pioneer aviator 'Sam' Cody, the first man to fly a powered aeroplane in England.

The Cemetery was designed by Sir Edwin Lutyens with J.R. Truelove.

Continue, turn left at Hellfire Corner and return to Ypres.

• *End of Itinerary Three*

THREE LONG EXTRA VISITS

LONG EXTRA VISIT ONE

Belgian Memorials, Kippe & Merckem; Houthulst Belgian Cemetery; (Optional Visit to Vladslo German Cemetery); Diksmuide: Trenches of Death and Ijzer Tower Round trip: 26.4 miles. Approximate time: 2 hours 15 minutes. (Round trip to Vladslo: 9 miles. Approximate time: 30 minutes).

The most convenient point to start this deviation is the Gas Memorial at Steenstraat (Map B6), Itinerary Two.

> *Continue on the N369 direction Diksmuide. Continue 200m to just before the building on the right before the bridge over the Ieperlee Canal.*

Here is the large white cross surmounted by a Crusader's sword which is the **Memorial to** the 162 officers, NCOs and soldiers of the **Belgian 3rd Regiment of the Line** (Map B7) who fell at Steenstraat from 24 April to 10 May 1915, in the later stages of the German gas attacks.

> *Cross the Canal bridge and pull in on the slip road to the left. Park.*

Here there is a sign 'Monument Gebruders Raemdonck'.

> *Walk to the Canal and turn right along the canal path which is a cycle path. Continue some half a mile to where a Flemish flag is flying by pylons some 200m after the pylons cross the canal.*

Memorial to the Brothers van Raemdonck. (GPS: 50.92075 2.84476).

A path leads to the impressive stone Memorial with large crosses on two of the sides. A Plaque commemorates the brothers Sergeant Edward (age 22) and Frans (age 20) van Raemdonck of 6 Komp 24 Linie and soldier Aimé Fievez of the same regiment. Many legends and myths have grown up about these three soldiers. In summary the company was ordered to cross the canal to take prisoners from the German position called the Stampkopstelungen. Frans was killed by a hail of bullets and against orders Edward insisted on trying to get his brother's body back. Some two weeks later their bodies were found (the story goes that they were locked in each others' arms) alongside the body of French-speaking soldier Fievez.

Memorial to Belgian 3rd Regiment, Steenstraat

The three were buried in Westvletern Belgian Cemetery under three marked headstones. In 1973 they were exhumed for burial in the crypt of the Ijzer Tower (qv). Only one coffin was discovered containing the mingled remains of the three soldiers. The headstones were left in situ and the remains moved to the crypt. Ironically this meant that a Walloon soldier was buried in this

Memorial to the Brothers van Raemdonck.

place sacred to Flemish Martyrs. Walloons maintain that Fievez was trying to assist the brothers and he has become a Walloon hero. Flemish nationalists revere the brothers as icons (Edward was a dedicated nationalist even before the war). Since the Ijzer Tower complex no longer welcomes extremist rallies, this area has become the focal point for their gatherings. The Monument was inaugurated on 19 August 1933 and is constructed from blocks from the Stampkop on a site that was in No Man's Land. There is a Plaque to their cousin, Clemens de Landtsheer, 1894-1984, who was a pioneer of the Ijzer Pilgimages and renowned film maker on nationalistic, military and folklore subjects.

Continue towards Dixsmuide, crossing three 'beeks' (the Lobeek, the St Jansbeek and the Langebeek).

On the left is a large concrete **Memorial**, which looks like a chunk of a pill box, to the **Belgian 3rd Division**, with its battle honours and ORBAT (**GPS: 50.94545 2.86189**).

Albertina Marker, Kippe.

Continue to the traffic lights at the crossroads in Kippe.

To the left of the crossroads is an **Albertina Marker (GPS: 50.95697 2.86572)** commemorating the one-day battle of 17 April 1918, when the Belgian forces succeeded in halting the German offensive. There were heavy losses on both sides.

N.B. Two small visits may be made here.

1. By turning left along Stationsstraat for just over half a mile to the old Town Hall of Merckem, three large metal **Plaques** – to the Victors of Merckem of 17 April 1918, **the** 1/4th, 9th, 11th and 13th Infantry Regiments (**GPS: 50.95263 2.85190**) – may be seen.

2. By continuing straight on for some 0.3 miles a fine statue of a young Belgian soldier, **Armand Victor Van Eecke, (GPS: 50.96195 2.86740)** age 22, killed on 9 September 1918, erected by his parents, may be seen on the left, surrounded on three sides by a tall hedge. On the base are his many honours and medals and a poem describing the loss of this young ex-student of Leuven High School who became Adjutant of the 5th Coy of the 3rd Inf Regt

Turn round and turn left direction Houthulst, through Jonkershove. In the centre of Houthulst turn right on the N301 signed Langemark-Poelkapelle. Continue to the large cemetery on the left at the edge of the forest. In 2016 the road was significantly enlarged.

Plaque to Belgian 13th Inf Regt, Merckem

The forest, which Napoleon called 'the key to the Low Countries', saw fierce action by the retreating Belgian army in 1914, when they suffered high losses. The occupying Germans strongly fortified the forest and from there directed their heavy artillery on the Allied lines.

There was more fighting here in 1917 and finally in September 1918 when it was retaken by the Belgians. In his Memoirs, the Prince of Wales tells of an incident that occurred at the end of 1917. "In a field near the Houthulst Forest I crouched for an hour in a dugout with the Welsh Guards while a

Statue of Armand Victor Van Eecke, Kippe.

French battery shelled us enthusiastically in the belief that we were the enemy – a misunderstanding that was happily removed over a fine dinner at the French Divisional Commander's Mess that night."

Large parts of the forest are restricted military areas, some used by the Belgian Army Disposal Service which carries out controlled explosions of the Iron Harvest that is still being dug up by the ton.

The Belgian Military Cemetery (GPS: 50.96654 2.94738) is now maintained and has been beautifully renovated by the War Graves Department of the Belgian MOD (see War Graves section below). It contains 1,723 Belgian graves (the majority of whom fell in the 28/29 September liberation offensive), and 81 Italian prisoners of war working in nearby German labour camps. It has an elaborate and imaginative lay-out which from the air would appear as a six-pointed star, within which are many circles, crescents and lines. There is now an **Information Point Shelter**, near which (but not visible) is a crypt where recent unknown remains are buried.

Outside the wall at the end of the Cemetery is an **Albertina Marker** to the end of the Battle of Houthulst Forest of 28 September 1918.

Belgian Cemetery, Houthulst: Italian headstone

Turn round and return to Houthulst. Continue towards Diksmuide on the N301.

Just before leaving the village, by a large white statue, is a grey stone **Marker** to the right, to the **Belgian 22nd Regiment (GPS: 50.97869 2.94457).**

Continue to the village of Klerken.

On the right in the far corner of W Coppens Plein is a small grey **Memorial to Heldhaftig Piloot Willy Coppens** *van de Belgische Luchmarkt* 1914-1918, erected on 13.8.1967 **(GPS: 50.99587 2.91090).** Coppens was Belgium's leading fighter Ace and, like American Frank Luke, specialised in shooting down balloons. He was knighted after the war, taking his title from the Forest at Houthulst.

Continue to the junction with the N35.

N.B. At this stage **Additional Visits may be made to the** *German Cemetery at Vladslo and the Kollwitz Tower & Lange Max Museum, Koekelare*. **Round trip: 19 miles. Approximate time: 2 hours 15 minutes.**

Memorial to Belgian WW2 Pilot Willy Coppens, Klerken

Belgian Headstones, Houthulst Belgian Cemetery

Turn right at Esen roundabout towards Roeselaere and then left towards Vladslo. Continue through Vladslo and keep on the same winding road following signs to Deutscher Soldaten Friedhof to the cemetery on the left.

German Cemetery, Vladslo (GPS: 51.07098 2.93010). By the forest known as the Praetbos, this Cemetery contains 25,664 burials. Many soldiers were buried in the woods, until in 1956, when the *Deutsche Kriegsgräberfürsorge* undertook a huge programme of concentration, the 3,233 remains buried there were moved into the present cemetery of Vladslo. Because of the density of burials in such a small space, the cemetery is virtually one mass grave. Around the graves with their standard flat marker, each listing several names, are some of the original, non-standard headstones of the early days of the war.

After a major renovation by the *Deutsche Kriegsgräberfürsorge*, the Cemetery was re-inaugurated in an important international ceremony on 7 October 2016. Half the €360,000 cost was subsidised by the Flemish Government.

The burial ground is enclosed by a beech hedge, the height of a man. Oak trees are planted amongst the ten plots. The visitor enters through a brick entrance hall where the roll of honour, in parchment books, is kept. At the back of the cemetery is the famous pair of statues, 'The Grieving Parents' created by the well-known artist and sculptress Käthe Kollwitz in memory of her son Peter, who is buried under the flat gravestone in front of the statues. (Her grandson, also Peter, was killed on the Russian Front in WWII, two years after her death.) For many years Peter Kollwitz's original wooden cross was preserved in the Cemetery.

Born in Konigsberg on 8 July 1867, Käthe, married to a doctor, was a graphic artist, specialising in etchings, woodcuts and lithographs. On 23 October 1914 her 18-year-old musketeer son, Peter, who had volunteered in Berlin, was killed near Esen, attacking the 11th Belgian Line Regiment holding the Yser at Diksmuide. It was a dreadful night. A Belgian officer described the seemingly suicidal attacks of the mainly young German forces in his diary:

The Grieving Parents by Käthe Kollwitz in Vladslo German Cemetery. Peter Kollwitz's name 9th from top

'The enemy has concentrated many fresh troops opposite Diksmuide and given the order to take the town, cost what cost. Scarcely an assault has been beaten off, when they arrive again, with ever-increasing strength. What have they been promised to let themselves be killed in such large numbers? What strong drinks have been poured out to give them such a wild courage? Drunk from blood, with devilish faces and howling like beasts, they charge again and again, falling over the heaps of dead, trampling down the wounded with their heavy boots. They are mown down by the hundreds but are coming on again. Some of them are able to reach the breast-works where it comes to cruel hand-to-hand fighting, striking with rifle-butts, sticking with bayonets. Skulls are smashed, bodies are torn open apart; but all in vain, nowhere are they able to break through. Eleven times in the northerly and easterly sector, fifteen times in the southerly sector, the waves were smashed to death.'

No wonder the Germans called these battles 'The Massacre of the Innocents'. Käthe sought to express her personal grief in a tangible, artistic form, but anguished for years over the form it should take. Should it be a monument for her son alone, or for the entire grieving legion of mourning parents? Should it be one figure or two, should the figure of the dead child be included? Käthe became bitterly anti-war and her art expressed her strong pacifist feelings and her revulsion to bloodshed. Her style and beliefs were anathema to the rising National Socialist movement after the war in Germany and, when the group of figures was reaching completion in 1932, its final form was reviled by the Nazis. The father's tight-lipped expression, the way he clutches his body with his arms to comfort himself: the mother's attitude of total sorrow, her head bowed, her hand pressing her long gown to her cheek - all were perceived as expressions of weakness by the new regime. German parents should be proud to have sacrificed their son for the Fatherland. The statues were erected in nearby Esen, where Peter was originally buried, in July 1932, probably just in time to prevent their destruction by the Nazis. In 1956 the 1,539 Germans, among them Peter Kollwitz, were moved here from the small cemetery called Roggeveld near Esen. The statues moved with them.

There has been much dispute between the German and Belgian authorities over the statues, now highly regarded as a work of art. Their soft stone is deteriorating and the Germans wished to remove them back to the Fatherland. The Belgians refused and are deciding how best to preserve the grieving pair. In the meantime, the statues are encased in green wooden boxes during the potentially damaging winter months.

A little further on and to the right in the Praetbos is a house built in typical German style. Now a farmhouse, it served during the war as a rest house for German soldiers returning from the front line, much as did Talbot House in Poperinghe.

Continue some 4.8kms to Koekelare and follow signs to the Centre and Kollwitz Museum. Park in the main square.

In the beautifully restored old town centre of Koekelare (well signed, **GPS: 51.08956 2.97878**) is the **Käthe Kollwitz Tower** which contains an exhibition of her life and work. **Open**: Tues-Fri 0930-1200 and 1330-1700. May-Nov 1330-1700. **Closed** Mon & Wed morning. Also Sat-Sun

and holidays in July/Aug. There are many charming restaurants and cafés in the vicinity, notably the **Koklikoo Bistro/Teahouse** (closed Mon, Tues) Tel: + (0) 51 72 74 13, and **De Volksbond** (closed Tues) with 'Tommy Tucker' menu. Tel: + (0) 51 77 98 38.

On the outskirts of Koekelare (at Clevenstraat 6, opposite No 15) there is a small **Museum** (featuring the **German Marine Corps In**

Kathe Kollwitz Tower, Koekelare

Flanders). **Open**: July/Aug daily 1400-1800. 1400-1800 **Closed** rest of year Mon/Tues. Tel: +(0) 476 21 68 59, www.langemaxmuseum. be (**GPS: 51.11681 2.98234**) **Coffee Shop**. In the Museum is the gun pit of the great 38cm German gun known as '**Lange Max**' or the Leugenboom Gun in what was the Pommern Battery. Its main target was the railway station at Adinkerke.

Interior Lange Max Museum, Koekelaere

Return to the junction with the N301. Continue and turn left at the T junction on the N35 to Diksmuide. Continue to the traffic lights in the town centre.

DIKSMUIDE

On 25 January 1920, Diksmuide was presented with the *Croix de Guerre* by President Poincaré, as it 'Won undying fame in the first days of the War by heroic, never-to-be forgotten combats. Proved herself worthy of this glory by the fortitude with which she daily supported bombardments and fires, confident that her sacrifices were helping to save the Country and the Common Cause.' Diksmuide was the only town to receive the *Grande Croix d'Italie* from Mussolini in 1922.

In the Grote Markt, the **Tourist Office** at No 6, (**GPS: 51.03312 2.86450**), is **open** 1000-1200 and 1400-1730, Tel: + (0)51 79 30 50, E-mail: toerisme@stad.Diksmuide Website: www.diksmuide. be It adjoins the picturesque and beautifully renovated Town Hall. Opposite is **a Statue to Gen Baron Jacques de Dixmude**, Commander of the 12th Belgian Regt of Line which defended the town at the end of October 1914. There is a variety of attractive **restaurants** in the Square (see Tourist section below). In the public park is a **Marker to the French Marines and their Admiral, Ronarc'h**, who defended the town from 16 October to 10 November 1914.

Continue to the canal.

On the left is the **Hotel Sint Jan**. Tel: +(0) 51 50 02 74. Email: info@st-jan.be Website: www. st-jan.be **Closed**: Fri. **Open**: Thurs 1000-1700. Rest of Week all day from 1000. This is on the site of the notorious Minoterie. Until the German occupation of World War II, there were preserved trenches here, which were destroyed when all metal was sent back to Germany to make munitions.

Diksmuide Town Hall, with Tourist Office right and Statue of Gen Baron Jacques de Dixmude

Cross the canal, turning immediately right along the bank, following signs to Stuivekensker with the River Ijzer to your right.

On the left is a large white **Calvary (GPS: 51.03549 2.85467),** a religious monument that was dedicated to all the soldiers and civilians who died in the Great War. On 23 September 1928 it was solemnly blessed by the Bishop of Bruges in the presence of the Duke and Duchess of Brabant, the future King Leopold III and Queen Astrid. The Calvary was once the object of large pilgrimages but this lapsed when the Ijzer Tower was built.

WW1 Memorial Calvary, Diksmuide

Continue and stop at the large red brick building on the right.

Trenches of Death (GPS: 51.04586 2.84297). In 1924 the Ministry of Public Works restored the infamous trench line, replacing the crumbling jute sandbags with concrete ones. The original entrance building was erected by the Touring Club of Belgium in 1927 and the Belgian Army maintained the site. After WW2 the Touring Club took over the site once more. On 2 June 1992 the site became protected and administered by the Ministry of Transport and in 1994 it was again taken over by the Ministry of Defence. Major restoration started in 1995 by the 11th Engineers and in 2002 the entrance building was completely rebuilt and continues to be updated, latterly in 2014, when 15 interactive Apps were installed. A 1915 German Bunker was also integrated into the site.

On 31 March 2004 it was inaugurated by M André Flahout, Minister of Defence and was manned by soldiers. It has toilets including for the disabled. Stairs lead to an upstairs room which gives superb views over the battlefield through panoramic picture windows. There are video displays in four languages showing footage of wartime scenes – many of them extremely rare. The displays of photographs of the Yser Campaign are vivid and very poignant. They were found by former Kapitein-Commandant Rob Troubleyn who has unearthed a marvellous cache of such photographs, maps and documents in the Royal Army and Military Museum in Brussels. They include pictures of the RND's abortive raid on Antwerp. There is also a **Plaque** to the 1927-1977 Touring Club of Belgium building and pictures of it.

Open: 1 April-15 November every day 1000-1730. 16 November-31 March 0930-1530 Tuesday and Friday. **Closed** 25 Dec-1 Jan. Tel: +(0) 51 79 30 50. E-mail: tourisme@std.diksmuide.be

Behind the entrance building is an imposing Memorial proclaiming 'Here our Army held the invader in check 1914-1918'. The trenches themselves are marvellously preserved and one can walk through them to the end to the Demarcation Stone and then return along the parapet. There are numerous Information Panels along the route. First one goes through the Horseman's Redoubt on two levels with machine-gun positions, shelters, signalling post and underground passage to the two parallel trenchlines with their

Trenches of Death Museum beside the Ijzer

View of the trenches and the Ijzer River   *Belgian Memorial at the Trenches of Death.*

galleries, shelters, firesteps and chicanes, concreted duckboards and sandbags giving a realistic idea of a working trench.

This was the Belgian forward defence line throughout the whole of the Yser battles (see 'Battles of the Yser' above) separated from the enemy only by the River Ijzer itself. For fifty months the men in it were subjected to attack by shell and mine, grenade and bullet. Sometimes the Germans infiltrated the trench and there was hand-to-hand fighting. Death was never far away, hence the sinister name, Boyau de la Mort.

After the land between Diksmuide and Nieuwport had been deliberately flooded at the end of October 1914 to halt the Germans, the trenchline was dug by soldiers totally exposed to German fire. Progress was then continued by saps. Sentry boxes and observation points were set up, the most famous being the Mousetrap, with loopholes on three sides of its concrete walls, which was erected in 1917. Lethal snipers from the trenches on the German bank were particularly effective. The Germans also built strong fortifications on their side of the river, one of the most notorious being the 'Flour Mill' (Minoterie) on the right bank opposite the present Ijzer Tower, with machine-gun and grenade launchers permanently targeted on the trench.

After the war the **first Belgian Demarcation Stone** (qv) was unveiled here on Easter Sunday 1922 by King Albert of the Belgians. Their Touring Club had raised the necessary 250,000 Francs for the erection of the Belgian stones. It was a glorious occasion, with flags and garlands, a huge crowd including many veterans and war wounded, and, according to the magazine, *Le Courrier de l'Armée*, 'vibrant' speeches from the representatives of the French and Belgian Touring Clubs.

Communications to the Belgian rear lines were made by two footbridges, well known to the Germans. One led to Kaaskerke, the village whose spire can be seen to the left. Over this bridge under the cover of darkness soldiers brought sacks of earth to repair their parapets. The other led to Lettenburg on the Nieuwport road and this was used to carry wounded to the rear and to bring up supplies and ammunition. A Decauville narrow gauge railway (like those built on the Somme) was constructed to bring up the heavy mortar shells. The soldiers manning the trench spent three days in its hell to be followed by three days of rest in the rear line villages.

Turn round and return to the crossing. Go straight over, following signs to Ijzer Tower.

Ijzer Tower (GPS: 51.03265 2.85410). Tel: +(0) 51 50 02 86. E-mail: info@aandeijzer.be. Website: www.museumaandeijzer.be

Listed as an International Peace Centre, the tower is a symbol of Flemish nationalism, which came to a head during the First World War. Its history is long and complicated and goes back to the 18th Century when the rich vein of Flemish culture – art, music and literature, which had been influential for centuries throughout Europe – was suppressed by the French-speaking regime. After Waterloo, new links with the Dutch promised a 'window' of Flemish renaissance and King William 1 of Orange permitted a Dutch-speaking University in Ghent. But the 1830 Revolution, led by the French-speaking nobility, closed the window and set the clock back. During the 19th Century, Flemish intellectuals began working

The Ijzer Tower through the Pax Gate

to build up a renewed Flemish identity, but when the First World War broke out in August 1914, all education was still being conducted in French and during the Yser campaign, 80 per cent of all officers in the Belgian army were French-speaking. The soldiers on the other hand were predominantly Flemish-speaking and resented their orders being given in French. Intellectuals, teachers, students and priests, disturbed by the situation, started a movement for Flemish identity that went far beyond the linguistic problem. To them it became a matter of human rights. At first the soldiers expressed their misery about the war in general through the medium of their desire for Flemish recognition, but soon the movement became more intensely nationalistic. In 1917 they addressed an open letter to the King expressing their unhappiness.

Although Albert was a fair and human man, he was above all a Belgian, and a French-speaking one at that. His advisers warned him that he had to keep his country together at all costs - it was the period of general unrest and dissatisfaction: the Russian Revolution, mutinies in the French army. The Germans, occupying 90 per cent of Belgium, were deliberately attempting to inflame the two different linguistic elements. In 1916 they had allowed the re-opening of the Flemish University at Ghent.

The letter was ignored. Outspoken Flemish soldiers were penalised by their French officers with heavy oppression. 'Martyrs' were created, as explained in the crypt of the Tower. The Flemish artist Joe English, born in Bruges in 1882 of Irish antecedents, became the artist of the Yser Front and dedicated his art to the emancipation of the Flemish. There are many examples of his work in the Tower. English, who was an active member of the Association of Flemish Catholic Students, designed the provocative headstones in the shape of a Celtic cross with the inscription 'Alles Voor Vlaanderen: Vlanders Voor Kristus' ('All for Flanders: Flanders for Christ') that were erected on Flemish martyrs' graves to replace what was thought to be the inappropriate official cross with a French inscription. You will see them in and around the crypt and also above the crypt in Zonnebeke local cemetery (qv). The military authorities defaced these 'Joe English' stones, which after the war could be seen in many local churchyards, by covering the inscription with concrete, or blowing them up and using the resultant rubble in road-building.

Aerial view of the Ijzer Tower complex. Just to the right and behind the top of tower the small Memorial Chapel to Comte Paul de Goussencourt (qv) may be seen in the fields.

'Rat-catcher' diorama - note the rat on the point of the bayonet and the dog) in the animals at War Exhibition, Ijzer Tower.

After the Armistice Flemish soldiers threatened to refuse to hand in their arms unless something was done about the language problem and a direct appeal was again addressed to the King. He promised palliatives but died in 1934 having done nothing radical to improve the situation. Flemish resentment ran high and what was to become an annual pilgrimage began in Diksmuide, the land around which was literally drenched with the blood of dead Flemish soldiers of the Yser campaign. What was originally a pilgrimage to commemorate the sacrifice of the Flemish soldiers of the Yser gradually took on a more political flavour. In the late 1930s language laws were passed to diffuse the situation.

On 16 March 1946 the opponents of Flemish nationalism blew up the 50 metre high tower that had been built in 1930 on the pilgrimage ground containing the graves of the most famous Flemish martyrs. The present 84m high tower - like a giant Joe English headstone - was soon built and a great Pax Gate erected using the rubble of the original tower. The new Crypt was inaugurated in 1958 and the Tower in 1965. It is still the focal point of an annual pilgrimage in the last Sunday in August which for many years was also used by European neo-Nazis as a meeting point. Happily the whole ethos of the complex has now changed. It now has some 80,000 visitors annually to the exhibitions in the Tower. The emphasis is on Peace and the rallies attract young people with such stars as Sir Bob Geldof. The more extremist nationalist rallies are now held near the Monument to the Brothers van Raemdonck (qv).

Today the country is still split between the more prosperous northern Flemish speaking area (about 60 per cent) and the southern French-speaking Walloons (about 40 per cent). In the middle is the uneasy capital Brussels, mostly French-speaking, but with bi-lingual street signs and duplicated ministries.

Stained glass window to the Brothers Raemdonck in the Chapel in the Ijzer Tower.

Extensive renovation has taken place over the past few years and the entire grounds are now enclosed and entry is through a reception building with book and souvenir stall. Further improvements have been made for the WW1 Centenary years from 2014. As one enters the site iron wreaths are a reminder of the prison camps at Arne and Avours where Flemish soldiers were incarcerated for their beliefs.

Open: Daily in Jan, Feb, March, Oct Nov, Dec 0900-1700 (Sat, Sun, Holidays 1000-1500). April, May, June, July, Aug, Sept 0900-1800. **Closed**: Dec 24-26, 31, Jan 1, 2 and for three weeks after the Christmas Holiday. Tel: + (0) 51 50 02 86. E-mail: info@ aandeijzer.be Website: www.museumaandeijzer.be

On entering the complex the visitor passes through the **Crypt,** at whose entrance is a Calvary, which has push-button talking machines in several languages which tell the story of the martyrs (**Joe English, Renaat de Rudder, the brothers Van Raemdonck** buried under the same headstone as the **Walloon Soldier, Aimé Fievez (qv), Frans Van der Linden, Frans Kusters, Bert Willems and Juul De Winde**) buried there. Above the crypt are the words, 'Here are our bodies, like seed in the sand, hope for the harvest, oh Flanders.' To the right of the Tower is an example of the wooden 'Barracks' which King Albert's Foundation supplied for post-war housing in the Ieper-Diksmuide area.

The tower complex, which was declared 'A Memorial to Flemish Emancipation' on 23 December 1986 and now recognised by the United Nations as a 'Peace Museum', has a large entrance hall with an audio-visual presentation of In Flanders Fields - WW1, a Chapel with stained glass windows by Eugeen Yoors (mainly from Joe English drawings) including one of the Van Raemdonck Brothers (qv), and a shop, drinks dispenser and WC. Then a lift takes you up to the Panorama hall with its 144 windows with magnificent views over the battlefield of the Yser, extending as far as Mount Cassel on a clear day. Around it is a panoramic painting aligned with the view from the windows, made from contemporary aerial photos, showing sites of interest on the surrounding battlefield. One scene shows an aeroplane being brought down. In a field on a line with the painting is a small Memorial Chapel erected by his parents in 1923 to Comte Paul de Goussencourt, Knight of the Order of Leopold II, an aviator who, with his observer, Lt de Crudd of the Artillery, was brought down by German fire on the site on 12 May 1917.

The floors on the way up have different exhibitions. They deal with the fight for the Dutch language, the Student Movement, the conduct of what they call the 'Stupid War', the Armistice, the consequences of War and growing Flemish power. Realistic dioramas and photographs chart the appalling hardships of the troops in the Yser Campaign and the life of the civilians – notably a little old lady who refused to be evacuated and rode through the trenches on her donkey giving comforts to the troops. She was decorated by the King after the war. Temporary exhibitions – on war and on peace - are changed regularly – in 2007 a superb 'Animals at War' exhibition was staged mostly from the collection of Philippe Oosterlinck. Some become so popular that they have virtually become permanent. Such is the superb 'Dugout Experience' with sound effects on the third floor, designed by Johan Vandewalle, co-author with Peter Barton of *Beneath Flanders Fields*. All the equipment, uniforms and arms used in the realistic dioramas are completely authentic. The 8 miles of planking were taken from old demolished houses and many original artefacts were brought from the dugout at Beecham Farm near Tyne Cot (qv) of which there are several photographs.

[N.B. If time is available, the Yser Campaign story can be completed by continuing on the N35 to visit Pervijze, where **'The Two', Elsie Knocker** – later Baroness T'Serclaes – and **Marie Chisholm**, set up their first aid post to support the Belgian Army having been rejected by the British, and where an annual ceremony of remembrance is held each year on 6 October], Nieuwport (the extreme left of the Allied line on the North Sea, where there is the impressive King Albert I Memorial, the British Memorial to 566 of the missing, the Communal CWGC Cemetery, the nearby monuments to Hendrik Gheeraert, 'the hero of the flooding' and Lt Calberg and his Coy of Engineers who controlled the flooding (to whom there are five other plaques in the area) and Koksijde/Coxyde, where the critic, philosopher and poet T[homas] E[rnest] Hulme (qv), killed on 28 September at Nieuwport with the RM Artillery, is buried and where the cartoonist Bruce Bairnsfather was attached to the French.) Also worth a visit is the excellent WW1/WW2 (including the Atlantic Wall) Museum at Raversijde on the coast at 636 Nieuwpoortsesteerweg, 8400 Ostende. (These are covered in *Major & Mrs Holt's Battlefield Guide to the Western Front - North*. See also Ariane Hotel, p 72.)]

Return to Steenstraat on the N369 and pick up the main Itinerary Two if appropriate.

LONG EXTRA VISIT TWO

The American Flanders Field Cemetery, Waregem. Round trip: 50 miles Approx time: 1 hour 30 minutes

The most convenient point to start this visit is at the junction with the Menin Road at Geluveld (page 106. GPS: 50.83455 2.99447).

Take the A19 motorway at the Geluveld N303 junction, direction Kortrijk and at the exit before Kortrijk filter right, signed to Ghent E403. Follow signs towards Ghent to the A14/E17 motorway and take Exit 5 before Ghent. Turn immediately right and then left following signs to

The Flanders Field American Cemetery & Memorial (GPS: 50.87372 3.45262).
This is the ABMC's smallest Cemetery and the only one in Belgium. At the entrance to the Cemetery grounds is a handsome 50ft high flag staff on which the national flag is raised each morning and lowered each evening. **The Visitors' Centre**, (built in 1923, the first house and centre to be constructed by the Commission) is a standard feature of all American Battle Monuments Commission Cemeteries overseas. In it are the Cemetery Registers, a visitor's book, a portrait of the current President, a 'Purple Heart' (whose order was established by George Washington in 1782 for 'distinguished service beyond the call of duty', which lapsed after the Revolution and which was not revived until 1932 as an award for all those wounded in combat and posthumously to those who died). Rest rooms with nformation sheets about the Cemetery and the Battle Monuments Commission are available. In April 2016 a major renovation of the Centre began, due to finish in 2017. The new 2,900sq ft area will contain an interpretative experience, with touch screen panels and small movie theatre. Exhibits show the different ethnic groups and walks of life from which American soldiers were drawn. The Staff Office will also be in the building.

The graves are of white Italian marble flecked with grey, set in immaculate emerald lawns. Among the Latin Crosses which mark them are several Stars of David, indicating Jewish burials, eight of them named. There is no special marker for atheists, agnostics, Buddhists, Hindus or any other denomination, thus a man is deemed to be Christian if not proved to be Jewish. However, there are a number of 'Known but to God' Stars of David and the Superintendent explained to the authors that the proportion of Jewish to Christian members of the American Forces killed in

Europe was known (say 1 in 12) and that proportion was respected when marking unidentified graves.

At the request of Marshal Foch, the 37th and the 91st American divisions were sent to add impetus to the offensive which had started in September 1918. They entered the front line on 30 October, as part of the Flanders Group of Armies under the command of King Albert and attacked towards the Scheldt at 0530 hours on 31 October. The 91st captured nearby Spaals-Bosschen, suffering heavy casualties from intense artillery and machine-gun fire. The 37th advanced under heavy fire to Cruyshautem and the next day, when it became evident that the Germans were retreating, both divisions pushed rapidly on to the Scheldt. They crossed the river on 3 November and were relieved the following night. They re-entered the line on 10 November in a successful attack near Audenarde which disorganised the Germans, who began a rapid and disorderly retreat during the night. When the Armistice was declared at 1100 hours the next morning both divisions were advancing practically unopposed.

The majority of the 368 burials (in 4 plots of 92 graves) are of the 37th and 91st Divisions, who suffered (with the 27th and 30th who also fought in this sector) 4,700 casualties. Twenty-one graves are of unidentified burials. The majority of the dead were repatriated at Government expense at the request of the families. (The overall proportion of American soldiers buried abroad for the two world wars is 32 per cent.) In Plot B, Row 4, grave 1 is **Lt Kenneth MacLeish,** of the USNR, killed on 15 October 1918, brother of the American Pulitzer Prize-winning poet, social critic, public servant and educator, Archibald MacLeish. Archibald visited his brother's grave with a delegation that included the American Ambassador and wrote a searingly moving poem entitled *Memorial Rain for Kenneth MacLeish, 1894-1918.* The poem intersperses the trite platitudes of the Ambassador ... this little field these happy, happy dead Have made America ...' '... Dedicates to them This earth their bones have hallowed, this last gift A grateful country ...' etc, with his own private thoughts which express his lonely grief and his desperate attempts to communicate with his lost brother. The wind has been blowing as MacLeish journeys from Brussels to Ghent and then to the new cemetery, and during the ceremony,

> The rain gathers, running in thinned
> Spurts of water that ravel in the dry sand,
> Seeping in the sand under the grass roots, seeping
> Between cracked boards to the bones of a clenched hand:
> The earth relaxes, loosens; he is sleeping,
> He rests, he is quiet, he sleeps in a strange land.

Co-incidentally, among the graves is that of Pte Condon, of 363 Inf 91 Div, killed on 31 October 1918. It is an unusual name, but there is also a Pte Condon (qv) in Poelkapelle CWGC Cemetery (qv). He was once thought of as aged 14 but it is now believed that there may have been confusion in discriminating between him and an elder brother.

In the centre of the beautifully landscaped Cemetery, with its linden, birch, maple, pine, purple plum and oak trees, ornamental and flowering shrubs, is the elegant **Chapel,** designed by Dr Paul P. Cret of Philadelphia, the consulting architect of the Battle Monuments Commission. Above the entrance, gilded with pure gold leaf, is the inscription, 'Greet Them Ever With Grateful Hearts'. The three figures in *bas relief* which symbolise Grief, Remembrance and History, were sculpted by A. Bottiau of Paris. The bronze entrance door has central portions, also gilded with pure gold. A soft yellow light suffuses the chapel through the window in the ceiling with its striking mosaics. The Altar is fashioned from Grand-Antique marble and its ornaments are of brass. The draped flags represent the United States, Belgium, France, Great Britain and Italy. The furniture is carved from black stained oak. At the request of Jewish visitors who felt that the religious symbolism in these beautiful chapels was uniquely Christian in nature, a stone, known as the Tablet of Moses, with the Star of David and the Roman numerals IX, is now a standard feature.

The names of forty-three American soldiers, missing in Flanders with no known graves, are inscribed on rose-tinted marble panels, framed in bronze and outlined in gold. Among them is

1st Lt Harold S. Morgan, MC, attd to the British Army, killed on 12 April 1918, and **1st Lt Ernest A. Giroux**, who joined the American Field Service on 21 April 1917, and was attached to Transport Section 526 until 6 August 1917, when he entered the American Aviation Service. On 20 November 1917 he was commissioned 1st Lt and attached to 103 Aero Sqn (the old Lafayette Escadrille). Giroux was awarded the *Croix de Guerre* and the DSC – 'No man living or dead deserved one more', wrote a fellow ace. He was killed on 22 May 1918 near Laventie, shot down in a dog fight against a superior enemy formation while 'endeavouring to protect his leader', and buried at Estaires in a grave that was subsequently lost.

Also attd to the British Air Service was **1st Lt John McGavock Grider** killed on 18 June 1918. Grider's family's original German name was Kreuter which was changed when the family settled in the town of Grider, Arkansas, which happened to rhyme with it. Grider enlisted in the Aviation Section of the Signal Corps in 1917 when America declared war and sailed for Europe in September 1917 for further training. He was diverted from his original destination of Italy to become one of the Second 'Oxford Detachment' for further ground training in the University city. The frequent moves that Grider made in his training show the thoroughness of the schooling the Oxford boys received. In November he moved to Stamford for flying training. In January 1918, Grider and his two friends, Springs and Callahan, known as 'The Three Musketeers', went to the Grantham machine gun school and then to Thetford, where he was thrilled to be flying at last. Grider also enjoyed the high life, partying with society ladies at the Savoy and quaffing Mumm champagne. At Oxford he lunched 'with Lord and Lady Osler, the famous doctor.' The Osler's son Revere (qv) had been killed on 30 August 1917. After final advanced flying training at Colney there was more schooling, including spells in the aerial gunnery school at Turnberry and in

Insignia of the Purple Heart

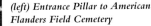

(left) Entrance Pillar to American Flanders Field Cemetery

Chapel interior: Tablets of Moses and mosaic ceiling

Ayr, then 'fighting school' at St Albans. Finally on 10 May he was posted to Hounslow and was commissioned a First Lieutenant on 1 April with 85 Squadron, which flew to Petite Synthe on 22 May. There Grider was very impressed by 'our Maj Bishop', who 'has shot down eight of them in the last eight days'. On 8 June the Squadron flew to St Omer to commence offensive patrols between Ypres and Nieppe. That day Grider reported that Bishop had now shot down twelve (he was to go on to claim seventy-two kills). On 17 June the Three Musketeers scored their own first victory. The following day they engaged an enemy plane which they saw 'go down in a vertical dive and crash near Menin Road'. After this Grider simply disappeared. The Germans dropped a message over the British lines informing them of Grider's death. He was buried by them at Houplines, but the grave subsequently disappeared. In Grider's belongings was his diary, which his friend Springs expanded by using Grider's letters. It was a huge success in 1926 when it was serialised in *Liberty Magazine* as '*War Birds, Diary of an Unknown Aviator'*.

On Memorial Day, 30 May 1927, nine days after his record-breaking cross-Atlantic flight, Charles A. Lindbergh flew over the cemetery in his famous plane, Spirit of St Louis, and dropped a cloud of poppies as a tribute to his fallen countrymen. Now on each Memorial Day (or the closest Sunday to it) each grave is marked with the flags of the United States of America and Belgium. This custom is observed in every American National Cemetery, with the flag of the host nation placed with the Stars and Stripes. It is a glorious sight and the ceremonies are attended by many local people each year. **Open every day except 25 Dec/1 Jan**: 0900-1700. Tel: (0) 56 60 11 22.

Return to Geluveld to pick up Itinerary One if desired.

Long Extra Visit Three

RB Plaque to Cpl of Horse William Leggett, Geluwe; Warneton Archives; Memorials to L/Cpl Andrew, VC, & Sgt Sciascia and Frelinghien – Christmas Truce Mem, German OP & Bunker; Comines German Memorial/Local Cemetery. One way trip: 30 miles Approx time: 2 hours 30 mins?

The most convenient start point for these visits is at Geluveld (page 107). GPS: 50.83455 2.99447.

Take the Menin Road (N8) away from Ypres. Continue into Geluwe following signs to Menin to the church on the left. The memorial is in front of the church.

Ross Bastiaan Commemorative Bronze Plaque to Corporal of Horse William Leggett, VC, 1st Life Guards /Local Modern Monument (GPS: 50.81006 3.07712).
This non-standard RB (qv) Plaque was unveiled on Sunday 26 August 2001 in the presence of members of the Leggett family, the Australian Ambassador and a delegation of modern-day Household Cavalry. It was made by students of the Academy of Arts Menen-Wervik supported by

three professional Belgian artists. It shows the young soldier, the first Australian to be killed in the Defence of Ypres during a skirmish with German Uhlans at Geluwe on 14 October 1914, with below him a sketch map of the site of the action and a descriptive text. Leggett was born in Lithgow NSW on 26 January 1887 and died of his wounds at the nearby Ghesquière Farm, age 23 and was buried in Gheluwe civilian cemetery. He is now buried in Harlebeke New Brit Cemetery (to the north of Courtrai). The Uhlans killed in the same action and originally buried with him were removed to the German Cemeteries at Langemarck and Menin.

Ross Bastiaan Plaque to Cpl Leggett, VC

As described in detail in *Major & Mrs Holt's Battlefield Guides to the Somme and to Gallipoli*, Ross Bastiaan, an old friend whom we met in Gallipoli when he placed the first of his markers, is an Australian dental surgeon, who has, largely at his own considerable expense and effort, placed these bronze plaques around the world in places where Australians have fought with distinction.

Beside the Plaque is an imaginative modern metal representation of the mechanised and traditional warfare in Flanders, with aeroplanes, lorries, carts etc with the figure of a falling airman in front.

Continue past the church to the roundabout junction with the N58 and take the first exit right direction Armentières. Continue on the N58 to the exit signed N336 Ypres and Warneton. Follow the N336 into Warneton centre and park near the Town Hall, Grand Place.

Archives of the Comines-Warneton Documentation Centre and small Museum (GPS: 50.75292 2.94891)

The architecture around the square, rebuilt after the War, is most interesting. The 1929 *Hotel de Ville* was designed by Louis-Marie Cordonnier. In front of it is the dramatic War Memorial. The 1922 Church of St Chrysole, rebuilt in neo-byzantin style, was one of the first to employ concrete in its reconstruction. In the grass public garden in the Square are two **WW1 guns** painted khaki.

The entrance to the **Documentation Centre** is at the side of the Town Hall. It contains a small museum charting the archaeology and history of the region from prehistoric to modern

times including, naturally, the Great War period. There is an important library containing many rare books and detailed personal accounts by local people. Many of these now appear in an incredibly detailed year book that has been published annually for over 20 years by the Comines-Warneton and District Historical Society. Those that cover the '14-'18 war are vivid and poignant, especially about the early days of the German occupation. They also include accounts of the actions at Plugstreet Wood, the Ypres-Comines Canal and other areas of '14-'18 activity – some translations from English diaries, regimental histories etc. There are research and educational facilities (by prior appointment). **Open:** Mon-Fri 0800-1200 and 1300-1700. 1st & 3rd Sat of the month in the morning. Tel: +(0) 56 55 79 66. E-mail: info@shcwr.org Website: www.shcwr.org **Contact:** Michel van Pottelberghe, Library Secretary.

WW1 field guns, Grand Place, Comines-Warneton

From the Place take the road opposite, the N15 rue de Lille, and continue to the bus stop on the left. Beside it is

Memorial to L/Cpl Leslie Andrew, VC (GPS: 50.74899 2.94054).

It was unveiled in an impressive ceremony by the NZ Ambassador to Belgium on 26 October 2008.

Cpl Andrew who won his VC at La Bassée when he was 20 years old went on to serve in WW2 and died, a Brigadier, in January 1969. His, together with that of Frickleton, VC (see page 137), was one of 9 VCs (including the exceptional double WW2 VC of Charles Upham) and other outstanding medals to have been stolen from the New Zealand Waiouru Museum on 2 December 2007. Lord Ashcroft (qv) and ex-US Marine Tom Sturgess put up a reward of NZ$300,000 which led to the return of the medals in February 2008. Lord Ashcroft then put up another large sum of money to help catch the thieves.

Memorial to Cpl Leslie Andrew VC, Warneton

Continue to a small turning to the right, rue de Neuve Eglise and continue up it on the track towards the railway line and the motorway. To the left is

Memorial to Sgt Sciascia (GPS: 50.74389 2.93313).

Sgt Charles Ranginawawahia Sciasia, born of an Italian father and Maori mother, played, with his brother John, for the Maori All Blacks in 1913. He enlisted in the 1st Bn Wellington Regt and served in Gallipoli. On 31 July 1917, age 25, he was reported Missing. The impressive Memorial has been built with Maori tradition in mind. It is 1.72m high – Sciascia's actual height, with a rounded top that represents the shoulders of a soldier bowed down by his heavy pack. It was unveiled, to commemorate the 90th Anniversary of his death in 2007, in the presence

of 40 of his descendants and local dignitaries. Sciascia is commemorated on the Messines NZ Memorial (qv).

Return to the N515. Continue. Join the N58 direction Armentières and continue on the N58 until it becomes the D7. Continue to the roundabout with the D945 and take the Frelinghien exit. Take the next turning left to Frelinghien. The Memorial is opposite the village football field.

Christmas Truce Memorial (GPS: 50.70616 2.92768)

The Memorial to the 2nd RWF and the Saxon *Infanterie-Regt* 133 and Prussian *Jäger-Bn* 6, who together took part in the 1914 Christmas Truce, was unveiled on 11 November 2008 in pouring rain but in excellent spirit by Margaret Holmes, the daughter of **Pte Frank Richards, DCM, MM,** of the 2nd RWF. Richards had described the Truce (in his memoirs, *Old Soldiers Never Die*), as had Capt C.I. Stockwell of the Regiment, whose grandson, Miles, was also present, as were Arnulf & Joachim, the grandsons of Hauptmann Freiherr von Sinner of *Jäger-Bn* 6. After some hesitation, Stockwell and von Sinner met during the Truce and toasted each other with beer and glasses provided by von Sinner, Stockwell providing the plum pudding.

Memorial to Sgt Sciascia, Warneton

Also in attendance was Penelope, the Welsh wife of then French Prime Minister Fillon and many members of the RWF Comrades Association and serving officers and men, including the current Commanding Officer, Nick Lock, of the 1st Royal Welsh, who with members of *Panzergrenadier-Bn* 371 *(Marienberger Jäger)* of the *Jägerbrigade Freistaat Sachsen,* provided the Guard of Honour.

On a simple plinth are Plaques – one with the RWF Badge, the other with the Badges of JB 6 and Saxon IR 133 (paid for by the *Deutsche Volksbund für Kriegsräber Fürsorge* as the *Bundeswehr* are not permitted to have anything to do with the traditions of pre-1945 units) - plus the words 'Christmas Truce 1914'.

Research for the project had been meticulously carried out by Dr John Krijnen (senior editor of Frank Richards's annotated books) in conjunction with the *Arbeitskreis für Sächsiche Militärgeschichte*. He co-ordinated events with the enthusiastic support of Frelinghien *Maire*, Michel Pacaux, and local residents Bernard Cousin and Lt-Col Jean-Pierre Deseure. M. Pacaux is determined that the village will keep alive the flame of memory for the events which took part in this area during the '14-'18 War.

After a fine and congenial lunch offered by the *Commune* of Frelinghien, a football match was played on the pitch opposite the Memorial between the Saxons and the 1st Royal Welsh, recreating the match which actually took place further south between the Saxons and the Seaforths. In 2008 the Saxons won 2-1 (the score in 1914 was 3-2).

Unveiling of Christmas Truce Memorial by Frank Richards's daughter, Frélinghien, 11 November 2008, with detail of Plaque

German Observation Tower, Frelinghien

View looking upwards inside the Observation Tower

Plaque at German Bunker, Frélinghien

There is a **replica trench** on the site of the 1914 football match **(GPS: 50.698764 2.927800)** and an interesting **German Observation Tower** on the D7 by the junction with Chemin de l'Aventure **(GPS: 50.691179 2.941575).**

Continue some 250 yards towards the village and take the second turning right, rue André-Marie Ampère. Stop immediately on the left.

Here, on the pavement and probably ivy covered, there are the sunken remains of a **Bunker (GPS: 50.70876 2.93125)** with a metal **Plaque** in French, English and German, stating that it is a German 2nd line support trench bunker. A *bas relief* sketch map show its position in the trenchlines. The top of the Bunker can be seen at road level.

Return to the D945 and turn left direction Comines. At the roundabout take the exit left signed 'Comines Centre'. On entering Comines continue on the main road, keeping to the right of the magnificent Art Deco Church. Continue through the shops and turn left up a very small, one-way road by a pedestrian crossing, rue du Bas Chemin (easily missed). Continue to the local cemetery on the right. You are now in France.

German Memorial, Local/Cemetery, Comines (GPS: 50.76581 3.01104).

The massive and impressive **German Memorial** is surrounded by ornate local graves and through its arch the *Tricolor* can be seen flying over the French plot. The remains of 4,283 German soldiers originally buried here were moved in 1956 to the German Cemetery at St Laurent.

The easiest way to return to Ypres (or Geluveld to continue Itinerary One if desired)) is to return to Comines centre and follow signs from beside the church.

German Memorial, Comines Local Cemetery

THE WAR UNDERGROUND & 1917 CRATER ROUTE

This section contains a do-it-yourself tour of the mine craters associated with the Battle of Messines.

Introduction

The war underground was a very specialised business and took some time to develop. Apart from the actions at Hill 60 in 1915 it was not until 1916 that extensive deep mining began.

At the beginning, underground activities were primarily for close support of infantry trenches but at the end of 1915 the control of mining was centralised under GHQ and future major battles above ground had their counterpart below. The most spectacular use of mine warfare in the Ypres Salient was on 7 June 1917 when a whole arc of mines was blown at the start of the battle of Messines. Grieve and Newman in their superb book *Tunnellers* declare 'Messines is to the Tunneller what Waterloo was to Wellington'.

In order to fight underground special tunnelling companies were formed to dig the tunnels and to lay the mines. One of the major difficulties faced was that of getting enough air into the shafts and tunnels for the men to breath and this led to the development of air pumps to replace the early blacksmith's bellows. Power pumps were also used to keep out the water, a special explosive (ammonal) was employed, listening devices were used to keep up with what the enemy was doing in case he was likely to break into one's own tunnel or planning to blow it up and scores of canaries and white mice were used to warn the diggers of the presence of poisonous gas. It was a highly uncomfortable, dirty and dangerous way of life and the preparation of underground works went on for months – in fact for Messines, an assault that General Plumer commanding the Second Army had decided should start with the explosion

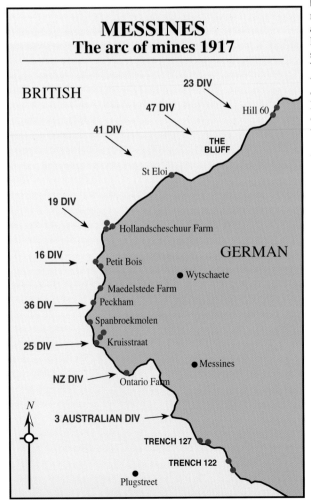

The arc of Mines 1917

The Cryer Farm Sanitätsunterstand (underground hospital)

of the arc of large mines, work began a year ahead.

In recent years much attention has turned to the war underground, with extensive work to preserve remaining tunnels, bunkers and craters, and it is a continuing process - hence this section of our guide-book. The Messines mines form the most important set of First World War craters on the Western Front and many of them can be visited. Thanks to the aerial photographs of Iain McHenry (Iain lives in Ieper and runs Trench Map Tours (qv)), several are illustrated below.

Between 1915 and 1918 the Germans built literally thousands of armed concrete constructions and some regiments (such as the 126th Infantry Regiment) required 150,000 kilos of cement and 300,000 kilos of pebbles each week to build bunkers between Gheluvelt and Hooge. From 1915 onwards there was much mining activity by both sides, some shafts as deep as 40m. At the same time huge underground chambers to be used as HQs, communication posts, hospitals etc were made, to house between 50 and 2,000 men (for example at Wieltje and at Hill 63). In 1918 about 25,000 Tunnellers, with as many infantrymen in support, were working on 200 dugout systems and there was more accommodation for people underground than there are inhabitants in the area today. One important bunker that has been cleared and cleaned (unpleasant work as it had been used as a cesspit until 1985) is the **Cryer Farm,** *Sanitätsunterstand* (qv) near Clapham Junction (Map I30a, GPS: 50.84439 2.96600). It was next to the light railway track which came from Hooge to drop off wounded soldiers, and built by the Germans in 1916. The two wide entrances (typical of a hospital function) were blocked off and the British made a new one which opened to their side after its capture on 15 September 1917 by a party under Lt R.N. Cryer of the 7th London Regiment. During WW2 it was used a shelter for local inhabitants. The 4.5 metre deep bunker is open to the public for special events and may be visited by groups on prior appointment with the **Zonnebeke Tourist Office** (reservaties@zonnebeke.be) and accompanied by a guide at a cost of €60 plus €2.50 per adult and €1.50 per student. See also the entries on Bayernwald (page 230), The Bluff (page 144), Bremen (page 127), Canal Bank at Essex Farm (page 189), Hill 60 (page 140), the Lettenberg (page 267), Vampir (page 128), De Dreve Café (page 134), Hill 63, Ploegsteert - The Catacombs/Château de la Hutte /Château de Rosenberg (page 256) etc.

The precise line of the German front line immediately before the Messines assault can readily be followed by walking from crater to crater – allowing for farm animals, wire fences and farmers! There are a number of expert groups and individuals who are engaged in the practical investigation of underground works and several books have been written about the results. In the Salient some formidable work has been undertaken between (a) Langemark, Zonnebeke and Heuvelland and their 16 villages (basically the old German Front), (b) Ieper and its 10 villages, Mesen… (basically the old British Front). More details of current work can be obtained from the relevant Tourist Offices.

THE ROUTE

The sketch map, 'Messines, The arc of mines 1917', on page 298, shows the positions of the 19 mines that were blown in the attack and the divisions involved. Most of the craters associated with the mines still remain, although some are on private ground. A tour is probably best made by starting at either the top or the bottom of the arc and working towards the other end. We suggest a start at the top and using the Holts' Map provided with this guide-book it should be relatively easy to navigate southwards following the battle line for 6 June 1917 marked as –•–●–•–●–•–

Hill 60 (Map N7a, GPS: 50.82354 2.92767)/Caterpillar Crater

It was here that the first British mine of the war is said to have been blown and considerable details of the actions in the area are given in Itinerary 1, page 140. Just over the railway line from the 14th Light Division Memorial and to the left is the Caterpillar Crater - so named because of the wiggly shape of the cutting beside the line. The crater is approached by a sometimes muddy, path that parallels the railway line. It was encircled by trees, including some lovely willows that lean over the water-filled crater, but some have been felled recently in the work for 'Entry Point – South' (qv). It is still a site of great peace and beauty. The early underground war in the area had involved both the 171st and the 172nd Tunnelling Companies, then the 175th and in 1916 the 3rd Canadian Tunnelling Company. Much of the work involved what was known as the Berlin Tunnel which was almost 30 metres underground and seemed to exude limitless quantities of mud and water. Despite German counter-mining, 53,500lbs of ammonal, packed in petrol tins to keep it dry, and

Remains of narrow gauge railway track found by the Diggers near Boezinge

7,800lbs of gun cotton slabs were tamped into position, between them forming two deep mines. But in August 1916 the whole of the Berlin Tunnel flooded and, to compound matters, the mine filled with gas. Eventually, with the help of electric pumps, the Canadians cleared the workings and found that the ammonal had indeed been protected by the tins. In November 1916 the 1st Australian Tunnelling Company took over the area. Originally it had been intended that the two mines should be used immediately but it was decided that they should form part of the Messines attack and to protect their workings the Australians constructed a steel-lined shaft to replace the incline that led to the galleries. The Australians also constructed a deep level defensive system to counter German attempts to locate and to destroy the charges and it is thought that if the Messines attack had been delayed by only a few days the Germans might have succeeded.

St Eloi (Map M17, GPS: 50.80912 2.89379)

The Crater visited in Itinerary Three is one of six that were blown together in 1916, but mine activity by the Tunnelling Companies began here as early as 1915. The Germans exploded mines under the area of The Mound just south-east of St Eloi (see the Holts' map) in March 1915 and in the ensuing fighting the British suffered some 500 casualties. A month later, on 14 April 1915, the

Germans fired another mine, producing a crater over 20 metres in diameter. Even when mining activities were proving successful here the British found it difficult to construct communication trenches forward to the captured ground and the idea of the 'Russian sap' was developed – that is to say a shallow trench with only a foot or two of cover that could be constructed before an assault and then broken out and rapidly joined up to the captured trenches.

Much of the British tunnelling in this sector was done by 172nd Company, commanded early in 1915 by Captain W. H. Johnston (qv), who had won his VC in 1914 and who was killed on 8 June 1915. Mining and counter-mining continued apace and in the planning for the Messines offensive it was realised that tunnelling for any substantial mine planned for St Eloi would have to start some way away. The work was begun by the 1st Canadian Tunnelling Company with a deep shaft named Queen Victoria in the area of Bus House Cemetery (Map M16) which was extended to the area of today's crater and tamped with 50 tons of ammonal, probably the largest single charge of explosive used during the whole war.

The sites of other craters can be seen in the area – one is further on beyond the obvious crater and another is hidden amongst the houses south of the memorial junction, but they are steadily being filled in.

Hollandseschuur Farm (Map M9b, GPS: 50.79772 2.86842)

The aim of the Messines offensive was to take the entire ridge but the logic behind the exact placing of the mines was to take out a number of small enemy salients that protruded into our lines. Hollandseschuur Farm was one such salient. In November 1915 250th Tunnelling Company sank a shaft to some 20 metres and then drove a tunnel over 250 metres extending well behind the German lines. Despite counter-mining, three charges were eventually placed and fired, the craters clearly visible in the picture here. The British attack of 1917 came from the bottom of the picture, north being the left hand edge.

Petit Bois (Map M11a, GPS: 50.78940 2.86540)

Like the Hollandseschuur mines, the work here was begun by 250th Tunnelling Company. Digging began about 170 metres behind our own forward lines and went down over 30 metres. As with many deep mines, compressed air and electricity were supplied from the surface and an interesting experiment was an attempt to use a mechanical excavator operated by hydraulic rams, similar to those used on the London Underground. The device weighed more than half a ton and when it was finally in position it promised to cut a tunnel about 2 metres in diameter. The idea has shades of the Allied black and white 1916 cartoon propaganda film the *U-Tube* in which the Kaiser planned to invade England via a tunnel from Berlin to Birmingham to be dug by a splendid machine. He ended up at the North Pole. The British device fared a little better. It managed about 5 metres in March 1916 and was abandoned. It is still probably where it was left.

The main gallery was taken out over 500 metres and had reached beyond the German lines when it was breached by enemy counter-mining. Twelve men were trapped in a collapsed tunnel over 30 metres below the surface and for six days miners worked frantically to rescue them. Sadly all that they found was one body after another until eleven had been uncovered. It was assumed that the twelfth man remained buried, yet at the end of the day he crawled out of the mud. After six and a half days buried his first words were 'For God's sake give me a drink! It's been a damned long shift!' His name was Sapper Bedson and he had already survived being wounded in the Salient and in Gallipoli.

Two mines were blown at about 600 metres. One of 41,150 lbs of ammonal and the other of 32,850 lbs, the craters are clearly visible from the air today. The Messines assault came in from the bottom of the illustration, the Petit Bois being the wood at the top right hand corner.

Maedelstede Farm (Map M4a, GPS: 50.78300 2.86579)

This was begun at the end of 1916 and forward workings began at a depth of about 45 metres. One tunnel headed towards Wytschaete Wood and the other towards Maedelstede Farm over

Hollandseschuur Farm Craters

Petit Bois Craters

*Spanbroekmolen
(Pool of Peace*

Kruisstraat Craters

Ultimo / Trench 122

Factory Farm

500 metres away. In order to remove the spoil from the workings a covered tramway was built running back behind the lines where the spoil was camouflaged to prevent the Germans suspecting what was going on. After a while it was realised that the Wood could not be reached in time and all efforts were concentrated upon the branch heading for the Farm. Just 24 hours before the offensive opened some 48 tons of ammonal were in place, tested and ready to fire.

Caterpillar Crater

Peckham Farm (Map M4, GPS: 50.78938 2.86638)

The shaft here was begun by 250th Tunnelling Company on 18 December 1915 and sunk to 20 metres, the heavy clay requiring much timber as the tunnel was driven forward. Despite strenuous efforts to work as silently as possible, including the use of clay kicking, German trench mortar activity caused many delays and flooding swamped much of the work causing some tunnels to be abandoned. However the main charge of 76,000 lbs of ammonal was placed below Peckham Farm as planned and, in time, some 400 metres from where the digging started. The crater is visited and pictured in Itinerary Three.

Spanbroekmolen (Map R1, GPS: 50.77658 2.86124)

The story of this mine is also told in Itinerary Three. Enemy counter-measures in this area were considerable and many camouflets (mines especially designed to blow in an opponent's gallery) were exploded. Major Paul Heinrici in his book *Der Ehrenbuch der Deutschen Pioniere* claims that the Germans had located the main gallery and had blown a mine well below our own workings but that it had failed to stop our drive. At one time the presence of gas was so overpowering that new tunnels had to be begun behind the current workings and it was three months before the miners were back to where they had started. The Messines attack came broadly from the bottom left hand corner of the picture.

Kruisstraat (Map R33/34, GPS: 50.77014 2.86491)

This was one of the small salients chosen as precise locations for the Messines mines and it is visited and described in Itinerary Three. In the illustration a small road runs along the edge of the cornfield just beyond the two craters and in front of the red roofed houses. It follows the line of what was Pill Road and to a first approximation the attack was directed along that line from right to left. To the right along Pill Road is RE Farm CWGC Cemetery.

Ontario Farm (Map R35a, GPS: 50.76439 2.87780)

The ground here proved very difficult to mine as much of it was sandy. Eventually, at the end of January 1917, 171st Tunnelling Company began a dig at Boyle's Farm which is just on the southern side of the N314. The shaft went down 30 metres and air and water pumps were installed. After tunnelling forward the miners broke into blue clay extending the depth to some 40 metres. After driving almost 200 metres the flooding was so bad that a dam had to be made and a new gallery started. Nevertheless the tunnellers arrived under Ontario Farm at the end of May and installed 60,000 lbs of ammonal with a day to spare.

Trench 127 (Map R23, GPS: 50.74772 2.90439)

The craters here, also known as the Ash craters, are gradually being filled in but at the time of writing could still be made out. It was in December 1915 that 171st Tunnelling Company began work and the shaft was completed to a depth of 25 metres within four weeks, however things did not continue so smoothly. After almost 310 metres the tunnellers faced a sudden inrush of quicksand and a concrete dam had to be built. A new drive was made under the troublesome area and by April 1916 the mine was ready – 50,000 lbs of ammonal over 400 metres from the initial shaft. The name Trench 127 indicates where the initial shaft was dug not where the mine was placed.

Trench 122 (Map R24) and Factory Farm (Map R25, GPS: 50.74294 2.91210)

Also known as the Ultimo Crater, the digging towards the R24 site was begun by 171st Tunnelling Company at the end of February 1916 from Trench 122, which was due west of the crater. The area was a complex of German trenches and by mid-May a charge of 20,000 lbs of ammonal was in place. Another shaft was started part way along the original workings and after another 200 metres a charge of 40,000 lbs of ammonal was set beneath the ruins of Factory Farm which sat on the German front line. The Messines assault came in from the left hand edge of each picture.

ALLIED & GERMAN WAR GRAVES & COMMEMORATIVE ASSOCIATIONS

AMERICAN BATTLE MONUMENTS COMMISSION

The Commission has been responsible for commemorating the dead of the American Armed Forces since 6 April 1917 – the date of America's entry into World War I – with 'suitable memorial shrines', and for 'designing, constructing operating and maintaining permanent American military burial grounds in foreign countries'.

General John Pershing who had commanded the American Forces in World War I was elected first Chairman of the Commission and served in that capacity from 1923 until his death in 1948. He was succeeded by General George C. Marshall, another World War I veteran, until his death in 1959. Then came General Jacob L. Devers, succeeded by General Mark W. Clark in 1969 until his death in 1984. General Andrew J. Goodpaster served in the post until 1991 when he was succeeded by General P. X. Kelley, followed by Gen Frederick M. Franks Jr. The current Chairman is Retired U.S. Air Force Chief of Staff from 1990-1994, Gen Merrill A. McPeak. He was elected in June 2010.

From its inception, the Commission offered relatives the choice of repatriation at Government expense or burial in an American Cemetery in the country of death. The Commission's post-World War I task included the erection of a non-sectarian chapel in each of the eight cemeteries to be built on foreign soil on land granted in perpetuity by the host country.

When visiting an American Cemetery, having recently walked through the peaceful gardens which are the Commonwealth War Graves cemeteries, through the starkly mourning German cemeteries with their massed graves and dramatic sculptures, through the neat standard ranks of French crosses, often with an ossuary, it is interesting to compare and contrast the different national sentiments that are being expressed. It is instructive, too, to compare the amount of information that can be inscribed on a headstone – the greater room afforded by the flat stones of the CWGC Cemeteries accommodates the regimental badge, date of birth and a poignant personal message from the family – in contrast with the limitations of the cross to be seen in American and French National Cemeteries. British and Commonwealth families felt strongly that they would have preferred a cross when the design for a personal marker was discussed and a petition with 8,000 names was signed to appeal for it. Questions were tabled in the House of Commons. In the end, the space afforded by the stone won the day over the cross. It is also interesting to reflect that, to the Americans, the State of origin is the dominating feature on the marker. To the British and Commonwealth it is the Regiment – the substitute family – that is all important. To the French it is *La Patrie*.

Understandably the Cemeteries of the vanquished are different in tone from those of the victors. There glory would not be appropriate. In an American Cemetery glory, even opulence, is perhaps the predominant overall emotion expressed. The cross or star bears the name, unit, date of death (but not of birth) as well as the home state of the soldier, nurse etc, whose grave it marks. Unknown burials are inscribed, 'Here rests in honored glory A Comrade In Arms known but to God'. Recipients of the Congressional Medal of Honor have a star and their inscription picked out in gold. This honour, ninety-four of which were awarded during World War I, is presented by the President in the name of Congress 'to persons who distinguished themselves conspicuously by gallantry and intrepidity at the risk of life above and beyond the call of duty and without detriment to the mission of their commands, while in action involving conflict with the enemy'. It equates to the British Victoria Cross.

More information about the Commission appears in the entry for the Long Extra Visit to Flanders Field American Cemetery above. The USBMC website where individual names can be searched is: www.abmc.gov **Head Office**: Courthouse Plaza II, Suite 500, 2300 Clarendon Boulevard, Arlington, VA22201, USA. Tel: + 703 696 6897. Website: www.abmc.gov European Office: 68 rue du 19 janvier, 92380 Garches, France. Tel: + (0)1 47 01 19 76.

BELGIAN WAR GRAVES

After the War, Belgian war graves were administered by the *Service des Sépultères Militaires*. In 1928 the care was taken over, in a somewhat half-hearted manner, by the Ministry of the Interior.

From 1 January 2004 Belgian war graves have been administered by the Belgian Army who have instigated a programme of renovation which will eventually cover all military cemeteries in Belgium – a huge task, resulting in a much higher standard of maintenance and restoration.

The nearest Belgian Military Cemetery to Ieper is in the **Forest of Houthulst**, (to the north of Poelkapelle on the N301 – qv) with 1,723 Belgian and 81 Italian burials (see Long Extra Visit above). The authors had read in early documents that there were originally 146 French burials in the Cemetery but they are no longer there and no information is now forthcoming about them. The Cemetery has recently been beautifully renovated with the replacement of all name plates with bronze plaques with the soldier's name polished so that it stands out. The colourful enamel roundels in the colours of the Belgian flag have also been renovated. There are three styles of this roundel. Most bear a cross, chosen by the Catholic authorities; soldiers with no religious affinity have a lion on the roundel and a roundel with neither cross nor lion indicates a new replacement. Some Plaques bear the insignia of campaign medals, such as the Order of Leopold II and the Victory Medal. Daffodils for the spring and roses for the summer are planted in front of the rows of graves.

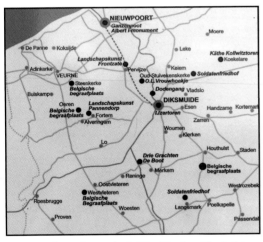

Belgian Military Cemeteries in West Flanders, Houthulst

There is also a Belgian Military Cemetery at **Westvleteren** (Map A1) signed *Militaire Begraafplats* up a narrow road. This concentration Cemetery contains 1,100 graves. Other Belgian Military Cemeteries are at **Keiem,** to the north of Diksmuide, with 628 burials, and **Ramskapelle near Nieuwpoort**, with 623 graves, 400 of which are unknown. There are two data bases for the Belgian 32,000 named and 10,000 missing dead of WW1.

There are Belgian graves in the following CWGC Cemeteries: **Birr Cross Roads, Duhallow, Nieuwkerke, Tournai Com and White House** and there is increasing co-operation between the Belgian MOD War Graves Dept and the CWGC.

Contact: Belgian War Graves, Institute for Veterans, Bvd du Régent 45/46, Brussels 1000, Belgium. Didier Pontzeele, or Yves Longeval, Tel: +(0) 0472871841 OR 0474270224. E-mail: info@warveterans.be OR wardeadregister@warveterans.be

A database giving Belgian military casualties (as well as a yet incomplete list of French casualties in the Salient) may be processed through The Documentation Centre, Flanders Fields Museum (qv).

It is interesting to note that the Belgian population during the war was approximately 7,520,000, and that between 1914 and 1918 some 378,000 men went through the army. Of them 26,338 died in combat or as a result of wounds, 14,029 were reported missing. This does not include casualties in Africa.

COMMONWEALTH WAR GRAVES COMMISSION

THE COMMONWEALTH WAR GRAVES COMMISSION IN THE YPRES SALIENT

Summary by Mr Colin Kerr, Director External Affairs

The Commonwealth War Graves Commission commemorates by name 205,090 of the British and Empire dead in Belgium from both World Wars. Of this number, the largest proportion, by far, relates to the area within the Ypres salient, from the First World War. The Ypres salient was the locus for five major battles:

- The 1914 fighting ("1st Ypres"), where the British Expeditionary Force, under French, held back the German dash for the channel ports; albeit at the cost of the core of the pre-war army. The end of the fighting left a bend in the allied lines around Ypres – this was the Ypres Salient

- The 1915 German attack ("2nd Ypres"), a diversionary attack linked to the German Gorlice-Tarnow offensive on the eastern front. This attack, with the first use of gas, was eventually held by British and Canadian forces under Smith-Dorrien's 2nd Army

- The 1917 Messines offensive, under Plumer's 2nd Army, where the detonation of a string of very large mines enabled the British salient to be "straightened out" in advance of the subsequent offensive

- The 1917 British offensive ("3rd Ypres"), which was aimed at the German submarine bases on the Channel, but which ground through, with appalling losses, as far as the ridge at Passchendaele. The offensive was carried out by 2nd Army and by Gough's 5th Army

- The 1918 German offensive ("Georgette"), which followed their successful offensive ("Michael") further south at Amiens. Plumer's 2nd Army eventually held the German offensive, but with heavy losses. Finally, in September 1918, 2nd Army began to push back, as part of the final Allied offensive which led to victory in November 1918

Further analysis of the numbers draws out the underlying horror. Of the 205,000 figure, exactly half of the casualties were never identified and have no known graves: their names are inscribed on memorials, which is their formal point of commemoration. Of this number, just under half – 48,000 – are represented by unidentified graves: "Soldiers of the Great War, known unto God", in Kipling's great phrase.

These numbers are reflected in the practical reality of the Commission's sites in the Ypres salient: the vast memorials, containing the names of the missing, and cemeteries where more than half of the headstones are for unknown soldiers.

The memorials are referenced in this excellent book and represent some of the most powerful images which the Commission can put forward: the sheer scale of these vast constructions, with lists of names so great as to be almost beyond modern comprehension. The three largest memorials to the missing are the Menin Gate in Ypres (designed by Blomfeld, with the names of 54,000 men), the extension (i.e. the back walls) of Tyne Cot cemetery at Passchendaele (with 36,000 names) and the Ploegsteert Memorial, south of Ypres, with most of the balance of names. The daily ceremony of remembrance at the Menin Gate now attracts thousands of people *each night* and is a deeply moving occasion. When the Menin Gate was opened, in 1934, Lord Plumer

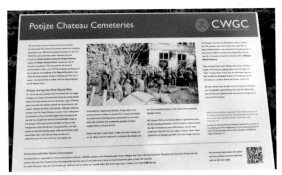

Typical CWGC Information Board, Potijze CWGC Cemeteries

(who, as General Plumer, had commanded 2nd Army in the Ypres salient from 1915 to 1918) declared "They are not missing, They are here".

The Ypres salient contains 150 CWGC cemeteries, all from the First World War. The most highly visited are Tyne Cot, Lijssenthoek and Essex Farm, all of which are referenced in this book. Tyne Cot, in particular, is the largest CWGC site in the world, with more than 12,000 graves from the Passchendaele fighting, although most of the men are unidentified.

Whilst CWGC welcomes the large numbers of visitors who continue to come to the Menin Gate, Tyne Cot and Essex Farm, many of the CWGC sites are visited rarely. Our message to visitors is to please pass to the other side of the street and explore the other 147 sites in the Ypres salient. Each has its stories and **all** of those men deserve to be remembered.

Colin Kerr,
March 2016

GENERAL BACKGROUND

If you are coming to the Salient to visit a particular grave do not rely on being able to locate it when you arrive without prior research. As described by Mr Kerr, the number of war dead buried and commemorated in the Salient is huge, many of them with no known grave. Nearly 100,000 names of these 'Unknown' soldiers with no known graves are recorded in the area, not only on the Menin Gate and at the Tyne Cot Memorial (qv) but also on the Ploegsteert Memorial, and the New Zealand Memorials in Buttes New Cemetery and Messines Ridge British Cemetery. **You are advised to look up the name you are seeking on the Commission's Website:** www. cwgc.org. The Commission holds information on all the 1.7 million Commonwealth servicemen and women killed in the two World Wars as well as some civilian casualties of WW2. Details of individual casualties can be found on the search-by-surname Debt of Honour Register which allows enquirers to carry out their own traces at no cost. Such has been the interest generated by the website, which now receives as many as half a million hits a week (compared with 40,000 enquiries a year before its introduction), that the Commission is currently putting more resources into improving the information available. For instance one can search by Name and Cemetery or – a by a particularly useful field, ' Additional Information'. Thus for finding out how many casualties came from a particular place – say 'Scarborough' – by leaving all fields blank except 'First World War' and 'Additional Information' and putting in 'Scarborough', one gets the figure of 834. However! Be cautious, because the finding and counting of the name 'Scarborough' may have been that of the name of a road.

Alternatively **Contact** the Commonwealth War Graves Commission (CWGC), Head Office, 2 Marlow Road, Maidenhead, Berks, SL6 7DX, Tel: + (0) 1628 634221, Fax: + (0) 1628 771208, E-mail: casualty.enq@cwgc.org before you set out, or the Ypres Office (qv) at 82 Elverdingsestraat, Tel + (0) 57 20 0118, E-mail: neaoffice@cwgc.org It will speed your enquiry to have as much information about the person you are seeking as possible, e.g. name, rank, number, unit, regiment, date of death. No charge is normally made for an individual casualty enquiry but researchers making multiple enquiries may be charged £2 per name and are encouraged to use the website register. The website provides general and historical information on the Commission, current news and details of publications. Information sheets can now be downloaded from the

Publications Section. Subjects of these excellent publications include Battles and Memorials of the Ypres Salient, Fabian Ware, Horticulture, Sportsmen and Women, War Poets and individual leaflets on Australia, Canada, India, S Africa and New Zealand's membership of the Commission. A Michelin map book showing the location of WW1 and WW2 Cemeteries on the Western Front is now available as is a teaching resource, 'Remember me – echoes from the lost generations'

Of particular interest is the Commission's monthly Newsletter. For details of how to subscribe, see the website.

The old-style Cemetery Registers are no longer published but the computerised system can produce tailored reports, including lists of those buried in individual cemeteries, together with historical notes and plans, details of those killed on particular dates, casualties with the same surname and from a particular regiment. Prices for Cemetery Reports start at £10. [It is interesting to note that in 1926 Maj-Gen Fabian Ware (qv) wrote to bereaved families with a proof of the entry to be made in the Registers that were then being compiled. They were offered copies of the completed Register for what was then the significant sum of three shillings.] More bespoke reports cost from £20.

The Cemetery Reports produced by the Commission are a mine of information. They summarise the burials by nationality and then list them in alphabetical order, reproduce the citation from the *London Gazette* for Victoria Cross winners, contain a map and often a historical background to the battles in the area of the Cemetery. Although the Commission aims to have a Cemetery Report in each of the bronze register boxes they can, sadly, go missing. This makes prior research even more important. At many of the Cemeteries the Commission has also placed stainless steel historical notices giving a summary of the campaign and notes on the Cemetery. These are supplemented with Information Boards bearing contemporary photographs and information about the locality during the War. We believe that in time it is planned to locate each headstone with a GPS reference.

The Commission's Annual Report published each November, makes engrossing reading It summarises the main refurbishment work carried out during the past year. To keep the Cemeteries and Memorials in the immaculate condition that visitors appreciate and have come to expect is a perpetual task. The Report details the vast budget required to carry out that work. It lists the 148 countries from A (for Albania) to Z (for Zimbabwe) where there are graves or memorials to maintain, and the number of graves and names recorded for the United Kingdom and for each of the Commission's member governments: Undivided India, Canada, Australia, New Zealand and South Africa. The total number of commemorations is a staggering 1,694,783. On 16 May 2016 Keith Simpson, M.P., a CWGC Commissioner, former Army Officer and sometime battlefield guide (with us), extolled the outstanding work of the Commission in a well-supported Debate in the House of Commons. See: https://hansard.parliament.uk/commons/2016-05-10/debates/16051033000001/CommonwealthWarGravesCommission

It highlighted the annual cost thus: 'Our work today is supported by member Governments of Australia, Canada, India, New Zealand, South Africa and, above all, the United Kingdom. Each of those countries contributes a sum in proportion to the number of graves it has. The United Kingdom contributes 78%, which comes from the budget of the Ministry of Defence. The annual budget is approximately £70 million, which works out at roughly £40 per commemoration per annum.'

A 47-minute VHS video, entitled a *Debt of Honour*, showing the world-wide work of the commission is available for £9. It was re-edited in 2002 with a commentary by Michael Palin. A shorter video, *Memorial and Memory*, aimed at a younger audience, is available free to schools.

For many dedicated years the Duke of Kent has

Headstones of Indian Soldiers, Railway Dugouts CWGC Cemetery

fulfilled the function of President and the current Secretary/Director-General is Victoria Wallace and the Rt Hon Michael Fallon, MP, is Chairman.

The Commission was the brainchild of Major Fabian Arthur Goulstone Ware, the 45-year old volunteer leader of the Red Cross Mobile Unit that came out to Lille on 19 September 1914 to care for the wounded. Before the war broke out, Ware had already had an interesting career. He had been educated in universities in London and Paris, and after several years in the teaching profession became Assistant, then Director of Education in the Transvaal. He was editor of *The Morning Post*, 1905-11. Ware was a liberal (with a small 'l') thinker and was interested in social equality. Once out on the Western Front he more and more concerned himself with identifying the bodies, registering the deaths and ensuring a standard, well-marked burial for them. He soon realised that the ad hoc wooden crosses erected over graves were ephemeral and could well be lost as the conflict raged back and forth over the land. He was also concerned that wealthy families were transporting the bodies of their loved ones home or erecting expensive markers over their remains in situ. By the end of October 1914 31,300 graves had already been registered and by March 1915 the army realised the importance of Ware's work and he was given sole responsibility for registering graves. Haig was quick to recognise the symbolic importance that the people would place after the conflict had been resolved, on the marking of the graves of those who had sacrificed themselves for the nation. He gave Ware (who had now left the Red Cross to join the Army) his full support. The next task was to negotiate with the French Government to protect the land in which soldiers had been buried. It was not an easy task as the French preferred the concept of mass graves or *'ossuaires'* as being more economical and also easier for relatives to locate than small, sometimes isolated, burial places. As seen in the description of the Ploegsteert Memorial (qv), this unwillingness to part with too much land extended to the post-war period when most of the Cemeteries and Memorials were built. In March 1916 a National Committee for the Care of Soldiers' Graves was established, with the Prince of Wales as President. On 21 May 1917 he became President of the Imperial War Graves Commission when it was established, with Fabian Ware as its Vice-Chairman. Its Charter (extended on 8 June 1964 to include the dead of World War II) was to mark and maintain the graves of the members of the forces of the Commonwealth who died in the war, to build and maintain memorials to the dead whose graves are unknown, and to keep records and registers. Each of the dead should be commemorated individually by name, either on the headstone on the grave or by an inscription on a memorial: the memorial should be permanent: the headstones should be uniform: there should be no distinction made on account of military or civil rank, race or creed. Ware's egalitarian wish that the wealthy and/or high ranking would get equal treatment in their burial with the poor and/or low ranking was fulfilled. The terms of the charter should be maintained 'in perpetuity'. There has been some concern as to the true meaning of 'in perpetuity' in French Law and that the land grant may cease once the 100th Anniversaries are over. In 1997 the Director-General of the CWGC, David Kennedy, stated that the 1951 agreement with the French granted land 'without payment and without time-limit'.

The work of commissioning architects, craftsmen, builders, stonemasons, carpenters and gardeners, of designing, building, landscaping and maintaining the Memorials and Cemeteries on the land scarred by shells (many of them unexploded) and exhuming bodies for burials in concentration Cemeteries was a task monumental beyond comprehension. It must often have seemed impossible for the Commission's executive officers. Sometimes the Commission's decisions were unpopular and controversial. They were trying to please the majority of the still grieving bereaved and the comrades of the dead. The genius and determination of Fabian Ware prevailed. The seemingly indefatigable Ware, who was knighted in 1922 and became a titular Major-General, returned to the War Office as the Director of Graves Registration during World War II, while still fulfilling his duties as Vice-Chairman of the Commission, a post he held until his retirement in 1948. He died in 1949 in his eightieth year.

The saga of the post-war years is described in Philip Longworth's book *The Unending Vigil*, which has an Introduction by Edmund Blunden (qv) who became literary adviser to the

Commission on Kipling's death in 1936. This has been reprinted and is available from the Commission.

CWGC Cemeteries

The tall white Cross of Sacrifice with its inset bronze-coloured sword was designed by Sir Reginald Blomfield and is found in most Cemeteries world-wide. Larger burial grounds also have a white sarcophagus-shaped 'Stone of Remembrance' (qv), designed by Sir Edwin Lutyens, whose inscription, 'Their Name Liveth for Ever More' was chosen from Ecclesiasticus by Rudyard Kipling, who was on the Commission's Committee and who became involved after his only son, John, went missing in the Battle of Loos in September 1915. The headstones marking the graves are a standard 2ft 8in high, normally of white Portland stone (although now, some stones are being replaced with Italian, smooth Botticino limestone) and bear, where possible, the rank, name, regimental number, regimental crest, unit, age, date of death and religious emblem (e.g. Latin Cross, Jewish Star of David, blank for agnostic etc.) At the bottom is a space for an inscription to be chosen by the family (a facility never offered to New Zealand soldiers). Most of the inscriptions, which are almost unbearably poignant to read, are accepting, expressing pride for duty nobly done as well as the pain of loss. Many are biblical or well-known poetical quotations. A favourite is from the Song of Solomon, 2: 'Until the day break and the shadows flee away'. An unusual exception is the personal message on the headstone in Tyne Cot Cemetery (IV.G.21) of 2nd Lt Arthur Young, 4th Bn attd 7th/8th RIF, died 16 August 1917 aged 26, born in Japan. It reads, in an allusion to H.G. Wells, 'Sacrificed to the fallacy that war can end war.'

Headstones for foreign and enemy soldiers buried in Commission Cemeteries have slightly differently shaped tops – e.g. the tops of the German headstones are straight, instead of slightly curved as are the British and Commonwealth, and civilians – such as CWGC workers – have varyingly shaped headstones as can be seen in Ypres Town Cemetery (qv). The inscriptions on the headstones and on the memorials are in a standard, pleasingly open and legible style of lettering designed by MacDonald Gill.

Headstones marking unidentified bodies have the inscription, also chosen by Kipling: 'A Soldier of the Great War. Known Unto God'. On graves whose markers were later destroyed but whose rough location was known, he chose the epitaph, 'His glory shall not be blotted out'. Kipling was also responsible for the poetic name, 'Silent Cities' for the many War Cemeteries he visited in his work for the Commission. The name may have been taken from the Urdu for Cemeteries: Shahr-e-Khamosham. In most Cemeteries there is a bronze box containing the

Kemmel Château Mil CWGC Cemetery

Cemetery Report and a Visitors' Book and a visit to a Cemetery should always be commemorated by a signature in the book.

The aim of the original designers, such as Sir Edwin Lutyens, Sir Reginald Blomfield and Sir Herbert Baker, was to create the impression of an English country garden (the original choice of plants and shrubs had been made by advisers from the Royal Botanical Gardens at Kew and Lutyens worked closely with the garden designer, Gertrude Jekyll). The influence of Sir Frederick Kenyon was also strong in this desire. The gardeners (and there are some 900 of them working around the world) are dedicated people, many of them being sons, grandsons or great-grandsons of soldiers who came out with the Commission after the war. They can be a useful source of local information.

Although today the Commission wishes to emphasise that it is so much more than a Horticultural Society, the peace and beauty of the Cemeteries with their well-tended trees, shrubs, bushes, and seasonal flowers, immaculate grass paths and lawns are immensely comforting to relatives visiting a grave. Presently the horticultural department is seriously concerned with the effect of climate change on the Cemeteries, when contrasts of drought and flooding are more increasingly occurring and new pests and diseases appear. Two Cemeteries have been selected in Belgium in which experimental planting to withstand these threats is being tried. They are Oostduinkerke Comm and Railway Château. The public's comments are welcome at feedback@ cwgc.org

Highly recommended is a stunningly illustrated book, *All Beautiful in Flanders Fields* by Annemie Reyntjens, pub Davidsfonds Uitgeverij nv, which shows the Cemeteries and Memorials in all weathers, in urban and rural environments, with human and animal visitors in an imaginative and original way, with much factual information about the work of the Commission.

Many misconceptions are held about the layout of the Cemeteries, and the design of the badges on the headstones, that have no basis in fact. Thus, for example, you may hear that all the headstones are placed to face the Cross of Sacrifice, or to face the direction of the battlefield: that the small crosses on the headstones are for Protestants and the large crosses (with the regimental badge inscribed inside) are for Roman Catholics. After a few visits where graves can be seen placed in circles (as at Railway Dugouts Cemetery), some plots facing the Cross and others with their back to it (as seen in Lijssenthoek Cemetery), and the same regimental badge (e.g. the Royal Artillery) can be seen engraved both inside a large and outside a small Latin cross, such stories can be seen to be false. Older gardeners maintain that the large cross with the regimental badge within was the original design, but that the smaller cross with separate badge was adopted as it was easier to carve.

The Cemeteries were laid out with a respect for the local environment (as at Buttes New Cemetery) and in some cases around existing wartime graves (as at Tyne Cot Cemetery). The occasional deviation from strictly consistent layout in the graves and on the headstones merely emphasises the humanity with which the Commonwealth War Graves Commission has always approached its work.

Memorials to the Missing

In 1918 Sir Frederick Kenyon, the Director of the British Museum and Chairman of the Committee advising on Cemeteries and Memorials, proposed that those men who were missing and had no known grave should be commemorated as near as possible to the spot where they had died. However, there was an inherent difficulty in such a proposal. If it was not known where a man had died how could a Memorial be placed near the spot? In any case the first thing that had to be done was to separate the names of the missing dead from the identified dead and to allow for the complications of returning prisoners of war, identified bodies that were being recovered from the battlefields and the, as yet, incomplete regimental casualty lists. A counter-idea to the geographical commemoration was that members of regiments should be commemorated together in allocated Cemeteries without reference to where they actually died.

Then there was the matter of 'National' memorials. At the end of 1919, at the suggestion of

Winston Churchill, a 'National Battlefield Memorials Committee' was created to report on 'the forms of National War Memorials and the sites on which they should be erected, together with estimates of costs.' These abstract Memorials were to be the responsibility of the Office of Works and quite separate to the work of the Imperial War Graves Commission that was concerned with the cemeteries and the memorials to the missing. The Cabinet was becoming apprehensive about the impending costs of the two commemorative authorities and it was agreed that a suitable compromise would be to combine the national memorials with memorials to the missing and to transfer the responsibility for them to the Commission. This would also solve the problem of trying to commemorate the missing on a geographical basis since it could now be done according to the dates of major actions.

New Zealand refused to agree to the idea and declined to be included when in 1921 it was decided that the Memorial to the Missing in Ypres (later to be known as the Menin Gate) should also be a national monument. The New Zealand forces had remained together throughout the war and complete lists were held of where they had fought and where casualties had fallen and so there was no problem in separating the known dead from the missing. Thus the New Zealand missing are commemorated on a number of memorials near the spot where they were lost according to the idea originally put forward by Kenyon in 1918. In a further departure from the general policy New Zealand also decided that the headstones of her soldiers would not carry personal inscriptions.

It is a rewarding and informative exercise to sit down with the Cemetery Report of one of the larger Cemeteries and read through the entries from beginning to end. The words of the entry were chosen by the family and represent their attempt to perpetuate their lad. Often the full names, addresses (the name of a pub or village store, for example) and posts held by grieving parents or wives and children are given; sometimes there are academic, career or sporting achievements; the fact that a father or brother had also been killed in the war; the manner of death (e.g. 'died of wounds, gas'); previous service (in South Africa, on the *Lusitania*); occasionally an American is shown as having gone to Canada to enlist; a man has chosen to serve under another name ... A rounded picture of the diversity of the social classes that made up the British and Commonwealth Forces of 1914-18 emerges. Reading the comments in the Visitor's Book is also interesting. Very often relatives give details of a grandfather, or a great-great uncle they are visiting. Children make comments such as, 'So sorry you had to die'. One young boy whom we took to Italy tried to walk to, and pause at, every headstone in a big cemetery, but had not finished when it came to leave. In the Visitor's Book he wrote, 'I am sorry that I could not visit you all'.

In 2017 the Commission will celebrate the 100th anniversary of its founding.

Joint Casualty & Compassionate Centre

In April 2005 the Army, Navy and RAF amalgamated in the Joint Casualty & Compassionate Centre (based at RAF Innsworth), part of Service Personnel and Veterans' Agency, to deal with any remains of service personnel (principally from WW1 and WW2) that are found. The Agency replaced the MOD PS4(A) Compassionate Cell.

They liaise with local embassies and the CWGC when remains are discovered and, if there is sufficient evidence with the remains to give hope for an identification, use historical case files and other appropriate means in their research. Once an identification has been made they use the media to trace any family. The wishes of the family are then paramount as to the form of burial (e.g. quiet or formal). **Contact:** Sue Raftree, Tel: 01452 712612 ext 6303. Email: historicso3.jccc@ innsworth.afpaa.mod.uk Any news will be reported on the general MOD website, www.mod.uk

The Recent Discovery and Reburial of WW1 Remains

The remains of soldiers of the Great War are continually being discovered in the Salient. Some examples: In 1999, 22 bodies were discovered, in 2000, 20, in 2001 14 and in 2002 14. More were then found in the excavations of the old Ypres-Roulers Railway line (qv). There were four burials of Unknown soldiers in Cement House Cemetery on 21 March 2007 and one in Hooge Crater

Cemetery. On 4 July an Unknown soldier of the Lancashire Fusiliers, found during the excavations along the old Ypres-Roulers railway line, was reburied in Tyne Cot Cemetery. Also on 4 July 2007 Pte Lancaster (qv) was buried with full military honours in Prowse Point Cemetery, together with two Unknown Soldiers, where Pte A.J. Mather was interred on 22 July 2010 and where Pte Harry Wilkinson was buried on 31 October 2001. On 4 October 2007 six Australian soldiers were reburied in Buttes New Cemetery with full military honours by the Australian Government. The remains were discovered in September 2006 when a new gas main was being laid in Westhoek. Four of the bodies were in a remarkable good state of preservation, with remnants of uniform and some artefacts. They were carefully excavated and removed by Franky Bostyn, Johan Vandewalle (see page 134) and their team and handed over to the Belgian War Graves Commission. Extensive research then ensued and it was concluded that the men were of the Australian 4th Division (probably of the 12th or 14th Bde) who fell during the attack of 22-30 September 1917 on 'Anzac Ridge' and 'Tokio Spur' near Zonnebeke Château. There then followed an intensive forensic investigation and the Australians mounted a huge publicity campaign with the ensuing results to try to discover DNA matches in order to make positive identifications of the four best preserved bodies. This follows the positive identification of a Canadian soldier, Pte Herbert Peterson, by this method after a three-year long forensic investigation involving family members, archaeologists, anthropologists and genealogists. He was re-interred with full military honours on 9 April 2007 during the 90th Anniversary Commemorations at Vimy Ridge in La Chaudière CWGC Cemetery, near to where his remains were discovered in 2003.

This use by Commonwealth nations of identification of WW1 soldiers using DNA ran counter to the long-held policy of the CWGC not to use this method - until the important and well-publicised discovery of a mass grave of some 250 Australian and British remains at Pheasant Wood, Fromelles in 2007. An impressive team of archaeologists, DNA specialists and war graves organisations set up quarters in the vicinity and, before the re-interment of the remains in the new Fromelles (Pheasant Wood) CWGC Cemetery, with its dedication on 19 July 2010, managed to identify 208 soldiers. The work of identification continues and in March 2011 it was announced that a further 14 Australian soldiers had been identified, bringing the total to 110. On 18 July 2016 the Centenary of the Battle was commemorated.

Remains of soldiers continue regularly to be discovered during new building and pipe-laying excavations in the Salient, the dignified and reverend burial ceremonies continue, with many in the last seven years alone…

FRENCH SERVICES DES SEPULTERES DE GUERRE / MINISTERE DES ANCIENS COMBATTANTS ET VICTIMES DE GUERRE

On 29 December 1915 a law was passed to guarantee a perpetual grave at State expense to every Frenchman or ally 'mort pour la France'. On 25 November 1918 a National Commission of Sépultures Militaires was formed to create cemeteries with standard concrete markers (Christian crosses, shaped headstones for Muslims, rounded headstones for Jews and non-believers) on graves laid out in plots, ossuaries, monuments, enclosures and gateways. On 31 July 1930 the cemeteries were declared 'national' and the Service des Restitutions de Corps' was created. The Tricolore flies in every French cemetery. Many of the damaged wartime cemeteries were concentrated into larger graveyards. On 29 June 1919 each signatory to the Versailles Treaty agreed to respect and maintain the graves of foreign soldiers on their land. On 11 July 1931 generous finances were allocated to the cemeteries and memorials, permitting the rapid completion of important sites such as Notre-Dame de Lorette, Douaumont etc. After the defeat of 1940 the burial of victims of war was left to municipalities, to private individuals or to the enemy. Once WW2 was over new cemeteries were created, several inaugurated by Gen de Gaulle. Between 1983 and 1990 many of the cemeteries were planted with flower beds (in most case with pinky-red polyanthus roses) and in recent years a programme of erecting Information Boards describing the combats in the region at the cemetery entrances has been undertaken.

The French National Military Cemeteries in or near the Salient are at St Charles de Potyze (Map I4) and the Ossuary at Kemmelberg (Map L3). There are large French Plots at Oostvleteren (Map A2), Woesten Churchyard (Map B1) and Lijssenthoek CWGC Cemetery. Other French graves are to be found in many CWGC Cemeteries. **Contact:** *Nécropoles Nationales, Ministère des Anciens Combattants et Victimes de Guerre*, 37 rue de Bellechasse, 75007 Paris, France. Tel + 01 48 76 11 35.

Researchers based in In Flanders Fields Museum are completing a database and website for the 12,000 graves in the Salient. It is estimated that there are approximately 50,000 French burials in Belgium and in French Flanders, of whom 38,000 have no name. Many bodies were repatriated to France in the 1920s. A joint project between the Museum and the French Ministry of Defence is a 1914-'18 *Chemin de Mémoire* (Remembrance Road) starting in Ieper.

VOLKSBUND DEUTSCHE KRIEGSGRABERFURSORGE (VDK)

The German War Graves Organisation provides a similar service to that of the ABMC and the CWGC in looking after the German war dead and in assisting relatives to find and, in many cases, visit the graves. In 1925 a treaty was signed between Germany and Belgium to organise care of the German dead from the Great War and from 1929 the Germans replaced the Belgians who had taken over the responsibility from the British, who had been in charge of all exhumations from 1919-1922. Until then the German dead lay scattered in 678 burial places, with one vast cemetery of 8,000 near the CWGC Aeroplane Cemetery outside Ypres.

[More details of the early days of the VDK may be seen in *Major & Mrs Holts' Definitive Guide to the Somme*.]

In Belgium many were concentrated in cemeteries at Langemarck and Roeselare. In 1954 a new convention granted more land and the dead from the remaining 128 small cemeteries were transferred to Langemarck, Menin and Vladslo. Hooglede remained as it was. Langemarck (the only German cemetery which is actually in the Salient) contains 44,294 burials, 25,000 of which are in the communal grave surrounded by bronze panels bearing the names of the missing. Hooglede (on the Roeselare-Ostende road) contains 8,247 burials. Menin (on the Franco-Belgian border) contains 47,864 burials. Vladslo (on the Diksmuide-Beerst-Torhout road) contains 25,664 burials and the famous statuary group of Grieving Parents by Käthe Kollwitz (qv). Further landscaping work was undertaken between 1970 and 1972, mainly by volunteer students during their vacations. The last major renovation took place on 7 October 2016.

Further work in Langemarck was completed in the late 1980s and in 2015 important renovation work took place. Under the mass grave in the Cemetery is a sealed Crypt, rarely opened – the last time being during the re-inauguration ceremony of 16 October 2015 (see page 170) for a re-interment service, after which it was resealed.

Floral tributes, re-interment service, Langemarck, 16 October 2015. Opening to Crypt is to extreme left

The German cemeteries present a stark contrast to those of the ABMC or CWGC. The predominant colours are dark and sombre and a strong feeling of grief for the dead is present. The grave markers are not standard like those in American and British cemeteries and vary from stark black metal crosses, to grey or reddish stone crosses, sometimes laid flat as in Langemarck. They bear, when known, only the soldier's name, rank and dates of birth and death. Usually there are several burials beneath each marker, symbolising comradeship in death as well as in life, and because less space was available to the vanquished nation. Most cemeteries contain mass graves for the unidentified with tablets listing the missing.

Sometimes there is a small chapel, an entrance/reception chamber with a WC and a dramatic piece of mourning sculpture is often present. Also symbolic is the presence of oak trees, which signify strength but there are no flower beds in front of the rows of graves (although flowering shrubs are sometimes planted on the mass graves).

A list discovered at CWGC HQ Maidenhead, of several thousand German casualties, is being researched by the Passchendaele Museum (qv) Contact: *Volksbund Deutsche Kriegsgraberfürsorge*, Werner Hilperstrasse 2, D-34117 Kassel, Germany. Belgian Office: Horst Howe, 35 Allée du Petit Pas, F-59840 Lompret, France. In 2007 Administration was taken over by retired Belgian Colonel Yvan Vandenbosch. **Contact:** Zwanebloemlaan 36, 2900 Shoten, Belgium. Tel: + (0) 36 46 08 75. Email: yvan.vandenbosch@skynet.be French Office: rue de Nesle Prolongée, 80320 Chaulnes. Tel: + (0)3 22 85 27 57.

THE YPRES LEAGUE

On 28 September 1920, veterans of the Salient formed an association which they called 'The Ypres League'. Its President was Field Marshal Lord Plumer, its patron HM the King and Haig, Allenby and Viscount Burnham (of the Anglo-Belgian Union) were Vice-Presidents. Membership was open to all those who had served in the Salient, to their relatives and friends to 'remember all that Ypres meant in suffering and endurance'. Members applied for their names to be enrolled and paid a subscription of 5s annually or £2 10s for life. A fine scroll certificate, bearing the arms of the Dominions and showing Britannia standing among stark crosses before a shattered Cloth Hall, was then issued, certifying that the person named thereon had 'served in the immortal defence of Ypres' or, for relatives, 'laid down his life for King and Country in the immortal defence of Ypres'. The certificate was designed by the *Punch* cartoonist and superb graphic artist, Bernard Partridge (who was knighted in 1925). Herman Darewski, the composer and theatrical entrepreneur who had worked on several productions of Bairnsfather musicals, wrote the League's Official March, Ypres, and the cover of its music sheet reproduced the famous drawing *Wipers* by the artist 'Snaffles' (C. J. Payne).

The League produced several editions of its own quarterly magazine and funded, from its Hostel Fund, the guidebook, *The Immortal Salient* by Lt Gen Sir William Pulteney and the author Beatrix Brice in 1925. A detailed map accompanied the book which showed all roads navigable by motor traffic, the cemeteries and all the memorials which had by then been erected. The authors warned, 'There is much delay over some, and others may never actually materialise'. Forty metal posts were erected on landmarks christened by the troops, and these too were shown on the map. They included Clapham Junction, Black Watch Corner and Fitzclarence Farm which lies between the two and which was named after the popular old Boer War VC, Brig Gen Charles FitzClarence (qv). Unfortunately, none of the posts has survived. The League also paid for the Demarcation Stones (qv) that marked the Germans' extreme limit of occupation in the British Sector of the Salient. Rik Scherpenberg (qv) believes that there were only six Demarcation Stones in the Salient (not seven as previously believed) paid for by the League. The Stone at Lankhof at Lock No 8 (Map M15) used to be 800 metres further south in Voormezele and Rik believes that it was counted twice, thus causing the mistake. In all there were 22 Stones erected in Belgium and during WWII these were removed for safety and replaced after the defeat of Nazi Germany. This also offers an explanation for the fact that the Stone at Pilckem (Map H26) is marked 'Boesinghe' and the one at Boezinge (Map H4) is marked 'Ypres'. The missing Stone from Wieltje was taken by the Germans. The last 'official' Stone was erected in 1927, making a total of 118, but one more private Stone was erected at Confrécourt to commemorate those who had died in the area, thus making 119. The Secretary of the League was happy to give 'expert advice and assistance' to any pilgrim wishing to visit the Salient and a Rest Room was set up for them in Ypres. Reunions were held in London and the Provinces and 'Ypres Day' was observed on 31 October.

Once the British Legion was formed the importance and influence of the League gradually declined.

THE ROYAL BRITISH LEGION

The horrific experiences shared by soldiers of World War I were so traumatic that few could talk of them to their families. Even on leave during the war men felt they were travelling into an alien, non-comprehending land from what had become their true home - the familiar, dangerous, uncomfortable environment of the front line. There their shared privations engendered feelings of comradeship and true brotherly love such as are beyond the comprehension of those who have not experienced them. In the anticlimactic post-war days, when Lloyd George's promised land fit for heroes to live in had not materialised, the need to keep alive the comradeship was very strong. Many ex-servicemen's organisations sprang up, such as the Ypres League described above. Although the war diminished the large gap that had existed between the classes and ranks before the war, many of these organisations were segregated into Officers' and Other Ranks' associations. In 1919 Sir Douglas Haig was created and voted a grant of £100,000 by Parliament. He then relinquished his appointment of C-in-C Home Forces in January 1920 and, according to Lady Haig, 'Practically all his time was devoted to the work of the British Legion and the formation of the British Empire Service League'. In the foundation of the former, 'Douglas saw the continuance of that wonderful comradeship born in the trenches and the inspiration of service to each other which had carried his men through the terrible happenings of the war ... Douglas realised that one united comradeship could achieve much more than several separate bodies.' At first his efforts, aided by Sir Ian Hamilton, to amalgamate the various associations into one, all ranks organisation, had little success. Finally agreement was reached and the British Legion was formed after a conference of all the other groups (e.g. 'The Comrades of the Great War ', 'The National Association of Discharged Sailors & Soldiers', 'The National Federation of Discharged & Demobilised Sailors & Soldiers' and the 'Officers' Association') in 1921. Haig became its President and worked tirelessly for it until his death in 1928. Many saw this devotion to the welfare of ex-servicemen as the expiation of the guilt he felt for the terrible losses of the war - especially of the Somme and Passchendaele - that led to the dreadful epithet 'Butcher Haig'. To others Haig was a noble man, little less than a saint whose vision and determination saw the country through to the final victory. In the revival of interest in World War I in the 1970s and '80s it was fashionable to portray Haig as incompetent, unintelligent, unfeeling: the 'Lions led by Donkeys' syndrome. Lately, revisionist historians (going against the popular tide of portraying heroes with feet of clay rather than reinstating their reputations) have done much to dispel this assessment and to show him as a man of his time, training and education, who was responsible for the ultimate victory. No doubt things will swing the other way again in due course.

The Legion received its charter in 1925 (although it did not receive its 'Royal' prefix until 1971) and the Prince of Wales was its Patron. One of the founding members was the remarkable Baron Fraser of Lonsdale, blinded on the Somme in 1916, who became Chairman of St Dunstan's in 1921, was called to the bar in 1932, became Governor of the BBC in 1936 and National President of the Legion in 1947. Funds were raised through the sale of the artificial red poppy, whose inspiration was John McCrae's poem *In Flanders Fields* (qv) to create employment for the disabled, to fight for decent pensions, to help the needy and organise Pilgrimages (not battlefield tours) to war cemeteries and memorials - all of which functions it still performs. The Poppy Factory was started in 1922 with five disabled soldiers working in a small room over a shop in Bermondsey. Despite these small beginnings, the first Poppy Appeal raised £106,000.

The Ypres Branch was formed in 1921 for the ex-servicemen who came out to work with the War Graves Commission. It lapsed during World War II when most members evacuated to the UK. In 1946 many World War II soldiers returned to stay in Belgium and work for the Commission. They married local girls, settled and joined the RBL. Later many Belgian veterans (most of whom had fought with the British Army) became Associate Members. Although their numbers are dwindling, they raise a considerable amount for the Poppy Appeal, provide hospitality to visiting UK branches and attend local ceremonies with their standards.

Ypres Branch: E-mail: ypres.secretary@rbl.community Website: www.britishlegion.org.uk/branches/ypres

National HQ: 199 Borough High Street, London SE1 1AA. Tel: + (0) 20 3207 2100. Website: www.britishlegion.org.uk

Pilgrimage Department. Website: www.remembrancetravel.org.uk

*   *   *

American War Memorials Overseas Inc
Non-profit organisation whose mission is to document, raise awareness of and care for, private American gravesites and memorials where the US Government has no responsibility, liaising with local, national and international organisations. **Contact**: Lil Pfluke. 6 rue du Commandant de Larienty 92210, St Cloud. Tel: (0)6 1173 1332 E-mail: info@uswarmemorials.org Website: www.uswarmemorials.org

Association des Paysages et Sites de la Grande Guerre
Founded in Paris in 2011 to undertake the enormous task of preparing an inventory and plan for UNESCO recognition of WW1 memorial sites on the Western Front. This involves 12 French Departments from Nord-Pas de Calais to the Haut Rhin, plus sites in Belgian Flanders and Wallonia, with a total of 45 major sites. A significant number of them are on the Somme battlefield. In 2015 the Association declared its aims to avoid the 'touristic Disneyfication' of the battlefield sites and to promote their moral value for humanity with the obligation of keeping alive the memory and the desire to learn.

Paysages et sites de mémoire de la Grande Guerre

The authors are proud to be *'Partenaires'* and totally support this aim. **Contact:** Secretaire-général Serge Barcellini, Controleur Général des Armées. E-mail: paysagesetsitesdememoire@gmail.com Website: www.paysages-et-sites-de-memoire.fr

Friends of In Flanders Fields Museum
Formed in October 2001, the Hon President is Governor Paul Breyne. Benefits include free entrance to the Museum, organised tours and an interesting magazine, VIFF Flash. **Contact:** Researchcenter In Flanders Fields Museum, Attn Friends of the In Flanders Fields Museum, Sint-Maartensplein 3 - B-8900 Ieper E-mail: vriendeninflandersfields@ieper.be Sec: Patrick Boone.

Friends of St George's Church
From 1933 the Old Comrades of the Queen's Own Royal West Kent Regiment were encouraged by ex-CQMS Len Dawson to support the upkeep of the Church and to make an annual pilgrimage to it which continued until 1939. In 1945 the Royal British Legion restored the slight damage that St George's Memorial Church had suffered during World War II, but it was soon apparent that ongoing funds would be needed to provide for the maintenance of the church. In 1955 the Association of the Friends of St George's Memorial Church was formed under Les Dawson, Col Donald Dean, VC and Maj-Gen Raymond Biggs, CB, DSO. Its objects were to promote interest in

the life and work of the church, to provide a link between members in the UK and overseas and the local community, to co-operate with bodies such as the RBL and the CWGC for the benefit of the church and to provide funds to help maintain the fabric of the church and its life. **Contact**: The Hon Sec: Mike Mckean. E-mail: mmckean@aol.com

Friends of the Tank Memorial Ypres Salient
Chairman: Lt-Gen (Retd) David Leakey, CMG, CBC. Vice-President: Ian Robertson, nephew of Capt C. Robertson, VC. Chairman: Chris Lock (ex R Tank Regt). **Contact**: Assistant/Sec: Milena Kolarikova. E-mail: asstchairman.memsec. fottys@gmail.com Website: http://tankmemorial.vpweb.co.uk/

The Guild of Battlefield Guides
When we began our battlefield tour company almost 40 years ago we were the only company running such tours. Since then battlefield touring has proliferated, with a wide and unfortunate variation in the quality of guiding. In 2002 Major Graeme Cooper, a devotee and battlefield guide of the Napoleonic period, determined that a 'kite standard' should be created validating the capabilities of those who offered their services as guides. The Guild was duly launched on 28 November 2003 with Prof Richard Holmes (who sadly died in 2011) as its Patron. The authors are founding Honorary Members. Its aim is to analyse, develop and raise the understanding and practice of Battlefield Guiding. It has since gone from strength to strength and the badge awarded to successful validation applicants is a mark of excellence and quality. The Guild has a magazine, *Despatches*, and regular members' tours and events, the highlight being the Annual Dinner Weekend.

The coveted and respected Badge of an accredited Guide of the Guild of Battlefield Guides

Contact: The Secretary, e-mail: secretary@gbg-international.com Website: www.gbg-international.com

Last Post Association
See full description on page 34.

Parliamentary All-Party War Graves & Heritage Group
Consisting of members from both houses the group exists to support the work of the CWGC, to further educational programmes aimed at increasing knowledge of war heritage and battlefield sites, to support campaigners seeking to conserve and promote heritage sites and to encourage

best practice in multi-disciplinary battlefield archaeology. It was formed in 2001 as a result of the threat posed to the Pilckem Ridge in the Ypres Salient by plans to extend the A19 motorway and is now concerned with battlefield sites in the UK and world-wide (including the threat to the area of the Hohenzollern Redoubt on the Loos Battlefield and the roadworks affecting the Gallipoli beaches). Co-Chairman Lord Faulkner of Worcester.

Contact: Professor Peter Doyle, 17 Fairlawn Drive, Woodford Green, Essex, IG8 9AW. Tel: 0208 504 0381. Email: doyle268@ btinternet.com

Ross Bastiaan Commemorative Plaques
These are a series of beautifully designed,

Ross Bastiaan with his Plaque to Monitor M33, Portsmouth

durable and informative bronze Plaques created and erected by Australian periodontist, Dr Ross Bastiaan, on sites where Australian Forces were engaged with distinction. He has now researched and placed well over 265 Plaques in 20 different countries (several new ones are planned for 2018, including one at Mesen (qv)) and has been awarded the Medal of the Order of Australia and other awards and is a Life Member of the Australian Returned Services League (similar to the RBL). Ross was inspired to this monumental and dedicated task by Lt Lawrence McCarthy VC [see *Holt's Battlefield Guide to the Somme*], whose only child, Laurence, was engaged to Ross's mother before he was killed at Bouganville in 1944. When she later married and bore Ross, the veteran VC treated him like a grandson and brought him up on tales of Australian WW1 valour. The authors first met Ross when he was placing his first plaque in Gallipoli in 1990 and later in Portsmouth when he unveiled a Plaque to the Monitor 33 at its inguration in 2015.

His Belgian Plaques are in Geluwe, Mesen, Passendaele, Menin Gate. **Contact**: rjbastiaan@gmail.com Website: www.plaques.satlink.com.au

Souvenir Français
An Association founded in 1872 after the Franco-Prussian War and revived after WWI. Its aim is to keep alive the memory of those who died for France, to maintain their graves and memorials in good *Souvenir Français Roundel* condition and to transmit 'the flame of memory' to future generations.

Quarterly Newsletter. Pres-Gen Serge Barcellini, Controlleur Général des Armées.
Head Office: 20 rue Eugène Flachat, 75017 Paris. Tel: +90) 48 7453 99. E-mail: infos@souvenir.francais.fr Website: lesouvenirfrancais.fr

Western Front Association (WFA)
Formed by John Giles in 1980 to further the interest in WW1 to perpetuate the memory, courage and comradeship of all who fought in it. Two excellent publications: *Stand To* and *The Bulletin*. Chairman: Colin Wagstaff. **Contact**: Hon Sec: Steve Oram, Spindleberry, Marlow Road, Bourne End, Bucks SL8 5NL. E-mail: secretary@westernfrontassociation.com
Website: www.westernfrontassociation.com

www.wo1.be/www.greatwar.be
An initiative of the Province of West-Flanders this inter-active website lists all military cemeteries, monuments, memorials and bunkers, craters and other sites of interest with thousands of photographs, also tourist information in the Westhoek. This is a truly brilliant site – comprehensive, well-researched and illustrated and totally reliable. **Contact:** vzw Westhoek, c/o Jan Matsaert, Markt 10, B-8957 Mesen. E-mail: info@westhoek.be OR Robert Missinne. Tel: + (0) 57 48 72 69/+ (0) 478 572 317 (Mobile) E-mail: wo1@westhoek.be

TOURIST INFORMATION

LOCAL GUIDED TOURS/WHERE
TO STAY & WHERE TO EAT

GENERAL NOTE. Parking is difficult during all the events and festivals described below and serious battlefield tourers are best advised to avoid them.

TELEPHONING. When phoning from the UK to Belgium, dial 00 32, then drop the first 0 of the local dialling code. From Belgium to the UK dial 00 44, then drop the first 0 of the local code followed by the number. From the UK to France dial 00 33 then drop the first 0 of the local code followed by the number.

Hotels, restaurants and cafés that are conveniently on the routes are also mentioned as they occur in the Itineraries. They are indicated by a **distinctive typeface**. In most cases the comments about them reflect the authors' subjective views but do remember they always depends upon the staff on duty that day. For a comprehensive list of hotels and restaurants, apply to the Tourist Boards mentioned below.

TOURIST OFFICES are also indicated by this **distinctive typeface**. It is the nature of tourist information to change! Although we have tried to make sure that all the details given in this book were correct at time of going to press, before planning your trip to the Salient it is advisable to contact **Tourism Flanders-Brussels**, Flanders House, 1a Cavendish Square, London WIG 0LD. Tel: 020 7307 7738. E-mail: enquiries@visitflanders.com Website: www.visitflanders.co.uk OR the **Belgian Tourist Office**, 220 East 42nd Street, Suite 3402, New York, NY 10017, Tel: +(0) 1 212 758 8130. E-mail: info@visitbelgium.com

THE WESTHOEK.

The Region which includes Ypres, Passchendaele, Zonnebeke, Langemark-Poelkapelle, Poperinge, Diksmuide…

THE WESTHOEK TOURISM, Koning Albert 1-laan 120, 8000 Brugge (Sint Andries). Tel: +(0) 50 30 55 00. E-mail: toerismewesthoek@westtoer.be Website: www.flandersfields.be

The northern region of the battlefields covered in this guidebook is in the Westhoek.
Battlefield tourism is a vital part of the economy of West Flanders - with visits by the British still among the most important - and the Westhoek, which covers the three 'Front Towns' of Ieper, Diksmuide and Nieuwpoort, has undertaken an important study, 'War and Peace in The Westhoek' of remaining battlefield sites in the Province which has taken several years to complete. The aim is to preserve the battlefield heritage and make more people aware of it. Some of the results are published in a remarkable magazine, *In de Steigers*, with wonderful photos and descriptions of well-known and almost-forgotten sites alike. Unfortunately it is only published in Flemish. There is, however, a booklet entitled *The Great War in Flanders* listing all the battlefield-related annual events to take place and booklets covering two battlefield routes – **The Yzer Front** (79km around Diksmuide by car) and **In Flanders Fields Route** (82km around Ieper by car). They are available for a small fee from the appropriate **tourist offices**. There have been, and are yet to come, many new initiatives for the Centenary years.

IEPER

IEPER/Westhoek Tourist Office, Stadhuis, Grote Markt, 8900 Ieper, Belgium, Tel: +(0) 57 23 92 20, E-mail: toerisme@ieper.be Website: www.ieper.be

This helpful office in the historic Cloth Hall provides up-to-date brochures and information about local hotels, restaurants, self-catering accommodation, camping sites, car and bicycle hire, museum opening times, events, special exhibitions etc. It has a well-stocked book and souvenir boutique.

In this age when people are becoming conscious of their 'carbon footprint' visitors may wish to park their cars and visit the battlefields on foot or on bicycle. Walking and cycling battlefield routes are now available from this and other local **tourist offices**, including a publication by Dominiek Dendooven (qv), *Tales For on the Road*, which has three routes (long, medium and short walks) with historical notes, through the Provincial Domein of The Palingbeek (qv) *From 'The Bluff' to 'die Grosse Bastion'*; The Messines Ridge Peace Path (3.2km walk); three thematic cycling routes round Ypres – 'Gas', 'The Ypres Salient' and '14-18' (30km). There is a new edition of the 'Pop' (Poperinge) Route and 'The Peace Route', a 45km long, signed cycling route which starts and ends in Ieper. Of special interest are the **3 'Entry Points'** (qv, see page 68 for details) and their following exploratory walking routes lined by Remembrance Trees with talking Information Boards

See also the entry for In Flanders Fields on pages 67 for much more detailed information about tourist plans for Ieper in 2017 and beyond. After the Armistice Anniversary of 2018 it is considered that visiting the battlefields will not have so much appeal to the general tourist. Emphasis will then be made on the attractions of the numerous events that take place in the picturesque town, its architecture, food and drink (especially the many specialist beers), the beautiful countryside to explore on the Flanders Hills and in the Palingbeek Estate, and the nearby coastal resorts from Dunkirk to Ostend. Hence the proliferation of walking and cycling routes with their explanatory literature freely available.

Of course there will never be a diminution of interest by military history buffs, Regimental Associations, student groups and the growing band of families researching their ancestors' participation in the Great War. They will ensure that the flame of remembrance will never be extinguished and it will be tended by the Last Post Committee.

Local Guided Battlefield Tours/ Military Bookshops

In addition to the tours by qualified guides offered by the Ieper Tourist Office there are some commercial Ieper-based organisations which run regular English-speaking tours in comfortable mini-buses or in your own transport. The first two are also well-stocked book/map/souvenir etc shops.

Salient Tours. Based in The British Grenadier Shop. Run by Canadian Steve Douglas, with a battlefield resource centre and computer facilities for looking up burials. A magnificent database of Canadian casualties, www.mapleleaflegacy.ca 5 Meensestraat. Tel: +(0) 57 21 46 57. E-mail: tours@salienttours.be Website: www.salienttours.be

Over the Top Tours. Run by André and Carol de Bruin from their attractive shop at 41 Meensestraat. Tel: +(0) 57 42 43 20. E-mail: tours@overthetoptours.be Website: www.overthetoptours.be

Flanders Battlefield Tours. Run by the popular ex-TOC H guide, Jacques Ryckebosch with Genevra Charsley. Tel: +(0) 57 36 04 60. E-mail: info@ypres-fbt.com Website: www.ypres-fbt.com

Lest We Forget Tours. Run by Chris Lock (ex 3rd R. Tank Regt) and Milena Kolarikova. Tel: +(0) 32 478 35 52 65. Mobile: +(0) 478 355 265/+(0)476 202 721. E-Mail: lestweforgettours@gmail.com Website: www.lestweforgettours.com

Trench Map Tours. Run by ex-RMP Iain McHenry. Tel: +(0) 57 48 61 31. Mobile: +(0) 473 762 710. E-mail: tours@trenchmaptours.com Website: www.trenchmaptours.com

Battlefield Exploration. Run by local enthusiast Bert Degrauwe. Westrozebekestraat 41a, 8980

Passendale. Tel: 0494 436 559. E-mail: bert@ battlefields1.com Website: www.battlefields1.com

Paul Foster, FRSA. Battlefield Guide, Lecturer, Author. Tel: +(0) 77 00 05 99 18. E-Mail: remembering@btinternet.com Website: www. remembering1418.com

The Grote Markt is always the scene of a bustling market each Saturday morning and in 1994 it received a major facelift when it was repaved and trees were planted, thus restoring it more to its pre-1914 aspect, so superbly documented in the photographs of 'Anthony of Ypres'. Some extremely 'modern' fountains were constructed at the same time which contrast strongly with the otherwise medieval appearance of the square. Nearby in May 1995 the Kiwanis erected a small bronze Model of the Cloth Hall with raised features so that blind people can experience its shape.

André de Bruin In the Over the Top Tours Bookshop

Further major renovations to the roads, removing many of the picturesque but bumpy cobble stones, were undertaken in 2016.

There is also a series of interesting events to attract the visitor throughout the year. The Flemish have a capacity for enjoyment of their festivals and fairs which belies their somewhat dour image and these events are fun to attend. The medieval custom of throwing live cats from the Cloth Hall Belfry (the symbolic killing of evil spirits as personified by the cat) has been revived – with velvet cats – in the Catsfestival, a colourful and popular parade which takes place on the second Sunday in May every third year (2018/2021). Other regular events are the 100 Kilometres Ieper March on the weekend after Ascension, the 24 Hours Ieper Automobile Rally on the last weekend in June, the Thuyndag Fair on the first two weeks of August, the four days of the Ijzer March in the week after 15th August, the Crazy Days, third weekend of June and the Tooghedagen 'Sales Days' on the first weekend in September when local and international traders and craftsmen display their wares. The colourful Procession of St Martin is on 10 November and the year ends with the Christmas Market and Ice Rink in the Square. Armistice Day is always celebrated on 11 November, whatever day of the week it falls on (not the nearest Sunday as happens now in Britain) and it is a public holiday. On that day there is a Belgian Memorial Service in St Martin's Cathedral and an English one in St George's Church, a 'Poppy Parade' and special ceremony at the Menin Gate. In the afternoon there is a Remembrance Concert in St Martin's Cathedral, organised by the Last Post Association. Hundreds of pilgrims come from the UK for this event and it is as well to apply early for tickets in the church. This commemorates the sacrifice of all those who fought and, in particular, those who gave their lives, many willing and proud volunteers, in the Great War in Flanders.

The **'T Kleine Rijsel pub, near the Lille Gate**, Tel: +(0) 57 20 02 36, even sells 'Peace Beer' in special earthenware pots.

Ypres is twinned with Sittingbourne in Kent.

You will probably lunch or dine in the main square in Ieper and it is difficult to get a poor meal there. Belgian cuisine is excellent and often has more appeal to the conservative British traveller than the more exotic French. What is not so easy is to get a quick one. Omelette/chicken/sausage and the magnificent chips for which Belgium is justly famous (but try them with a dollop of mayonnaise for sheer sinful heaven) are favourite battlefield tourist dishes at lunch-time. If you have more time, sample some of the juicy mussels - cooked in a variety of sauces - that the locals order by the ton, or a tender pepper steak.

Around the square are to be found the following: the three-star **Regina Hotel**. with 17 refurbished bedrooms, and two restaurants (one of which is 'gourmet'). Tel: +(0) 57 21 88 88,

E-mail: info@hotelregina.be Nearest to the Cloth Hall is the **In't Klein Stadhuis**, Tel: +(0) 57 21 55 42 and next is the **Anker** restaurant where a fine meal can be had, Tel: +(0) 57 20 12 72, but allow plenty of time. **The Trompet** (which serves a great mixed salad and chips), Tel: +(0) 57 20 02 42, is very convenient and popular, especially for lunch. The **Kolleblume** (Poppy) Tel: + 57 21 90 90, and the **Café Central**, Tel: +(0) 49 70 66 67 43, are reasonably priced and serve snacks as well as full meals. **The Vivaldi tearoom/restaurant** has undergone a major enlargement but still provides the same mix of snacks and full meals, Tel: +(0) 57 21 75 21. **The Old Tom** (one-star). Tel +(0) 57 20 15 41. E-mail: info@oldtom. be Website: www.oldtom.be also has some hotel beds.

Karel Vandaele in the Chocolaterie, No. 9 Grote Markt

Local specialities are on offer in most of these restaurants. There are several hundred varieties of beer to choose from to wash them down, from thick dark brown to light lagers or even raspberry flavoured!

A few hundred grammes of the renowned Belgian hand-made chocolates – on sale in half a dozen or so outlets in the square – make a perfect end to a calorific spree. Highly recommended – especially **Patisserie/Chocolaterie Vandaele** (qv) at No 9. Tel: +(0) 57 20 03 87. Email: info@vandaele-ieper.be Website: www.vandaele-ieper.be

If really pressed for time, buy a carton of those crisp chips (with a choice of sauces, most popular is mayonnaise) from one of the *frituur* windows and eat them on the hoof. If you want the maximum time on the battlefields, then there is a choice of shops/supermarkets around the square, along J Coomansstraat or Meensestraat to buy the makings of a picnic. Along J Coomansstraat/A Vandenpeereboomplein is the **'t Ganzeke** (Goose) restaurant with a varied menu. Worth a visit to see the superb posters of Ypres from post-World War I to the 1950s. Tel: +(0) 57 20 00 09. Further along, if you want a change, is the large **Chinese Restaurant, Shanghai City**, Tel: +(0) 57 20 06 52. E-mail: info@newshanghaicity.be Website: www.newshanghaicity.be

Continue past the Theatre on your right to the right-hand corner of the square and continue along the small Boezingestraat and Veemarkt.

Members of the 'A Team', Hotel Ariane Reception

*The Bairnsfather cartoon on the Old Bill Pub*

Ahead is the four-star, **Hotel Ariane**, (see also page 72). Tel: +(0) 32 57 21 82 18. E-mail: info@ariane.be www.ariane.be GPS: 50.85461 2.88233. It is within an easy stroll of the Menin Gate and the Grote Markt and the best hotel in Ieper for battlefield tourers. It has spacious, well-equipped rooms, a superb restaurant, bar and a warm welcome by owners Natasja and chef Johann. Attractive enclosed and outdoor terraces extend the dining area to a spacious and elegant foyer which has WW1 exhibits and book stall. There is a large, safe, car park, resurfaced in 2016. The hotel is continually being improved.

The **Novotel** group has a smart, 122 bedroom modern three star hotel in Sint-Jacobsstraat just off the Grote Markt and near the Menin Gate. It has underground parking, fitness room and sauna. Tel: +(0) 57 42 96 00. E-mail: H3172@accor-hotels.com Under new ownership and refurbishment planned. Opposite the Novotel is the **Old Bill Pub**, whose pub sign, a Bairnsfather cartoon, originally hung outside the Regina Hotel in whose cellar a pub and private club was opened on 8 March 1969 when the distinguished historian Dr Caenepeel made a speech about Bruce Bairnsfather (qv) and the artist's links with the Salient

Also in Sint Jacobstraat is the elegant three star **Albion Hotel** in a converted Flemish renaissance building with 20 ensuite rooms, no restaurant but an attractive lounge where breakfast is served. Tel: +(0) 57 20 02 20. E-mail: info@albionhotel.be

For restaurants on Meensestraat as you walk towards the Menin Gate, see page 31.

Agriculture thrives again in the fields around Ieper and there is a growing industrial estate in the northern suburbs. This is served by a modern hotel, the **Best Western Flanders Lodge** (formerly the Rabbit), Tel: +(0) 57 21 70 00. E-mail: bw-ieper@skynet.be Website: www.bestwestern.com 40 Rooms. Restaurant **Open:** 1200-1400, 1830-2130. **Closed:** Sun.

It is built in wood like a Swiss Chalet, with thirty-nine rooms with en-suite bathrooms, jacussi, restaurant and attractive bar, which is also used by visitors to the battlefields.

At No 54 D'Hondestraat (off the Grote Markt and site of the old Shell Hole) is now the

How do they do that? Ieper Ring Road

Niek & Ilse welcome you to the Hooge Crater Museum Café (qv)

Corner of The Auberge, Ploegsteert

renovated **Ambrosia Hotel**, with 9 ensuite bedrooms, run by Vincent Vandelannoote and Wona Danik. Bed and Breakfast and bar. Tel: +(0) 57 36 63 66. Email: info@ambrosiahotel.be Website: www.ambrosiahotel.be

A handy place for a quick lunch is the **Café** at the Hooge Crater Museum. GPS: 50.84634 2.94388. Tel: +(0) 57 46 84 46

COMINES-WARNETON

COMINES-WARNETON Tourist Office (GPS: 50.785574 3.005978) 6-46 Chemin du Moulin Soete, Comines. Tel: +(0) 56 55 56 00. E-mail: office.tourisme.comines-warneton@belgacom.net. Website: www.villedecomines-warneton.be This covers the area of Ploegsteert/St Yvon and Warneton. Lists of *gîtes and chambres d'hôte* in the area. **Note that the area is French-speaking.** The region is showing an increasing interest in developing its historical WW1 sites (see Last Post at Ploegsteert Memorial) with well-researched and illustrated Information Panels at cemeteries and sites of historical WW1 interest in the area. These were written by Ted Smith (co-author with our dear friend Tony Spagnoly - who sadly died in 2008 - of books about the area) and Claude Verhaeghe (qv). Many new initiatives are always in progress, especially at the Plugstreet '14-'18 Experience. See also page 246.

There are opportunities for lunch breaks in Ploegsteert - **L'Auberge**, (see also page 243) opposite the Memorial. **Closed:** Wed. Tel: +(0) 56 58 84 41. E-mail: restaurant@auberge-ploegsteert.be. Variety of menus. Can take groups on prior reservation. HQ of Last Post Committee. Owned by Claude & Nelly Verhaeghe (qv).

Hostellerie de la Place, next to the Town Hall, Ploegstreet. Tel: +(0) 56 58 86 77.

DIKSMUIDE

DIKSMUIDE Tourist Office, Grote Markt 6, 8600 Diksmuide, Tel +(0) 51 79 30 50. E-mail: toerisme@stad.diksmuide.be Website: www.diksmuide.be See also pages 284.

Market day is on Monday, the Cheese and Butter Fair is on Whit Monday, Ijzer Tower

Pilgrimage, last Sunday in August, Flemish 'Day of Peace' 11 November. You can hire a canoe or a small motorboat for trips up the Ijzer or hire a pedal cart to explore this attractive town and helicopter flights can also be made to get a bird's eye view over the battlefield – details from the tourist office. The picturesque Grote Markt, with its statue of Jacques of Diksmuide in the centre is the best bet for a lunch break with a good choice of restaurants and snack bars from Chinese to *frituur* and a two star hotel/restaurant **Polderbloem** with 8 rooms, Tel: +(0) 51 50 29 05. Website: www.polderbloem.be and **De Vrede** with 14 rooms, Tel: +(0) 51 50 00 38. E-mail: de.vrede@skynet.be. At Heilig Hartplein 2 is the four star Best Western **Hotel Pax** with 378 rooms, Tel: +(0) 51 50 00 34, e-mail: pax.hotel@skynet.be On the Ijzer bank opposite the Peace Tower (qv) is the three star **hotel-restaurant Sint Jan** with 10 rooms, Tel: +(0) 51 50 02 74. E-mail: info@st-jan.be Website: www.st-jan.be Restaurant: **Closed** Fri.

LANGEMARK-POELKAPELLE

LANGEMARK-POELKAPELLE Tourist Office. Kasteelstraat 1, Tel: +(0) 57 49 09 41. E-mail: toerisme@langemarck-poelkapelle.be **Open:** Mon/Tues/Fri: 0900-1200. Wed: 0900-1200 & 1400-1600. Thurs: 0900-1200 & 1400-1830. **Café/Restaurant/Hotel 't Munchenhof.** Markt 32, Tel: +(0) 57 48 83 13 www.munchenhof.be

Varlet Farm B+B. Wallemolenstraat 43. **GPS: 50.93805 2.97208.** Tel: +(0) 47 02 11 654. E-mail: info@varletfarm.com Website: www.varletfarm.com (see also Page ??) The original farm was named by the British and taken by the Hood Bn of the RND in October 1917. An attractive venue, with en-suite rooms (from single to 4-bed family, can sleep up to 22), open all year, very popular with battlefield tourists, but group bookings in advance essential. Many WW1 artefacts and displays in and around the farm buildings. Advice on local touring and cycles to rent.

MESEN/MESSINES

MESEN/MESSINES Tourist Information: In the main Market Square, on the left at No 22, in the site of the old Town Hall (now in the fine building opposite) and Museum. **Open:** Mon-Thurs 0900-1200/1330-1700. Fri: 0900-1200/1330-1600. Tel: + (0) 32 057 22 17 14. E-mail: info@mesen.be/toerisme@mesen.be. www.mesen.be. Guided tours available and literature on local accommodation/events/walking tours etc

Adjoining it is a smart new unmanned TIP (Tourist Information Point) which tells the story of Messines in WW1 and its general history.

Messines Peace Village, Nieuwkerkestraat 9A. See also page 236 Hostel with 32 four-bedded studio-type rooms with bath or shower, restaurant, games room. Designed for student or low budget groups. Facilities for the disabled. Nieuwkerkestraat 9a, 8957 Mesen. Tel: +(0) 57 22 60 40. E-mail: info@peacevillage.be Website: www.peacevillage.be

POPERINGE

POPERINGE Tourist Office, (see also page 201) Stadhuis, Grote Markt, B-8970 Poperinge, Tel: +(0) 57 34 66 76, e-mail: toerisme@poperinge.be Website: www.poperinge.be. There are many cultural and folkloric events here (e.g. the annual Hop Festival in September, and there is a signed, 54km 'Hop Route' around the area). Market day is on Friday (as it has been since the Count of Flanders granted permission for a market in 1187).

They produce a leaflet called Poperinge in the First World War as well as the POP.ROUTE booklet (qv) (for which there is a fee). Information about hotels, b&bs, self-catering, camping

Poperinge Town Hall

Typical appetising lunch, T'Jagershof Restaurant, De Lovie

sites, cycle hire, horse and carriage hire etc. Samples of Poperinge's famous beers (such as Poperings Hommelbier and St Bernardus beers) and Dutch gin (Genever) and delicious cakes (such as Mazarinetaart) are available in many of the shops and restaurants in this pretty town.

Today 'Pop' makes a good base for touring the Salient. Around the Market Square are a variety of hotels, restaurants and cafés – this is ideal for a lunch break or an overnight stay when touring the Salient – for example the three star **Hotel Amfora** with its neo-Gothic façade and gastonomic restaurant, Tel: +(0) 57 33 94 05. E-mail: info@hotelamfora.be; at No 16 is the **La Poupée/Café De Ranke** (qv) Tel: +(0) 57 33 30 08. E-mail: geeraerdvandermoere@gmail.com which makes a good lunch or tea break and specialises in sinful cream and chocolate cakes. **Du Tram Snackbar** at No 8. Tel: (0)+ 47 23 19 056. **Hotel de la Paix** at No 20. Tel: +(0) 57 33 95 78, E-mail: info@ hoteldelapaix.be. Website: www.hotldelapaix.be

Up Gasthuisstraat, at No 48, is **Talbot House** (qv) (Toc H) with self-catering accommodation in this evocative and historic House (qv). Tel: +(0) 57 33 32 28. E-mail: info@talbothouse.be Website: www.talbothouse.be

In Ieperstraat is the three star **Palace Hotel with restaurant** and bar with 100 beers! Tel: +(0) 57 33 30 93. E-mail: info@hotelpalace.be For a touch of elegant luxury there is the four star **Hotel Recour** with gourmet **Pegasus restaurant** on Guido Gezellestraat. Tel: +(0) 57 33 57 25. E-mail: info@pegasusrecour.be Website: www.pegasusrecour.be

ZONNEBEKE

ZONNEBEKE Tourist Office in the Passchendaele Memorial Museum (qv), Château Zonnebeke, 7 Ieperstraat. Tel: +(0) 51 77 04 41. E-mail: toerisme@zonnebeke.be Websites: www. paschedaele.be/www.zonnebeke.be/www.toerismezonnebeke.be **Open:** Daily 0900-1800. **Closed:** 16 Dec-31 Jan.

Details of guided battlefield tours by the Museum's expert guides and local accommodation and eateries available. Many fascinating WW1-related events are organised by the Museum throughout the year and absorbing educational packages for students are available. The grounds of the Château are quite delightful to stroll or to take your picnic in. In them is the **Koklikoo Bistro/Tearoom/Restaurant**. Tel: +(0) 51 72 74 13. **Closed:** Mon & Tues. Opposite on Ieperstraat 26, is the **De Volksbund Café/Restaurant**. Tel: +(0) 51 77 98 38. **Closed:** Wed & Thurs. 'Tommy Tucker' menu for student groups.

Another attraction in Zonnebeke is the Old Cheese Factory which has the **Oud Kaasmakerij Café/Bistro**. Tel: +(0) 51 77 70 05. See www.deoudekaasmakerij.be for opening times.

KEMMEL

HEUVELLAND/Kemel Regional Tourist Office, Kemmel (see also page 267). Tel: +(0) 57 45 04 55. E-mail: toerism@heuvelland.be Website: www.toerismheuvelland.be The helpful and

informative Heuvelland/Kemel Tourist Office manned by Ingried Tierson is due to move by February 2017 to the old Vicarage by the church, at Sint-Laurentiusplein 1, Kemmel. **GPS: 50.78423, 2.826**36. It provides information about accommodation, camping sites and restaurants in the area, details of local attractions, festivals and events, information and leaflets on sites related to the Great War. There will be several interesting exhibitions here, both temporary and permanent. Apply here for a ticket to the **Bayernwald** (qv) and for a ticket to the fascinating and well-preserved **1963 Cold War Command Bunker** which is at 64 Lettingstraat, Kemmel. It is important to reserve in advance as only small parties are permitted at set times: 1000; 1145; 1330; 1515. Allow 90 minutes. Open Tues & Sat.

Ingrid Tierson, Tourist Office, Kemmel

Hostellerie Kemmelberg. (See also page 260). This upmarket hotel with gourmet restaurant is at 34 Kemmelbergweg. Tel: +(0) 57 45 21 60. E-mail: info@kemmelberg.belg Website: www.kemmelberg.be Superb views from the terrace. 16 individually furnished rooms. Completely renovated (with lift) and beautifully designed throughout by new owners, Kristine and Philippe Vercoutter in 2012. Restaurant: **Closed** for non-residents, Mon & Tues night. Annual closing 4 Jan-11 Feb.

GOLF

For those who wish to combine a tour of the battlefields with some golf there is a superb and peaceful 18-hole course designed by Harold J. Baker at the Golf and Country Club in the region of Palingbeek, that has been listed as a provincial recreation area since 1978. The clubhouse is the pavilion of the old château of Voormezele, Eekhofstraat 14, 8902 Hollebeke, Ieper. Tel: +(0)57 20 04 36 E-mail: golfpalingbeek@skynet.be Website: www.golfpalingbeek.be

BELLEWAERDE PARK

The theme park, with its hair-raising rides, is the most popular family attraction in the area. Take Exit 3 (Beselaere) from the E17-A19. Tel: +(0) 57 46 86 86. E-mail: belinfo@europe.sftp.com Website: www. bellewaerde.be

Graduates celebrating in the Beer Bus, Pilckem

FRANCE

CASSEL Tourist Office of Cassel Horizons, 20 Grand' Place Tel: 00 33 3 28 40 52 55.
See also page 49. Tourist information on local events and a plan of the town are available here

and an interesting film on the area and its history is shown. This picturesque and historic town would make a delightful base or lunch stop. A favourite spot for hikers and bikers one of the attractions is the Windmills of Flanders Route.

Beyond the *Mairie* in the Grand' Place is the welcoming **Café-Brasserie Au Charles Quint**. Tel: 00 33 3 28 42 48 57, specialising in crêpes, gaufres and other local specialities. Quick snacks or a variety of menus. Beyond that is the 2 star **Hotel/Restaurant Foch**. Tel: 00 33 3 28 42 47 73 with regional and Flemish specialities. At No 38 rue Maréchal Foch is **Le Sauvage** (qv) no longer a hotel, but a restaurant Tel: +(0) 3 28 42 40 88. Further along the road is the historic Hotel Schoebeque (qv), now the 4 star **Châtellerie de Schoebeque** lavishly and lovingly restored and converted by Muriel and Hervé Diers to its old glory but with all modern comfort. There are 14 rooms/suites, all imaginatively and contrastingly designed with named themes (e.g. *Suite Maréchal Foch, La Vie*

Windmill, Mont Cassel

en Rose, etc). There is also a heated outdoor pool and spa with treatments. Tel: +(0) 3 28 42 42 67, E-mail: contact@schoebeque.com Website: www.schoebeque.com

ACKNOWLEDGEMENTS

Our thanks go to all the hundreds of people who helped us with our researches over the last 40 years, and in particular with the earlier and latest editions of this book: Chairman M Benoit Mottrie, Jan Matsaert and Ian Connerty of the Last Post Association; Colin Kerr & Ian Small, CWGC; Piet Chielens Director In Flanders Fields Museum; Peter Slosse, Ieper Tourist Officer, (for his support over the years); John Krijnen for information about Frelinghien Christmas Truce, Bunker and Observation Tower; Gertjan Remmerie for new information about Talbot House; Chris Lock & Milena Kolarikova for Tank Regt Memorial and other info; Steve Douglas, Genevra Charsley & Jacques Ryckebosch for keeping us up-to-date on many things and for their friendship; Marc Decaestecker for Welsh matters at Hagenbos; Robert Missine of wo1@westhoek.be; Johan Vandewalle and Bert Degrauwe for information about the Brothers-in-Arms project and to Natasja and the team at the Ariane for their hospitality and support during our many research visits. Finally, to Elaine Parker for 'keeping us on the road' and to the whole of Charles's team at Pen & Sword - invidious to mention individuals, as all offer us encouragement and indulgence, but we just have to give special thanks to David Hemingway for his extraordinary understanding and speed of response in the design of the book and also Lisa Hoosan for patient trouble-shooting whenever required.

PICTURE CREDITS

To all those who helped us in previous editions and to Ieper Tourist Office for the interior of In Flanders Fields Museum; CWGC for Colne Valley Cemetery; Jan Matsaert of The Last Post Association for photo of the authors and Benoit Mottrie and of Jessica Wise with the Buglers and the front cover image; Paul Foster for Langemarck German Cemetery burials; Robert Missine for the B12 Ceremony; Nigel Parry, BBC TV Wales for the photo of the authors and new Peace Monument, with instigators, at the Welsh Dragon; Steve Douglas for Tyne Cot aerial view; Chris Lock for Polish Memorial; Jessica Wise for Buttes Cemetery, De Dreve Café, Clay Figures.
All other contemporary photographs have been taken by the authors.

INDEX

FORCES

These are listed in descending order, i.e: Armies, Corps, Divisions, Brigades, Regiments, Battalions ...

MEMORIALS

National and 'Military' Memorials are listed first, followed by 'Personal' Memorials. See also 'VCs' under 'General'

MUSEUMS/INFO CENTRES

WAR CEMETERIES

GENERAL INDEX